KENYA

THE KIKUYU AND MAU MAU

David Lovatt Smith

Published by
Mawenzi Books,
Swanmore, Church Road,
Herstmonceux, East Sussex BN27 1RJ

ISBN 0-9544713-2-6

By the same author
Amboseli – Nothing Short of a Miracle
My Enemy: My Friend
A History of the Kikuyu Guard – Ed.

Cover design by Tessa James

Printed and bound by
Antony Rowe Ltd.,
Eastbourne

THIS BOOK IS DEDICATED TO THOSE OF ALL RACES
WHO SERVED IN KENYA DURING COLONIAL TIMES
AND WHO FOUGHT AND DIED TO MAKE IT
A BETTER PLACE

Contents

Appendices

Illustrations

MAPS

Acknowledgements

A book dealing with such a wide ranging subject as this could not have been written without a great deal of assistance from many sources. Several people have given their time to reading the draft in whole or in part and have made constructive comments and suggestions which have been incorporated in the text. Others have gone to lengths to answer questions and provide data. Many have contributed their experiences and anecdotal memories of their time in one or other of the services in Kenya, and I wish to thank all those who have helped. I would particularly like to mention the following people: Andrew Barnett: Stan Bleazard MBE; John Blower; John Boulle; James and Caroline Breckenridge; John Butter CMG, OBE.; John Campbell CVO, CBE, MBE, MC.; Ian Campbell-Clause; Sheilagh Candler; Dick Cashmore Phd.; Noel Cossins; John Cowan MBE.; Dr. Geoffrey Cunningham; Roy Davies; Roger Draycup; John Dykes; Francis Erskine; Peter Evans; Ian Field MC.; James Foster; Alan Francis; Peter Fullerton; Charles Gardner; Terence Gavaghan MBE.; John Golds MBE.; Ed Green; Pam Gwyer; George Hales BEM.; Ian Henderson GM & Bar, QPM, CPM.; Mike Hudson; Ossie Hughes; Pascal Imperato MD, MPH & TM.; Sir John Johnson KCMG.; Alan Jones MBE; Anthony Kirk-Greene CMG, MBE; General Sir Frank Kitson GBE, KCB, MC, DL.; Peter Lloyd CMG, CBE.; Ivor Lopes; Peter May; James McCarthy; Fergus McCartney; Neil McDonald; Rhoddy Macleod; George McKnight; Chris Minter; Mike Morland; Dick Moss; David Nicoll-Griffith; Bob Otter; Ian Parker; David Peters; Gordon Potts; Bruce Rooken-Smith; John ('Rusty') Russell; Bert Selley; Phil Sykes; Graham Tudor; Brian Turner; Ian Wallace; Hugh Walker MBE; Elisabeth de Warren-Waller; Len Weaver CBE.; Michael Wenden; Alec Wilkinson; Geoff Winstanley and Henry Wright;

I am indebted to Dr. John Lonsdale for his encouragement to write the book in the first place, and for reading a first draft and making comments and suggestions vital to historical records, without necessarily agreeing with the conclusions or tenor of the book. Also to Mike Prettejohn who started me off on the hunt for evidence and helped considerably to keep me on the right track; to Laurie Slade who allowed me to use his father's letters from Kimathi. Willoughby ('Tommy') Thompson, from whose unique and vitally important memoirs I have quoted liberally and to John Hvass for his detailed knowledge and memories of the conditions we encountered in Fort Hall, as well as providing me with his father's journal parts of which I have included in appendix 8.

Finally and especially, my gratitude is to Roy Spendlove who has had close personal involvement in issues of government and colonial disengagement since 1944 including service in the Provincial Administration and the Ministry of Agriculture in Kenya 1952 – 1963. I am indebted to him for agreeing to write the Foreword to the book. Without his erudite knowledge of Kenya coupled with a first hand grasp of Whitehall's policies and influence on colonial Kenya's destiny, it would not be possible for the book to boast the same authenticity nor its legitimacy.

.

PREFACE

In the 21st century, the impacts of Western Europe's imperial role on the wider world over the last three hundred years, are but vaguely understood, important though such understanding is to the global challenges that have faced us since. Those who have studied the subject objectively will know the demands and responsibilities it put upon the ruling powers and the differing extents to which those powers succeeded in shouldering their responsibilities. Great Britain played the major role in the evolution and development of the continent of Africa and in the enlightenment of its Black people, a role of which she can justifiably be proud.

It is regrettable then, that through misrepresentation of the historical facts, it has become increasingly fashionable to look upon Britain's role with shame and ignominy. Shakespeare put the effect into words ...

> *The evil that men do lives after them*
> *The good is oft interred with their bones*

Shakespeare: Julius Caesar

This book is a personal contribution to the better understanding and interpretation of a critical phase in Great Britain's administration of one part of the British Empire: the Colony and Protectorate of Kenya. It forms, perhaps, a microcosm of the challenges that faced Britain during the height of her own imperial role, a task, the records reveal, that as far as East Africa was concerned, she undertook with great reluctance.

I have been associated with Kenya and its peoples for more than fifty years and during that time I have witnessed the integrity, creative leadership and consistency of purpose shown by those of all races, who brought Kenya and its peoples through difficult times to the threshold of independent statehood. In my research for the book, from the origins of the British presence in East Africa, through the European farming settlement, to the illegal insurrection that developed into Mau Mau, I draw heavily on eye-witness accounts, complemented where relevant, by my own experience. In the course of writing, I have been surprised at the support and encouragement I have received from surviving contemporaries who served in Kenya in one capacity or another and am extremely grateful for their contributions to this book.

In developing the subject, I am conscious of the predisposition of many who may read it, to have based their opinions on the less than well-researched material presented in the popular media. In too many cases, academic compositions are based solely on the writings and utterances of those who lay claim to being 'experts' but whose credentials and experiences are often as limited as those who seek to copy them. These compounded errors, in recent years, have led to a systematic distortion of the historical background of the colonial period and through misrepresentation of the facts, there has been an excess of denigration of the British administration of Kenya, especially during the Mau Mau period. This is a censure Britain does not deserve and this book is written with the express purpose of breaking that mould and introducing a modicum of hard evidence into the history of Kenya's colonial period.

The book attempts to provide the reader with an overview of the wider, historical, geographical and evolutionary context of the period. It endeavours to clarify the record so that the reader is able to judge for himself, the reasons why Britain took on the development of eastern Africa and the effects the colonial phase had on the Black population, leading to the transfer of power and the consequential independent sovereign state. The origins and nature of the threat posed by Mau Mau and the effects of it are considered in some detail as are the reasons why the conflict ended as a victory for none, other than the supremacy of law that breeds order, virtue and morality. For:

'The only liberty I mean, is a liberty
connected with order, that not only exists
along with order and virtue but which cannot
exist at all without them.

Edmund Burke (1729 – 1797)

The communications I have received during the course of writing[1] show there is unanimity of concern by those who served not only in the Colony and Protectorate of Kenya, but also in the far reaches of the Empire as a whole, regarding the way in which the subject of colonialism is not only neglected in teaching institutions throughout the United Kingdom and elsewhere, but also,

---

[1] Due to lack of space, it has been impossible to include many of the letters and emails I have received from over two hundred people, which in themselves provide a valuable history. A selection of these have been deposited for safe keeping in the Rhodes House Library, Oxford.

where it does see the light of day, the prejudiced way in which it is presented. The flames of such prejudice have undoubtedly been fanned by the inclination of the populist media to melodrama, distortion and uninformed sensationalism as well as a particular group of academics who are bent on revising the records, to suit their own somewhat obscure agendas. Hopefully the book may help to douse these flames a little, and with the aid of solid evidence and informed argument presented, I hope, with sensitivity, bring some perspective to the subject.

If the evidence may seem unconvincing to today's students – children of the new and commendable age of tolerance that swept the Western world in the 1960s (an attribute that carries with it perilous dangers from those extremists who would seek to take advantage of it) – if it is unconvincing to them, maybe later generations of scholars, unencumbered by illusory consciences about their forebears' generation of 'jingoists', will be able to study the subject without rancour and with the objectivity it warrants. So it is to them that the book is primarily directed.

The historic perspective of the evolution of a sovereign state must surely take account of its primal origins. So when the Union Flag was finally and symbolically lowered over Kenya on 12th December 1963, it would have been the seventy year old Kikuyu, Masai or Luo elder who would have been the one best qualified to give a true appraisal of the legacy the British left behind them, and their conduct during their period of suzerainty. He is the one who would have known whether or not they handed back to Kenya's inhabitants a country that was more peaceful, more enlightened and a better place to live than when the same flag was hoisted some seventy years before.

DLS December 2004

FOREWORD
By Roy Spendlove CVO.

The Interplay of History and Geography
in the Hinterland of the Sultanate of Zanzibar.

"This event is intended to make the different races of the Empire better known to each other and to demonstrate to those that visit it the almost unlimited possibilities of the Dominions, Colonies and Dependencies together. "

King George V at the British Empire Exhibition
at Wembley Stadium, 23 April 1924

The author of this assertive account of the Mau Mau Emergency in Kenya during the period 1952-1960 has undertaken a most timely mission. He and I met for the first time shortly after a much and rightly criticised programme broadcast on 17 November 2002 in the BBC TV programme entitled "White Terror". We discovered that we were simultaneously serving in the Central Province of Kenya, then the critical focus of the Emergency period. We quite independently one of the other found common ground in being deeply concerned that the history and the facts of this time were so grossly misrepresented in much teaching and media comment. I have therefore a very real sense of the importance to the lives and public service of which we were proud and privileged to be members, and to posterity, of having, at the author's invitation, this opportunity to contribute a Foreword to his careful composition.

In 2004 no one can be wholly ignorant of the human tragedies which have struck successive communities of the Black People of Africa since the Great Scuttle from Africa which swept the Continent during the 'fifties and 'sixties of the last century. Kenya has by no means escaped some portion of them, though none perhaps as grievous as many of those with which TV audiences may be vaguely and sedentarily familiar. The author tells the story of a comparatively brief and geographically quite limited crisis in Kenya prior to its emergence as a sovereign state. Left to fester or irresponsibly dealt with by those responsible for governance at the time, the period might well have sown the self-destructive seeds for post-Independence troubles which have characterised the history of so much of the Continent. Though there have been and remain serious problems, no knowledgeable critic would yet be wise to describe Kenya as a 'failed state', though in Africa much of life hangs precariously on a thread today as from time immemorial. The promise of its foundation years can still be realised even if the omens may not be good.

The history of the indigenous peoples who now claim for their home the land which comprised Kenya Colony and Protectorate was shaped by the harsh personal disciplines of internecine conflict, animal disease, human afflictions and adaptation, in competition with the untamed herds of the savannah and forest, to uncertain cycles of the rains and drought on fragile soils and isolated from benign innovation. The advent of new and radically different influences on their lives at the end of the nineteenth century was to change much of this. The Colony of Kenya and the Sultanate of Zanzibar had formally come together under the governance and suzerainty of the British Crown in 1906. Just over fifty years later, on 12 December 1963, Kenya Colony became an independent state within the Commonwealth and a member of the United Nations. The Independence Act approved by Parliament bluntly declared that

" ... on and after 12 December 1963 (Parliament)
shall have no responsibility for the governance of the
Colony of Kenya and the Protectorate of Zanzibar. . . "

The birth of the new state of Zanzibar, thus provided for the recognition of Muslim interests there, but an uprising on the island in January 1964 was put down by the Tanganyikan Special Police and together with the near-by island of Pemba, was later incorporated into Tanganyika, the whole being renamed Tanzania.

In the brief three quarters of a century prior to Independence it is possible to recognise in Kenya a singular story of the Continent encapsulating all principal themes of development and change evident elsewhere in Africa south of the Sahara, except that of exploiting mineral resources. Of them there were virtually none. The foundation for Kenya's livelihood as an emerging independent state would depend principally on its people's ability to manage soil and water, sustain animal and public health and population growth in tandem with a complex, technically demanding constitutional structure bequeathed by the departing colonial government in a last minute hope that the future government would and could remain a respected guardian of the new state's heritage and the legitimate reciprocal interests of its diverse peoples.

The accession to statehood was accompanied by predictable optimism by many, and by concern among others who had nurtured the territory from the beginning of the century and through the Mau Mau Emergency and the prior, brief phase of Internal Self Government, that the practicability of making a success of the undertaking might prove disappointing. The timing of the decision to move to full independence assumed that the recent evolution of the putative state had developed deep enough roots for it to survive birth and adapt to a challenging world, *"standing"*, as President Nyerere of Tanzania had staunchly contended for Tanzania, *"on its own feet"*. Would the new state, in all its constitutional, cultural and economic complexity, as it had evolved from a primaeval history of poorly resourced, tribal peoples in chronic conflict one with another, jointly with innovative, adaptive and energetic immigrants moving into their second and third generation, successfully sustain the legal and economic foundations on which the emerging society depended for its success as a self-reliant, sovereign state? To many closely involved this seemed likely to prove, at best a qualified, if not forlorn hope. The Mau Mau episode and the much more beside discouraged great optimism.

The practical significance of the security crisis giving rise to the Emergency can only properly be understood in the context of three key sets of wider inter-locking and all-pervasive factors which variously influenced events and contributed to maintaining the forward thrust of public policy toward Independence. In brief, they are:

* the imperial context and vision
* the indigenous, local cultures and the profound impact of change for them
* the interplay of race and culture on the development of institutions and their economic underpinning

---

The Imperial Context and Vision

The unique historical phenomenon of the British Empire as it had evolved by the beginning of the twentieth century was based on achieving a wise, practical balance of interest between Great Britain at the centre and the Dominions, Colonies and Dependencies at the periphery in a consistently nurtured framework of accountability, law and development. As in many other parts of the world since the 18th century, successive British governments had somewhat drifted into becoming entangled in events which arose from a perceived duty to protect British people and British interests in a world which seemed to burst with ever wider opportunity and challenge. Not surprisingly this led to an acceptance that the protector might legitimately expect some degree of compliance, especially where protection was associated with a significant measure of territorial control by those seeking protection.

This became a matter of central importance in the nineteenth century in the increasingly influential colonies of Canadian North America, and of Australia and New Zealand, all 'colonies of settlement', where limited practical communication of any sort inhibited the protecting power from readily intervening. By the end of the 19th century, Great Britain had extended her influence widely into Africa south of the Sahara, South Asia, South East Asia and the Pacific. Given the immense diversity of and within these areas, any inclination to ride roughshod over 'alien' peoples of other cultures had long been tempered by the realisation that any tendency to clumsy arrogance would be, and was, self-defeating. Effective public administration of necessity rested on respect, mutual understanding and restraint. Inescapably it involved the importation of sometimes alien juridical systems and practices while, in the context of a need to nurture the interests of local societies and sustaining the integrity of local law and custom.

It was against this very wide background that in British practice ideas of suzerainty and protection evolved along with a need to define the limits of 'local' legislative and executive power which might be exercised. As the author considers further below, this was a matter of considerable practical importance in the early relationships of the Sultanate of Zanzibar with the British during their initial exploration of the coastline and hinterland over which the Sultan claimed jurisdiction. Where outside the area designated as the Protectorate, colonial government took root, more complex procedures and legal precepts needed to be in play, if those exercising the Crown's authority were to have effect. In the lands of the hinterland the foundations of colonial government were progressively laid so that, by the end of the Second World War, the Governor, appointed by the Crown, had responsibility for the executive acting through a Council and subject, in exogenous law, to the oversight of staunchly independent and highly professional courts.

This system, already in many aspects reflecting the ultimate goal of autonomous self-government, had deep practical origins. By the mid-19th century and adaptively in the context of lessons learnt from the dramatic events in North America both in 'the thirteen Colonies' and Canada, Britain had learnt the over-riding imperial imperative and paradox that the inescapable premise on which successful rule rested was that it should be rooted in real local control over local destiny and on governmental structures which were not, in territorial terms, over-centralised. This conclusion, arrived at in the Durham Report of 1839, reflected the growing appreciation that to be effective, colonial governmental structures required a high degree of autonomy and local accountability and, in many circumstances a sufficient degree of decentralisation. In this context, in 1865 Parliament at Westminster enacted the Colonial Laws Validity Act with in mind, in particular, the emerging but already advanced federal structures of Canada, Australia and New Zealand. The effect of the Act was not intended to fetter colonial legislative power, but to ensure that any colonial law should not be repugnant to any Act of Parliament. Order or Regulation made by Parliament, approved and applicable to any specific colony. In practice this important principle contributed to ensuring in the foundation years a consistency of approach to the development of Kenya's laws through the Emergency years and beyond. When Kenya became a colony in 1920 its affairs immediately came to be locked into the embrace of principles of law and administration compatible with those deemed appropriate at the time and subsequently, throughout Great Britain and the emerging Dominions. The well-tested principles and precepts of the Common Law, the rules of evidence and the independence of the judicial system were the foundation on which each colony's own autonomous system rested.

Two particular Acts of Parliament at Westminster were relevant to an understanding of the public policy ideas underlying London's approach toward self-government and independence in the years after World War I and reinforced by the experience of World War II. Underlying policy toward British imperial relationships was an affectionate regard and high respect for the peoples of the Dominions and Colonies who had generously and often at great sacrifice rallied to the Allied cause during times of conflict. It was simply stated by George V King Emperor when he formally opened the new Wembley Stadium on 24 April 1924. His vision of munificent potential was complemented by constitutional vision. In 1931 Parliament enacted the Statute of Westminster and, in 1935, the Government of India Act, each, in different ways, pointing the way to constitutional changes eventually applicable in Kenya as it followed many other territories in Africa and elsewhere to independence after World War II, less than twenty five years later. Whatever immediate factors may have expedited moves toward Kenya's independence during the post Emergency years, the history of British public policy is indelibly marked by recognition that autonomy and equality of status under law was the ultimate goal for all 'the Dominions, Colonies and Dependencies' in the emerging Commonwealth. Similarly, the Government of India Act followed the precedents of Canada and Australia in recognising the need for decentralised governmental structures if lasting foundations were to be made in geographically extensive and ethno-culturally diverse territories. No public documents could more clearly make these principles evident in all their demanding intricacy and as the lodestar for Kenya's future than the official Summary of the Proposal for Internal and Independent Self Government than HMSO Cmnd. 1970 published on the eve of Independence at Westminster in 1963.

London had been exceptionally active after World War II, during the years of colonial disengagement both in South, and South East Asia and in Africa in a search for constitutional systems which might sustain regional/ inter-state cohesion in situations which, without such systems, might tend to be driven apart, thereby generating conflict rather than economically fructive, cooperative cohesion. It was in this field that the concepts built into the very substantial and complex pattern of legislation shaping the legal framework for autonomy in North America, the Antipodes and the Sub-Continent may be identified as reflecting the policy approach to structures devised for Self Government throughout East Africa. In December 1961, under the aegis of the Commonwealth Development and Welfare Act, 1959, the East Africa Common Services Organisation (EACSO) was established. This was to provide structures to manage reciprocally useful services (eg. crop research, railways and inter-state roads) between the new states of Kenya, Uganda and Tanzania. As with much else in this field, this imaginative endeavour eventually failed. By 1977, largely because of the intransigence of Amin in Uganda, it had fallen apart completely. Given the deep-seated and short-term irredeemable deficit in experience and skills for such interstate activity and its fiscal costs, the collapse of EACSO had some merit in at least not distracting from the central task of resourcing the institutional structures of new states themselves, but it was symptomatic of the all pervasive institutional weakness in over-hasty change.

Indigenous Cultures and the Impact of Change.

Regardless of the imperial context in which events unrolled after Kenya became a Colony, it was at the grass roots of tribal life that the ambitions implicit in over-arching precepts of government or constitutional ambition would be realised, if at all. It was there that the unforeseen consequences of such matters would determine the reality of political and human outcomes. The raw material did not promise a smooth passage. Neither history nor geography promised a helpful contribution to impatiently looked-for immediacy.

Until the last years of the 19th Century, the hinterland of the East Coast of Africa had been of little more than tangential interest to outsiders as a source to overseas buyers of ivory and slaves through Arab intermediaries associated with the Sultanate of Zanzibar, itself a supplier of cloves. Since the 16th century, the haven of Mombasa, 140 miles north of Zanzibar and within the jurisdiction claimed by the Sultan, had attracted seafarers from the maritime states of Western Europe. The Portugese, with characteristic boldness, built a fort on its shore to protect their trade en route to India and the East Indies. The haven remained important for Arab dhows trading from the Gulf into the Indian Ocean and beyond. Following the construction of the Suez Canal in 1869, Mombasa's importance grew simultaneously with Britain's continuing desire to end the trade in human beings and with the intensifying imperial rivalries, between, in particular, the British and the French in Upper Egypt and the Sudan.

From this rivalry British curiosity was more specifically aroused in what lay behind and beyond the littoral. In the 21st century in an age of greatly improved communication, it is easy to be unappreciative of the practical significance of vast distance and seemingly unoccupied space. So it undoubtedly seemed to anyone venturing into the hinterland of East Africa. With no understood or evident boundaries, they discovered that the geographic heart of the land did not lie in a great river basin but in the unique and highly complex geological fault, the Great Rift Valley, running north-south for vast but then unmeasured distance from the Ethiopian Highlands to places yet ill-understood, but evidently linking unexplored lakes and grazing lands of untold scale. To the east lay the imposing massif Kirinyaga – Mount Kenya, and to the south west the largest inland water of Africa, Lake Victoria. The tentative probes of the British were directed primarily at the Lake. To get there they crossed vast areas occupied by often warring tribes of Nilotic, Hamitic or Bantu cultures, each very different one from the other, leaving Mount Kenya to the north of their westerly line of march.

The Nilotic and Hamitic tribes were nomadic cattle people, originating in the Nile Valley and the western areas of the Ethiopian Highlands, or in the

Horn of Africa to the north-east. Their lives were inexorably linked to the savannah and the natural cycle of the rains and the quality of grazing in the plains in competition with the prolific animals of the veldt. Their physical prowess and intimate understanding of land and water, flora and fauna, enabled them to maintain personal life on narrow margins always threatened by outbreaks of endemic and often lethal disease infecting them or decimating their stock. The often hard disciplines of long-tested tribal structures protected posterity in a world whose wide de facto and ever variable reach called for vigilance and provoked conflict as, in hot dry periods, they pressed into cooler forested, or better watered areas in competition with others – the Bantu tribes.

The Bantu were more settled peoples of the higher lands, practising primitive forms of 'shifting' agriculture. Such empiricism resulted in moderated use of forest and cleared land at higher altitudes as fertility waxed and waned with land use, a practice which enabled them more readily than the nomads of the plains to produce surpluses in barter from the soil or the forest, should uncertain opportunity arise. Among the Bantu were in particular, the Kikuyu, Embu and Meru tribes clustered round the 4700-6,000 ft. contours of the forested outliers of Kirinyaga (17,000ft.) and adjoining the Aberdare Mountains (11,000-13,000 ft.) to the west with Nyambeni Hills (6,000 ft.) to the east, overlooking the vast and arid plains drained by the Tana River eastward to the coast at Lamu. It was predominantly, though not exclusively, along the southern edge of this mountainous region and to the east of the Rift Valley that, of the three Bantu tribes in these temperate higher altitude lands, the Kikuyu who were drawn or tended eventually to be drawn into the Mau Mau. The Meru to the north-east and the Embu to the south-east sides of Mount Kenya were noticeably less compliant either in its brutalising practices or by its myopic distortion of historic truths. It was usually along the forest boundaries with the tribal lands, and in the interface of the settled lands of Nanyuki to the north of the mountain that they lent fitful support.

Regardless of the tribal group into which an African person was born, from time immemorial, life was moulded by tradition, custom and discipline defined by ritual and binding forms practised through successive generations and sealed by traditionally administered oaths of fealty and obedience in service to the tribes' needs. Tradition was nurtured by the elders; the cohesion of the tribe was secured by proper restraint and enshrined in customary practice. It was from this deep well of unrecorded human experience that each generation secured the future of the succeeding one on an assumption that no external factor upset the calculations on which customary practice rested.

During the first fifty years of the twentieth century, tribal societies were to experience an unprecedented number of radical upsets. Each change built on the impact of the other to create unprecedented disturbance to traditional practice born of the harsh struggle for survival. Accelerating diversity opened challenging but more benign opportunity. Colonial government was the midwife of change, but also a reconstructive palliative for its impact. Pacification had diminished the tribal warrior and undermined the timeless rituals which cemented them into the tribe as the keystone of tribal strength and protection. Bit by bit tribal barriers and languages gave way to the widespread use of Swahili and English. Where tribal life relied on experience and day to day judgement, the patterns of life increasingly became shaped by a need dramatically to revise introspective tribalism and to agree and establish fixed or variable boundaries in order to avert conflict in the extensive and increasingly intensive use of land. The impact of alien settlement and the emergence of entirely unprecedented marketable volumes of meat and crops began to change expectations and promote a sense of market value for land where historically there had been no currency by which to measure any such quantum. The implications of these changes for systems of law in customary law African courts and magistrates courts as well as in public administration were as far-reaching for tribal people as they were radical in their impact on life and livelihood and on future generations.

It is a tribute to the adaptability, intelligence and fortitude of tribal leaders through the years of change which ensued upon the first explorations of the interior and of the hinterland, that, with few exceptions, they accepted challenge and led their people patiently, wisely and with gratitude through this profound, dramatically new but, to them, manifestly benign phase of change. To many of these wise people and those who courageously followed, the Mau Mau offered their bitter, unimaginative, deconstructive and febrile opposition.

The Interplay of Race and Culture on Economic and Institutional Development.

By 1952, the year in the October of which the Emergency Regulations became effective, towns, trading centres and diverse urban communities, linked by well constructed and maintained roads had become established widely across the territory. The access of the Central Province tribes people southward had

23

been much enhanced by the growth of what had become the Colony's capital city, Nairobi which with the tribal lands to the north, became a magnet and focus for tribes people from all over the Colony as they increasingly became aware of new and stimulating opportunities and involved themselves in the newly evolving patterns of economic, social, and institutional life. Entirely new interfaces for tribes peoples were to prove significant for novel forms of politicisation significant though tribal identity remained. Nairobi had, in a quiet and modest way, become the centre not only of government but also of a relatively sophisticated cosmopolitan society in which indigenous and immigrant races mixed adaptively and without friction.

Three critical non-governmental factors had generated this rich genesis. The extraordinarily vitalising impact on the Colony of the the white settlers, that energetic, imaginative, and often highly cultivated minority, who had come to Kenya in substantial numbers before and between the two World Wars, were complemented by a no less enriching South Asian immigrant element. By the closing years of the 19th century it had become evident that the climate and soils of the high plateau from which the snow capped mountains of Kilimanjaro and Kenya rose majestically into the sky, although straddling the Equator, were potentially amenable to high quality agricultural production and stock rearing. Within the first four decades of the twentieth century a resourceful trickle of innovative and imaginative European farmers had established a highly productive constellation of industries associated with the agriculture and firmly rooted in high quality research units, and internal and external market outlets. Roman Catholic and non-Catholic missionaries had set up schools, hospitals and teacher-training colleges in a quiet and vitally enriching bid to fill the void left by the breakdown of tribal self-confidence. With a contemporaneous influx of South Asians into the few new municipalities and the growing rash of townships, the foundations for a prosperous and versatile, self-supporting national economy were being laid, interlocking across the whole territory.

In the brief period of half a century a dramatic human, institutional and environmental change had swept across the land. Painful lessons learnt by tribes people and immigrant farmers alike, had led to all-pervasive and inter-related programmes for land, forest, grassland and water management throughout the country. The implications of all this needed to be effectively audited, invigilated and skilfully managed both by government at the centre and by staff cadres in the increasingly influential Districts and Provinces.

During those several decades life for the Black People had drastically changed. Out of traditional tribal structures and in tribal lands, modern forms of local government, the African District Councils, customary law courts, magistrates courts, hospitals, schools and teachers' training colleges, well-developed agricultural and veterinary services and marketing organisations had all become powerful and influential contributors to welfare and wealth. The impact of the introduction of education policies for all races began to generate a balanced flow of trained minds to staff the rapidly growing institutions, contributing, inter alia to a growing sense of personal identity and affection for the country known as Kenya. Change had created a need to redefine land use especially in relation to new ideas of the public and sectional interests including the development of municipal and township land, tribal land and alienated agricultural land. Economic horizons were hugely widened. By the mid 'fifties, after years of patient advice and skilful management, African coffee produced by the Meru and Kiambu Kikuyu was beginning to be cooperatively marketed in the Kenya Coffee auctions in Europe along with award winning arabicas from Thika and Ruiru; by the early 'sixties African tea, underpinned by Commonwealth Development and Welfare funding, was beginning to be marketed. In Africa south of the Sahara, the Government of Kenya and the communities of Black, Brown and White had, in five brief decades, established benign foundations for a prosperous evolution unique in the history of its peoples.

It was into these uniquely creative advances of human welfare in Black Africa that the backward-looking delusions and destabilising impact of the myopic promoters of the Mau Mau intruded their moribund and narrowly self-serving ambitions.

It is on that foolhardy and self-destructive digression that David Lovatt Smith's important contribution to a rounded understanding of this most critical episode in Kenya's evolution, throws light. Public servants in the Colony and Protectorate during those critical years would, with him, ask only that those who now pass judgment on events which, for them, can only ever be judgment on remote echoes or fitful and insubstantial shadows, make their judgments on incontrovertible evidence to which this Foreword is an unabashed contribution.

P. R. Spendlove.
Wimbledon   15 November 2004

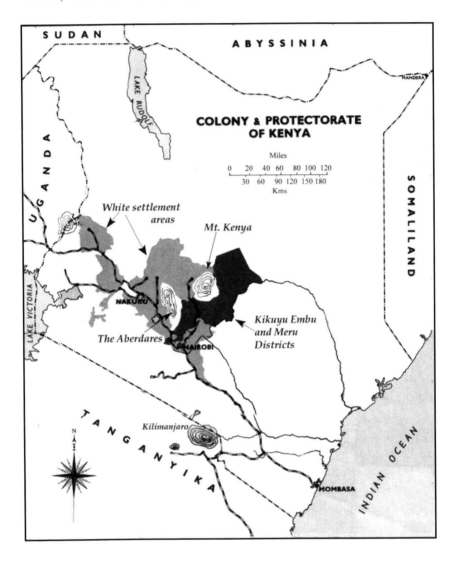

THE COLONY AND PROTECTORATE OF KENYA AS AT 1950

CHAPTER ONE

ORDER OUT OF CHAOS

'Old England is an Island,
And this is my complaint,
Why does Old England mess about
With Continents that ain't?'

A.P. Herbert: 'Foreign Policy'

'For it was slavery that first brought East Africa to Britain's special attention.'

Charles Miller: 'The Lunatic Express'

Any recent history of the Kikuyu people and particularly that of the Mau Mau conflict, cannot be taken in isolation from the previous history of East Africa. Certainly, any history of the colonial period can only be understood if it is taken in the context of the reason why the British were in that part of Africa in the first place – a natural enough question. Were they in Kenya by chance? Were they invited in by the local rulers? Did they have designs on the land or the minerals it might contain, or did they simply march in and take it over to gain a strategic advantage over other European powers who had also shown an interest in it? In fact, all those reasons played a part in the British Government's reluctant decision to become involved. But to understand clearly the prime and overwhelming reason why they were in the vicinity in the first place, one must go back further into the history of that part of Africa.

Who can say when the history of a country first begins? How far back is the historian supposed to go to trace the origins of his subject? Must he, in this case, go back to 'Lucy', the lady from whom all mankind is supposed to have descended, who herself, lived in East Africa more than two million years ago? One day, academics may have the tools for such a complete history book, but for the present we must be content to go back only as far as there are recorded events to report, or to artefacts that can be positively identified and dated.

The recorded history of eastern Africa is comparatively young. No records survive beyond the time when the first ships from Asia and Egypt came to trade along the coast. For it was trade that brought the first foreigners to its shores. East Africa had few resources that were sufficiently attractive to warrant exploration by merchant sailors. Unlike its neighbours to the south, it did not have gold or diamonds in any quantity nor at first sight, did its land appear to be particularly fertile. But it did have one major commodity that merchants would risk their lives to seek out, and there was plenty of it for those who were willing to make the dangerous and often years-long safaris into the interior to barter with those that harvested the merchandise. The product was, of course, ivory, and it is an interesting thought that as long as four thousand years ago, visitors were coming to East Africa to seek out parts of the same animal that still represents the major attraction in Kenya today. Ivory, a product of Africa's wildlife, was the most sustainable and valuable resource that East Africa has ever had, but today, thankfully, its producer, the elephant, does not have to be killed in order for its value to be realised, though sadly, its true value has yet to be appreciated by Governments.

A London Ivory warehouse in the 1890s

There was, however, a commodity of lesser value than ivory that had always been harvested together with the ivory. Indeed the two were complementary. There was no easy method of transporting the cumbersome and heavy ivory over the long distances from the hinterland to the coast. There were no roads, no trains, indeed the wheel had yet to be seen in eastern Africa except at the coast. So humans were the obvious means of conveying the huge bulks of ivory. And humans were cheap. All a trader had to do was to surround a village at night, set light to the thatch on the huts and catch the occupants as they tried to escape. Sometimes it was possible to pay the headman of a tribe or clan at war with their neighbours to seize a whole bunch of people from their enemies and have them ready to pick up the next time the trader passed that way. The cost of feeding them was minimal and the convenience great. It made sound business sense then, for the carriers themselves, having reached the coast and completed the transportation job for their Arab masters, to be sold off at the same time as the ivory. The two commodities would be stockpiled at one or other of the coastal ports, for onward shipment to the island of Zanzibar, where the main market for ivory and slaves had existed for centuries.

Nor was the trade a minor one. In the two decades up to 1873, 75% of the world's ivory originated from the Zanzibar markets. In the one year of 1863-4, for example, US$930,000's worth of ivory was exported from Zanzibar[2] (equivalent to £11m in 2003), which, at the average price of US$1 per lb. represents between ten and twelve thousand elephants. And the trade in humans was no less profitable. It is reliably estimated that some 30,000 slaves arrived at the coast annually during the six years 1870 - 1876[3], and this figure represents only a proportion of those that were actually taken from their homes, the balance having succumbed to maltreatment and illness on the long and arduous journeys to the coast.

Few of these slaves were actually taken from what is now Kenya. Most came from Tanganyika, the eastern Congo and as far south as Mozambique. The fierce Masai people were probably the reason for this. Their ferocious and bloodthirsty nature was legendry and few Arabs would dare to risk their whole caravan of ivory being plundered by a horde of the renowned Masai warriors. So the slave hunters always avoided Masailand.

Amongst the many eyewitness accounts of slave caravans heading towards the coast, this by A.J. Swann[4] is typical:

As they filed past [our camp] we noticed many chained together by the neck. Others had their necks fastened into the forks of poles about six feet long, the ends of which were supported by the men who preceded

[2] Esmond Bradley-Martin: 'Zanzibar. Tradition and Revolution' Hamish Hamilton p. 37
[3] Ibid p.32
[4] A.J. Swann: 'Fighting the Slave Hunters in Central Africa' Seeley & Co., 1910 p.84

them.[5] The women who were as numerous as the men, carried babies on their backs in addition to a tusk of ivory or other burden on their heads.

It is difficult adequately to describe the filthy state of their bodies; in many instances not only scarred by the cut of a 'chicote' (a whip made of hide), but feet and shoulders were a mass of open sores, made more painful by the swarms of flies which followed the march and lived on the flowing blood. They presented a picture of utter misery, and one could not help wondering how many of them had survived the long tramp from the upper Congo at least 1,000 miles distant. Our own inconveniences sank into insignificance compared with the suffering of this crowd of half-starved, ill-treated creatures who, weary and friendless must have longed for death.

The headmen in charge were most polite to us as they passed our camp. Each was armed with a rifle, knife and spear, and although decently clothed in clean cotton garments, they presented a thoroughly villainous appearance. Addressing one, I pointed out that many of the slaves were unfit to carry loads. To this he smilingly replied, "They have no choice! They must go or die!"

Then ensued the following conversation:-

"Are these slaves destined for Zanzibar?"

"Most of them, the remainder will stay at the coast."

"Have you lost many on the road?"

"Yes, numbers have died of hunger!"

"Any run away?"

"No, they are too well guarded. Only those which become possessed with the devil try to escape: there is nowhere they could run to, if they should go."

"What do you do when they become too ill to travel?"

"Spear them at once!" was the fiendish reply. "For if we did not, others would pretend that they were ill in order to avoid carrying their loads! No, we never leave them alive on the road; they all know our custom."

"I see women carrying not only their child on their backs, but in addition, a tusk of ivory or other burden on their heads. What do you do in their case when they become too weak to carry both child and ivory? Who carries the ivory?"

"She does! We cannot leave valuable ivory on the road. We spear the child to make her burden lighter. Ivory first, child afterwards!"

---

[5] A forked pole that held the slave's neck fast by a metal bar across the fork.

Speke writes of whole areas of country around Lake Tanganyika that had been depopulated by the Arab slave traders. Tippu Tib was perhaps the most renowned slaver of all. It was normal for many of the smaller tribes to be constantly at war with each other. The victors would enslave the vanquished and would keep them corralled until Tippu Tib came along on his next safari when they would sell them to him together with any ivory that had also been collected. In this way great swathes of land became depopulated between the coast and Lake Tanganyika and Speke conjectures that if the slave trade was not soon stopped, the whole of the interior would be devoid of humanity.

Ronald Hardy[6] writes:

> There was, of course, nothing new in a Muslim Arab trade in slaves. Slavery in one form or another had existed since the earliest inland expeditions. But by Livingstone's time, the trade had increased dramatically. It was organised with a fearsome energy. Funds flowed from Indian sources in Zanzibar. Firearms could now be bought and the caravans went further and further into the interior. Ivory was the goal. Those were the days of the great elephant populations and money hung, it seemed, from the heads of the tuskers in inexhaustible supplies. But there was no wheeled transport. Only men could carry it. The caravans penetrated deeper and deeper, even as far as the Great Lake. There on the shores, where the tribes were concentrated, was an abundance of bone and muscle. The arrangement was perfect in its simplicity. Both commodities, ivory and people, were obtained at little cost. By the middle of the nineteenth century, some fifty thousand slaves were passing through the Zanzibar market. ...For each to survive the rigours of the long march down (Livingstone estimated) perhaps ten had died. These were the statistics of misery; these the revelations which were to rekindle in the British nation the dormant passion for philanthropic crusade.

Only a few of these slaves originated from present day Kenya, but all those that survived the journey to the coast, would eventually be sold through the Zanzibar slave market where foreigners from Europe would come face to face with the horror and misery of it all.

When Speke arrived in Zanzibar on 20th December 1856 he found a situation far worse than anything he could imagine. He writes of seeing dogs

---

[6] Ronald Hardy: *'The Iron Snake'* Collins 1965. p.17

on the shores of the island, devouring the flesh of the sick and dying humans that had been thrown overboard from the holds of slave dhows that plied along the coast. And when he entered the town itself, he found that slaves '...*roamed through every street, men, women and children, those who had been domesticated by years of captivity, and those who had just arrived from the interior and who were half mad and half dead through hunger and maltreatment'*.

The markets themselves were the ultimate humiliation for the slaves. Alan Moorehead describes the scene witnessed by Thomas Smee, commander of the British research ship Ternate, who visited Zanzibar in 1811:

The show commences at about four o'clock in the afternoon. The slaves, set off to best advantage by having their skins cleaned and burnished with cocoa-nut oil, their faces painted with red and white stripes, which is here esteemed elegance, and the hands, noses, ears and feet ornamented with a profusion of bracelets of gold and silver and jewels, are ranged in a line, commencing with the youngest, and increasing to the rear according to their size and age. At the head of this file, which is composed of both sexes and all ages from 6 to 60, walks the person who owns them; behind and at each side, two or three of his domestic slaves, armed with swords and spears, serve as a guard.

Thus ordered, the procession begins, and passes through the market-place and the principal streets; the owner holding forth in a kind of song the good qualities of his slaves and the high prices that have been offered for them.

When any of them strikes a spectator's fancy, the line immediately stops, and a process of examination ensues, which, for minuteness is unequalled in any cattle market in Europe. The intending purchaser, having ascertained there is no defect in the faculties of speech, hearing etc., that there is no disease present, and that the slave does not snore in sleeping, which is counted a very great fault, next proceeds to examine the person; the mouth and the teeth are first inspected and afterwards every part of the body in succession, not even excepting the breasts etc. of the girls, many of whom I have seen handled in the most indecent manner in the public market by their purchasers; indeed there is every reason to believe that the slave-dealers almost universally force the young girls to submit to their lust previous to their being disposed of.

The slave is then forced to walk or run a little way, to show there is no defect about the feet; and after which, if the price be agreed to, they are stripped of their finery and delivered over to their future master.[7]

Alan Moorehead goes on to record that in the forty-five years between Smee's official report and the arrival of Burton and Speke in Zanzibar, slavery had been abolished within the British Empire and consequently the trade from the Atlantic coast of West Africa had been closed down. The British public were therefore shocked when they heard that a thriving slave trade was still being carried on by the Arabs on the east coast of Africa. When reports reached England from British naval ships that intercepted the slave dhows and found horrific conditions on board, there was an outcry. Palmerston, as Foreign Secretary, made strong representation to the Sultan of Zanzibar through whose country most of the slaves had to pass.

Palmerston had been largely responsible for bringing the end of the Atlantic slave trade, a crusade that had been initiated by William Wilberforce. He was incensed by reports received from Naval captains and from letters published in newspapers giving eye-witness accounts of the horrific conditions suffered by the slaves on dhows that were stopped and searched on their way from Zanzibar to Arabia and Persia and to the French Possessions of Mauritius and Réunion where they were used on the vast sugar plantations. David Livingstone was appalled at what he found on his travels through Central and East Africa. He called the trade *'this open sore of the world'* and writes: *'If my disclosures should lead to the suppression of the slave trade, I shall regard that as a greater matter by far than the discovery of all the Nile sources together.'*

Charles Miller[8] , author of 'The Lunatic Express', perhaps the most objective, complete and readable version of the history of eastern Africa who comments: *'I think the British Empire with all its horrendous failings, was on balance a good thing. I mourn its passing.'* writes:

It should be borne in mind that this was an era which saw Britain's ideology of empire taking its shape largely from the Palmerstonian credo of world domination through free-trade and moral influence—although backed up, when necessary, by the threat of force. British policy in East Africa, such as it was, turned on two objectives: to put down the slave trade and to utilise Zanzibar's geographical positions (as well as its ties with Oman) as a sentry post, guarding the southern route to India. Hand

[7] Alan Moorehead: *'The White Nile'* Hamish Hamilton , 1960 p.11
[8] Charles Miller: *'The Lunatic Express'* Futura 1972. p. 68

in glove with these aims went a third policy: tacit yet uncompromising rejection of any colonial acquisitions.

The last sentence might surprise those who believe the British to have had imperial designs on this part of Africa. But Charles Miller was not wrong. He had done his homework.

It was, in fact Hamerton, the British Consul in Zanzibar who negotiated a treaty with the Sultan Seyyid Said in 1845 forbidding the export of slaves from any of the Sultan's east African dominions. The Treaty, which was to take effect on 1st January 1847, allowed for the Royal Navy to search and confiscate any vessels on the high seas belonging to the Sultan, which were found to contain slaves.

Palmerston in London wrote to Hamerton: *"You will take every opportunity of impressing upon these Arabs that the nations of Europe are destined to put an end to the African Slave Trade and that Great Britain is the main instrument in the hand of Providence for the accomplishment of this purpose"*[9]

That Hamerton was able to dictate to the Sultan in this manner was possible, because the Royal Navy was the most powerful force on the high seas and ruled the sea lanes, not only on the Indian Ocean but over most of the globe. Zanzibar was an island in the Indian Ocean, and all its wealth came from the mainland, across barely twenty miles of water. Ivory and slaves came to Zanzibar from Mombasa, Bagamoyo, Kilwa and other small ports along the coast of what is now Kenya and Tanzania. All its exports of ivory, slaves, copra and spices had to travel several hundred miles across an ocean that gave plenty of time for cruisers of Royal Navy to find and intercept them. Better, the Sultan reasoned, to have such a powerful navy as an ally rather than an enemy though it took another thirty years to convince him and his successors finally, to end the trade altogether.

Hamerton even offered the Sultan £2,000 a year for the first two years in order to offset the loss of customs duty that would have been payable on the slaves. While accepting the offer, the Sultan pleaded that the part of the trade to be abolished by the projected Treaty was actually closer to £10,000 a year – a figure by today's equivalent of over half a million pounds!

It should be no surprise then that the trade was still going on and in fact

---

[9] R. Coupland: *'The Exploitation of East Africa 1856 – 1890'* Faber & Faber . p.150

increasing in anticipation of its inevitable closure 28 years later when the British Government finally issued an ultimatum to the then Sultan Barghash through their Consul, John Kirk. His orders were: '...*to inform the Sultan that Her Majesty's Government requires him to conclude the Treaty ...and to take effectual measures within all parts of his dominions to prevent and suppress [the slave trade]*' The signal to Kirk from Lord Granville, the British Foreign Secretary states: '*You will state to the Sultan that if the Treaty is not accepted and signed by him before the arrival of Admiral Cumming, the British naval forces will proceed to blockade the island of Zanzibar*'.[10]

Admiral Cumming was Commander in Chief of a task force of one battleship and three cruisers on their way to Zanzibar from the U.K. The Americans also had a Cruiser in the vicinity and were prepared to offer assistance if necessary, but interestingly, the French, no doubt with an eye to their sugar plantations in their southern Indian Ocean islands, sided with the Sultan and secretly advised him that the British would not press home their threat. Sultan Barghash and his Council did not trust de Vienne, the French consul, and under the very real threat of a naval blockade, gave in and signed the ratification of the 1845 Treaty on 5th June 1873. [11]

Other European countries were now beginning to take an interest in eastern Africa, notably the French, the Germans, the Belgians and even the Americans whose interest was boosted by the stories of Henry Stanley, an American citizen, and his travels to the interior of that vast and untamed continent to look for and eventually to find Livingstone. The Germans particularly were entertaining ideas of colonising parts of the interior, and explorers were bringing back reports of fertile highlands around the snow-capped mountain Kilimanjaro. But before anyone could reach Kilimanjaro, or anywhere else on the mainland, they had to get permission from the Sultan of Zanzibar. His Highness laid claim to a strip of the mainland coast of eastern Africa from Mogadishu in the north, to Cape Delgado, some 800 miles to the south, so that anyone landing at Mombasa or at any other of the mainland ports, had to pay his dues to the Sultan first, necessitating a visit to Zanzibar.

No one could arrive in Zanzibar without the knowledge of all the residents, and the British were the first to know who had arrived and what their business was. The Sultan feared and respected the British more than the

---

[10] Ibid p.207
[11] The full text of the Treaty, translated from the Arabic text. Ibid p.212 - 213

others, because of their naval power. He also trusted their advice more, as was evident when they were asked to arbitrate over a dispute between three brothers as to which one of them should succeed their father as Sultan (The Canning Award)[12]

By the time the slave trade was finally shut down and the slave market in Zanzibar closed its gates for the last time, Britain was beginning to realise there was more to East Africa than ivory, slaves, copra and spices. It was clearly a good hunting ground for missionaries, some of whom were bringing back interesting news about the country behind Mombasa. No less than four British Missionary Societies had been plying their trade since Krapf of the Church Missionary Society founded the first mission station at Rabai, near Mombasa in 1844. By 1880 these societies, together with a few intrepid explorers, had been bringing back reports of vast areas of unoccupied land covered in herds of wild animals; of snow-capped mountains, crystal clear rivers and fertile valleys; of uninhabited sunlit uplands simply waiting for occupation by the technologically advanced European farmers.

Britain, though, had always respected the independence of the Sultan's realm. It had signed a Declaration with the French in 1862 that both countries would respect the independence not only of Zanzibar Island itself, but also of the Sultan's *'dominions and dependencies on the mainland of East Africa'* (even though it may be doubtful where the western frontiers of those dependencies lay). The British maintained that the Sultan's land was inviolate, and that the guarantee of independence must be firmly upheld. Zanzibar had, by now, acquired the international status of an independent State in the Society of States. *'It had concluded treaties with several other states on a footing of equality; and if it had concluded one particular treaty under duress,[the 1847 - 1873 treaty to close down the slave trade] it had yielded, as sovereign states have often yielded, to 'force majeure' without losing its independence'*[13].

Moreover, the Sultan was not averse to the British having a hand in the administration of his dominions on the mainland. Indeed, *'...the moment he signed the Treaty of 1873, he established so close a relationship with the official agent [Kirk] of that foreign [British] Government, took him so fully*

---

[12] R. Coupland: *'The Expoitation of East Africa 1856 – 1890'* Faber & Faber p.*26-31*
[13] Ibid. *p.266*

into his confidence, became so increasingly dependent on his advice as to endow that agent... with a personal authority in his dominions scarcely less respected than his own. Kirk, the British consul-general, became a sort of unofficial prime minister of Zanzibar.[14] Kirk was also recognised by most of the Arabs trading in the interior as being on an equal to the Sultan himself, and even the German consul, Schultz, looked upon him as *'the real Governor of Zanzibar'*. In the twelve years between 1873 and 1885 the close trust and friendship between Kirk and Sultan Barghash proved to be an ideal foundation on which to extend their influence into the interior by the two men.

All this was an important prelude to the future administration of East Africa by the European powers. The legal trade that was now being carried on in the interior in ivory, cotton, spices, beads and indeed weapons, and the increasing numbers of missionaries entering the country to take up residence there, meant that inevitably the country would continue to be opened up and some form of official administration would become necessary sooner or later.

The murder, then, of an English missionary named Penrose, in 1879, near Tabora in Tanganyika, brought things to a head. The thug elements that carried out this murder caused considerable concern to the Sultan. Such elements, he realised, and such incidents were bound to weaken his claim on the lands behind the coastal strip. The Sultan recognised that if it was seen that he was unable to control *'his'* people, and murders took place of foreigners who were there quite legally and with his permission, it would be a good excuse for the governments of those foreigners to take the law into their own hands and bring in their own peace-keeping force, which would soon lead to a take-over of the whole country. The murder of Penrose some 400 miles from the coast therefore, precipitated prompt action by the Sultan who was, according to Kirk, *'...prepared to ...place the administration of the interior in the hands of a European Officer, providing ...a settled government along the main lines of trade'*[15]. This came about because he was unable to police the country himself with his lack of expertise and relatively meagre resources.

The British government, however were not at all keen to get involved with administering a land that had no perceivable benefit to them. They had, by then, done their bit by single-handedly putting a stop to the slave trade, and the Foreign Office was preoccupied with the aftermath of the Indian Mutiny,

---

[14] Ibid *p.266*
[15] Ibid p.374

the Afghan wars and Home Rule for Ireland to take on yet more dependencies however needy they might be. They were simply not interested and communicated this to Kirk. Coupland points out the importance of this attitude: *'For if British imperialism in the nineteenth century had been as grasping and unscrupulous as is often represented, the murder of a British Missionary would have provided an admirable excuse for forcible intervention.'*[16] In the event, the British did nothing.

Such was the standing of Kirk and the British in Zanzibar that even when the Sultan suggested in 1880, that the British appoint a Governor General to administer his dominions, which would include virtually all of what is now East Africa, the British were not interested, and refused to accept any new responsibility. They were happy for their man in Zanzibar to help and guide the Sultan in his policies, but they were not willing to take the matter any further than that.

Sultan Barghash, however, was not giving up that easily. By now, he desperately wanted someone, and preferably the British, to give him greater assistance in controlling his domains, because he knew he was not going to be able to do it on his own and he did not want to lose it to some European power that might threaten his very seat of government in Zanzibar. A year later, in 1881, in a fit of panic, and unbeknown to anyone, he drew up a Deed *'of such historical importance'* that Coupland gives the whole text of it in his book'.[17] This would have given effective control of the whole of East Africa to the British, virtually handing them his Regency on a plate. The Deed, on his death, put control of Zanzibar and all its dominions and dependencies at the disposal of what he calls 'The Great Government'— the British.

But the British still did not budge, and Kirk's orders were politely to refuse. As an excuse the British cited the Anglo-French Declaration of twenty years previously: *'To Respect in all matters the Independence of the Sultanate.'* The French, by this time, had in any case become more interested in Madagascar and the Comoros Islands than East Africa, and had bowed out of the picture by then.

It wasn't, in fact, until the Germans began to show a more assertive interest in the coast of East Africa, that the British government really began to look at the situation more closely. Kirk himself was dead against a colony as

---

[16] Ibid *p.374*
[17] *Ibid p.377*

such. He was still much more in favour of the British remaining the main influence supporting the Sultan's independent sovereignty, so that British tradesmen, British missionaries, British scientists and British sportsmen could travel there and ply their trades, expertise and pastimes. Mindful of these new German interests, though, the British Government ordered Kirk to ask the Sultan to sign a Declaration that he would *'not accept the protectorate of any nation whatever, nor cede [his] sovereign rights or any part of [his] dominions...to any Power or Association without consulting the English...'* The Sultan signed the Declaration the same day Kirk presented it to him.

It was clearly the British government's intention that the development of East Africa should be influence, not annexation: the Sultan's flag, not the British, but especially not the German.

But it seemed the Germans had got the bit between their teeth, and were not going to be put off so easily. A flotilla of German warships arrived off Zanzibar as a demonstration of their power and intentions, and had it not been for Kirk's diplomacy and Whitehall's strong representation to Berlin, things might have turned in favour of the Germans. No one, least of all the Sultan was more mindful of the fact that Zanzibar was unable to protect itself in the face of great naval powers like France, Germany and Britain. Therefore if Britain did not take on the job of protecting the Sultan, then Germany certainly would. And if anyone had to do the job, it should surely be Britain. After all it was her explorers that first put the place on the map by discovering the source of the Nile; her missionaries who had borne the brunt of opening up the hinterland and calming the natives, but most of all it was she that had been of the greatest service to the real owners of the land, the indigenous population themselves, who had, since time immemorial been carried off by slavers, their land despoiled and left to waste. It was left unsaid, but doubtless thought by Kirk and the British that the Arabs had never done any good to the country as a whole. Indeed they had only brought harm. All they had done in the several hundred years they had been there was to exploit its only two natural resources, ivory and slaves, and had grown exceedingly rich on the pickings thereof.

As German interests in the coastline of Africa rose, the British Government realised they could not simply ignore the fact that if they didn't take matters in hand soon, other powers would, and that might well affect Britain's access to harbours on the coast of East Africa for ships on their way either from the Cape or from the Suez Canal to India and the Far east. The

French had by now annexed Madagascar and the Comoros and other islands in the Indian Ocean. Now, it appeared, Germany wanted to take over the key ports along the rest of the mainland coast of eastern Africa. Britain as a leading naval power, could no longer afford to disregard the likelihood of losing the strategically important ports of Zanzibar, Mombasa, and Tanga to another sabre-rattling European country, Germany.

It came to a head, when a German explorer Dr.Carl Peters took it upon himself to persuade the local chiefs of four areas within the Sultan's dependencies on the mainland to sign 'treaties', making over their land to the German Emperor Bismarck. Peters had no authority whatsoever from the German government to do this, and these 'treaties' could by no means be considered legal — the chiefs were illiterate and simply signed with crosses. Nevertheless, when Peters returned to Berlin and waved them in front of the German Emperor, they were enough to show him and the German Government, that for all the Treaties and Declarations the British had signed with the Sultan, this land was there for the taking.

Germany had few colonies up to that time, and she was beginning to feel left behind in the race to build an empire, on which her neighbours Britain, France, Belgium, Holland, Portugal and Spain had been employed for many years, and in the case of the latter two, for centuries. Germany could see that she would not be able to sit round the tables of the European powers that were slowly but surely amassing great swathes of the globe, unless she also could boast an empire. At that jingoistic time, empires were important indicators of a country's standing in the world's corridors of power, and Germany was anxious to sit at the tables within those corridors, particularly if she happened to know of countries that were there, just for the taking.

Carl Peters' buccaneering and somewhat audacious act, brought the reluctant British Government up with a jolt. They realised at last that they could not continue to hide behind the 1862 agreement to respect the Sultan's independency. The writing was now clearly on the wall. The days of the Sultan's 'dominions and dependencies' wherever they were, were inevitably numbered.

A Conference was hastily convened in Berlin towards the end of 1884 in which the British and the Germans agreed once and for all, the 'spheres of influence' they sought. They somewhat generously 'allowed' the Sultan to keep his islands of Zanzibar, Pemba and Mafia, together with a narrow strip of mainland coast ten miles in depth and six hundred miles in length, and the rest of the interior they divided up in more or less equal halves. Germany was to have the southern half which became German East Africa, then Tanganyika and finally Tanzania, and Britain the northern half – the present day Kenya. The western boundaries were left undefined for the moment for none of the powers were particularly interested in lands to the west, populated by primitive peoples and lorded over by despot kings or Kabaka.

On March 3rd 1885 the day after the close of the Berlin Conference, the German Government published an Act accepting suzerainty over the four areas Carl Peters had so conveniently found. The die was now cast. The future boundaries of the interior would now be settled and the security and well-being of its inhabitants, many of whom had been so cruelly exploited for so long, was assured for the next seventy-five years or so.

Later, the Sultan leased a two hundred mile coastal strip of the British section, which included the port of Mombasa, to the newly formed Imperial British East Africa Company. Thus the British, de facto, came to administrate an enormous piece of land that they did not want, for the sake of securing the strategically important port of Mombasa.

Charles Miller[18] writes:

> …the building of the Imperial framework in east Africa was anything but a deliberate or even a conscious act of British Policy. …Any suggestion that England might have been seeking to plant the Union Jack over such a quagmire, would have appalled every responsible Prime Minister and Cabinet member of every major Party. Until the final two decades of the century, the least conspicuous feature and the least desired goal of British Imperial thinking was territorial expansion in Africa.

If Britain had had its way, the control of eastern Africa would have been left to the Sultan of Zanzibar, using Britain as its consultant in political matters in much the same way as Britain was doing for Egypt in the Sudan. The port of Mombasa would have been leased to the British, and Zanzibar's income, if correctly used and accounted for, would have been sufficient to pay for the cost of basic administration of its mainland dependencies. But it was naïve of the British government to think that one or other of the great European powers would be content to see a minor Arab state acquire such a large proportion of the African continent without lifting a finger, and that one or other of those

---

[18] Charles Miller: *'The Lunatic Express'*, Futura, 1972 p.68

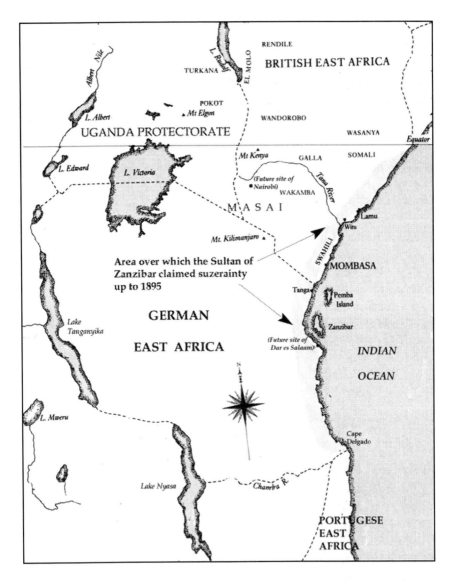

**EASTERN AFRICA, FOLLOWING THE DIVISIONS MADE AT THE BERLIN
CONFERENCE IN 1885**

powers would not, sooner or later, step in and grab it.

As it was, on September 3rd 1888, the Imperial British East Africa Company received its royal charter and the Company's headquarters were established at Mombasa with an advance post set up at Machakos some 250 miles inland. Thus the preparations were complete for the effective occupation and governance of the interior, reaching westwards towards the boundary with the recently agreed Congo Free State to which the Belgians laid claim. The western half of the British area was to be known as Uganda, after the Buganda people.

Uganda was, however, of some importance to the British because of the source of the Nile and the effect this geographic quirk had on Egypt and therefore on the Suez Canal, which was of the greatest importance to the British. Having accepted responsibility for the northern half of East Africa at the Berlin Conference, they realised the necessity of ensuring that the source of the Nile at least, came within the boundaries of their jurisdiction. It took a British Army officer, patriot and empire builder named Frederick Lugard, in 1890 to put down the tribal and internecine wars that had so tormented the country up to that time, to settle the boundaries and to bring the modern state of Uganda under British protection where it remained until 1961.

The Buganda tribe were the most influential of the peoples in that region and perhaps the most advanced of all East Africans. But they were ruled over by a despotic leader known as the Kabaka, and when he declined the invitation to come under British protection, he was virtually frog-marched to the conference table by Capt. Lugard to sign the treaty that gave his people the protection of Britain in return for British suzerainty. Once the Kabaka had signed, the other Kings and leaders fell into line or were easily 'persuaded' to sign. At that time, Capt. Lugard was employed by the Imperial British East Africa Company (IBEAC) who were the official agents of the British Government.

Uganda initially included nearly half of what is now Kenya. This status remained until 1902, in order to ensure the somewhat nebulous objective of cost-effectively protecting the sources of the Nile and securing the northern shore and islands of Lake Victoria against German competition, whilst avoiding complications which might arise from alien settlement. Uganda was always a Protectorate, not a Colony. No European settlement took place and the clear intention of the British Government was to leave as soon as a democratic system of self-government could be introduced. This would require education of the masses and political maturity, which the British realised might take some time. Sadly, as it turned out, the British decided to leave after only 70 years, well before the electorate were sufficiently well-versed to judge the political maturity and trustworthiness of their politicians. For in a comparatively short time after the British left in 1963, the rise to power of two tyrants, Amin and Obote, one after the other, brought the country to its knees, from which it will take years, perhaps even generations to recover.

It is quite clear, therefore, that Britain was a most reluctant participant in the scramble for the eastern part of Africa. Apart from the port of Mombasa, Uganda seemed at the time, to be the most important asset gained, but even that turned out to be a 'white elephant' in the end, and cost the British taxpayer dearly in terms of administrators and infrastructure for little in return, except the satisfaction of knowing they had alleviated some of the pain the inhabitants were suffering and had set them on the road to becoming a nation.

Kenya was a different matter. Once it was realised there were great swathes of land in areas of high elevation where the climate all the year round was not dissimilar to summer in the U.K., and that most of these lands were occupied by nothing more than herds of wild animals, interest began to be aroused. Here, the first administrators reasoned, there could be farms managed by technically advanced Europeans who, in return, would not only employ the local inhabitants, but would also show them better methods of farming in order to obtain the maximum production from the land so that the people would no longer starve in years of drought, and attack their neighbours in order to steal their food and crops and their women and children as they had done with monotonous regularity up to now. At the same time, a strict Administration would calm the natives, introduce an orderly system of government and stop them from killing or enslaving each other. The resulting pacification would provide an opportunity for introducing methods of government capable of providing self-sustaining stability and scope for productive development of local communities able to manage their own affairs.

Sir John Kirk, who was not only the originator of British presence in East Africa, but also its inspiration and its representative for the first twenty years (1866 – 1886), died in 1922 at the grand old age of 90. He must be seen as the first British commissioner in East Africa who initiated the new order regarding the inviolability of the indigenous African's rights to their land. He was the first to realise that black peoples, for all their backwardness, could not be treated as a race apart from the rest of the world; that they could not be denied the opportunities of 'life, liberty and the pursuit of happiness' accorded to all other peoples.

In the same year that Kirk died, the League of Nations bestowed on Great Britain the Mandate for Tanganyika after Germany's defeat in the First World War. That Mandate, which could equally be applied to all three territories, required that the British Government, and therefore the British

Sir John Kirk after his retirement

people, are pledged *'to promote to the utmost, the material and moral well-being and the social progress of the inhabitants and to help them, in the course of time, to stand by themselves in the world'*. Kirk would, I believe, be proud of the record of the following forty years until Independence was granted to those three countries, a record which he himself so ably, if reluctantly, set in motion.

CHAPTER TWO

CIVILISATION BETTER THAN BARBARISM

'If I didn't mutilate the innocent, how could I make the guilty fear me'

King Kabarega of Bunyoro

To come to terms with one's history, whatever it may reveal, is to learn from the lessons it can provide; it is to understand the progress society has made, and to fully appreciate one's present situation. The examples it teaches must spur one on to work for even better conditions for one's descendants and for future generations of society.

Less than four hundred years before the Kenya Emergency was declared, an English Queen ordered her henchmen to burn alive hundreds of people, for no greater misdemeanour than professing the protestant Faith in a predominantly catholic England. Later, her sister, Queen Elisabeth 1 ordered her own advisers, if she believed them to be traitors, to be hanged, drawn and quartered — a very messy business where the body was first disembowelled and then dismembered. The bits were then buried, and it was deemed to be the height of disgrace for the surviving family. In the eighteenth century, the French laughed and drank wine during the spectacle of thousands of their countrymen being decapitated by a guillotine — an even more messy spectacle. Even as late as the twentieth century, men were being shot on the battlefields of France on the orders of their own officers, for displaying what they perceived to be 'cowardice or desertion in the face of the enemy', and this was forty years before the murder of six million innocent people in the holocaust and the killing of tens of thousands at Hiroshima and Nagasaki. These are all things Europeans would prefer to forget. All countries and all peoples of the world have 'skeletons in their cupboards', which they would prefer to keep there, with the doors tightly closed.

But it is impossible to escape from one's history. Better by far to accept that this was how things were, and to learn from the mistakes of one's ancestors and aim to create a still more perfect society.

In 1885, when, during the Berlin Conference, portions of eastern Africa were shared out between the Germans and the British, the indigenous inhabitants of those lands had been living in a state of turmoil and misery since time immemorial. Fear was the all-consuming affliction. Fear of one's enemies; fear of the slavers; fear of starvation; fear of wild animals, fear of disease. Life was one long battle against a host of adversities and deprivations. Women had even more to fear than men. In a male dominated society, typical of most African tribes, a woman was little more than a beast of burden: a chattel. Indeed some African tribes today in 2004 still pay more respect to their cattle than they do to their womenfolk. Only now, in the twenty-first century, are numbers of Masai girls even at primary school age, beginning to equal the numbers of boys. Secondary and tertiary colleges have yet to catch up.

No white man had been near Kikuyuland until 1883. The people had no notion of the outside world and of other ways of life. They could scarcely have been more isolated from the rest of the world than if they had been living on the surface of the moon.

When the first missionaries and explorers arrived in this part of sub-Saharan Africa they found the indigenous inhabitants were extraordinarily primitive. While much of the rest of the world had for centuries been gaining in their battle against the fearsome trials of life: developing new weapons with which to fight their enemies; inventing new methods of agriculture to guard against starvation; exterminating wild animals that were a threat to them and developing new medicines with which to combat diseases, the people in this part of Africa were still living in what can best be described as the stone age. The element of imagination among the people had not yet fully developed, for imagination is the antecedent of invention leading to development and progress. Technology was virtually absent, though some smelting of iron ore was being carried out by an elite Kikuyu clan, and primitive metal weapons were being made. Even the wheel was not yet in use. Infant mortality was rampant. Life was not the precious thing it is today. Homicide was a necessary means for survival, and to those who could not imagine a better life, death was a comparatively minor affair and must have been an attractive option for those for whom life became totally unbearable, particularly the women.

Scoresby Routledge, who in general holds a high opinion of Kikuyu society, gives an example of the extraordinary lack of value in which the Kikuyu held their own life.

> The Kikuyu man seems to possess the peculiar faculty of letting himself go until he is absolutely gone. A man will publicly say that he intends to die, and within a few days or weeks he will be dead. He does nothing

actively, but simply mopes about for a while, getting weaker and weaker, then lies down and fades out.

As a case in illustration, one of my men told me he had, in special circumstances, lost his wives and his flocks, and that now he had just heard that his brother was dead; he therefore meant to die too. Had no notice been taken, I have not the least doubt that within a month he would have done so. I, however, formally called him to me and said to him, "I have heard what you have said; your words are the words of a fool. With much trouble I have taught you to grasp intelligence, and now you say you want to die? A spirit not your own has come into you. I say it is to go immediately, and you will be well and happy. If I see you miserable, then it has not gone, and it must be driven out by beatings. Come every day at the third hour and tell me whether you need a beating by the guard." The sufferer replied that, as we were friends , of course he would not die if I objected. The evil spirit left him: the man was a changed being in a few hours. I have no doubt that he owed his life to me.[19]

If his own life means so little to him, it must follow that the lives of others, outside his own family, are virtually worthless.

In 1880, Thomson, on his first exploration of East Africa, mentions a Chief he visited called Lusinga who had just begun to appreciate the market value of slaves and ivory. The former could only be obtained by war and Thompson writes that Lusinga had depopulated two hundred square miles of the most fertile land in the interior. Later, on visiting Pamililo, the chief's village, he found it *"protected by a very high and strong stockade. This was grimly ornamented by a few hundred human skulls in all conditions, from the freshly stuck up head to the bleached cranium...the ground outside was strewn with human bones."[20]*

Slavery was practised by most of the tribes throughout East Africa but surprisingly not by the Kikuyu, though it is well documented that the neighbouring Kamba people would raid the Kikuyu to take slaves and sell them to the Arabs. Leakey writes of this practice in his book 'The Southern Kikuyu Before 1903'. *'The Akamba made a definite practice of raiding Kikuyu women and girls with the intention of selling them to the Arabs, and not a few*

---

[19] W. Scoresby Routledge: *'With a Prehistoric People'* Frank Cass 1968 p.272
[20] J.A. Golding – Introduction to *Colonialism – the Golden Years* Birlings 1987

Kikuyu were, therefore, taken to the coast as slaves through the agency of the Akamba'[21].

The Kabaka of Buganda would send his troops out to neighbouring islands or shores of Lake Nyanza to bring back men, women and particularly children to his palace at Mengo Hill near present-day Kampala. When John Hanning Speke arrived at Mengo in 1862, he found that Kabaka Mutesa, in his excitement of meeting the first white man he had ever seen, had sacrificed *'fifty big men and four hundred small ones'* at the prospect. Most of these would have been the thoroughly expendable slaves.

A favourite pastime of some minor Kings, was to mutilate their subjects, particularly their faces and hands. This practice of mutilation was, in fact, so widespread that it was often used with impunity for medicinal purposes. The Rev. Arthur Fisher, who went out with Bishop Tucker as a missionary in 1892, was interviewed by Dan Mannix after he retired. In his book 'African Bush Adventures' written in 1954, Mannix records his conversations with the Reverend Fisher who described in detail the conditions he found when he took up his first posting in the small village of Mityana some fifty miles west of the modern city of Kampala. Mannix records his conversation with Fisher at his retirement home at Eastbourne in Sussex:

'Did the natives object to having you interfere with their own religion?' I asked.

'No, I can't say they did,' said Mr. Fisher thoughtfully, 'You see they really didn't have a proper religion of their own. It was mainly what might be called devil worship. A man would pay the priests to give him a fetish to keep off evil spirits or, if he or his family were sick, he'd pay the priest to drive off the evil spirit that was troubling them. The priest usually did this by mutilation. If a child cried, the mother thought he was possessed by a demon, and the priest would brand the child with a hot iron or cut off the poor little mite's ears to drive out the spirit. You never saw a child that didn't carry the marks of the branding iron or the knife. In fact, natives would stop and stare at the children of our native converts because they weren't mutilated. They called them "Jesus Children." The natives had no idea of sin. They couldn't understand why we thought it was wrong for a man to beat his wife to death or for a strong community to conquer their neighbours and sell them to the Arab

---

[21] L.S.B. Leakey: *'The Southern Kikuyu before 1903'* Academic Press 1977 p.53

slavers.[22]

In common with most missionaries even up to the present day, Fisher had to learn the local language in order to 'teach' his flock. He was aided by a bible that had recently been translated into Luganda, the local language, by a dedicated missionary named Pilkington and printed by another missionary, Mackay, who carried a small printing press all the way to Mengo from the coast seven hundred miles away. *'The natives'*, Fisher recalls, *'were fascinated that "paper could talk", and were desperately eager to learn to read.'*

But Fisher spoke with passion on the subject of giving material help without first instilling a sense of morality into the natives. He gave Mannix an example of a man whose cattle were being decimated by a lion. *'Even though I have a spare gun to give that man to shoot the lion, I must not give it to him, because I know that having shot the lion he will immediately go and shoot his neighbours to gain their property. First I must teach him to have religious scruples, which will enable him to use the gun wisely.'* In other words, when you are the only person with a gun in a community whose only weapons are spears, you automatically become that community's leader, no matter whether you are a tyrant or a saint.

Fisher was later sent to Hoima, in the Bunyoro country north west of Kampala. The warrior King Kabarega of Bunyoro had left a country ravaged by frequent wars and starvation. *'There was not a single man who did not show the marks of either the knife or the branding iron.'* When Fisher asked him why he mutilated innocent men, the King answered in surprise, *'If I didn't mutilate the innocent, how could I make the guilty fear me?'*

John Hanning Speke encountered much the same behaviour. As early as 1858 he had noted in his diaries the attitude of some African mothers to their children as he wended his way through the interior to look for and eventually to find the source of the Nile, at Lake Victoria Nyanza, accompanied by his caravan of 132 porters and 8 Beluchi soldiers from the Sultan of Zanzibar's own personal guard:

> The mothers of these savage people have infinitely less affection than many beasts of my acquaintance. I have seen a mother bear, galled by frequent shots, obstinately meet her death by repeatedly returning under fire while attempting to rescue her young from the grasp of intruding

---

[22] J.A. Hunter and Dan Mannix – *'African Bush aAdventures'* Hamish Hamilton 1954 p.66

men. But here, for a simple loin-cloth or two, human mothers eagerly exchanged their little offspring, delivering them into perpetual bondage to my Beluchi soldiers.[23]

Conversely, Masai mothers were more caring of their offspring. It was well documented by L.S.B. Leakey that Kikuyu women were often given children by the pastoral Masai women so that they would have a better chance of survival living with the agricultural Kikuyu who usually had plenty of food.

In certain tribes the diabolical practice of forcibly fattening women was common. On another expedition, Speke describes the Palace of Rumanika, the King of Karagwe:

> Custom condemned the princesses of the royal house to stagger about like huge black whales, burdened by layers of undulating fat. The girls' almost obscene rotundity fascinated Speke...whose fascination soon began to exceed his natural sense of propriety. One of the king's sister's in law, being especially vast, he made up his mind to measure her. ...After getting her to sidle and wriggle into the middle of the hut, ...I took her dimensions. ...I tried to get her height by raising her up. This, after infinite exertions on the part of both, was accomplished when she sank down again fainting, for the blood had rushed from her head. Meanwhile the daughter, a lass of sixteen, sat stark-naked before us, suckling at a milk-pot, at which her father kept her at work by holding a rod in his hand; for, as fattening is the first duty of female life, it must be duly enforced—by the rod if necessary.[24]

The way in which the bodies of the dead are dealt with may also be an indicator of the attitude a society has towards the respect for human life and the absence of feeling in which it holds its fellow beings. In Kikuyu and Masai folklore only the most senior and revered leaders of the tribes were actually buried. It was a very expensive matter to bury a body. Undertakers, usually from a different tribe, had to be employed to carry out the burial as it was considered unwise and dangerous to touch a corpse that had died of 'natural causes' as opposed to those who had been killed in battle. When a member of one's family died suddenly and without warning, the body could not be removed from the hut because it was considered dangerous to touch a body that

---

[23] J.H. Speke: *What led to the Discovery of the Source of the Nile* Blackwood, 1862, p.235
[24] Speke: *'Journal'* Blackwood 1862 p.137

had succumbed through illness or old age, so a hole was cut into the hut wall to allow hyenas to come in and dispose of the body naturally. The animals were not allowed to enter the hut through the door, as this was a sacred entrance for humans only, and a hyena entering the hut through the door would have defiled those who used it. The hut was then burnt. Routledge recalls a macabre incident where he witnessed a body being towed out of a hut by string tied to both its feet. Neither he nor the removers were sure whether or not the 'body' was yet a corpse.

In Kikuyu tradition, when a family member was known to be dying, the normal procedure was that the sick person, with their complete acquiescence, would be taken from their bed and put in a small hut that had been specially prepared for the purpose. Here, they would be tended by a near relative until death came when an opening would be made in the hut sufficient for hyenas to enter and take the body[25]. In the case of the Masai, the person would be left in the shade of a tree. I have witnessed this procedure myself when I came across an old man lying under a tree in the Amboseli area in 1952. The old man could still talk and when I offered to take him to hospital, he replied that he just wanted to be left alone to die. While this procedure owes more, possibly, to practicalities of the situation than to any lack of feelings about one's relatives, it must be the ultimate in environmentally acceptable recycling.

Dr. L.S.B.Leakey in his three volumes entitled *'The Southern Kikuyu Before 1903'*, writes in detail about the culture, traditions and history of the Kikuyu people. It is the only definitive work on that specific subject, written in 1939 but only published after his death in 1977. It gives the most detailed accounts of the culture and traditions of the Kikuyu and the way in which they lived prior to the influence of Western Man when the inevitable changes began to occur. As a blood-brother Kikuyu himself, being brought up with them (his parents were two of the first missionaries to Kenya) he knew more about them than perhaps any other European, and what he did not know, he found out from the elders, some of whom clearly remembered seeing the first white men in that part of Kikuyuland. The result is a tome of tremendous authority and information, and while the author is at pains to explain that the information is concerned with what he calls the 'Southern Kikuyu' only, i.e. those who lived south of the Chania River, in what was later known as the Kiambu District, he believes that their culture represents closely that of the

---

[25] W. Scoresby Routledge: *With a Prehistoric People* Frank Cass 1968 p.168 - 173

rest of the Kikuyu speaking peoples of Kenya. His writings must therefore be taken seriously and the volumes treated as the definitive history of pre-Westernised Kikuyu Man. Leakey later wrote at some length about the Mau Mau Emergency and his works on this will be considered in later chapters.

Leakey explains Kikuyu society as being cultured and well-ordered, the traditions and rites being sensible and with good reason. He shows that they had a good sense of justice and respect for their age-old traditions and their leaders. As with any society there were those that tried to circumvent the rules, who, when found, were severely punished. He tells of the 'Njama' or local police warriors, who were strong and kept strict order, describing them as *'Men who take the lead in wartime – persons of power and position. They consist of young men, and all are eligible to join the ranks, but newcomers can only be received by consent of the body as a whole. Their powers include judicial attributes and generally speaking, the keeping of order especially in regard to affairs outside the immediate homestead.'* Each district is served by an 'Njama' with a renowned leader. One such leader in the area around Fort Smith was Waiyaki.

Kikuyu Warriors or *'Njama'* c.1905

To start with, the British were on good terms with Waiyaki. He sided with them against the recalcitrant Kikuyu and helped Francis Hall and other Administrators to calm and pacify the local inhabitants. However, he fell foul of the British when, one evening having consumed a great deal of liquor, he went into one of the Administrator's rooms and started attacking him. A fight developed, and Purkiss, the Administrator, seized Waiyaki's sword and with help, managed to tie him up. The next day, the man was unrepentant and truculent, so it was decided, perhaps rather foolishly, to banish him to Mombasa. On the way, at Kibwezi, the party which was guarding him, found him dead one morning, apparently from a complication of a wound to the head that he suffered during the fight with Purkiss and the struggle to calm him down. Sixty five years later, Waiyaki was reborn again as a folk hero, and many stories have been written about him and his deeds as leader of the Njama around what is now Dagoretti, near Nairobi. One of the main thoroughfares out of Nairobi is named after him.

The practice of drinking blood direct from the cow is also well documented. The cow or bullock having been restrained, and the jugular vein identified by means of a thong tied around its neck, someone shoots an arrow with a half-moon shaped arrow-head on it, into the vein. The blood shoots out. *'Somehow everyone seems to get a mouthful; at least everyone gets smeared with blood, whilst those who have been really lucky and have succeeded in swallowing a lot, often vomit it up. The splendid figures of the nude men beautifully greased, groomed and ornamented, all smeared with blood: the weapons, the shouts, the movement, the hour and the stage, make a tableau that is not easily forgotten'.*[26]

Both Leakey and Routledge mention the Agumba people whom the Kikuyu cast out when they took to the land south of the Chania River. The Agumba must have been overrun and died out before the first explorers came on the scene as there was little evidence of them by the 1880s. They appear to have been very small in stature, perhaps a race of pygmies, who lived either in caves or in the ground. Excavations carried out by Routledge in places where he was shown they had once lived, revealed obsidian arrow heads and other artefacts, suggesting their existence comparatively recently.

Routledge also gives the probable origin of the name 'Kikuyu'. Several different species of fig trees grow in that part of Kenya and they are all revered by the people — some species more than others. 'Kuyu' is the generic term in the Kikuyu language for a fig tree and 'Ki' is the locative. 'Kikuyu', therefore, is simply 'The Place of the Fig Trees' and 'Gikuyu', 'the People of the Place of Fig Trees'.

---

[26] Routledge *'With a prehistoric People'* Frank Cass & Co, 1968 p.175

CHAPTER THREE

THE SAVAGE WARS OF PEACE

Take up the White Man's burden—
Send forth the best ye breed—
Go bind your sons to exile
To serve your country's need;
To wait in heavy harness,
On fluttered folk and wild—
Your new-caught sullen peoples,
Half devil and half child.

Take up the White Man's burden—
The savage wars of peace—
Fill full the mouth of Famine
And bid the sickness cease;
And when your goal is nearest
The end for others sought,
Watch Sloth and heathen Folly
Bring all your hopes to nought.

Rudyard Kipling

No one likes to be reminded of their ancestors' darker days. Some of the issues raised in these first three chapters of this book might seem to attach too much importance to revelations of the past. But it must surely be essential, if one is to take an entirely objective view of the subject, to get a clear understanding of the conditions existing at the time the first records of East Africa were written. To draw a veil over the first fifty years of Kenya's modern history would be doing a great injustice, not only to the first administrators, many of whom gave their lives in the service of making Kenya a better place for everyone, but also to the Africans who were the subject of their administrations who underwent a sea-change in their lives. Most of the colonial officers worked hard to bring a better life for the people under their control, and in the twenty years between 1895 and 1914 one in nine officers of the

Administration died while in the service of Kenya[27]. The conditions they encountered when they first took up their posts, must be fully explained and interpreted in order that subsequent events might be more clearly understood. Likewise, the sudden revolution experienced in the social morphology of the indigenous peoples, who were the subject of those administrations, has to be carefully explained. That the Kikuyu people in particular underwent such traumatic changes in so short a time – changes that took the Western world more than a thousand years to achieve successfully, and, with the exception of Mau Mau, that they have come through them so far virtually unscathed, is a fact that must also be recognised and applauded.

In the Africa of the nineteenth century, human life was cheap. Generations of social stagnation had conditioned people to a life of one long fight against disease, starvation, belligerent neighbours and wild animals. Death was a common factor that had to be faced daily. *'To the M'Kikuyu, the fact that a stranger has accepted his hospitality, has eaten his food and slept in his hut, is not sufficient reason why he should not murder him, if for any reason such a course seems desirable. Conversely, the stranger who has sought and been accorded hospitality feels himself under no moral obligation to refrain from treacherously taking the life of his host.'* [28]

How then, one may reasonably ask, was it possible to pacify this primitive humanity and bring them into what most of the rest of the world considered was a happier state of life, without dealing out strong measures in the beginning, which they understood? The savage wars of peace had to be fought.

> In Raum's words, the African child becomes conditioned to a morality whose demands become less stringent the remoter they are from the initial situation of the family. So that without the tribal group, or in one's dealings with outsiders who have been seen as evil, the traditional rules not only have no application, but are positively incorrect. The outsider has no rights, and, if that outsider has inspired fear and hate, the vilest of behaviour is appropriate. ...But in indigenous African behaviour, life was cheap and full of fear. Only too often one's own life was only saved by violence and the sacrifice of helpless creatures (animal or human) which must have been a familiar experience even in the lives of children.

---

[27] Cashmore T.H.R. 'Imperialism, the State and the Third World' 1992 Note 11 p.133
[28] W. Scorsby Routledge *'With a Prehistoric People'* Cass 1968 p.247

So that in the hierarchy of 'power', which was the background of the African attitude to life, the dangerously powerful or the wholly powerless, inspired behaviour patterns which were the converse of those normally applied within the group.[29]

This behavioural pattern could not surely be expected to disappear in one or two generations. It would, as it had in Europeans, persist until bred out in later generations who would be shown that it is possible to live in peace with one's neighbour and that survival is easier and more certain if humans can live without enmity towards each other.

So it is not unreasonable to expect that the conduct of a few Kikuyu in the times of Mau Mau, less than two generations later, was simply a vestige of that behaviour manifesting itself. Even today in 2003 Africans have not yet thrown off the yoke of some ancestors' genes, as events in Rwanda and the Sudan as well as most other African countries have demonstrated.

When members of one's family died or were killed, it was, no doubt, distressing, but in order to exist one had to be pragmatic. A death in the family at the very least meant one less mouth to feed. If, to survive, the mother had to sell her child for a hatful of corn, then it must be done, for the corn will be the means of her survival, and by surviving, she will be able to produce more children in hopefully better conditions, in the same way that an eagle with two chicks, and an uncertain food supply, will feed only the strongest chick and let the other die. Compassion was a luxury no East African could afford. In a world ordered by the survival of the fittest, a compassionate man would soon be a dead man, either from starvation or from his enemies who would find him an easy pushover.

Kenneth Ingham[30] writes:

At the opening of the last quarter of the nineteenth century East Africa was still an almost completely unknown territory so far as the outside world was concerned. The Arab slave- and ivory-traders probably knew more about the interior than anyone, but they had no desire to attract commercial rivals or the attention of humanitarians by communicating their knowledge to others. European explorers had added greatly to the accuracy of the geographers' maps and had told something of the lives

---

[29] Dr. J.C. Carothers – *The Psychology of Mau Mau* 1954 p.3
[30] Kenneth Ingham, Professor of History, Makerere University, Uganda: *'A History of East Africa'* Longman's, London. 1962 p. 115

of the peoples of the interior to interested listeners. But they had inevitably been restricted in their travels to the well-trodden routes of the traders and vast areas were unknown to them. A clearer picture of conditions in the heart of the continent was beginning to be collected by missionaries, but their work had barely started. African society, although on the verge of a revolution, was unaware of the fact. Some tribes, living along the slave routes, had seen their normal life disrupted by the constant threat of raiding parties or by their own active participation in raids, and at the coast, traditional tribal hierarchies had been replaced or overlaid by Arab authorities. Elsewhere, although the shrewd Mutesa of Buganda might scent danger, the tribes of East Africa lived as they had lived for generations. ...Change would only come from without, and the forces of the outside world were poised for attack.

So when the first administrators began to take up their posts in the countries now known as Kenya, Uganda and Tanzania, they found most of the tribes to be dominated by the wealthiest, either in terms of land, cattle, slaves or weapons. Tyrant leaders like Mutesa paid scant attention to the welfare of the people themselves. Some tribal leaders, notably of the Masai, were more benign towards their members, and it is interesting to note that the Kikuyu who were organised on what today would be called the committee principle, i.e. leadership that was disseminated throughout the local clans, were more stable and less violent than those that had one dominant 'King', who, it seemed, always turned out to be a tyrant.

One of the first requirements for the European administrator was to create Chiefs and Headmen who would be paid to act as intermediaries between him and the local people. It was important to have an open channel for the exchange of information, and the administrator needed to know as much as possible of what was happening in his area. Existing leaders were usually chosen, but where they were thought to be untrustworthy, others within the society had to be recruited, sometimes leading to jealousy as the traditional elders saw such choices as unwelcome competition. But it was necessary for the administrators to know as much as possible of what was going on from people they could trust. As money was unknown to the people and the main currency was sheep or goats, payment by the administrators for the services of Chiefs and Headmen was in lengths of cloth.

Local labour here is cheap; they are paid ½ yard of calico a day, worth about twopence per man per day, and have to feed themselves. In this way I have had nearly all the stones for two sides of the Fort [Smith] carried from the quarry about 800 yards away, by fifty or sixty people working daily.[31]

The tribes were constantly in a state of rivalry with belligerent neighbours and every tribe had its warriors who could attack and plunder neighbouring tribes if there was a good reason, for example, if they were thought to be weaker. It was, and always had been at matter of the survival of the fittest. If a tribe became weakened with disease it was pounced on by a neighbour who would plunder its livestock and food supplies and carry off its people to enslave them.

In the late 1890's the pastoral Masai, once the strongest and most fearsome of all East African tribes, were so weakened by internecine war, the sudden onset of the two fatal diseases of rinderpest in cattle and smallpox in humans, and by a near fatal drought, that by 1904, their numbers had dwindled *'to between 25,000 and 12,500 in the whole of British East Africa, the latter number being the latest, and perhaps the most correct'*.[32] Had it not been for the British, who by then were beginning to keep the tribes apart, they would have been brought to the edge of extinction and probably beyond, by the neighbouring Kikuyu and waKamba within a matter of months. Francis Hall in his letters home writes of encountering a war party of between 1,000 and 1,200 waKamba warriors on the Kaputei Plains. They had been out *'looking for Masai'*, whose numbers had presumably by then, been so decimated that the waKamba warriors were returning unsuccessfully from their hunt.[33]

Hall was Commissioner of an area known as 'Kikuyu', which extended from the Kaputei Plains in the South East, through Ngong in the South West, to Mt. Kenya in the North and the Aberdares in the North West, an area of several hundred square miles. The District headquarters was at Fort Smith in the village of Kikuyu. This was one of the first two administrative stations in Kenya, the other being Machakos.

One of Hall's first jobs was to bring a modicum of peace between the warring Kikuyu and Masai. The Masai were so reduced in numbers and were so fearful of neighbouring tribes that the remnants of the Kaputei and Kekanyuki sections asked for, and had to be given refuge in Fort Smith by

---

[31] Francis Hall *Unpublished letters home - October 16th 1900.*
[32] Hollis *'The Masai'* Oxford 1905 Introduction by Charles Eliot p.xiv
[33] Francis Hall. Unpublished letters home – June 24th 1893

Hall. He recounts what happened one night soon after the Masai were taken into the Fort.

> That night I got two and a quarter hours sleep, and at daylight the war cry sounded all around the country. The hills were soon black with Kikuyu and things began to look a bit serious for the Masai, for I was afraid I would not be able to hold the Fort against such numbers. I sent for some of the [warrior] chiefs and told them that any man who approached too close would be fired upon, so they went off and told the people and then came back and we had a great pow-wow. ...this pacified the Kikuyu a bit but they begged me to send some of the Masai out of the country as there were too many.
>
> The following day I started the Masai off with an escort of 40 men. These blackguardly brutes of Kikuyu [secretly] followed them out of the bush, and after my men had returned, fell on the Masai and carried off as many women and children as they could and killed many more. I called the chiefs [leaders] at once and after cursing them until language failed me, I ordered them to return all the Masai they had captured and pay a fine of 100 goats within three days or I would wipe them off the face of the earth.[34]

That Hall was able to pacify the tribes was due entirely to the respect in which the tribal leaders held him, together with his vastly superior weaponry. *'The greatest compliment I had... was from one of the Kikuyu'* (who had been out shooting game with him). *'He said he must go back at once and tell his people [about me] because it was no good for them to go against a white man when I, with my little gun, could kill a lion and a wildebeest together'*. Hall concludes, *'They will be more frightened of us now, which is perhaps a good thing.'* [35]

Hall had been sent to Kikuyu in 1892 by the Imperial British East Africa Company (IBEAC) who were Agents for the British Government. The IBEAC had been acting as proxy for the British Government since 1888 after the Berlin Conference three years before, and had sent out administrators to begin the work of pacifying the natives and opening up the country. Hall's back-up or 'police' force were Swahili men from the coast who had been trained in the use of firearms. Their march up from Mombasa through the Taru desert to Machakos and on to Kikuyu had taken 32 days. Hall's main brief was to bring

---

[34] Francis Hall. Unpublished letters home – July 5th 1894
[35] Ibid. June 24th 1893

peace to the countryside so that everyone, Kikuyu, Masai, and waKamba, as well as the administrators and their employees could go about their daily routines without fear of being attacked. Thereafter, he was to set up a depot to provide food for caravans travelling to and from Uganda, to align a permanent road for those caravans, and to prepare the way for missionaries and traders to carry out their work in comparative safety.

Hall's letters home to his father reveal in stark reality, his day to day work and the dealings he had with the local people. He soon found that the Masai and the Kikuyu were deadly enemies – the Kikuyu the more treacherous and the Masai the stronger and more dignified. That he succeeded in his task was a tribute to his firm but even-handed policies.

In October 1893 he arranged a meeting between the leaders of the Masai and of the Kikuyu. Hall describes the scene:

> After a walk of about 3 miles, I came upon a large party of Kikuyu, all armed, and further on a body of Masai squatting in an open plain. I took 20 of my askaris (soldiers) who carry long Snider rifles, and sword bayonets and marched up in good form with fixed bayonets. There was the usual pow-wow for about an hour and then, all preliminaries and terms of agreement having been made, they were ratified by the slaughter of a goat with great pomp and ceremony. One headman for each party held the goat while my representatives, flourishing the knife, made a great speech. Then the dire effect of breaking such a solemn pledge were enumerated and from what I could make out, seemed to include all the curses of this world and the next. For each pledge, a stick was thrown onto the goat. At last… the head was severed from the body, completing the business. Then arose a mighty shout and both parties executed triumphant war dances, while my Sergeant-major, not to be outdone, marched my men about in all sorts of formations doing manual and bayonet exercises at lightning speed. The whole scene was extraordinary and very impressive.
>
> At last all parties mingled and shook hands and pow-wowed all round and then all started for home seeing who could sing the loudest.[36]

Although the Masai and the Kikuyu had made treaties before, they were usually broken fairly easily when, by accident or design, a chance killing or stealing of cattle annulled the treaty and they were back to square one. So this

---

[36] Ibid. October 28th 1893

was a remarkable achievement for Hall as the two tribes had been fighting each other on and off for as long as anyone could remember. Hall later recalls that the treaty was strictly adhered to by the Masai but some factions of the Kikuyu continued to raid the Masai villages and had to be punished by Hall for so doing. In the next letter home he reports that a small band of Kikuyu, who, by virtue of the peace accord between the tribes, had inveigled some Masai to their village and treacherously murdered them in the night. Hall received the news at 11pm at night and went straight out to the culprit's village about 6 miles away. He continues:

> I determined to take them by surprise by prompt action. Luckily several of the friendly [Kikuyu] Chiefs were with me at the time so I told them to call their men together at once and in less than an hour, my men, together with a large party of friendly [Kikuyu] were on the road. They [the culprits] had not yet driven off their stock, so my fellows swooped down on them quite unexpectedly and made a grand haul of over 1000 goats and 6 head of cattle. A good deal of ammunition was wasted (chiefly in jubilation on the way home) but we did kill nine [men] and wounded 5 with 600 rounds, which is above average for Swahili shootings. On our side there were no casualties.

The next day Hall distributed the stock he had commandeered amongst the friendly Kikuyu that had accompanied him on this foray who had helped him to apprehend their aberrant kin and teach them a lesson. He also sent a cow and 50 goats to the Masai Chief as recompense for the people who had been killed.

It is interesting to note that when it was shown that some of their people had gravely misbehaved, the Kikuyu leaders were quite willing to side with Hall and his men, and readily agreed that the troublemakers had to be punished. Hall writes to his father:

> I gave Lane [Hall's assistant] a bit of an outing to go and punish an m'Kikuyu chief who had been doing a little murdering on his own account and refused to come in. Our Force was joined by all the natives for miles around and Lane says that when he arrived on the ground, about 25 miles from here [Kikuyu], he had a following of about 4,000. So 'our friend' made himself scarce and left Lane to collect his goats and cattle without opposition.[37]

---

[37] Ibid. – January 28th 1897

This tendency of the Kikuyu that 'right' should prevail has very important implications for what happened fifty years later during the Mau Mau conflict as we shall see in later chapters. Most of the traditional leaders sided with the Government forces against Mau Mau. They formed the Kikuyu Guard and took up arms against the insurgents — many losing their lives in the process. Moreover, some of those who initially fought with the Mau Mau, when captured, were easily 'turned' to fight against their erstwhile colleagues in the forest, when they realised their mistaken allegiance.

Hall makes no secret of the fact that as tribes go, he prefers the Masai who are more aristocratic and honourable than the Kikuyu who will break a treaty or an agreement with impunity. But as he gets to know them better, he revises his first impressions of the Kikuyu leaders.

In his letter of June 10th 1894 he writes: *'I received a visit from some of the Kikuyu from Meranga, the District at the foot of (Mount) Kenia. They are a far more peaceful lot than those about here and begged me come up there and establish a station just now. I gave them a letter and a flag... and promised to visit them the first chance I get.'*

His letters are full of instances where Kikuyu have killed his men or his men's followers. The Kikuyu used poisoned arrows as well as spears when out raiding. Hall describes the culminating battle he had with a particularly troublesome group who had been raiding the Masai villages and even killing employees from the station if they found them on their own outside rifle range of the Fort.

'I had sent some men out on Christmas Day [1893] and they returned empty-handed having been warned by some friendly [Kikuyu] that a trap had been laid for them and unless they cleared off at once, they would all be murdered. I sent a messenger to enquire into the matter but he was caught and beaten and all his arms and ornaments taken away and he had to run for his life. I then sent three friendly Kikuyu to gather news, but they ran back as soon as they saw danger.

Hall then realised he would have to deal seriously with this particular *'mbari'* or clan of Kikuyu and teach them a lesson.

I started my men off at one in the morning and they reached the place, six miles off in good time and surrounded the kraals [villages]. At daybreak they got to business. My fellows fought splendidly, I hear, and as the enemy came so close, couldn't miss them and the slaughter was heavy. But at last the natives got sick of it and drew off. We lost two killed and three wounded. I have since heard that the enemy lost over 90 killed, of which their Chief was one of the first. My men [casualties that were wounded] were all shot with poisoned arrows. The Sergeant Major got the only nasty wound through the inside of the arm, just missing the artery. Directly they got back here I attended to him, though I was afraid it was too late as he was already drowsy. But I poured whisky and ammonia into him and poulticed the wound every 15 minutes and though he was slightly delirious in the night, he got better as the poison returned to his arm which swelled up like a football [38]

With skirmishes like this, the Kikuyu soon learned that it was not worth messing with the British administrators and their employees. They were there to stay, so better they fall into line and accept their fate.

It may seem iniquitous to us now, over one hundred years later, for Hall to sanction the killing of ninety men with no better cause than that they had murdered his employees and had broken the Treaty with the Masai. In order to understand the necessity for carrying out what seems in the twenty-first century to be a massive over-reaction, one can only put oneself in the position of that person in that situation at that time. This is not to justify the actions nor is it to condemn them. It is to come to terms with the situation as it was then, just as much as it is necessary to accept that it was quite in order to burn people alive for their perceived transgressions in sixteenth century England. It was how life was led. There was no International Court of Justice to bring to book those who committed what would now be labelled 'atrocities'. They were not atrocities then. Even in the so-called Western World, the sanctity of human life was not looked upon as sacrosanct as it is in 2004. The battle of the Somme had not yet taken place, and the Holocaust, Hiroshima and Nagasaki were still 50 years in the future.

It is not easy for the historian to articulate the perspective that Africans, at the dawn of their Westernisation,[39] had on life in general and on human life in particular, without appearing to be either callous, racist or to be defending the actions of the colonial administrators. While Africans' behaviour and morality had remained the same for generations, Western compassion and sensitivity towards life in general and human life in particular had been

---

[38] Ibid – January 14th 1894
[39] I use the term *'Westernisation'* indicating enlightenment or edification

growing with each generation until in 2004 it is difficult to perceive a world without the International Court of Justice or of Human Rights. This has made it difficult for a Westerner who has no experience of Africa, to understand that only a hundred years before, humans—African or European—could have treated life so cheaply as to condone the killing of ninety people in one small foray. Nor is it easy to come to terms with the horrific accounts of mutilations, castrations, rape, murder, slavery and mass slaughter that had been going on since time immemorial in sub-Saharan Africa. That continent is still, in Western terms, comparatively violent, as confirmed by the massacre of hundreds of thousands of Hutus and Tutsis in Rwanda in the 1990s. The danger for the student of African social history is to make comparisons between sub-Saharan Africans one hundred years ago with the Westernised, compassionate and tolerant societies of today. To compare the values of Kikuyu Man in 1900 with the values he might hold today, or his behaviour then with the morality he has learnt to practice since then, is to make comparisons between the primitive and lawless Anglo Saxons and the technologically superior Romans or the subjects of Elizabeth the First with those of Elizabeth the Second. As Sir Joseph Chamberlain, Colonial Secretary, put it in 1895: *'You cannot have omlettes without breaking eggs; you cannot destroy the practices of barbarism, of slavery, of superstition ...without the use of force.'*

So if Hall had shot just one or two instead of ninety, it would not have had the necessary salutary effect. This is verified by the attitude of the friendly Kikuyu that he had gathered around him at Fort Smith who not only condoned the punitive expedition but willingly and voluntarily took part in it as well. Hall's reasoning was that it is kinder to take strong measures in the beginning, in order to save an even greater loss of life later. Had Hall and his fellow administrators not carried out punitive actions on this scale, lessons would not have been learnt, and the more brutal elements could not have been dragged kicking and screaming through three thousand years of evolution from something akin to the stone age to the age of computers within a matter of two or three generations. And the British administrators as well as the people themselves can be proud of the fact that they have got through that transformation relatively unscathed.

The hypothesis of being cruel to be kind is given credence by so many eyewitness accounts of the early missionaries, explorers and administrators. Perhaps the best example is of an Administrator called Purkiss who was left in charge of Fort Smith while Hall was away. Purkiss was a young inexperienced administrator, who had only been in the country a short time. His one assistant, an Arab by the name of Maktub had been set upon and murdered together with ten armed Swahili men, by a dissident faction of Kikuyu known as the Waguruguru. Instead of taking immediate action against the perpetrators, Purkiss hesitated because he had lost his only assistant and had not been given sufficient back-up by his employers. His apparent indecision encouraged other Kikuyu to flaunt their belligerency and attack more members of the Fort Smith staff, until it soon became impossible for anyone to go outside the Fort without being heavily guarded. Purkiss, by his inaction, had given the impression that he was afraid of the Kikuyu, and by so doing had allowed the more savage elements to risk their inherent treachery and so set back the work that Hall and other more assertive officers had carried out through their positive, but by today's standards extreme reactions to misdemeanours. *'Purkiss was even warned by the few friendly chiefs that had stood by him so far, that unless he took [decisive] action a general rising against the Company's authority might be expected'.*[40]

Macdonald, who was one of the engineers employed on constructing the Mombasa to Uganda Railway, which at that time had reached the area of Fort Smith, wrote of the incident in his journal: *'Vacillation and indecision cause in the end a vastly greater amount of bloodshed than the strong hand and the personality which commands obedience. ...Africa needs the right men—men of decision and of character and individuality. Where such men are in charge, you will rarely hear of bloodshed and reprisals.* [41]

But punitive killing was only carried out when no other alternative presented itself; there was compassion shown in equal quantities. During the terrible drought and smallpox epidemic of 1898/99, Hall in Kikuyu and his colleagues in Machakos and elsewhere lost no time in starting a famine relief operation. On 17th October 1899 Hall writes:

> I have an awful job on now with the famine and the smallpox. I have an average of 370 famine-stricken people to feed daily. It is the most pitiful job I have ever had. Poor beggars, owing to the drought their crops failed. Not all [are the same], but the poorer people who live entirely on the proceeds of their land. A large fund has been raised here to assist, but when one considers that the Govt. is feeding thousands at Mombasa,

---

[40] L.S.B. Leakey – Academic Press 1977 *'The Southern Kikuyu before 1903'* p.78
[41] Ibid p.75

1,500 at Kibwezi, 1,500 at Machakos while I have 370 here, our efforts are very puny. If 'Min' [Hall's sister in UK] could see her way to raise only a few pounds for our Famine Fund, it would be a grand thing. Every man in this country is getting subscriptions to help and I think Tonbridge ought to be in it with all its connections with these parts.[42]

Anyway, Hall's policies worked, because the inter-tribal fighting ceased, and by the time he left Fort Smith in 1899 he had won the trust and respect, not only of the surrounding Kikuyu people and the remnants of the Masai, but also of the waKamba people on the south eastern fringe of his District. He eventually lived up to his promise and went to form the new station at Mbirri near Muranga, which after his death in 1901, officially became Fort Hall. He died after only two years in that station while still a young man in the midst of the work he so strenuously believed in. He was buried in the cemetery at Fort Hall, which was at the centre of the areas to be affected by the Mau Mau conflict, fifty years later.

Hall was not alone among appointees of the IBEAC in achieving a reputation for severity. In May 1902, another Empire builder, Richard Meinertzhagen, unlike Hall, professed it with unabashed enthusiasm. He found himself responsible for pacifying the pastoral Nandi tribe in central parts of the Rift Valley. This, he thought, necessitated the slaughter of men on both sides, but more so on those that had to fight with swords and spears rather than with guns. The Nandi were a particularly warlike tribe and they did not see why 'strangers' should occupy their land, nor be subjected to laws that were often diametrically opposed to those that they had lived by for generations, and through which they had grown strong. But dialogue was not in Meinertzhagen's vocabulary. When he was stationed with a hundred soldiers amid a population of some three hundred thousand, in cases of emergency they had to act quickly and decisively, and this simply meant shooting the attackers. There was no alternative but to use such force to subdue them.

The Government's official policy was to wait until things became so bad that there was sufficient reason for action to be taken against the Nandi, but Meinertzhagen, an army officer with the Kings African Rifles, who was trained to believe that the best method of defence is to attack, disagreed. His method was that for every person the Nandi murdered without good cause, ten

---

[42] Francis Hall's unpublished letters home – 17th October 1899. (Hall's family home was at Tonbridge in the U.K. where he was educated at Tonbridge School, as was this book's author.)

of them should be 'taken'. *The fact is that Bagge [the Commissioner] hates the idea of an expedition against them. He prefers to wait until it is forced on him by circumstances. ...I told him I thought this was a dangerous policy which would be interpreted as weakness by the belligerent Nandi'.*[43] Eventually Meinertzhagen contrived to meet the local leader of the Nandi whom he had found out was the cause of all the trouble. Meinertzhagen was told by his informers that there was a plan to kill him at this meeting and when he presented himself and went forward to shake hands, a spear thrown by one of the Laibon's body guards narrowly missed him and he shot the Laibon at close range. The rest of the war party then fled and the conflict subsided, though Meinertzhagen was castigated by his superiors for using more than 'minimum force' to put the rebellion down.

Meinertzhagen in his 'Kenya Diary (1902 – 1906)' admires the way in which the warriors fought so courageously. Elspeth Huxley, in her Preface to the book writes, *'It is hard to imagine a sentiment more out of keeping with the notions of today. One only has to dip into these diaries to apprehend how profound has been the revolution in our attitudes within the lifetime of many still alive.'*[44]

Here is the epitome of what some might perhaps see as the unacceptable face of colonialism. One or two British army officers backed by gun-toting N.C.Os of Indian origin together with Swahili or Nubian soldiers, hoisting the Union flag on a bare patch of ground and telling the local population that they must no longer kill their neighbours, and must abide by the laws imposed with rifle and Maxim machine gun. It is the nub of the argument that is often used to condemn colonialism. The spectre of a man who today would be accused of 'crimes against humanity', was at that time hailed as an empire-builder. And those of us who strive to reason with the points and explain the situation at the time, have the most difficult task of reconciling the attitudes of men like Hall and Meinertzhagen with today's standards of morality and justice.

Elspeth Huxley's eloquent description of the problem we have, cannot be bettered:

> If, today, the white man's burden has become a burden of guilt, there is little here of comfort for the black man either. No one likes to be told that his ancestors were barbarians with certain nasty habits and

[43] Richard Meinertzhagen *Kenya Diary* Eland Books 1957 p.211
[44] Ibid - Preface by Elspeth Huxley p.v

uncivilised ways. I have little doubt but that a Romanized Briton living in luxury in a villa equipped with hypocausts, baths and tessellated floors, fluent in the Roman tongue, clothed in the Roman toga and given, perhaps, to quoting from the odes of Horace, did not care to be reminded that his early British ancestors were clothed in skins and woad, lived in miserable huts and were generally ignorant of the refinements of life in Rome. So may today's African Minister, senior civil servant, banker, academic or whatever, living in luxury in a Nairobi villa and with a chauffer-driven limousine, resent Meinertzhagen's unadorned descriptions of the lifestyle of his tribal ancestors. Time, I feel sure, will mellow this resentment; might even bring about a reversal of attitudes? Just as the self-made man will boast of his humble origins, so may the Westernised African come to take pride in the speed and wit with which so many of his people have crossed the cultural gulf to which I have referred.[45]

But in the end, and with the advantage of hindsight, most modern Kenyans who have taken the trouble to study the past, now agree it was the only way to bring their forbears into the twentieth century. Something that, once they saw the benefits of it, they wanted and indeed, later, demanded. David Nicoll-Griffith, a District Officer in the Kipsigis homeland in the 1950s sums up the dilemma.

The popular view today is that explorers, having once opened the path, should have withdrawn and left everything as they had found it. But even if they had done that, the reports of what they had found aroused such interest, that having opened the path they had also effectively opened the gate to missionaries, anthropologists, map makers and, inevitably, to traders and developers, and thus began the whole process of civilisation.

Before any progress could be made it was necessary to establish law and order, and this had certain consequences. Preventing tribes from fighting each other meant demarcating the areas which each tribe could call its own, and at the same time educating them in better use of the land – whether for crops or livestock – so that they could continue to draw a livelihood without having to move on to land now assigned to others. The Masai, because of their military ascendancy, by the time the

---

[45] Ibid. p.vii

British arrived, ended up in control of a hugely disproportionate amount of land relative to their numbers, and much of it— particularly in what later became the Rift Valley Province—was fertile, well-watered and ideal for dairying and crop-growing, and therefore not put to best use by a people who were exclusively subsistence cattle ranchers. There was, too, an increasing need for the country to help pay its way. One cannot launch government services (security, law, agriculture, veterinary – later education and all the rest) without paying the people who carry them out and giving them tools and equipment as well.

The chief result of all this was that the country had to produce what people were prepared to buy, not just for local consumption but also of a sufficiently high quality to attract overseas customers. This in turn meant building proper roads and, above all, a railway to link the interior with the port of Mombasa. There were no easily-worked mineral deposits and it was decided, on purely economic grounds, to concentrate on agriculture, dairying and cash crops. But the need was immediate, and farming would have to be started by people who already knew what they were doing; it would have taken decades to instruct the indigenous people in modern, efficient farming methods and production.

Thus it was that substantial areas of the Highlands were set aside, and leased to farmers from outside Kenya. Among those who came were many from Great Britain who had been demobilised at the end of the First World War and who, uncertain of job prospects at home, seized on the challenge and chance to make a productive contribution in East Africa.

Not all of them found themselves blessed with good fertile land, however, and even those who did, were faced with a great deal of hard work and struggle. A certain Capt. F.O'B. Wilson was offered 40,000 acres of eroded hillsides near Machakos, vacant land which not even the local tribesmen wanted but which, at a farthing an acre leasehold, he could just about afford. He worked hard, planting trees to induce rainfall and prevent erosion, building dams and introducing good cattle strains. When I came to Kenya, nearly 40 years later, he and his sons had developed the land to the point where they were able to supply Nairobi and Mombasa with 9,000 gallons of milk a day, and indeed were under contract to do so.

During the same forty years, families in the now demarcated Tribal Reserves had multiplied but their land had stayed the same size. They had continued to produce the same number of children as before, but instead of most of them dying from warfare or disease, most of them survived thanks to education, medicine and the rule of law. The result was that the family plot, which had been sufficient for the family, was now totally insufficient when divided up between several grown sons. So they turned their eyes to farms like that of F.O'B. Wilson and said, "That is our land which you stole from us, and we want it back. It is we who should be benefiting from its riches, not you!"[46]

---

[46] David Nicoll-Griffith – personal comm.. The Wilson farm is now run by the Agricultural Development Corporation, a parastatal organisation that took over a number of highly developed farms after Independence. Now, in 2003, they are being run in much the same way, with much the same success as they were in the days before Independence – a small yet significant example of the ideal originally planned by the British for the running of the country by its own people.

CHAPTER FOUR

THE DRILL SERGEANT

'Colonialism was the drill-sergeant of East Africa's forced march into modernity'
Dr. John Lonsdale

'**M**odernity'? Perhaps Dr. Lonsdale would agree that a more descriptive word in this context might be 'Westernisation'. In the late nineteenth century Western Man's culture embodied all the literate societies that lived in, or had originated in Europe. These had been developing over previous centuries and had, to some extent merged into one relatively similar way of life. As America had no influence in Africa at that time, it is more convenient in this context to refer to Western Man as 'European'. Similar cultures had been developing in parallel for much longer periods in other parts of the world, but these also had had no influence over Africa apart from trade at the coast.

When the appointees of the IBEAC first planted the Union Flag in Machakos and Fort Smith, they became the harbingers of changes which were to lead the tribes people out of timeless turmoil into the potentially enriching western world of the twentieth century. It was to be a governance predicated unashamedly on commerce and Chistianity. Britons, exemplified by Hall and the missionary Leakey, felt it was their right and their *duty*, having taken over responsibility for governing these primitive people, to teach them, and if necessary to impose on them the values of order and virtue and the principles of morality that they had always held dear; to show them the methods of European-style government and law and to teach them to read and write their own and other languages.

This is illustrated well by W. Scoresby Routledge, an anthropologist who visited Fort Hall in 1902 to study the traditions and culture of the Kikuyu, before they were under Western influence.

> Soon after my arrival at Fort Hall, to which I travelled with the sub-commissioner [Sidney Hinde] returning from leave to take up his command, three native elders came to see him and to tell him that the people of their district were prepared to accept the White Man's Government, and that therefore they would not oppose its orders by force of arms. These three old men had, they said, started as a company of five, but two of their number had been killed on the road by fellow-

tribesman of another district which was opposed to submission to the white man. Mr. Hinde received the survivors cordially, explained at great length to them what the advent of the white man meant, gave them presents, and dismissed them. Not one of the three ever reached home. They were all murdered en route by those who were opposed to their mission.

On the news coming in, the leading men of the guilty district were summoned to the Fort. They came without hesitation or mistrust. The sub-commissioner then explained to them that the government would not permit the murder of its friends or sanction the misdeeds that were constantly occurring, and that they must now either surrender the murderers and pay a heavy fine in cattle, or accept war. A date was fixed for compliance and the futility of resistance to the power of the Government was clearly pointed out to them, and they were told to go home and think it over.[47]

Presumably the guilty parties paid the fine and gave up those who carried out the murders because Routledge goes on to explain that had they not complied, the result would have been: *'some five hundred Masai would be summoned and they, together with some regular native troops and police would scour the country. The men would be killed and the women and children and herds would be taken captive until such time as, experience having been dearly bought, another meeting procured the requisite submission.'*

Africa, the missionaries and administrators felt, was like a warehouse, cluttered with useless goods: a mass of wasted space waiting to be cleaned out and replaced with more worthwhile commodities. The door was open and the owners willing to accept better, more modern goods now on offer. And everyone who saw it wanted to fill it with the very best articles produced by Western man. Africa, the new arrivals found, was a veritable depository waiting to be filled with all that a thousand years of European civilisation had to offer. Here in East Africa were human beings ready and willing for instruction; populations who had undergone millennia of savagery, fear and turmoil, without even the comfort and succour of a Christian religion.

But those who were about to carry out the instruction might sensibly have been more circumspect, for as Corfield warns, *'It is the African himself who is the raw material of the evolution in African countries, not the*

---

[47] W. Scoresby Routledge *'With a Prehistoric People'* Frank Cass 1968 p.x

European, and it is his characteristics which will determine the form of this evolution. [48]

To begin with, Africans were model students and eager to learn. Of their own volition, they sought to follow and emulate the Western way of life. Through the good offices of the European governing power, Africans had unfettered access to Western values, Western education, Western religions and Western-style governance and most of them, with the exception of the pastoral and ultra conservative Masai, were eager to follow and learn. Europeans believed this to be a good thing. With all its failings, Westerners believe they have the best of a bunch of imperfect ways of life, and actively seek to persuade others of its benefits. From the very earliest Crusades in the 12th century, Europeans have felt strongly theirs is the only way of life, and in the past, they were even prepared to make war on those that refused to adopt it.

Even now, in the twenty-first century, though the reasons have altered somewhat from religious fervour to democratic ideologies, they believe it is sometimes necessary to impose their standards on those who they think might, sometime in the future, cause them to expend their resources and the lives of their own sons and daughters in quelling tyrannical regimes, or in the case of Africa to subdue chaotic anarchies. That they did so in the 12th Century, and continue to do so now, must, as Marx and Engels realised, in the end be seen as progress, because the alternative, an absence of control over tyrannical regimes in primitive Africa would, with the advent of modern weaponry, have inevitably led to the nemesis of vast populations, as events in Rwanda, Liberia, Uganda, the Congo, Zimbabwe, Angola—the list is endless—have so vividly and tragically demonstrated. It remains to be seen whether or not the continued imposition of Western democratic principles will have the same positive effect it did then, but with the analogous dangers of even more perilous weaponry now available, it may yet prove to be an even greater necessity.

To take Dr. Lonsdale's analogy further, the 'forced march' has by no means arrived at its final destination, though the drill-sergeant had to take early retirement after harsh words from his charges, and some questionable advice from his 'senior officers'. The unsupervised march has consequently lapsed into a disorganised rabble with some members following different routes; others taking frequent rests by the wayside and a few even returning down the road from whence they came.

---

[48] Frank Corfield *'The Origins and Growth of Mau Mau'* Sessional Paper No.5 1959/60 p.29

Few historians and surely few Africans themselves would disagree that the forced march was necessary in order to arrive at some essential way marks, and that a drill-sergeant needed to accompany it, anyway for the first few miles. It is the behaviour of the drill-sergeant, rather than his charges that has now become the contentious issue.

The transition from one way of life to another is a slow and difficult process. The Ancient Britons were subdued, pacified and enlightened by the Romans who came to Britain in AD 42 — an event that bears a striking similarity to that of the Kikuyu by the British nearly two millennia later. Compared to the Romans, the Ancient Britons were savages and barbarians. They worshipped the sun and the moon; their 'witch-doctors' were Druids who built strange stone circles some of which, like Stonehenge, are still visible today. They were illiterate tribal people, often fighting each other and enslaving their captives. The houses were thatched rondavels, similar to a Kikuyu hut, and they lived in defended settlements surrounded by an invader-proof fence not dissimilar from a Masai *'enkang'* or village. They wore skins of animals and carried spears. The Britons, like the Kikuyu, must have found it difficult to change when the Romans arrived, and many sought to follow the Roman culture and way of life. The Romans brought with them technology and literacy, but they also brought leisure and recreation, and most important of all, the Romans, through their firm and ordered rule, stopped the inter-tribal fighting, so that by the time they left nearly 400 years later, they had laid the foundations for a nation rather than a collection of warring tribes.

There was, however, one marked difference between pre-literate Africans and the Ancient Britons. Africans proved to be significantly more adaptable and more eager to learn. Only the most intelligent Briton learned to speak the Roman language, whereas administrative officers in Kenya were embarrassed at the ease with which their subjects learnt English, and the eagerness they displayed at wanting to learn it. The officers themselves were only obliged to learn the *lingua franca*: Swahili. What problems could have been averted, what misunderstandings could have been forestalled and how much smoother might the road to independence have been if it had been obligatory for all official administrators to learn the vernacular of their district instead of Swahili! Apart from other considerations, there is a certain respect attached to someone who takes the trouble to learn the local language when going to reside in another country. Could it have been the reason why the missionaries were so successful in East Africa and worldwide was that they were, and still are, never allowed to start their ministrations until they have at least a working knowledge of the local language? Dr. Louis Leakey, son of one of the first missionaries to Kenya believes it was the major cause of friction between the administrative officials in the field, and their charges. In his book 'Kenya'[49] Leakey gives the failure of the British Government to insist that all their District Commissioners should learn the local language of their districts, as the cardinal error made by the British Administration.

The inability of the District Commissioners to understand clearly the fears and aspirations of the people whose future lay so demonstrably in their hands, must surely have been the cause of many misunderstandings and frictions that arose with the Africans. It also had very serious repercussions later, in the Kikuyu unrest that led to Mau Mau, when there was an absence of vital intelligence emanating from the European administrators. Leakey is perplexed at the reason for such a basic error by Whitehall. He gives, as the main reason, the continual movement of officers from one District to another. In his appendix to the book he cites—he says at random—the movements of officers from one District to another: fifteen different District Officers and three changes of District Commissioners in South Kavirondo District in the four years 1928 to 1932. In Kiambu there were sixteen changes of District Officers between 1928 and 1935 and ten different District Commissioners between 1929 and 1935. He lists examples of the changes that eighteen different officers had between the years 1928 to 1934, figures that average out at a change of District every 10 months for each officer. Leakey makes a strong case that the two factors, the continual movements of officers from one district to another and the lack of direct communication between the officers and their subjects, were the main reasons why the administration of the country fell short of the success it could have been, and was certainly one of the prime reasons that the British, particularly in the higher echelons of the Administration, were slow in appreciating the seriousness of Mau Mau.

This lack of continuity and the inability to have direct communication, was clearly a considerable drawback to the 'Drill Sergeant's' rapport with many of his recruits. It made a difficult task more complicated particularly when the African could not understand the European's methods of dealing

---

[49] L.S.B. Leakey 'Kenya' Methuen 1936 p.65 and Appendix

with such basic issues as land tenure, crime and punishment and morality, where the European's interpretation of these matters was so different. Corfield again spells out the problem:

> There is a fundamental difference between the European and the [pre-literate] African social system. In the European system the customs and laws are based primarily on the right of the individual ...and it is as an individual that he contributes to the well-being of the community; original modes of thought and action are the life-blood of Western society. But in a [preliterate] African society the individual is of importance only in so far as he is a member of a group and conforms to the accepted patterns of behaviour of the group: it is the group that counts.[50]

It was, though, noticeable that in Kikuyu culture the individual counted for more than in most other tribes. W.H. Thompson, a District Officer in Fort Hall explains how the Kikuyu governed themselves before the British took over:

> The traditional concept of dynastic rule by hereditary chiefs and headmen did not apply to the Kikuyu. Tribal rule was exercised by clan elders who derived their strength from a mixture of wile, guile, respect due to them as older persons, and the descended mysticism of Gikuyu and Mumbi through their clan-forming offspring. Taken all together, a powerful mixture which, when allied to the tribal predilection for secret oaths, gave local elders enormous powers'.[51]

It is an interesting trait of the Kikuyu that he seldom harbours a spirit of revenge. Mercenary that he is, if his relation has been murdered, he is far more concerned about wresting reparation from the murderers in the form of money or, traditionally, sheep or goats, than he is to avenge the killing. Routledge asks his Kikuyu mentor Munge, an elder and acknowledged seer, what the elders would say if the son of a murdered man wanted to avenge his father's death. The answer immediately came back *'the old men would say better to make an agreement for recompense than there should be another death'*. *'But what would happen'*, Routledge persisted, *'if the son had already killed the slayer of his father?'* The answer was *'two men are dead: the affair is ended'*.[52]

---

[50] Frank Corfield *'Historical Survey of Mau Mau'* Sessional Paper No. 5, 1959/60 p.8
[51] W.H. Thompson Unpublished memoirs 1976 p.62
[52] Routledge *With a Prehistoric People' Cass 1968 p.219*

In addition to the difficulty for the Kikuyu to understand some of the more bizarre laws imposed on them by the British, there was also this barrier of communicating the reasoning behind the laws, that helped to bar the way to understanding. But they were quick to learn and sometimes found it easier to learn the hard way as Francis Hall points out in a letter home to his father.

'I have been digging into my old friends the Kikuyu in the hills again, and have made things a bit lively. Some of the brutes murdered two of our men within a quarter of a mile of the Fort [Smith]. I was on their trail pretty sharp with twenty guns and a horde of yelling Masai. But our raid was obviously expected for I found most of them had already cleared out of their homesteads with their livestock. I was fairly mad, for I had seen one of my old hands who had been with me for a long time, hacked to pieces, and I thirsted for revenge. We made a mess of all their villages, but the ones remaining would not stand to fight.

'Even so, they still come and lie up in the scrub to kill any man who strays too far away from the Fort. So I called up all the Chiefs and told them that in future, any man seen carrying a spear or a shield will be shot first and interrogated later. They have obeyed alright and now only carry sticks, so there is likely to be less bloodshed from now on. I also told the Chiefs that unless the people worked like others in the country, they would eventually be wiped out and others brought in who would work. The general effect has been wonderful. I got thirty of them to carry food loads for Smith and when I called for 100 to go to Machakos to fetch loads for me, no less than 170 turned up, and 105 were signed on and brought the loads in good time and were delighted with their pay. This is the first time the Kikuyu have ever carried loads so it is a feather in my cap. How long the fit will last, remains to be seen, but I hope by letting them down a bit easy at first, they will soon get into the way of it.'[53]

That they did 'get into the way of it' and became probably the hardest workers and the most successful traders in the country, shows that a potential was always there, and that it only required a catalyst to bring it out from them.

In order to overcome some of the difficulties with the lack of communication, the 'Drill Sergeant' found that certain measures would help to create a better understanding. From the very beginning, District Commissioners were instructed to bring in local inhabitants of known character and

---

[53] Francis Hall – unpublished letters home – 6th August 1894

leadership qualities to help bridge this gap.

> By the time I arrived [1947], a well-tried pattern of appointment for chiefs and headman had worked itself throughout Kenya. Each location had a chief in charge, directly responsible to the District Commissioner [a European]. In turn, headmen were placed in charge of sub-locations.[54]

Thompson goes on to explain how these chiefs and headmen were chosen.

> When a chief retired, the District Commissioner (D.C.) would call a *baraza* (meeting) of all adult men and women in the location at which he would ask for the names of their nominees. A week or so later, the selection would take place with each of the contenders forming up in line with their supporting voters to the rear. Most often the result would be clear-cut, but sometimes the count would be close and the factions vociferous. In this case, having dismissed the contenders with the lowest number of votes, the D.C. would call for a re-vote in the hopes that the resulting redistribution would provide a clear answer. In the event of all the variations having failed, the D.C. would have to make the final choice being careful not to create a puppet. Puppets are useless in a dynamic administration, which, if it is to be any good, has to put across its policies receiving as much in return as is possible to garner.
>
> If my memory serves me right, only once, during my entire time in a district was an elected nomination rejected. It speaks volumes for African good sense that many times, hopeful contenders were laughed to scorn because everyone knew of their uselessness and their inability to lead.[55]

(What a tragedy it was then, that after the British left, in their haste to emulate 'Western style democracy', the new government of Kenya, instead of carrying on with this tried and tested method of selecting local leadership, insisted on the election of leaders by ballot, a system that inevitably led to universal corruption that has pervaded sub-Saharan Africa ever since, and has been one of the major limiting factors on their progress.)

Although it had not been part of Kikuyu culture to elect chiefs and headmen, it was necessary for the European Administration to have people they could rely on to serve as a two-way information agency. It was not a question of 'divide and rule', it was the only fair way to bring a semblance of

---

[54] W.H. Thompson Unpublished memoirs 1976 p.62
[55] Ibid p.62

democratic governance to the countryside.

The wider the geographical horizon, the more complex the challenge. Achieving success in East Africa faced the specific challenge which Lugard had recognised in West Africa, but which had long been identified as a crucial contributor to imperial success in India and further east: how far, and to what extent, could authoritative influence be achieved by working directly, or indirectly, with the local people. With whom might the new ruler best work to win acceptance without seeming to threaten irredeemable hostility? How should inter-ethnic and inter-tribal relations be defined and managed whilst ensuring balanced human and land management?

Answers would inevitably emerge only empirically in the light of very local circumstances – circumstances in which internecine squabbles were endemic. Practical solutions would emerge only through patient give-and-take, in processes of mutual acculturation governed fundamentally at the local level through the emerging government of Kenya and by the application of the Colonial Laws Validity Act (1865)[56], an Act increasingly influenced by changes in international expectation. The often violent flux in European and global society during the first half of the twentieth century (leading to the Treaty of Versailles and the UN Charter) induced fundamental changes in concept of inter-nationalism and the assertion of liberal 'open society'. It was therefore fortunate that the tribes people and the new ruler had, early on, pragmatically worked out practical and mutually acceptable solutions to the challenges facing each, by working through respected tribal elders and members of the tribe and respecting tribal practices, in a bid to reconcile the very divergent objectives of maintaining the integrity of the tribe at the same time as allowing the peaceful pursuit of objectives which would progressively undermine it.

In this situation, tribal groups practising a primitive agriculture would increasingly be faced by a range of challenges quite different from those facing nomadic tribesmen. This divide was to become the source of much of the inherent though quite localised conflict as Kenya became an established Colony of White settlement and emerged in 1963 as an independent state. The cohesion of the tribes people in its dependency on ancient rituals associated with age-groups of the young men and of women, was regulated by the most experienced in conclave with outstanding individuals achieving personal dominance while recognising

---

[56] Defined as '*An Act to Remove Doubts as to the Validity of Colonial Laws*'.

interdependence as a precondition of group and personal survival. The tribespeople of Kenya had not established quasi-monarchical systems of government which compared with the Baganda or the Zulus. This added to their vulnerability against Arab traders before the Europeans arrived and made easier the intrusion of Europeans. But a precondition for European success was their establishing a relationship of goodwill by compromises with the particular elders in the ascendant at the time and with younger men of influence in the tribe prepared to do business with them without undermining tribal governance.

Against this uninviting and unstable background, elders emerged as recognised Chiefs with whom an emerging alien governance could do business; young men emerged as potential interlocutors for the tribe in the interface of its members with the intruder. Reciprocally, too, the sinews of customary law in all its diversity and external law which increasingly would override indigenous systems both conceptually and actually, began to interact in a manner which bridged the divide between customary and imported law and created a legal system for a modern state and a progressive society. Inevitably such processes were slow to mature. Given the sources and human factors operative in potentially conflicting systems, inevitably there were lapses in the component parts. But bit by bit they were reconciled with a developing sense of personal responsibility in a rapidly changing legal system. These were to be especially evident during the brief interlude of the Mau Mau challenge to both lawful customary and external authority. They expressed themselves in extreme cases such as where Mr. Justice Cram[57], unaccustomed to Africa's ancient methods of self-determination, criticised local Africans for unlawfully presuming to assert 'unconstituted' authority, and even more dramatically where a gathering of some 250 Meru tribesmen in a remote location with a negligible government presence decided quite coolly and ruthlessly to protect themselves from the threat of Mau Mau, by seizing and killing three strangers thought by them to be Mau Mau oath administrators, in front of the Chief and District Officer.[58]

The impact of foreign governance was slightly different on each of the tribes in East Africa, but the effect on the agriculturalist Kikuyu was greater than on most of the other tribes. The pastoralist Masai, for example, simply treated the

---

[57] See also page 169
[58] Roy Spendlove - *Pers. Comm.*

British arrival with dignified and proud disdain and carried on with life as though little had happened. They wanted none of the material comforts of the European. The Kikuyu were entirely different.

Routledge sums up the difference between the pastoralist Masai and the agriculturalist Kikuyu, written at a time when the British had already begun to pacify the tribes:

> The Masai is by nature greed personified—sulky, morose and vindictive; a born thief, an arch liar; absolutely devoid of the sense of gratitude or the spirit of hospitality. He is material that civilisation cannot grind up in her mill. The isolation that brought him into being has ceased to be. Change has come, but he cannot change. …The nations that he formerly drove back into the forest, the Kikuyu and the waKamba, will now rapidly creep out again and re-occupy the country under the aegis of the white man whose purpose they serve, and the Masai will remain but a name. …His old enemies and victims, the Kikuyu are displaying a marked degree of those qualities a native race must exhibit if it is to survive: hard-working, intelligent and adaptable, peaceful and prolific. The Kikuyu is the coming man under the altered conditions of today.[59]

At first, after the initial reconciliation and peacemaking, they began to see the new arrivals as an opportunity. Essentially a hard-working, agricultural, people who had always traded their produce with other tribes in times of famine, the Kikuyu were not slow to see the benefits of bartering with these newcomers who had seemingly endless wealth and needed food, not only for themselves, but also for their retinue of porters and employees; and so they made the best of that opportunity.

But later, as they came to see the way the Europeans lived, and the material comforts they enjoyed, they began to covet and adapt to that lifestyle. The Kikuyu were almost unique within Kenya, in that they had an inherent desire to better themselves, and because of the recession of the Masai people through internecine wars and famine in the 1890's, they were poised to take over parts of the vast lands the Masai were vacating, had not the British intervened at the precise time, and later taken some of that land for themselves. Moreover, the British provided them with an impetus to make the transition from a primitive clan-based culture to a more competitive and trading one, as well as a more peaceful one. But as Corfield warns, if this transition is too

---

[59] W.S.Routledge *'With A Prehistoric People'* Cass 1905 p.348

sudden, it can lead to problems later on.

The danger lies in the transitional stage; the strain on both the tribe and the individual is very great. If the latter is brought up in the environment of the old tribal culture but in adolescence he comes into contact with a different culture, this may make a nonsense of many of his primitive beliefs. Once he goes into the outside world, he has lost most of his traditional moorings. His magic modes of thought persist, but the old restraints are gone. The comforting cloak of his tribalism has disappeared and he is left to act as an individual—a new state of affairs which places upon him a great strain. He often becomes rudderless and it is all too easy for him to identify his trouble with the European, who has indirectly brought on his troubles.[60]

The difficulty the Kikuyu were experiencing in their self-imposed transition from one culture to another, should have been more fully appreciated by the British administrators. Had they realised the mental turmoil that some of the younger Kikuyu men were going through, and the inevitable vacuum that was being created as a result of their rapidly changing life, they might have been more aware of the possible outcome that manifested itself eventually in Mau Mau.

As the old Basuto proverb puts it so nicely: *"If a man does away with his traditional way of living and throws away his good customs, he had better first make certain he has something of value to replace them."* Easier for a community – more difficult for an individual.

The transition Africans were trying to make, from one system to the other, brought out some extraordinary quirks, especially during Mau Mau.

This rapid transition has produced a schizophrenic tendency in the African mind — the extraordinary facility to live two separate lives with one foot in this century and the other in witchcraft and savagery. ...Mau Mau revealed the almost inexplicable extent to which it could go. A Kikuyu leading an apparently normal life would, in one moment, become a being that was barely human. A most notable manifestation of this was the murder of the Ruck family at the end of 1953. Mr. Ruck's groom, who led a gang of terrorists, enticed Mr. Ruck from his house at night on a spurious statement that a gangster had been arrested. He was battered to death in front of his wife who had come out to assist him, and she was then murdered. On the instructions of the groom, their small son,

---

[60] Frank Corfield *'Historical Survey of Mau Mau'* Sessional PaperNo. 5, 1959/60 p.9

aged 6, hiding in terror in the house, was then slashed to death. The groom, who led this attack, had only a few days previously carried the boy tenderly home some miles from the house after a riding accident. But even more unaccountable was the reverse process which was the basis of the formation of the pseudo-gangs which were the deciding factor in the final defeat of Mau Mau in the forest. On surrender, a gangster, who had been in the forest for years and had taken a succession of the vilest of the Mau Mau oaths, almost immediately volunteered to lead the Security Forces to the hide-out of his previous gang and, if an opportunity arose, would willingly dispose of his recent comrade-in-arms. Nor was he led to this course of action by an inducement of clemency. It was a spontaneous and willing course of action.[61]

But it came as no surprise to those of us who worked in pseudo gangs during the emergency. We were able to see at first hand, the dilemma these young men faced. Working with them necessitated living very close to them, and this gave us a unique insight onto what went on in the minds of these young Kikuyu men torn between two cultures, several thousand years apart. They had been born into a primitive society whose culture and lifestyle had remained the same for generations, but then, encouraged by the missionaries, their parents sent them to school. Thus they were thrust into a system totally foreign to anything they had experienced up to that time. A young adolescent Kikuyu boy, probably taught by a white missionary, saw the way the Europeans lived, and with his innate desire to better himself, tried his damnedest to emulate them. But the European had behind him generations of forbears who, over the millennia, had gradually lost the cloak of tribalism and community dependency, and had found he could lead a better life by acting on his own, as an individual. This individualism, inherent in the European, was anathema for the community-dependent Kikuyu who needed a mooring on which to attach himself. Like space dust, he gravitated to the nearest larger object and attached himself to it and felt better. Once he had left school and the bosom of his family he still needed something to cling to, which traditionally would have been his age-group warriors, of whom he would have been an indivisible part and with whom he would have always acted in concert. In those early days, if one asked a young Kikuyu warrior his opinion on something to which he did

---

not readily have the answer, he would invariably say, *'first let me discuss it with my friends'*, (i.e. his co-warriors) *'and then I'll give you my answer'*.

But the age-group was not part of the new system. It was not possible to work in an office or on a European farm for a monthly salary while being a member of a warrior group. He was on his own for the first time. So if something then presented itself that was akin to his longed-for warrior buddies, it was tempting to gravitate towards them. If they happened to be a forest gang, claiming to be fighting for some cause or other, that was ideal particularly if he was told he was fighting for a good cause, and would be paid for his services; but if circumstances changed, and he saw a better chance of survival by attaching himself to a different object—one that also gave him a modicum of companionship—that was also perfectly admissible. Loyalty did not come into the equation. Unlike the Masai and other pastoral tribes in Kenya who were sufficiently content to accept the status quo, the young semi-educated Kikuyu man was torn between wanting the companionship of the warrior age-group, and at the same time wanting to earn money with which he could become more like the European, but lacked meaningful scope for achieving his goal. He was ripe for the gangland fraternity of Mau Mau.

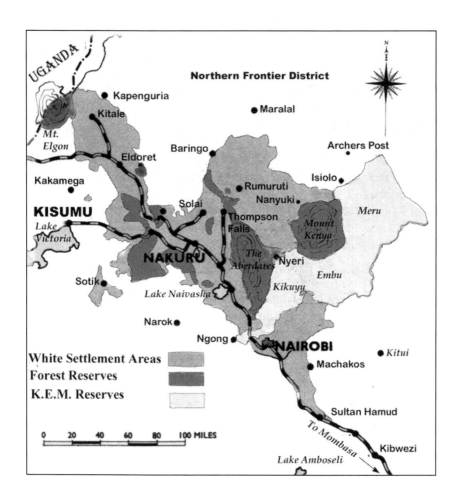

CENTRAL KENYA AS AT 1950

Showing the railway, the townships, the forest reserves, the White settlement areas and the Kikuyu, Embu and Meru tribal reserves.

CHAPTER FIVE

SUNDOWNERS AND SWEAT

*'British imperialism was not merely a cheap planting of flags, but basically an
essential driving of new furrows.'*

Elspeth Huxley: *White Man's Country*

It was almost inevitable that European explorers, seeing so vast a country so suitable for farming and, in large part, virtually uninhabited, should turn their attention to the possibility of settling in Kenya. At that time the western prairies of Canada and the United States were being opened up for European settlement; railways had been built, the natives 'pacified' (or otherwise disposed of), and the wildlife removed, so why not here in Africa, in areas that had much the same climate as an English summer day, all the year round.

The explorer's ideas were soon taken up by the British administrators and within eight years of the start of British rule, the first white farmers arrived to try their luck. They were the pioneers of a movement that in the end was the making of Kenya's farming industry, which up to then, had been by the indigenous people for their own, or their family's subsistence. There were no altruistic thoughts of planting crops for their cousins in other parts of the country, though in good years, the Kikuyu were happy to grow a surplus as a means of currency to trade with their neighbours the Masai.

At first, European settlement was slow. The Christchurch plains of New Zealand, the Pampas of Argentina as well as the Prairies of Canada were more appealing and carried fewer risks than the untried highlands of East Africa. But later, having proved that the climate and the soil were suitable for large scale food production, farmers from South Africa and European countries converged on Kenya and settled with their families to make a life for themselves. The farming required the breaking of new land and the discovery of new methods of husbandry. Like most farming in those days, it required hard work for precious little in return. Unfortunately, with typical journalist hype, the settlers name later became tarnished because of a small section of that society who became notorious for leading an extravagant and scandalous lifestyle and won themselves a licentious image as the infamous 'Happy Valley' set.

So much has been written about the disgraceful behaviour of that small circle of white settlers in Kenya, characterized in the book *White Mischief*[62], and so little about the far more important, hard-working majority of the settlers, that a casual observer may be forgiven for thinking that that behaviour was typical of all Kenya settlers. If it were so, the indigenous Africans would have been right to get rid of them as quickly as possible after Independence. But it wasn't and they didn't. One of the first things Jomo Kenyatta did when he became Prime Minister of the independent Government just before Independence, was to speak at a meeting of settlers at the Stag's Head Hotel in Nakuru, the heart of the White Highlands, in August 1963. He made it very plain that Kenya could not do without the settlers and that their contributions to the prosperity of the country were absolutely vital. That he did so, is testament enough that all but a tiny band of renegades, were hard-working dedicated farmers who had the country, the land and the people at heart.

Confirmation of this is best summed up by one who was born and brought up in the midst of the 'Happy Valley' set and its small band of drop-outs.

> It was my destiny to grow up among a small group of people whose reputation for behaving badly has earned them a place in the history of colonialism. The Happy Valley set was a unique phenomenon. Shallow, spoiled and self-centred, they were by nature metropolitan consumers who, set down in the Garden of Eden, found it dull. Beneath the froth of the dancing, the drinking and the overt liaisons, there lurked an element of the frantic. Many became addicts either of drink or drugs [or both]. The cheap cost of living bestowed the kind of comforts only enjoyed by the super-rich at home; there was no nine-to-five routine to regularise their life and blunt their energy; as for setting an example, who cared, with only the natives watching? The images of June Carberry [her step-mother] and her friends downing yet more drinks, heedless of the servants trying anxiously to save the roast which is already hours late, of Lady Idina parading naked in front of her servant, tell the story.
>
> The people who built the Colony were very different. They were doughty, decent men and women who earned their sundowners by the sweat of their brow; who left farms, hospitals, hotels, businesses and newspaper empires behind as a testament to their industry[63]

---

[62] James Fox – *'White Mischief'* Jonathan Cape 1982
[63] Juanita Carberry – *'Child of happy Valley'* Heinemann – 1999 p.192

Settlement of the land by White farmers has often been held as the reason for the uprising of the Kikuyu people in the illegal insurrection that came to be known as Mau Mau. It is an over-simplification to give it as a direct result, but the existence of White farmers on land which they were reported to have stolen was used very successfully for propaganda purposes by Kikuyu politicians who found it a most convenient tool in their attempt to win over the Kikuyu population to the course of action they planned, a course very different to the

The railway passing through the European settled area in the White Highlands - 1950

one they advertised and the one so erroneously given today in 2004.

The question of 'stolen lands' has been addressed *ad nauseam* by many authors, the most conclusive of which must surely be Frank Corfield's version in *'The Origins and Growth of Mau Mau'*. The evidence shows that the excuse for a minority of Kikuyu to take up arms over land they were told had been 'stolen' from them fifty years before, was a gross over-reaction. But the issue of land, was nevertheless such an emotive one, that it was put to good use by the politicians, particularly by Jomo Kenyatta himself, as a rallying cry to unite the tribe behind him and as a means of verbally attacking the British administration.

However, while the claim that the British stole land from the Kikuyu in the early days of their administration lacked solid evidence, there may have been an element of truth in it.

The findings of the 1929 Committee of Kikuyu Land Tenure and of the Kenya Land Commission of 1934 chaired by Judge Morris Carter, are available for all who doubt that when land was being assigned for European settlement, the British went to considerable lengths to ensure not a single acre was taken from anyone who could genuinely show they owned it or that it had been under cultivation by them at the time, and that if any had been taken inadvertently, to make sure it was either returned to the owners or they were adequately compensated.

The 1929 Committee under the chairmanship of the Chief Native Commissioner, G.V. Maxwell, and on which Dr. L.S.B. Leakey also served, were unable to make any meaningful adjudication on the disputed lands, owing, largely, to the convoluted and sometimes incomprehensible system of Kikuyu land tenure which made it almost impossible to come to a fair conclusion. But later, the 1934 Carter Commission persisted with the complexities and was much more thorough. It went into every aspect of doubts that had emerged over the years since 1900 concerning the alienation of land for European (and Asian) settlement – doubts that came mainly from the Nandi, Masai and Kikuyu areas as well as some from the Northern Province and the Coast. Aggrieved people were invited to attend the Commission and present evidence to it. Over 300 claims were made by the Kikuyu, Embu and Meru people alone, and many of the 147 Kikuyu who gave evidence to the commission, claimed they had once owned land that had since been apportioned to European settlers. The Commission's job was to look into these claims and where they were found to be correct, to advise the Government to return the land to its rightful owner or to compensate him. The Report, which the British Government accepted in its entirety, runs into 618 pages, and the evidence taken amounts to a further three volumes, nearly 3,500 pages, of which the first volume of 1,174 pages is on the disputed Kikuyu areas alone.[64]

The three members of the Commission took evidence from several hundred people during the eighteen months of their deliberations, which included visits to some, but not to all of the disputed land.

The areas in the Kikuyu land unit were the most difficult on which to adjudicate, particularly the areas around Limuru and the south western part of

---

[64] Dr. John Lonsdale of Trinity, Cambridge, an authority on Colonial Africa, regards the Commission's evidence as being one of the most important records of oral history anywhere in Africa.

Kiambu where, before the onset of British rule, the Masai had always grazed their cattle up to the very edge of the forest within which the Kikuyu had their settlements. The Kikuyu lived inside the forest which they had not yet cut down, the easier to defend their settlements. While the Masai would graze their cattle up to the edge of the forest, they would never enter it. Joseph Thomson in his book *'Through Masailand'* describing his first contact with the Kikuyu in 1884, writes, *'The Masai have made repeated attempts to enter into the [Kikuyu] country, but they have found that the Wa-Kikuyu were more than a match for them in their dense forests. They have failed miserably on every occasion. ...No caravan has yet been able to penetrate into the heart of the country, so dense are the forests and so murderous and thievish the inhabitants. They [the Kikuyu] are anxious for coast ornaments and cloth, and yet defeat their own desires by their utter inability to resist stealing or the fun of planting a poisoned arrow in the traders. These things they can do with impunity, sheltered as they are by the forests which are impenetrable by all but themselves.'* [65]

The Masai warriors, fierce and bloodthirsty though they were, did not have it all their own way. The Kikuyu had a well-equipped and organised militia or *'njama'* of their own who were more than a match for the warlike Masai warriors when it came to fighting in the forest, where the Kikuyu would use poisoned arrows to great effect. The *'njama'* were a kind of police force of warriors that not only defended their settlements in times of warfare, but also kept order at markets and communal meetings. Later expeditions that went through the Kikuyu lands had first to make their peace with these warriors before they could begin their exchange of goods for the Kikuyu produce. Leakey instances examples of the work the *'njama'* had to carry out. When some of the Kikuyu traders got out of hand and started pinching things off the Teleki and von Höhnel expedition, the *njama* went to work on them. *'The young warriors, however, soon restored order, drawing their long knives or swords, and laying about them vigorously, with the flat sides only, though some blood was drawn. One native snatched a bundle of beads out of Qualla's hand, another stole the turban off Maktubu's head, but the warriors themselves caught and flogged the thieves, compelling them to restore the property taken'.*

Leakey continues:

---

[65] Joseph Thomson *'Through Masailand'* Sampson Low 1885 p.308

Here we have an interesting statement which confirms the evidence of the Kikuyu people that long before the Europeans took over the government of the country they had a well organised police system. A section of the warrior organisation was known as the 'njama' and they were the tribal police responsible for seeing the laws were obeyed and thieving punished. Von Höhnel gives us a striking picture and one of the only ones we have from outside sources of this tribal police force performing its duties prior to European control of Government.[66]

The complications faced by the Carter Commission were immense, particularly in the areas where the Masai land bordered the forests within which the Kikuyu lived[67]. In the period just after the European administration began, between the years 1888 to 1903, the Masai suffered enormous losses through the 1898 rinderpest epidemic. The ensuing famine and the previous internecine wars weakened them and drastically reduced their numbers. So that by 1904, when areas were being surveyed for European settlement, the Masai had pulled back from the forested areas, and the Kikuyu, ever resourceful, stepped in and began planting crops where Masai cattle had only recently grazed. When evidence was being taken by the Commission some thirty years later, both the original Masai and the later Kikuyu claimed tenure of the same land. Each of these claims had to be looked at carefully before judgment could be given. If it was indeed judged to have been Masai land, it could be alienated for European settlement by virtue of the Masai Treaty of 1904.[68] If it was judged to have been owned or cultivated by a Kikuyu, it had to be returned to its rightful owner or he had to be compensated accordingly.

Further complications arose when the waNdorobo were invited to give evidence. The Kikuyu had a history of 'purchasing' land from the waNdorobo, a hunter-gatherer people who also laid claim to land both inside and outside the forested areas, particularly in the Kiambu district west of the Chania River. The waNdorobo people lived almost entirely off the natural land. They grew no crops, neither did they raise livestock, therefore as they were no competition for either the Masai or the Kikuyu, they were friendly to both. Their numbers were also very few and their homesteads scattered. The

---

[66] Dr. L.S.B. Leakey – 'The Southern Kikuyu Before 1903 p.61

[67] Vestiges of these forests can still be seen in the Nairobi National Park

[68] Masai Treaty of 1904 allowed the removal of the remaining Masai families to south of the railway thus enabling the securing of land for European settlement

Commission found it extremely difficult to conclude whether or not certain parcels of land had or had not been purchased in this way. Witness after witness gave evidence to the Commission that such and such a parcel of land had never been cultivated, and yet the Kikuyu still claimed it was theirs. The Commission tended to believe the waNdorobo rather than the Kikuyu whose claims, they concluded, were *'based on a process which consisted partly of alliance and partnership and partly of adoption and absorption, partly of payment and largely of force and chicanery''*.[69]

Many of the difficulties and complications arose because of the changes that occurred in the years between the time when the first European administration of the area took place in 1888, and the demarcation of the land some twelve to fifteen years later when things were very different. These changes may well point to the source of the disputes that came later.

Anthropologists such as Leakey, Lambert, Routledge and others are able

to show strong evidence that the Kikuyu settled in the forested area of what became Fort Hall District, in the sixteenth century.[70] They began clearing the forest that once covered the whole of the eastern side of the Aberdare mountains, land into which they gradually expanded over the years, clearing the forest as they went and cultivating the extremely fertile soil. Even in 1960 the remnants of that forest could be seen on Nyeri Hill, a forest which, according to the change in soils, must have reached to the old Thika to Nyeri road alignment. Now, the only remaining indication of the existence of this

One of the last remaining trees on
Nyeri Hill - 1960

immense forest, is *'the deep red earth derived from volcanic tuffs and*

[69] Sorrenson – *'Land Reform in the Kikuyu Country'* OUP 1967 p.8
[70] Ibid – p.6

the humus from the heavy forests that once clothed the country'.[71]

By the time the first records were written by European travellers, the Kikuyu had reached the Thika and Chania rivers, and had begun purchasing land from the waNdorobo people in what was to become the Kiambu district. But those who lived on the extremities of their land had to contend with the Masai, particularly in the triangle marked by Ngong, Limuru and Kiambu.

The New Zealander historian Sorrenson gives a clear indication as to who these pioneering Kikuyu were likely to have been:

> As a result of growing pressure on the land after several generations, the tenants were likely to suffer an increasing insecurity of tenure in the face of the demands of lineage members. ...There was also likely to be friction between various families, especially where one branch of the founding family had prospered and grown and another branch had been relatively stationary. The former family naturally required and often obtained land at the expense of the latter and the prospect of large areas of [hitherto] uncultivated land—as for instance existed on the borders of Fort Hall District, between the sixteenth and nineteenth centuries—was a standing temptation to adventurous members of the *mbari* [family] to migrate. Despite the dangers that any pioneer had to face—hostile occupants of the land in question, bands of marauding Masai, the difficulties of establishing a new homestead in the bush—there was the prospect of substantial reward.[72]

Thus the first European travellers to discover the Kikuyu and record their meetings with them, came in from Masailand over the Athi Plains to Ngong and Dagoretti. The explorers found the Kikuyu a forest-dwelling people and describe their settlements as enclosures surrounded by forest. A Hungarian/German expedition headed by Count Teleki and von Höhnel in 1887 provided the first record of how the Kikuyu people lived, when the Masai were at their strongest and before the advent of the British influence. This expedition was the first to go right through the Kikuyu country from Ngong en route for Mount Kenya, and Leakey refers to their journals as the clearest record of how those forest-dwelling Kikuyu arranged their settlements in order to defend them against the marauding Masai. Leakey quotes a relevant extract from the Hungarians' journal when they were entering the Kikuyu area

---

[71] Ibid – p.3
[72] Ibid – p.12

between Ngong and Kiambu to buy food from the Kikuyu for their caravan. There are no markets exactly like those in other parts of Africa, as the Kikuyu do not venture out of the forests from fear of the Masai, and caravans have to seek them. A well-armed contingent from a travelling party goes into the woods and calls the attention of the natives by firing two or three shots. In a few minutes the signal is answered by the appearance of some envoys [probably the Njama]. A time and a spot are fixed on for the holding of a market and in due course the traders make their way to the rendezvous soon joined by hundreds of men and women laden with the superfluous produce of their fields.[73]

It is clear from this and other accounts from early expeditions, that the only way the Kikuyu could defend their settlements in these border areas of their territory was by having them well inside the forests. In the more populated areas of Muranga (Fort Hall) and Nyeri that had been settled for many years, they were able to live a more open existence without the necessity of well defended enclosures, as the Masai were a long way from them. But in the areas at the limit of the Kikuyu territory, they could only clear small glades deep within the forest and build their huts and enclosures some distance from the forest edge. For although the Masai warriors would graze their cattle up to the very edge of the forest, they would not enter it and the forest perimeter formed the Kikuyu's first line of defence.

Only a few years later, after 1888 when the British, from their base at Fort Smith near Kabete, began to mediate between the Masai and the Kikuyu and impose a truce, a stop was put to the warfare between the two tribes. The Kikuyu then began to venture out of the forest more, as confirmed by Francis Hall who was stationed at Fort Smith from 1892 to 1899. Later still, when the Masai numbers decreased so drastically and they vacated these areas, the Kikuyu gradually came out of the forest and began cutting it down in order to cultivate more land, and use the timber for building their huts and for firewood and charcoal. The disputes that arose later over the Limuru land, originated from this time when the Kikuyu began to cultivate outside the woodland, and eventually to build their settlements on land which had, up to that time been denied to them by the Masai. The disputed land to the east of Kiambu was a different matter and was simply a question of whether or not the land had been purchased from the waNdorobo.

---

[73] Dr. L.S.B. Leakey – 'The Southern Kikuyu before 1903' Academic Press 1977 p.58

The legality of alienation of land for European occupation was given by Law Officers of the Crown, who, in 1899, gave the opinion that as the country was legally dependent on Britain, in that as far as international law stood at the

A typical Kikuyu homestead in 1950

time, she was legally bound to administer the country: *'The right* (therefore) *to deal with unoccupied land accrues to Her Majesty by virtue of Her right to the Protectorate.'* [74] The East Africa (Lands) Order in Council 1901, gave legal effect to this opinion. The Order was specific as to exactly what land could and could not be alienated, and the surveyors that undertook the task of marking out the parcels of land and mapping them, were government surveyors brought from the U.K. specifically for the job. It was clearly stated in the Ordinance that *'no land that was under cultivation or showed signs of having been under cultivation could be alienated'*, and the surveyors had to follow this rule to the letter.

One of the main causes for the disputes that surfaced in the 1920s and later gave rise to the rallying cry of 'stolen lands', lay in a specific area near Kiambu where the land was particularly fertile. This came about in the early days of settlement. Surprisingly there were insufficient numbers of Europeans

---

[74] Foreign Office Confidential Print 7403 No. 101 16th February 1900

taking up the offers of settlement. The U.K. farming community were uncertain as to the suitability of the Kenya climate for Europeans; they did not know the nature of the crops that would grow in East Africa, nor the diseases to which both crops and animals might be prone, and they were concerned as to the whereabouts of markets for their produce. So the initial response for settler occupation from the U.K. was slow. By 1903, there were still only a hundred or so settlers who had taken up land, so in an attempt to encourage more settlers to come and try their luck, the Governor, Sir Charles Eliot, sent word to South Africa advertising that land was available in Kenya for settlement. The response to this was almost immediate and there was a sudden flood of hopeful applicants who knew all about the vicissitudes of farming in Africa.

The response to this mission was extremely good, so much so that early in 1904 a wholly unprepared Land Office was besieged with requests for land from several hundreds of South Africans, few of whom had money to waste on waiting in Nairobi until land could be surveyed. This hold-up was accentuated by the Government's insistence upon the whole paraphernalia of British practice in regard to survey and the registration of titles. An administrative officer, J.O.W. Hope, was instructed to demarcate as swiftly as possible a line to the south of the Kikuyu country defining the unoccupied area available for settlement. The land granted in this area proved to be among the richest in Kenya, but the grants marked the beginning of the clash between European and African claims on land which was to extend over a much wider area and which in due course was to be one of the main sources of dispute between the two races. In spite of a sincere attempt to reach a fair decision, Mr. Hope had insufficient time to investigate historical rights in land, much of which had been further complicated by the recent decimation of the Kikuyu in Kiambu as a result of the smallpox epidemic.[75]

There is no doubt that the Kikuyu method of land tenure was extremely complicated. It is not possible to say that the land was *owned* by anyone as ownership requires title and the only titles to land in those days recognised by the British, were the ones given to the new European settlers. But in Kikuyu culture there was a system by which land could be cultivated but of which no right of ownership existed. It is very likely that this complication gave rise to

---

[75] Kenneth Ingham *'A History of East Africa'* Longman's 1962 p.213

portions of land in Kiambu being alienated by Mr. Hope and his team. He would have seen land that was covered in bush and showing no signs of cultivation, without means of knowing that it had, in fact, been cultivated some years previously by *'athami'*[76] ('tenants') who no longer lived there nor worked the land, but nevertheless considered themselves to be the rightful tenants, if not owners of it. Much of the acrimony that arose over the land issue at Kiambu was on land which was, on the face of it, deserted. This occurred because the owner, *'mwene githaka'* or the 'tenant', *'muthami',* had died or had been unable to cultivate the land for some years owing to the reduction in the size of his family through the small-pox epidemic and coincidental droughts that decimated the population between 1898 and 1902. Francis Hall writes about these plagues vividly in his letters home. Land left idle in Africa soon reverts to nature. Anyone, then, carrying out a survey, who came across land that showed no sign of occupation, with zebras grazing on it and giraffes browsing the trees, would naturally assume it was unoccupied and had never been cultivated. Some of the disputed Kiambu land had undoubtedly been cultivated by people years previously who, by the time Hope arrived, had returned to their traditional homes miles away beyond the Chania river, in Muranga (Fort Hall). They would, therefore, not be around to show the unsuspecting, but nevertheless perfectly amenable surveyor that this land actually belonged to them. By the time the owner/landlord was next able to visit his land in Kiambu, he may well have found it fenced, with coffee bushes growing on it and a white Farmer living there with his family.

This, then was the muddle that Judge Carter and his team were expected to sort out.

One of the Kikuyu who gave evidence to the 1934 Commission was Andrew Gathea, a member of the Anglican Church.

He spoke not so much of the grievances of his own land-owning corporation or *mbari*, but of matters of principle. He wondered why settlers were expelling African labour tenants off their farms at the same time as the Commission was sitting; why 'native reserves' should be so called when they covered African owned land, not held in reserve for some other purpose; why elephants in game parks should have more security than Africans in reserves; why the British did not believe that Africans had ever had laws of property and why government should take

---

[76] There is no equivalent word in English. The singular *'muthami'* is best described as one who is given, or assumes both building and cultivation rights on a piece of land.

African land when the British had come 'with peace, not with a sword; not by conquest but by treaty'.

'If a man cannot get justice for himself he leaves the matter over for his son. Unless you can do something for us and make an end of our troubles', Gathea concluded, 'we will have to leave them for our children to carry on, and we will pass on to them that our land was bought by us originally and then taken from us by force'.[77]

Andrew Gathea was not, apparently, asked why, when the land was supposed to have been taken from them 'by force' in the early 1900's, the Kikuyu who had the strong and well-disciplined 'njama' warrior force at that time, meekly allowed the British to come in and 'steal' their land and settle on it when the settlers had little with which to defend themselves and no police force to guard them.

There was, for example, during the *Iregi* age-group in the mid eighteenth century, a determined effort by the Somalis who came down from the north east, to settle on the fertile and verdant Kikuyu land and take it from them by force. Both Routledge and Leakey explain how the Kikuyu warriors repulsed the Somalis and sent them back to their own lands with a bloody nose. So they were not averse to defending their land against intruders, as the Masai also found to their cost.

It is inconceivable, then, that the rightful landowners, had the land been under cultivation, would simply stand idly by and watch it being taken by the Europeans. There is no record of any Kikuyu at the time, protesting that his land had been stolen, not, that is, until the Carter Commission started taking evidence. If then, the rightful owner or his relatives were not around at the time the demarcation was carried out, but had temporarily (or permanently) abandoned the land because they had no current use for it, they surely cannot blame the surveyors for taking it in for settler occupation when there was no sign of cultivation having taken place, and the only animals on it were zebra and giraffe. Is it not surely more likely that the Carter Commission was seen by the ever resourceful Kikuyu to be a chink in a door that could be opened wider by those who dared? Wasn't there a chance here for those who were adventurous enough and who could make up a good case, to get some free land?

---

[77] Dr. John Lonsdale '*Jomo Kenyatta and the two Queens*' Paper to Oxford Commonwealth History Seminar 2003

Another complainant was Senior Chief Koinange, who had been appointed to that position by the British, some years previously. He maintained he had only been given back one tenth of what had been his before the British surveyors arrived. He mentions nothing, however, about the land being taken from him 'by force'; nothing about the surveyor being told the land was already owned, and nothing about the local *njama* being employed to give the Europeans that arrived to take up their plots, 'a bloody nose'.

Archdeacon Beecher assisted the Carter Commission with translation from Kikuyu to English. Beecher ran the Church Missionary Society's mission at Kahuhia in Fort Hall in the 1920s and '30s He was later appointed Archbishop and head of the Anglican Communion in East Africa. Having attended most of the Commission's inquiry into the Kikuyu claims, he commented *'If the Kikuyu that gave evidence [to the Commission] had not told so many blatant lies, they might well have got more land than they did out of the commissioners'*. He found little to criticise in the Commission's findings.[78]

In his book, *'Facing Mount Kenya'*, published in 1938, four years after the Carter Commission report was published, Kenyatta accuses the British of trickery regarding the report. *'The Gikuyu lost most of their lands through their magnanimity; for the Gikuyu country was never wholly conquered by force of arms, but the people were put under the ruthless domination of European imperialism through the insidious trickery of hypocritical treaties'.* [79] One can only wonder whether or not Kenyatta ever actually read the report, or if he did, whether he hoped by its somewhat onerous length, no one else would.

Some fifteen years later, in 1950, the Kikuyu population had more than doubled from what it was in 1900.[80] It was then that the Kikuyu began to make out that the Commission did not do its job properly or did not come to the correct conclusions. This is not only to cast aspertions on the integrity and independence of the eminent people who sat on that commission, it also smacks of opportunism. The real problem, one that was never mentioned by the Kikuyu claimants, was that by 1934, after more than forty years of British rule which had brought peace, a modicum of prosperity and proper healthcare to the people, the Kikuyu population was burgeoning and they were beginning to run short of land. By 1950 they had simply run out of land. This was the

---

[78] James Foster – Biographer of Archbishop Leonard Beecher Pers. Comm.
[79] Jomo Kenyatta *'Facing Mount Kenya'* Mercury Books 1938 p.47
[80] In 1902 the Kikuyu population was estimated at 451,500. By 1950 it was estimated to be over 1,000,000

reason they were so ready to pursue the stolen lands issue. It is also fair to point out that part of their shortage of land was brought on themselves by their resistance to change from their poor agricultural husbandry and food production practises to far more productive methods – something the British had been teaching them and trying to persuade them to do (and which they have now done) since the first Agricultural advisors were sent there in 1946. *'Right up to the beginning of the Emergency it was a fight to get better methods of husbandry across. In 1946-47 when I was concerned with community development [in Fort Hall], I worked closely with the Agricultural Officer who had a very difficult job indeed; even trying to move them towards compost-making was extremely difficult'*[81]. Instead, it was much easier to blame the British for stealing their land.

The first Europeans had begun to take up small parcels of land in the Kenya Protectorate by 1896, some six years after the Imperial British East Africa Corporation had sent its first administrators to take control of the country. It was not, in fact, the Government's intention initially, to develop the country for settlement. With the exception of South Africa and Rhodesia, the British Government saw its function of administering its African Dependencies, as protecting and pacifying the natives, providing basic infrastructure, and thereafter to bring the populations to a state of literacy and enlightenment where they could eventually be left to govern themselves. But Kenya turned out to be somewhat different. It was largely the influence of the pioneer, Lord Delamere, who persuaded the then Governor, Sir Charles Eliot, to consider the idea of encouraging white settlers to establish themselves in the highlands of Kenya. Here, Delamere argued, was fertile soil, adequate rainfall, a healthy climate and most important of all, unoccupied land—all the prerequisites of settlement.

That much of the land was empty is confirmed by all the early explorers. In 1900, away from the forested areas in the higher, more fertile and well-watered lands where the Kikuyu people lived, one could travel all the way along the railway line in the Rift Valley from Nairobi in the south for nearly a hundred miles to Nakuru in the north without seeing a single human being except for the occasional Asian railway worker.

---

[81] W.H. Tommy Thompson - Pers. Comm.

It was inevitable, therefore that the emptiness of the land should be the first feature to strike and even astonish the European eye. A man could walk for days without catching sight of a single human being, save perhaps for a wild little Ndorobo hunter, with his bow and arrow and a hyrax-skin cloak, or a slim Masai herdsman standing alone with his spear and his sheep on a plain that stretched to meet a far horizon. It was only natural that some of the early-comers should begin to ask for land.

Once the railway had arrived it was obvious that the uninhabited country through which it passed would somehow have to be filled up and utilised. Good land could not be left fallow for ever when a £9,500-a-mile line passed through the middle of it.[82]

Every train that ran along the line, did so at a heavy loss, and the Governor was charged with finding a method of making it pay for itself. Sir Charles Eliot was told that the British Taxpayer could not go on making good the deficit for ever. The native population on its own could not be expected, for the foreseeable future at any rate, to provide passengers for the line or to send sufficient goods or crops along it. Most of them, with the notable exception of the Kikuyu who had some of the most productive land between the 5,200ft (1,585m) and the 7,000ft (2,135m) contours, couldn't even produce enough for themselves let alone export it. The only hope was to fill the empty spaces along the line with farmers who could, with European technology and machinery, turn the fertile land into productive farms and produce crops that the railway could carry and who would import goods and machinery that would need to be brought up from the port of Mombasa by the railway.

In any event, Sir Charles Eliot reasoned that European farming settlement was in fact an economic necessity for the good of the country. When he took office in 1900 Eliot witnessed the aftermath of one of the most damaging famines in the country's history. He argued that with their superior technology and machinery White Farmers would reduce the effects of such famines in future years, and would show the African farmers how to make better use of their land which would be good for the population as a whole.

But Elspeth Huxley, writing only thirty years later, and at the time the Carter Commission was sitting, argued that the reason for white settlement was more than simply a means to pay for the railway. In this passage from her book 'White Man's Country', Elspeth Huxley, surely Kenya's most articulate,

---

[82] Elspeth Huxley – 'White Man's Country' Chatto & Windus 1935 p.74

sensitive and prolific authoress, who grew up in a family of settlers, sums up the much wider and more important argument for European settlement in Kenya. It vividly and eloquently portrays the context in which settlement took place and was justified—something that any serious student of Kenya's history cannot afford to overlook, however unattractive its ethic may appear to be in an age when *'the pioneer has exchanged the glamour of a hero for the ignominy of a blackleg'* — the age in which this book is written.

When settlement [in Kenya] started, there was a world-wide need for raw materials, a need to which no limit could be seen. So long as industrialised countries demanded products of the soil, it was inevitable that that demand should be met. To lock up any productive region of the earth's resources in the interests of a tiny group of inhabitants, was considered to be a crime against humanity as a whole. This was the meaning of one arm of 'The Dual Mandate' [83]—the mandate held by a colonising power on behalf of the world 'to develop the resources of any area over which it had control, to the maximum extent'.

So long as the world continued to want more raw materials, the man who brought a new field under the plough, who pushed the limits of cultivation a little further out, who drained a swamp or watered a desert—the pioneer—was a benefactor to humanity. By adding to the world's wealth, he was adding to its prosperity. This was the justification for moving forward, if necessary on to land which he could put to better economic use than its previous owners. British Imperialism was not merely a cheap planting of flags, but basically an essential driving of new furrows. The theory of 'beneficial occupation of land'—land that in the long run must go to the man who can turn it into the greatest productivity—was part of a world system founded on reality.

This theory was not then regarded as it sometimes is today, as a specious excuse for filching land from its rightful owners. For the opposing theory that land belonged exclusively to the people already there however sporadic their occupation or inadequate their husbandry, could be pursued *in reductio ad absurdum*. Should the whole continent of North America have been left to the two or three million natives who roamed over it? Should New York, San Francisco, Chicago and Montreal remain forever unbuilt? Should Australia have remained unsettled …in the interests of a handful of aborigines? Should New Zealand never have

---

[83] The mandate by which the League of Nations charged Britain with ex-German colonies after the First World War.

produced cheap butter and meat ...for fear of disturbing the Maoris, who had themselves reached the island only two centuries before the British?[84]

This, then, sets the scene for the opening up of land in Kenya for White settlement, something which both Heads of State since Independence have recognised has benefited the country out of all proportion to the numbers who actually farmed the land, and still do. Now, more than 100 years after the first Whites came in and struggled to learn how to work this African land, there are second, third and even fourth generation White Kenyans living in harmony with their African countrymen, carrying on the work their pioneering forbears began, showing their African colleagues how to make the best use of their fertile soil and contributing to making Kenya a better place for everyone.

One method of teaching that helped both the farmer and his 'student' was to invite Africans onto the European farms and allow them to 'rent' an area to grow their own subsistence or cash crops and graze their own livestock. These men who usually brought their immediate family with them, were known as 'squatters' and their rights were strictly controlled by government legislation. The 'rent' they paid was to work without pay for 180 days a year on the host farm, but with any additional days worked, paid for by the farmer at the going rate. This proved a mutually satisfactory arrangement particularly during the slump years of the 1930s when farmers everywhere were suffering from the worldwide recession. The squatters' children went to schools that were usually provided by the farmer himself (or a neighbour) who was also able to employ wives or other members of the family when there was extra work available on the farm. While it was a very amenable settlement, it was never meant to be a permanent compact and both parties knew this.

The arrangement continued to work well until towards the end of WW2 when Africans returning from the war now wanted a better lifestyle which they had experienced while fighting for the Allies against the Japanese in Burma and on other fronts. A feeling of resentment began to spread amongst the squatters.

This unrest was fuelled by other factors. More and more White farmers wanted to come to Kenya, now becoming known as the 'White Man's

---

[84] Elspeth Huxley *'White Man's Country'* – Chatto & Windus 1935 p.73/79

Country'– an ideal place to settle and bring up one's family. As land prices rose, the acreage of the farms reduced as the larger ones were divided up into smaller units. Coupled with this was the steady increase in the African population particularly that of the Kikuyu – an increase that had been building up over the past fifty years, since the British put a stop to the fighting amongst the tribesmen and had introduced better health care and veterinary services which resulted in a drastic reduction in the mortality of both humans and their stock. More Africans were therefore seeking the attractive squatters rights on farms and in an effort to cater for this increase, the acreage given to each squatter by the host farmer was reduced giving rise to yet more unrest.

This unrest was put to good use by the politicos bent on whipping up anti-European feeling amongst the Kikuyu – a convenient recipe and another pretext for the country's worst conflict: Mau Mau.

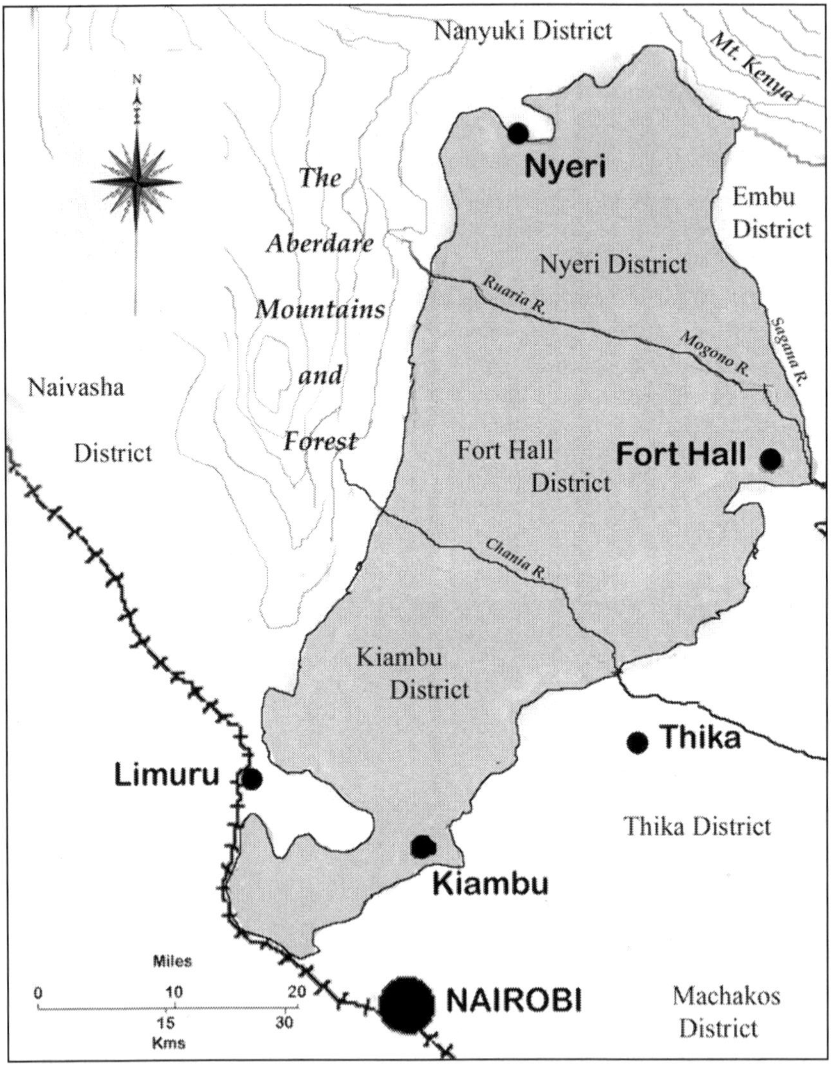
Nanyuki District
Mt. Kenya
N
Nyeri
The
Aberdare
Mountains
and
Forest
Embu
District
Nyeri District
Ruaria R.
Mogono R.
Sagana R.
Naivasha
District
Fort Hall
District
Fort Hall
Chania R.
Kiambu
District
Thika
Limuru
Thika District
Kiambu
Miles
0
10
20
15
30
Kms
NAIROBI
Machakos
District

THE KIKUYU TRIBAL RESERVE AS AT 1950

CHAPTER SIX

KENYATTA AND MAU MAU

'Mau Mau was a violent and wholly evil manifestation of nationalism'

Frank Corfield

There are various possible origins of the name *'Mau Mau'*, but none can be said to be definitely and historically correct. However, one that perhaps bears the most credence is contained in the book *'Mau Mau Detainee'* written by Josiah Mwangi Kariuki. He believes he has the real origin of the name, and because of its simplicity, it is hard to disagree.

> Kikuyu children when playing and talking together often make puns and anagrams with common words. When I was a child I would often say to other children 'Ithi, Ithi' instead of 'Thii, Thii', (meaning 'Go away, Go away') and 'Mau, Mau', instead of 'Uma, Uma' ['Get out!' 'Get out!']
>
> One evening, people went to a house in Naivasha area where the oath was being administered. It was always the duty of the oath administrator to see that there was a good guard to keep watch outside while the oath was being given. That evening, the guard was given instructions that, if he heard footsteps and he suspected it was the Police or an enemy, he should shout the anagram 'Mau Mau' so that those in the house could escape. It would be a clear sign only for those in the house, for the enemy would not understand what the words 'Mau Mau' meant.
>
> That night the police did come to the house and the guard shouted out. The people left the house. When the police came they found only the paraphernalia of the oathing. When they reported back to the Police H.Q., they said that they heard the words 'Mau Mau' as they approached. From then on the oath was given the name 'Mau Mau' [by the Police and the authorities] though the members of the movement did not call it by that name.[85]

Twenty five years after his demise in 1978 is too short a time to pass

---

[85] Josiah Mwangi Kariuki *'Mau Mau Detainee'* Oxford University Press. 1963 p.23

judgement on Jomo Kenyatta's term of office as the first President of Kenya. At this time, most objective commentators would opine that Kenya could have done a lot worse than have Kenyatta as its first President. He did, after all try to unite the country into a nation – itself an almost impossible task with so many different factions, tribes and languages, and he did reign over a comparatively peaceful period when many other states were in turmoil – not the least of which was his neighbour, Uganda. Other commentators might point to the fact that he did head some of the worst poaching of wildlife the country had ever experienced, particularly of elephant ivory and rhino horn, something that will be seen in years to come as Kenya's greatest natural asset and one that it could ill afford to fritter away. They will also point to the elements of corruption within the police and judiciary that took hold during his Presidency, from which the country has yet to recover, and to the mould of corruption generally from himself and his wife downwards.

But it will be for his controversial role in the Mau Mau conflict that he is most likely to go down in history.

As a political culture began to emerge in the years following WW2, there was, alongside it and parallel with it, a growing sense of fear, hostility and tension. This unfriendly attitude first manifested itself in Nairobi. The mood of sullen uncooperativeness soon started spreading to the Kikuyu tribal areas north of Nairobi. By 1951 it had become evident that this unfriendliness towards the Europeans was spreading fast, not least in association with a few Kikuyu leaders of whom Jomo Kenyatta was seemingly, but by no means exclusively, the most culpable. Evidence began to emerge that the means by which this was being fomented was not primarily in public meetings, though these were indeed a cause, but more importantly in widespread secret meetings held at night both in Nairobi and in the Kikuyu homeland. There was growing evidence from both the local District Officers and indeed from eye-witnesses of an emerging cult knit together by the administration and receiving of oaths leading inexorably to acts deliberately intended to subvert both tribal and Common law.

A District Officer in Fort Hall during the hey-day of Kenyatta's seduction of the Kikuyu people through the clever manipulation of tribal traditions, sets out his recollection of the man.

In 1922, when a handful of Kikuyu rioted in Nairobi, Kamau wa Ngengi, alias Johnston Kamau, alias Jomo Kenyatta, then about 30 years of age, joined the Young Kikuyu Association, which in 1926 became the Kikuyu

Central Association (KCA). Backed by this association he travelled to England and on to Moscow several times. At a time when few East Africans travelled abroad, all this coming and going and rumours of meetings with influential white men gave him an important and intriguing image back home amongst his peers in Kenya. Those that associated with him, began to see that through him there may be a way of partaking in some of the seemingly limitless wealth in European and Asian hands—not an unreasonable aspiration.

In 1929, two events of fundamental importance took place, both having a profound effect on Kikuyu pride and politics and on Kenyatta's political status within the tribe. The first was a decision by the Church of Scotland Mission to adopt a firm, but as it turned out injudicious, stand against female circumcision: an ancient custom, abhorrent to European thought, regarded by the Kikuyu as an essential part of their social frame-work. A wave of violence followed during which an elderly woman missionary was mutilated and murdered. The Church of Scotland pronouncement was seized upon by the Kikuyu Central Association and used to provide a powerful fillip to its anti-European teachings. Both as a political thinker and propagandist Kenyatta used his now considerable influence to lead a breakaway from mission schools. His use of the Kikuyu-language newspaper, *'Mwigwithania'*, which he had founded only the year before, was particularly adroit. The outcome was the setting up of two separate independent education bodies - the Kikuyu Independent Schools Association and the Kikuyu Karinga Education Association, which soon became very powerful vehicles of Kikuyu nationalism.

At about the same time, the Kikuyu Central Association provided funds for Kenyatta to go to London to present a petition of Kikuyu grievances. Accompanied by an Asian lawyer, of known Communist affiliations, he duly presented the petition at the Colonial Office, where it was ignored on the grounds that his going over the head of the Kenya Government would create a dangerous precedent. Undoubtedly many of the points in the petition were spurious, but some had substance, and the visit to England and its unsatisfactory outcome could possibly have been avoided if the Kenya Government had given them thought.

Frustrated and disappointed, and again with funds provided by Communist contacts in the British Trade Union Movement, he went off to Russia where he joined the Communist Party[86]. After a few months he was back in England, but in early 1930 went to Germany where he attended the Communist organised International Workers' Congress in Hamburg, going on to be a guest of the Communist Party of Berlin. Communism and Africa do not go well together, and 1930's Communism was far different from that of today, but I have recorded this background not to show that Kenyatta was a thorough-going Party Member but to illustrate why and where much of his natural political skill was honed, polished and prepared for long-term action. In fact I do not believe that he ever was a Communist. Certainly he did not preach it.

On his return to Kenya he made a strong bid for the leadership of the K.C.A., but Kikuyu politics being what they were he was not immediately successful. However his strong mark had been made and he was already unstoppable. It was not until 1935 when his arch rival Harry Thuku, who by comparison, was a moderate in favour of something approaching constitutional methods, withdrew, leaving the Association in the hands of the extremists, indicating that Kenyatta's time had come at last.

At this point a bogus and self-styled "Archbishop"[87] appeared on the scene. Associating only with Kenyatta and the K.C.A., the "Archbishop" worked under the auspices of the Kikuyu Independent Schools Association baptising converts and 'ordaining' priests for a newly formed Kikuyu African Orthodox Church which was intensely Kikuyu and political. It is not an over-statement to say that by the 1950's Kenyatta was the new church's deity. My own knowledge substantiates this. All these ingredients in the hands of a most skilful cook made an awful and costly cake.

During the war [WW2] Kenyatta was in England [working on Iford Farm, Lewes in East Sussex for the Robinson family] where he married an English girl. On his return home in 1947 he brought all his teaching and native talent together starting a well thought out campaign of agitation among the Kikuyu. He also imposed an oath of secrecy upon all council members of the K.C.A. This was the moment of the birth of Mau-Mau.

...This is the point at which I should attempt to sum up my

---

[86] With the recent opening of the Moscow archives, this has now been disproved.
[87] William Daniel Alexander a bogus 'archbishop' who was brought to Kenya from South Africa in 1935 by the Kikuyu Central Association. See *'The Origins and Growth of Mau Mau' Frank Corfield p.173*

feelings about this man who went on to become the first President of post-Colonial Kenya. Looking back over a quarter of a century of increasing detachment, taken together with the advantages of hindsight, I know full well that had I been him, my political targets would have been in the same direction. There is nothing wrong in having political drive and vision. His scheme to dominate his tribe, and then to dominate all the other tribes, actually failed as was more than amply demonstrated by their reactions during the State of Emergency. Be that as it may, as a result of his eventual incarceration as a detainee and a convicted person he became the right person in the right place. The late Tom Mboya with the backing of the Kenya African National Union and with much money from the American 'Kennedy Fund for Africa' foresaw all this and projected Kenyatta right to the forefront of Kenya affairs. What Mboya [who was not a Kikuyu] did not see, was that he in turn would have to be out-manoeuvred and destroyed.

I still believe, and from the testimony of my own ears and eyes, I know that Kenyatta built up a murderous, and murdering, organisation that killed thousands of his own tribesmen. I remember only too well the day he exhorted the Fort Hall Kikuyu to "Go out and water the Tree of Freedom with blood". And I was there the very next morning when the machete-hacked bodies of seven persons known to be his opponents were brought into my District Headquarters.

Never did Kenyatta express regret over his clandestine Mau Mau activities. His apparent eventual return to the Christian fold and his quite splendid enactment of the part of a solid, respectable world statesman, was, I am quite sure, nothing but a front.

His aims are now acceptable to me. His methods are not.[88]

It will probably never be known exactly how much Kenyatta had to do with setting up the Mau Mau organisation, but that he fanned the flames of it cannot be denied. His speeches certainly record his feelings about the 'stolen lands', though he was not a man for reading up his facts, or if he did, he conveniently left them out of his rhetoric. Corfield makes the point.

Land had already become a political issue, but it did not become a burning issue until the return of Jomo Kenyatta [from Europe] in 1946. In the intervening years, the old balance of nature had gone; the increasing population in the Reserves had led to an ever increasing

---

[88] W.H. Thompson – unpublished memoirs

pressure on the land, and Jomo Kenyatta and his associates saw all too clearly that the exploitation of land hunger was a sure way of furthering their own ends of uniting the Kikuyu against the Government in general, and the settled European farmers in particular. The juxtaposition of a crowded Kikuyu Reserve and the more spacious settled areas of the White Highlands made this all too easy. The claims on the White Highlands became more insistent and were supported in public by statements which bore no relation to the truth.

[In Kenyatta's rallying speeches] the Kikuyu agricultural labourers were asked, "Why continue to work for a pittance on land which is yours by right and was stolen from you by those for whom you are now working?"

The fact that much of the overcrowding in the Reserves was the direct result of the spread of the civilising influence of the European, and the failure of the Kikuyu to adapt his agricultural methods to the needs of the land, was ignored. Jomo Kenyatta and his associates went much further as they fought to oppose by propaganda and intimidation, all the efforts made by the Government to encourage proper use of land in the Reserves. It was entirely against the interests of their subversive movement that there should be a contented peasantry.

It is also of interest to note that as late as October 1951, The District Commissioner Kiambu reported that it was clear, from detailed discussions he had had with Jomo Kenyatta, that the latter had little understanding of the recommendations of the Carter Commission. Also, that many of the younger generation of Africans appeared genuinely to believe that Africans had been evicted from vast areas to make room for Europeans.[89]

As Corfield points out, it must be remembered that almost all the land occupied by the Kikuyu people had always been between altitudes 5,000 and 7,500 feet (1,525m and 2,280m), and situated on the slopes of Mount Kenya and the Aberdares: '...*probably the richest block of agricultural land in Kenya and as good as, if not better than much of the land in the area of the White Highlands.*'

Thus it was not difficult for Kenyatta, grand orator that he was, to give the masses what they wanted to hear, that vast areas of land had been stolen from them fifty years ago, and now was the time to get it back. The fact that

---

[89] F.D. Corfield – '*The Origin and Growth of Mau Mau*' Sessional Paper No. 5 of 1959/60

the British Government went to the extent of paying for a learned Judge to head a team to come out to Kenya and spend several weeks looking into every aspect of the land issue, taking evidence from witnesses, and making recommendations that, as far as the Kikuyu were concerned, added a fair and reasonable acreage to their land, cut no ice with Kenyatta. It is extremely unlikely that he ever read the Carter Commission report, because to acknowledge its fairness would defeat his main objective: to lead the Kikuyu people into a conflict where the battle cry was 'to regain the stolen lands'.

Jomo Kenyatta in 1945

On the face of it, Kenyatta's speeches given before his arrest in 1952, bear little similarity to the man who was believed to have been the architect of Mau Mau and its ensuing evil. So maybe he didn't expect the idea of Mau Mau to gather such momentum so quickly. Francis Erskine, that ardent anti-colonialist and fighter on the side of 'Kenya for Kenyans', came to know the man well and describes him as *'a true Kenyan fighting for independence for all of us and not just the Kikuyu people. He never took any of those bestial Mau Mau oaths but the political wing of that organisation adopted him as their leader as they had no one else'.*[90]

(Perhaps it was not easy, as Goebels discovered in 1938, to jump from an express train when you find it is not going in the direction you expected it to.)

It must, however, be made very clear that any typescript of Kenyatta's speeches which are still available today, are just a shadow of what was actually said, or at least what was implied at the time. A good Kikuyu orator does not spell out his message in words of one syllable. He speaks in proverbs and innuendos, in implications and ambiguities so that only those who are familiar with the deeper meanings of the phrases and the cliché can interpret them in

---

[90] Francis Erskine Pers. comm..

the way the orator intends his message to come across. A good example is his reference to the Tribal Policemen, whom it was well known Kenyatta disliked intensely. Red jerseys were part of the Tribal Police uniform and instead of referring to them simply as Tribal Police, he would call them '*the rain-birds*'. Now the rain-bird was actually a cuckoo with a red chest (*Cuculus solitarius*), a common enough bird with an easily recognised call: '*it–will-rain, it-will-rain, it-will-rain*'. Everyone knew the bird and knew the chick always hatched out before the other eggs and threw them out of the nest so that it could monopolise the food from its foster parents. It was one of the tales every Kikuyu child grew up with. So his audiences knew exactly what he meant when he talked about '*the rain birds*'; the analogy suited his purpose well.

Jomo Kenyatta became president of the Kenya African Union (KAU) in 1947 after his return from Europe. It was then that the flame of the 'stolen lands' issue began to grow again in the minds of the younger generation of Kikuyu, a flame that was fanned by a few political opportunists who found it a convenient device to use for the somewhat different agenda they had in mind. Originally the KAU was open to all Kenyan Africans, but by 1951 it was so dominated by Kikuyu politicians that it was virtually an exclusively Kikuyu club, thus emphasizing the fact that they were the only ones spoiling for a fight to attain independence from the British. All the other tribes were happy enough with the status quo—a situation that remained throughout the ensuing Emergency.

The publicly stated aim of the KAU was to have the 'stolen lands' at Kiambu and Limuru returned to them from the white settlers' but the carefully kept secret agenda of the KAU leaders was not only to get back the 'stolen lands'—bonus though that would have been—but to take over the leadership, not only of the Kikuyu, and later of the Embu and Meru tribes, but in so doing, of the whole country as well. This was to be achieved through the removal of the colonial government, which would be accomplished through the murderous intimidation of the settlers who would flee their farms, when the government would be expected to cave in. Then, because it would be seen that the KAU were the ones who fought and defeated the colonialists it would fall to them to assume governance.

African intelligentsia often show an incredible self-confidence, and it is fair to surmise that given a situation such as that in pre-Emergency

114

Kenya, such persons would assume not only that the Europeans could be driven out of the country at will, but also that they could rule thereafter in idle ease by virtue of the 'power' within them. The converse is of course true, that when the 'power' bubble is pricked, this omnipotence collapses and gives way just as easily to an opposite conviction in which they see themselves as a victim of an unkind world.[91]

Kenyatta believed he had the qualifications to lead the peoples of Kenya, and the rhetoric to carry out a leadership programme. He had the support of several left wing members of the British Parliament who no doubt egged him on for their own political ends, and he had contacts in the Soviet Union, who liked to befriend countries with potential for strategic importance to them during the Cold War.

In order to carry out this programme, Kenyatta and his cronies realised it would be essential to have the support of the Kikuyu people. Without that support, nothing could be achieved. They would have to be persuaded by fair means or foul to follow the aims of the programme, even if it meant that in order to make examples of them, some of the Kikuyu people who worked for the government would fall victim to the same fate as the settlers. By far the best way to obtain this essential support, was to keep stressing the stolen lands' issue. It was an essential part of the scheme, therefore, that every opportunity should be taken to impress upon the people the way in which the European settlers had taken their Kiambu and Limuru land. The KAU leaders knew only too well that land was the most emotive issue that could be brought before the Kikuyu people, and good use of it was certainly made. Corfield makes the point.

It is not easy to convey to those who have had little contact with, or understanding of primitive societies, the intense emotional attachment that those societies have to land. Apart from the livelihood it affords, the spirits of their ancestors continue to dwell and have their influence in tribal lands: and what is perhaps even more important, in a society which has not yet advanced to a more modern cash economy, land is the insurance for old age. As anyone who has had to deal with land disputes knows, passions are inflamed and reason and truth go by the wind.

The attitude of the Kikuyu to land is summed up well in the

---

[91] Dr. J.C. Carothers – *Psychology of Mau Mau* 1954 p.14

following words by Mr. Eliud Mathu. *"It is on the land that the African lives and it means everything to him. The African cannot depend for his livelihood on profits made through trading. We cannot depend on wages. We must go back every time to the only social security we have—the piece of land. The land stolen must be restored, because without land the future of the African people is doomed. God will hear us because that is the thing he gave us."*

Corfield continues later:-

Again the expression "stolen lands", which after forty years of constant and intensive propaganda, was firmly embedded in the minds of every Kikuyu, bore little relation to the true facts. ...The cardinal point to bear in mind is not whether these claims to the "stolen lands" had any real substance, or whether such as were justified were dealt with equitably by various commissions set up by Government; it is that a sufficiently large number of Kikuyu believed they were true enough to enable agitators to make full use of this highly explosive source of discontent.[92]

So the first and most important part of KAU's plan was carried out at mass meetings, firstly in Fort Hall and later in Kiambu and Nyeri.

The leaders had to have some binding method of getting the population to adhere to the Mau Mau initiatives, because they knew that both the Government and the Missions would to try to steer people away from it. Christianity, ever since the first missionaries arrived, was firmly entrenched by 1950, having swept through East Africa like wildfire. The Mau Mau hierarchy knew they would have to use every means available to trounce Christianity and the missions.

In the nineteen thirties there began in Ruanda-Urundi a remarkable movement of religious revival. This movement has slowly spread throughout East Africa, and has had a great influence for good in Kenya. Its influence threatened the plan of the Mau Mau leaders in several ways. Its enthusiastic Christian teaching overcame the old Kikuyu fear of the supernatural on which the Mau Mau depended so much for the efficacy of their oath. It formed a common meeting ground for all races who were able to join together in a common fellowship on equal terms. To the Mau Mau such a common fellowship between different races was anathema as they wish to foster race hatred of the Black against the

[92] Frank Corfield *'Historical Survey of Mau Mau' p.11*

White. Finally, anyone who had been influenced by this movement of revival could no longer be trusted to confine his thinking to the narrow nationalistic channel prescribed by the Mau Mau. The result was that the Mau Mau opposed this movement of spiritual revival. They included a clause in the Mau Mau oath which was administered in the areas where the East African revival was strong, by which the oath-taker specifically agreed [on pain of death] to have nothing to do with Christianity in general, and with this revival movement in particular.[93]

The easiest way, of course, to defeat this movement was simply to murder those who were responsible for spreading the word, and many a Christian Kikuyu suffered in this way together with several white missionaries. There was, however, another factor the Mau Mau had to address.

The second factor which threatened the Mau Mau plan was the implementation of the Report on African Education in Kenya which had been published in 1949. It is commonly called the Beecher Report from the name of the chairman of the Committee [later Archbishop Leonard Beecher]. This Report recommended a system of greatly increased grant-in-aid for Africa education, together with a greater measure of control of the staffing, curricula and finance of the schools. This meant that those schools which had been the main channel of Mau Mau propaganda had to come into the new system or be closed. These schools were run by the Kikuyu Independent Schools Association (KISA) which was formed in 1930, and by other similar bodies such as the Karing'a Schools Association which was a direct descendant of the KCA. The Mau Mau could not afford to lose control of its centres of propaganda, and so in most cases the schools refused to accept the new grants-in-aid. This immediately lost them the sympathy and support of the great mass of the people, who had a great love of education and had no wish to see its educational facilities reduced. Thus by 1951 the Mau Mau movement was in danger of losing the support of many of its former sympathisers, and of failing in its attempt to unite the Kikuyu tribe behind it unless it acted swiftly. First, it tried to close the Mission schools, by various means, legal and illegal. When this attempt was not successful it turned to methods of violence. Forcible administration of the Mau Mau oath became widespread. Those who refused to take the oath and those who were thought to support the Beecher Report were beaten up or had their

---

[93] J. Wilkinson M.B., *'The Mau Mau Movement: Some General and Medical Aspects.'* East African Medical Journal July 1954 p.297

houses and property burned, especially in the South Nyeri District. Firearm thefts mounted. By the end of 1952 a major crises was inevitable. Meantime there was an increasing opposition party in the tribe led by such men as Harry Thuku and Chiefs Muhoya, Nderi and Waruhiu. Chief Waruhiu had rallied the Christian and moderate elements of the tribe in Kiambu district, and had denounced the Mau Mau and its methods at a great mass meeting. His murder on 7th October, 1952 was one of the factors which determined the declaration of the State of Emergency. With this declaration the police acted swiftly and detained Jomo Kenyatta and other suspected Mau Mau leaders.[94]

The following account written at the time by W.H. Thompson, a robust District Officer in Fort Hall, gives a clear indication of what was happening in his district more than five years before the Emergency. The account also shows how the first cracks began to appear in the solidarity of the Mau Mau movement between the easily persuaded masses who attended these rallies, and the more perceptive Kikuyu who could see what was in store for the Kikuyu people if these rabble-rousers were allowed to get away with their inflammatory speeches and achieve their revolutionary aims.

By midday on 24th August 1947, the village green at Kahuro, in the heart of the Fort Hall Reserve, was packed with thousands upon thousands of Kikuyu men and women, colourful in their Sunday best. They listened eagerly, intently, silently to the cunning words of hate poured forth by the orators who had driven up from Nairobi. Time and again they would burst forth with the menacing shouts and murmurs of an inflamed mob.

Many were the Sundays on which they had attended such meetings. After hours in the sun listening to the speeches they would feel so surfeited with abuse and suspicion that they would drift off to their homes, there to go about their normal affairs until word went round that another meeting had been called.

It took a brave man to approach a meeting of this sort, let alone to speak in a sane, sensible manner. But Ignatio Murai, a forty-five year old Chief and a staunch Catholic who had previously been a schoolmaster, was not one to know fear, as he proved repeatedly five years later. He calmly walked into the crowd that Sunday in August 1947, and, accompanied only by his two Tribal Police constables, arrested the two leading mob orators. He then took them back to his camp half a mile down the road.

The crowd, drunk with the subtle words on which it had been fed throughout the morning, took a little time to react, then they saw that this Chief, who stood for decency and orderly progress, represented all that they had been led to despise and loathe. They picked up sticks and stones and set off in pursuit. Chief Ignatio and his two constables refused to panic. When they saw the mob was out of control and were closing in to attack they opened fire. One rioter fell dead, another was wounded. The rest disappeared.[95]

Ignatio Murai was, of course, a Chief, appointed and paid by the British government, and having learnt something of the British ways, he knew all too well that the colonialists would not simply give up, and leave Kenya. He also understood the kind of might that western technology could unleash on the Kikuyu people if it came to a fight. The action taken by the Chief was by no means simply an act of loyalty to the British; it was in respect for the Kikuyu people themselves. He could see where this type of perversion of their culture would lead them, and he believed it was totally wrong and was prepared to stand up and say so.

In the months to come, this act of bravery was to prove typical of traditional Kikuyu who were prepared to risk their lives to attack these upstart orators who had no mandate from the people, and who were not part of the kiama, the traditional local committee that had been the lawful authority since time immemorial. Yet here they were, warmongering and preaching sedition that would lead the Kikuyu people into a fight that could seriously weaken them and one they could not possibly win. Chiefs had the authority to intercept these meetings; others who did not have that authority but may have felt the same indignation, just didn't go to the meetings. Later, they had their chance to show their opposition by joining the Kikuyu Guard, and sadly, many paid with their lives for taking the stand they believed was right.

Thompson, who served in the Fort Hall District during the five years that preceded the build up of Mau Mau, discusses the period in his own words.

If one looks back one can see the set pattern of Mau Mau agitation from that incident in 1947. After it, everything went quiet, very quiet indeed, and it was quite obvious that Jomo Kenyatta, with his friends James

[95] Jock Rutherford 'A History of the Kikuyu Guard' Ed. David Lovatt Smith 2003 p.5

Beauttah and Petro Kigondo of Fort Hall, decided to look around again and replan. Their plan took the form of arousing people against the Government at the frequent meetings of the Kenya African Union at Fort Hall. Kenyatta and his friends always remembered the shooting by the two Tribal Police at the time of the early attempt on Ignatio's life, and he made the mistake of shouting at the Tribal Police and ranting against them at every single meeting he held. This was one of the reasons why the Tribal Police were basically against Mau Mau.

An early sign of Kenya African Union and Mau Mau agitation was the painting of the famous Kenyatta shield and spear upon the doors of the native buses. The great strength of the Kenya African Union, and certainly of its financial support, came from certain locations in Fort Hall.[96] They were: Location 4 in the Kandara Division, the northern part of Location 7 in the Kigumo Division, and whole of locations 12 and 13, with particular emphasis on the areas around Kangema and Gituge. The worst of all came from Gituge.[97]

Thompson, in common with most officers serving in the Kikuyu homelands, knew what was happening but was unable to get the seriousness of it through to his seniors in Nairobi and thence to Whitehall. The reason given was that with the axiom of 'freedom of speech' so firmly embedded in the British order of governance, it was not thought important enough to warrant firmer action. Nor, perhaps, was it possible. Under the existing administration of the Colony and Protectorate of Kenya, the Constitution did not allow for 'serious internal disorder'. The responsibility for internal security rested with two separate Government Departments: that of 'Law and Order' and of 'African Affairs', a third arm being the Governor himself who was also the Commander in Chief. Prior to 1952, Kenya was considered a military backwater, answerable only to the Commander-in-Chief Middle East, with Headquarters in Cairo over two thousand miles away. It was not until six months after the Declaration of Emergency in May 1953 when it was agreed to separate Nairobi from Cairo and appoint a Commander-in-Chief East Africa, that things began to be taken seriously.

In any case, in the five years preceding the Emergency, the Governor, Sir Philip Mitchell was nearing the end of his term of office and did not want

---

[96] 'Location': an Administrative sub-division of a district.
[97] 'A History of the Kikuyu Guard' 1957 Ed. D. Lovatt Smith p.5

anything to 'rock the boat'. An officer of the Kenya Police who rose to be an Assistant Superintendent, in a private communication to me, writes of his exasperation at the time when Mau Mau was known about but had not yet reached the masses and was therefore still controllable.

> We were feeding lots of information about Mau Mau through to the Government, but Sir Philip was near to retirement and wanted nothing but a quiet life and a peaceful retirement. Nothing was being done, and we in the field were becoming increasingly exasperated. You must also bear in mind that in those days the Kenya Police were not allowed to go into the [Kikuyu] Reserves; they were the sole preserves of the [civil] Administration. If it was necessary for us to go in pursuit of a criminal or some such person, we first had to obtain permission from the local District Commissioner, and if permission was granted it would probably be on condition that we went with a District Officer. The Kenya Police knew nothing officially about what was going on in the Reserve, but those of us whose job it was to know, had a pretty good idea. Then we had those awful weeks when Mitchell had left before the new Governor Sir Evelyn Baring arrived when we were without anyone who could take decisions. By the time Baring had realised how serious things really were, it was too late to nip the thing in the bud.

So the mass rallies continued unabated. There was no difficulty in organising them neither was there anything to stop anyone holding a meeting as long as they informed the authorities of the date and the venue. There was no difficulty either, in attracting people to the meetings. Word was passed from lip to lip, from family to family, from ridge to ridge and from location to location. Within a week, the whole district would know the day of the meeting, and where it was to take place. At the meeting, the speakers had to be careful they did not let out too many secrets, as there were bound to be chiefs and headmen who would be opposed to their aims, and who would inform their senior officers what was being said. But by clever use of the Kikuyu language, speeches were cloaked in duplicity and disguised so that to those who were not familiar with the subtleties of the language, particularly those not familiar with the local dialect, they might appear perfectly harmless, when in fact they were getting the message across loud and clear.

The language barrier and the absence of a clear understanding of what was being said or inferred in these speeches, was a matter of some frustration to the District Officers. Most of the Europeans who could speak the language, were either youngsters, brought up by Kikuyu nannies, who would be totally incapable of attending such meetings and writing down translations, or local missionaries who did not attend such meetings, as they did not want to become embroiled in political issues between their 'flock' and the government. Speeches made at this time by Kenyatta and others were being translated and written down from notes and from memory after the event. They were not recorded verbatim and one of the two European Policemen who attended the largest and most important of all the rallies, remembers well the day it happened. While this person was not fluent in the Kikuyu Language, his colleague was and between them they made the translation that has come down to us as one of Kenyatta's most important pre-Emergency speeches that took place at the Ruringu Sports stadium, on the outskirts of Nyeri in July 1952.

The meeting is for ever firmly imprinted on my mind. It was a fine and sunny Saturday morning. I think we were the only 'whites' present. We sat together on the inner perimeter surrounded by thousands of Kikuyu [later estimated to be at least 30,000]. The meeting, naturally, was conducted in Kikuyu, and my colleague who was fluent in the language, took copious notes. He had grown up on his parents farm at Mweiga in the company of Kikuyu children and spoke the Kikuyu language as a native.

The meeting went on for most of that Saturday morning. Jomo Kenyatta arrived with the ubiquitous fly-whisk and the inevitable wooden staff. These appendages were waved and used to emphasise points. Jomo was a past-master at implying all manner of things without actually putting them into words. But he made sure the words were nothing we, as policemen and upholders of the law, could bring as evidence that could be used against him in Court.

The most memorable thing that happened that day, as far as I was concerned, was when, at a certain signal, the women started ululating. This is a primeval sound at the best of times, but when some 10,000 women started up in unison, you can imagine it was a most frightening and memorable experience. The hair on the back of our necks was literally standing on end. My colleague recorded in his notes that it would have only taken one sign from Kenyatta for knives to be brought out and for us to be hacked into little pieces and sent home to our mothers in small envelopes!

But although the meeting was a tinder-box, ready to explode at any second, violence did not erupt due solely to the influence and eloquence of Kenyatta. In the fullness of time, the meeting ended and we all filed away. My colleague and I went back to his office and spent the rest of the day using his notes to make as fair a record of the meeting in English as we could. That record remains the only one in existence[98]

The same Special Branch officer was responsible for keeping tabs on Kenyatta and his cronies and was given the task of making sure that if any of them made the slightest slip-up, they could be arrested. He continues:

Anarchy thrives when good men do nothing and this was all happening during that dreadful three month period when the outgoing Governor of Kenya, Sir Philip Mitchell had retired, and before the newly appointed Governor, Sir Evelyn Baring, was able to take up his post. By then it was too late to do anything. In the end, all we could do was to detain the ringleaders on minor charges such as 'Managing An Illegal Society' until after the Emergency was declared when we had the backing of Detention orders signed by the new Governor. We could have beaten Mau Mau before it started but by the time the new Governor was sworn in, we were far too late and our efforts were futile. The ball was already rolling down the bowling alley and the skittles were about to be flattened. We did not even succeed in mitigating the effects of Mau Mau — quite the opposite.

However, Kenyatta and his cronies did not have it all their own way. A District Officer recounts what happened in part of his Division which encompassed the Nyambeni Hills, to the north east of Mount Kenya in the Meru District. The Meru people are an offshoot of the Kikuyu, and their language is very similar.

In mid-1954 the Administration in Meru District were concerned that the Mau Mau should not undermine the District which was then developing an unusually prosperous, high quality export coffee industry along the 5,100 to 5,200 ft contour on Mount Kenya under the strong and able leadership of Departmental officers .

The Department had already begun to think that it might next be possible similarly to develop small-holding tea production further east in the less densely inhabited and climatically very favourable area of the Nyambeni Hills overlooking the Tana basin. There had long been disturbing evidence of gang activity in the forest and oathing in the rich coffee land above Meru township. It was therefore of evident concern

---

[98] The record of the speech is given by Frank Corfield in his Report on *'The Origins and Growth of Mau Mau'* p.301

when the Chief responsible for Nyambeni reported an encounter with three Kikuyu strangers who were unable to account for their very surprising presence in an unused road mender's hut. They seemed to him, after interrogation, to be involved in attempts to recruit and encourage oathing as a preliminary he feared, to extending Mau Mau in parts of the District which were inaccessible to regular access by Administration staff. The Chief reported his concern. The District Commissioner asked one of his District Officers to call on the Chief.

In the event, the District Officer accompanied by Tribal police immediately went to Nyambeni, and on arrival found that the Chief had assembled a subdued gathering of elders and younger men armed with spears and clubs and clad, as was the practice, in grey or brown blankets and battered hats. They were assembled in an open space close to where the 'strangers' had been caught earlier in the day hiding up in the forest. With them were the three whom they had arrested. Typically speech was quiet and the mood sombre.

The Chief welcomed and thanked the visiting officer for coming, asking him whether he would wish to say anything. The District Officer, speaking in Swahili through a kiMeru interpreter thanked the Chief for his timely report and action which 'Bwana DC' took very seriously. He expressed his concern that the local people and their Chief should have found evidence of the contagion of Mau Mau in the Nyambeni, an isolated and remote location, but one with an excellent climate, fertile soils and promise of a future which they needed to protect. The seizure of the three was evidence of a need for the people of Nyambeni to be vigilant and to protect themselves and their families from the destructive contagion which Mau Mau would bring if it were allowed to take root.

The Chief thanked the District Officer in Swahili and then spoke briefly to the motionless gathering who listened attentively throughout. The Chief's speech ended in subdued tones. The crowd uttered no more than a long, low voiceless murmur of assent, and with of an almost primeval moan, rising to a slight crescendo, whisked the three hapless and voiceless figures away to a silent but no less vigorous clubbing to death by the guard of the Chief's retainers.

After this awesome and quite disturbing demonstration of self-assertion by a tribal leader, there was no further evidence of Mau Mau infiltration from the Nyambeni Hills throughout the whole Emergency.

Not long after, the Commonwealth Development Council took the first step in introducing tea cultivation on smallholdings on the slopes of the Nyambeni Hills.[99]

At least two years before the Emergency was declared, it was decided in secret by the Kenya African Union (KAU) hierarchy in Nairobi that Mau Mau would operate as the militant wing of the KAU. Oaths, binding the population to loyalty would be administered universally. Arms would be obtained by whatever means possible. Murders of European settlers in the White Highlands would then take place. These murders would be condemned in public by the KAU leadership who would attribute them to the more violent elements of Nationalism, while in the seclusion of the committee rooms they would be acclaimed and honoured. The KAU leaders, in their naïveté, imagined that the Mau Mau, having murdered a few settlers, the rest would flee from the country and the government would cave in, leaving a vacuum into which they, as victors, would immediately step. But while the British were still around they had to appear not to condone the murders, describing them as 'the unacceptable face of nationalism'. It was, after all, too easy for the Nairobi politician, knowing the absence of a reliable translation of their public speeches, to condemn Mau Mau in their best Oxford English in one breath, while in the next vernacular breath, urge the population towards militancy.

The murders of Europeans started soon after the Emergency was

Cow with its hamstrings slashed by Mau Mau

declared on October 20th 1952. Eric Bowyer, an old farmer living near Thomson's Falls was brutally hacked to death in his bath. His two Kikuyu house servants were murdered at the same time. From then on gangs of Mau Mau thugs terrorised the settled areas. One of their favourite activities was to slash cattle. They knew that to a dairy farmer, cattle were his pride and joy so they would not

[99] The District Officer who recorded this event wishes to remain anonymous

necessarily kill the animals, but would maim them so that when the farmer came out in the morning to collect his cows for milking, he would find them with their hamstrings severed so that they could not walk and had to be put down. Sometimes they would disembowel them and leave them alive with their intestines hanging out or their foetuses on the grass beside them. It became essential for every European living in areas where there were Kikuyus to arm themselves the whole time, day and night. Everyone, men and women had to know how to use a pistol or revolver, and it was unsafe to walk around one's farm unarmed. House servants, whether they were Kikuyu or another tribe would be intimidated into telling the gangs the routine of the household so that an attack could be planned for the time when the European would be least expecting it. Any refusal by the servant would be met with slashed limbs or cut throats.

The following is an extract from the statement of Thuku Muchiri, one of five men accused of murdering a European farmer Charles Fergusson and his visitor Richard Bingley at Ol Kalou on 1st January 1953.

I took the Mau Mau oath during the month of November last year, I think it was on 11th of the month but I am not certain. The ceremony took place in the hut of a man named Karimu, a mzee [old man] on the farm of Bwana Neli, a neighbour of Bwana Fergusson in the Ol Kalou area. I can remember the names of the [34] other people who took the oath at the same time. Nearly all of the womenfolk of these men were also present. Guards were posted to keep a look-out, and other persons were sent out to bring in people to take the Mau Mau oath. I think that nearly every Kikuyu in the area of all ages and sex have taken the oaths. The other tribes have not taken the oaths as far as I know. I myself, was a houseboy employed by Bwana Fergusson. I have actually taken the oath three times. I took the oath twice at one ceremony at the hut of Karioki on Bwana Fergusson's farm on a day not long before Christmas [1952]. The second oath was a very strong one to prevent me from disclosing anything at all. The third oath was taken on the night of Wednesday after Christmas [31st Jan 1952] at the hut of Mwangi on Bwana Fergusson's farm. That morning, Bwana Fergusson's tractor driver came to us in the kitchen of the house and inquired as to the number of firearms in the house. I replied that we had taken the firearms with the Bwana into Ol Kalou and that none remained. That evening, myself and Karanja the kitchen boy went to Mwangi's hut and found that a sheep had been slaughtered and the meat prepared. The oath was given by Karioki.

The next day, Thursday [1st Jan. 1953] Karioki came to the kitchen at about 7 pm. He took some tea and sugar and said he would be seeing us later on. He returned at about 9pm and wanted to talk to me but I refused as I had to take in the Bwanas' dinner. Karioki then called Karanja. I then took in the soup to Bwana Fergusson and Bwana Bingley, and then came back for the toast. I then went to clear the drinking glasses from the sitting room and waited for the bell signal to show that the soup was finished. I then removed the soup plates and was placing the plates for the second course and was serving Bwana Richard [Bingley] as the guest, when the door opened and Bwana Richard turned his head to see Karanja entering through the dining room door which he had opened. The two Bwanas were sitting at the table, Bwana Fergusson at the head of the table and Bwana Richard at the side. Karanja was carrying a simi [short sword] and he was the first to hit Bwana Fergusson on the head with his simi. Many other people then crowded into the room. They were all armed. I dropped the food plate in my surprise. Bwana Richard managed to stand up and make for the doorway but he

was hit several times with pangas and simis. I saw both the Bwanas try to get to the sitting room but they fell on the ground close together on account of their wounds. I tried to get out to the kitchen but two men were on guard at the place where the hats are kept and they detained me. Both of the Bwanas had their revolvers in the pockets of their dressing gowns which were over their pyjamas, but they had no opportunity to draw the weapons when attacked.[100]

The mutilated body of Richard Bingley murdered by Mau Mau on 1st January 1953

The man who made this statement was the prime suspect accused of these murders and together with four others was formally charged, tried in

---

[100] Statement made by Thuku Muchiri at the trial of himself and four others at Nakuru Supreme Court, April 1953

Nakuru Court, found guilty and hanged.

Some farms close to the forest edge would be spared these raids, and for a good reason. Peter May was manager of Squair's Farm at Ngobit, an area formerly grazed by Masai cattle, and not part of the Kikuyu homeland. It is now known as Gatarakwa and divided up into small plots owned mostly by Kikuyu people. In a personal conversation, Peter told me why his cattle were never killed or maimed by Mau Mau.

I farmed 16,000 acres of good grazing land close to the [Aberdare] forest edge. We had a dairy herd of some 60 pedigree Ayrshires and several herds of Boran cross Ayrshire beef steers, a total herd of some 500 head altogether. The farm bordered the forest for about two miles, where we knew there were several Mau Mau gangs. I employed about 150 Kikuyu men and women as labourers on the farm and I have no doubt most of them had close contacts with the gangs. During the early part of the Emergency, we would lose up to 30 animals a week to the Mau Mau. The gangs would come down at night and round up the animals they thought they could take up without losing too many on the way, and several gangs would share the remainder out between them. So many were going, that at one stage I felt I was keeping these cattle simply for the Mau Mau! We used to follow their tracks the next morning and pick up any stragglers we found. I lived at the farm on my own and had excellent relations with my work force, I was never attacked though my neighbour, Mr Thorpe was. He was actually captured by a gang and taken from his house, but they relented and let him go when the leader recognised him as the person who saved his life as a child, from a lethal snake bite.

In the end, I had to corral the steers at night and employ Turkana or Lumbwa *askaris* [night watchmen] to guard them. But I still lost one or two almost every night until the gangs in the forest were eventually routed by the security forces." [101]

Peter used to sleep in a different room of his house every night in order to try and trick potential attackers. He had a VHF radio transmitter and an SOS rocket launcher that he could fire from inside the house in the event of an attack. He would go to bed with a shotgun at his bedside and a couple of hand grenades with which to defend himself. The nearest neighbour was about eight miles away and the nearest police post about twelve miles.

---

[101] Peter May – Pers. comm.

It was comparatively easy for those who had taken the second, third and subsequent oaths, to kill the enemies of Mau Mau with impunity and without due conscience. Once an oath was taken, it became totally binding. So, to the ordinary members of the community who were easily led, these oaths were similarly binding. It did not matter that the oath administrator was not a *mwene githathi*, one of the elite clan of medicine-men whose age-old tradition was to administer oaths; it did not matter that the oath-taking was being carried out in secret, often under cover of darkness when traditional oath-taking was done in daylight in front of a large gathering; it did not matter that the oaths were being used for seditious, political reasons and not for lawful, cultural purposes; it did not occur to the ordinary oath-taker that the intention of these illegally constructed oaths was not part of their culture, that it was not something introduced for the good of the community as a whole. They could not see it for what it was: black witchcraft, negative oathing for subversive purposes — subversive, because it twisted the elemental Kikuyu tribal

The leading members of Ihura's gang at the height of their infamy - The Aberdare forest 1953

'General' Ihura is far right holding the flag. This gang, numbering more than 50 members, carried out many atrocities and murders during 1953. Second from left, Kimani Kirugo is captured on 17th December 1954. He recuperates and is persuaded to work for the Security Forces in the author's pseudo gang. (This photograph was taken by a Mau Mau sympathiser who went to the forest with a camera and took photos of various gangs. The film was given to a Nairobi Chemist to develop and print where a keen-eyed technician noticed the photos and handed them to the authorities. When the man came to collect his film he was detained.)

concepts and prepared the oath-takers for yet worse to come.

There were several thousand Mau Mau insurgents in the forests of Mount Kenya and the Aberdares at the height of the attacks on settlers early in 1953, but when it was found that some of the Kikuyu in the Reserve were beginning to side with the government and that some had even formed themselves into an armed resistance against them, some of the gangs were recalled to the forests above the Reserves to deal with those Kikuyu who were now fighting for the government in units known as the Home Guard, or the Kikuyu Guard.

A few fighters kept diaries in the forest. The following is a abridgment of a typical diary found on a fighter captured by the author in October 1954. It is necessarily a summary as the full diary contains many names and places of no interest.

> I took the first oath in Nakuru on 30.9.52. Later, I was given the work of administering the oath to others, by the Mau Mau committee in Nakuru. I also collected the money for taking the oath, and handed it over to 'Major' Muraguri.
>
> On 2.2.53 we were detained by the Security Forces [in Nakuru] and put into a camp surrounded by wire for 6 days where we secretly continued to administer the oath. On 8.2.53 we were repatriated to our home locations in the [Kikuyu] Reserve.
>
> On arrival at my home, the local committee commander immediately enrolled me for work as a Mau Mau fighter. On 15.2.53 'Field Marshall' Mbaria Kaniu arrived at my home and we began to administer the second oath to very many people. After that we were secretly posted to different troops. My troop consisted of 25 men. On 28.2.53 we administered the 'batuni' oath to 22 men. Besides being an oath administrator, I was also given the work for finding food for the people in the forest. We collected a lot of food from the Reserve and sent it up to the fighters in the forest. One day in March 1953 I took 12 men to the home of a Kikuyu Guard and we stole eight cows.
>
> On 5th May 1953 I was told to go to the forest to be a fighter. I joined a platoon of Mbaria Kaniu. We fought many battles against the Kikuyu Guard and killed many of them. We also had casualties and I was given the work of dressing the wounds of our casualties. In July 1953 I went with 52 men over to the Kinangop to collect weapons from a hut where they had secretly been stored. Unfortunately someone had already found the weapons and the hut was burnt. We returned to the hideout in the forest. In August 1953 we attacked the Kikuyu Guard Post at Kiamuturi. In September 1953 our hideout was attacked by the Security

Forces and we were for three days without food.

From then we suffered from hunger but were able to steal cows from the Reserve and take them to the forest. In July 1954 we were led by General Ihura to Kijabe to collect more food. The Security Forces followed us and found us because of the fire we lit. There was a terrible battle, worse than Burma [WW2]. We were dispersed and I had to look after 15 wounded people, but because of too much blood was pouring from the wounded, the Security Forces were able to follow us. They captured 14 of the wounded. I left with 1 other person back to our hideout in the forest where I still am today 25.9.54.[102]

It is interesting that from the end of 1953 the main entries in the diary are about the lack of food, and how they were occasionally able to make sorties into the Reserve to steal cows and sheep to drive them back into the forest where they would be butchered. However, the tracks left by the cows were easy to follow, and the butchering had to be carried out quickly before the Kikuyu Guard or other Forces found them.

By now it was clear that the Police, the Civil Authority, would not be able to cope with this insurgency on their own. The army had to be called in to support them. From then on, right to the end of the Emergency, the use of the army was strictly limited to the support of the civil power. The conflict never developed into a war. It was never a state of conflict between the British and the people of Kenya as a whole. The conflict was purely against those terrorists who endangered the lives of other Kenyans of whatever race or creed.

In May 1953, when the murders of Kikuyu who were showing hostility towards Mau Mau became unacceptably high, together with the increasing number of murders of European farmers, the matter at last had to be taken seriously. General Sir George Erskine was appointed Commander-in-Chief East Africa, and several more battalions of British soldiers were flown to Kenya to swell the numbers already there.

Having taken stock of the situation in the Reserve, General Erskine came to the surprising conclusion that the cause of the violence was simply "bad

---

[102] Document written by 'Sergeant' Gaturu Kabuthi of Fort Hall, captured by the author in October 1954. The translation of the diary in his possession. (See also Appendix 5)

administration", though he accepted that Jomo Kenyatta was *"the father and mother of the whole movement".[103]*

On his appointment, General Erskine wanted to have overall command, not only of the military forces but of the civil administration also, in effect, martial law. This was refused him by the British Government, though he was given a letter (that he always carried around in his spectacle case) authorising him to take over the civil government if at any time he thought it necessary — which it never was. The reason it was unnecessary to declare martial law was that only a relatively small area of the country and a tiny fraction of the population was affected, the rest of the inhabitants being perfectly loyal to the government. Although the Declaration of a State of Emergency in October 1952 gave the government the widest powers over legislation, they did not replace the basic Laws of Kenya which were backed by the Colonial Laws Validity Act, 1865, an Act of the British Parliament, where the army and the rest of the security forces, were simply operating 'in aid of the civil power', i.e. the Kenya Police. The security forces could only use their weapons without challenge in certain specially demarcated uninhabited areas of forest and mountain bordering the Kikuyu homeland which were declared 'Prohibited Areas'. The obligation under the law was strictly *'to protect the population from a felony using minimum force'*. Any suspect who was detained or captured had to be passed to the Police, being the official civil authority, who, for a conviction, had to show that the suspect had broken the law. That they were operating only *'in aid of the civil power'* was drummed into every officer of the British Army, over and over again.

Where it became impossible to prosecute a person who was suspected of a felony, which could include taking an illegal oath or belonging to a proscribed society such as Mau Mau or by then, the Kenya African Union, under the Emergency powers, the Government had the power to issue Detention Orders. These allowed the detention in secure camps for an unlimited period, and led to the internment of many thousands of Kikuyu suspects. This subject is dealt with in detail in Chapter 10.

The death penalty, one of the basic laws of Kenya, was given for murder, sabotage, the illegal carrying of weapons and even for certain types of oath administering. It was also available for the supplying and aiding of terrorists, but was seldom if ever used for this offence. Between 21st October 1952 (the

[103] Erskine to Lady Erskine unpublished letters 16th July 1953

first day of the Emergency) and 1st January 1955 when a general amnesty was declared, a total of 796 executions took place. This may seem an enormous number in these days when capital punishment has been outlawed in most of the Western World for decades. But it was not so then, and is not so now in the independent states of sub-Saharan Africa. Learning by example is, and was then, seen to be the best way of controlling capital offences, and although critics will accuse the British of using extreme measures, they will be taking the issue out of context. To have punished murder with prison sentences would have sent messages to the population that they could not understand, and would be seen as a demonstration of weakness, in the same way it was with Francis Hall at Fort Smith in 1892, and they would not have kept the vital support of the Chiefs and Headmen, together with the rank and file of the Kikuyu Guard. 'Why keep a man in prison for the rest of his life', the population would ask, 'at a cost to us taxpayers, when he has committed such a major crime? Either execute him and send a clear signal to others, or if he has a good excuse, let him go so that we as tax payers do not have to spend our money keeping him in prison'.

The possibility that of the 796, some innocent person may have been executed, cannot be overlooked. Such is the price paid and the lesson hopefully learnt by those who seek to impose their ideas through the gun and the *panga* rather than through sensible argument or the ballot box.

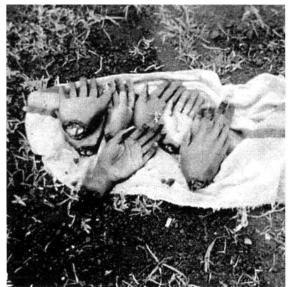

The severed hands of terrorists

The practise of cutting off hands of those terrorists that were killed in the forest in order to fingerprint them and enable their deaths to be recorded was stopped immediately it became known to the authorities

Soon after General Erskine took over command of the Security Forces he became appalled at what had been described to him as *'the indiscriminate shooting'* of suspected terrorists and rumours of *'scoreboards'* recording 'kills' by competitive units of the K.A.R. and the British Army. He also came to hear about the practise of cutting off the hands of dead terrorists, shot or killed in the forest, in order that their fingerprints could be taken and their names verified for the records and for the notification of their families. It was often impossible to bring the bodies down to the edge of the forest where fingerprinting could take place, so this was deemed to be the best method of proving their identity. Because of this and other unacceptable practises, he issued a directive, under confidential cover, to all officers of the army and police. This is the full text of that directive.

It must be most clearly understood that the Security Forces under my command are disciplined forces who know how to behave in circumstances which are most distasteful.

I have the greatest confidence in the Army and Police to uphold their honour and integrity while dealing with the present situation.

I will not tolerate breaches of discipline leading to unfair treatment of anybody. We have a very difficult task and I have no intention of tying the hands of the Security Forces by orders and rules which make it impossible for them to carry out their duty —I am a practical enough soldier to know that mistakes can be made and nobody need fear any lack of support if the mistake is committed in good faith.

But I most strongly disapprove of beating up the inhabitants of this country just because they are inhabitants. I hope this has not happened in the past and will not happen in the future. Any indiscipline of this kind would do great damage to the reputation of the Security Forces and make our task of settling Mau Mau much more difficult. I therefore order that every officer in the Police and the Army should stamp on any conduct which he would be ashamed to see used against his own people. I want to stand up for the honour of the Security Forces with a clear conscience - I can only do that if I have absolutely loyal support and I rely on you to provide it.

Any complaints against the Police or Army which come from outside sources will be referred to me immediately on receipt and will be investigated either by the Police or the Attorney General as I may, in consultation, direct. There will be full mutual co-operation between the Police and the Army in regard to all such investigations and in no circumstances will either deny information or assistance to the other.

Signed: George Erskine, General, Commander in Chief. 23rd June 1953.

One of the reasons General Erskine sent out this directive was because he had become aware of the case of a Major Griffiths who had been charged, together with two hapless National Service Subalterns of murdering an African. Griffiths, who owned a Farm in Kenya, was in command of a K.A.R. Company, when some twenty Somali men under his direct command killed two Africans, of which he was charged with the murder of one. A Court Martial was ordered, but Griffiths was acquitted on a technical point after the prosecution failed to prove the identity of the victim. During the Court Martial, Griffiths' Company Sergeant Major, a European, said in evidence that he had been told by Griffiths that he could *'shoot anyone he liked so long as they were black'.*

Griffiths was, however, put on trial again, charged with torturing prisoners. Two of the specific charges were that he had removed a prisoner's ear, and that he had drilled a large hole in another prisoner's ear. Griffiths was convicted on these charges, cashiered and sentenced to five years imprisonment. *'The truth was that he had known psychopathic tendencies and should never have been put in command of such a Company of fellow hotheads. He often wore a samurai sword and had other non-issue weapons. He loathed the Mau Mau, particularly as (I think) they had cut the hoofs of two of his horses'*[104]

The attention this case provided in the U.K. prompted a debate in the House of Commons with the result that a Court of Enquiry headed by a Lieutenant General was appointed to look into the conduct of the British Army in the Mau Mau Emergency. Its terms of reference were limited to the period following Erskine's assumption of command, except in the cases of the British battalions that came in at the start of the Emergency. Its enquiries led to a report in January 1954, of which a summary was made public. The Court of

---

[104] Personal communication from a fellow officer.

Enquiry found no incidence of inhuman conduct other than the 'kill' competitions already abolished, and the incidents that led to the replacement of the K.A.R. battalion commander. In its hearings, the Court took evidence from 147 witnesses, including the Director of a government African hospital and a Roman Catholic Bishop. The Christian Council of Kenya was invited to forward allegations, but they had none to offer. The Times subsequently commented that it was excellent that the Army should be thus vindicated, but public disquiet centred round other arms of the Security Forces, particularly the Kikuyu Guard.

On Day One of the Emergency, the first battalion of British army soldiers started arriving at Eastleigh airport from Egypt. These soldiers were split into small units and scattered around the troubled areas as support for the Police — the civil authority. Later more battalions of British army personnel arrived to swell the numbers of other Security Forces including the Kenya Police Reserve, the Kenya Regiment, the Tribal Police and a few weeks later, the Kikuyu Guard. Two squadrons of Royal Air Force bombers were also sent, comprising North American P.16 Harvard fighter bombers and nine Avro Lincoln heavy bombers that carried 1,000lb bombs. While the bombers had an effect on the morale of the gangs, they had very little success operationally. Few, if any terrorists were killed by bombs though some were thought to have died of wounds from shrapnel and machine-gun bullets. By bringing such a mighty force to bear on the insurgents in the forest and in the Reserves, the British Government hoped to get the thing over quickly so that costs could be kept to a minimum and it could get back to the main programme which was to continue its strategy of working towards self-government for the Colony eventually leading to Independence. It was to find that, as in most wars, this one would take longer to finish than most would have hoped, and one of the reasons was the efficacy of the oath.

CHAPTER SEVEN

THE OATH

'If I do not kill a person who is against Mau Mau, even if it is my mother or my father or my sister or my brother or my wife or my child, may this oath kill me'
Part of the Mau Mau 'Batuni' oath

From the earliest records available, the Kikuyu people always enjoyed some of the most fertile agricultural land in Kenya which they used well, growing plenty of food for themselves with enough left over to sell to other tribes during times of famine. Later, they realised the surplus could be sold off at a better profit to European safaris that went through on their way from the coast to Uganda. Even the largest caravans with hundreds of porters were able to stock up from the abundant supplies they found for sale in the forest clearings of Kikuyuland. The very first to go right through from Ngong towards Mount Kenya was the caravan of the Hungarian Count Teleki and the German von Höhnel in August 1887. Most of the inhabitants had never seen a white man before and were fearful of this new kind of human, but being Kikuyu, their timidity was soon overridden by their natural inclination to trade and barter produce with the caravan. Von Höhnel wrote of their journey and his account makes interesting reading:

> 'We had, however, no need to be anxious about provisions. Even large caravans such as ours could easily, in normal seasons, buy food for several months off the Kikuyu in a very short time. There are no markets exactly like those in other parts of Africa, as the Kikuyu do not venture out of the forests, from fear of the Masai, and caravans have to seek them. A well-armed contingent from a travelling party goes into the woods and calls the attention of the natives by firing two or three shots. In a few minutes the signal is answered by the appearance of some envoys [*njama*]; a time and spot are fixed for the holding of a market, and in due course the traders make their way to the rendezvous, soon joined by hundreds of men and women laden with the superfluous produce of their fields, which they are very glad to dispose of.'[105]

Francis Hall, stationed at Fort Smith, near the village of Kikuyu in the centre

---

[105] L.S.B. Leakey *'The Southern Kikuyu Before 1903'* Academic Press 1977 p. 58

of the Southern Kikuyu, was charged with purchasing food from the local people for the surveyors working on the Mombasa railway alignment. On October 8th 1896 in a letter to his father he explained how easy it was to buy food from the local Kikuyu: *'Within 12 days I supplied about 20 tons of grain, all purchased in small lots. ...Now I have to supply 33,000lbs [approx. 15 tonnes] of grain monthly'*. Later in July 1897 when the railway workers were in his area building the Mombasa to Uganda railway he was able to purchase *'nearly 50 tons of native flour'* within a 16 day period.[106] This would have been millet meal as maize was not introduced until later.

To help in their quest for the best and most auspicious times for planting their crops, the Kikuyu would consult medicine men or seers who would, for a consideration, and with the aid of a variety of paraphernalia, give the enquirer the best information he had available. The same medicine men would also be available to perform important ceremonies for the bringing of rain if and when the crops were in jeopardy of failing because of the lack of it. These men must have been good at their jobs, for the Kikuyu, primitive as they were in other ways and unlike most of the other tribes of Kenya, seldom went hungry.

Before the onset of Westernisation, most Kikuyu consulted medicine men or *'mu'undu mugo'* to diagnose and treat diseases. The man was part witch-doctor, part prophet, and part psychologist, and it was a revered profession handed down from father to son. It was quite normal to seek advice for the most propitious times for marriages, for journeys and for the removal of curses thought to have been laid on them by an enemy or rival. It might be necessary to travel many miles to obtain the services of a good medicine man, and the best were often thought to be Masai 'Laibon' who were famous for their supernatural powers. (In 1988, I recorded an interview with the great grandson of Lenana, the greatest of all Laibons, who lived near Namanga. This highly revered man named ole Saitoti, was at that time the senior member of the Laibon's community: the elite *Enkidong* clan. He told me that many of his 'clients' were Kikuyu who travelled more than 100 miles from Nairobi, to consult him.)

Similar men, known as *'Mwene Githathi'*, would also be available to perform certain traditional rites at times of initiation and circumcision when oaths would have to be taken by the young men and women as part of their launch into manhood or womanhood. These rites, the equivalent of the

---

[106] Francis Hall's unpublished letters home from Kikuyu 31st July 1897

Christian baptism or confirmation or the Jewish bar mitzvah, probably originated hundreds of years previously, and throughout the ages, no doubt were honed and perfected to make them as relevant as possible to the purpose for which they were created. Ceremonies were always happy affairs and causes for celebration by the whole locality who were invited to attend, where a feast was prepared for the occasion. While the taking of oaths was central to the ceremonies, carried out with great seriousness and solemnity, they were always performed in daylight and in public so that everyone could see and hear what the oath-taker had vowed. The oath administrator was a highly respected person. He was believed to have direct access to the God *Ngai*, and to be able to call upon supernatural powers. He was, perhaps, the equivalent of the Druids in the ancient English religion.

The Kikuyu, in common with most primitive Africans, had always believed firmly in supernatural powers. Dr. L.S.B. Leakey, that monumental 'bridge', whose works do more than any other to help span the enormous gulf between modern Western Man and pre-literate Kikuyu Man, who left a positive treasury of books that bring a closer understanding between the two cultures, writes:

> It is not easy to draw a dividing line between religion and magic in Kikuyu society, nor between white magic which is beneficial and black magic or witchcraft which is anti-social. The Kikuyu methods of administering oaths are intimately connected with the belief in magic and witchcraft and some understanding of the effects of oaths is essential if we are to fathom the methods which have been so successfully used by Mau Mau.[107]

Leakey accentuates the effect of oath-taking upon the Kikuyu. *'It was this absolute fear of magic powers that was the foundation stone of all Kikuyu ceremonies of oath-taking, and in consequence the taking of a solemn oath was an act never lightly undertaken, and once sworn, its effect upon the taker was very great.'* He gives as an example a judicial case where both parties firmly believed that they were in the right. An oath-stone was brought that had seven holes in it symbolising the seven apertures of the human body. This ceremony, in common with all oath administration, had to take place in daylight and in public and be administered by as distinguished a *mwene githathi* as the parties

---

[107] L.S.B. Leakey *'Mau Mau and the Kikuyu'* Methuen 1952 p. 47

could afford. Both parties were called upon to insert a stick into each of the seven holes declaring solemnly at the same time that if the claim made before the assembly was false, the claimant accepted the penalty that the oath-stone would not only kill him but also the members of his family. Such was the enormity of entering into an act of this magnitude and outcome, that, in the certain knowledge of the consequences, many participants lost their nerve at the last minute, and cases would be settled, so to speak, 'out of court'.

Oaths and oathing was also the traditional way of confirming agreements such as the settling of boundary disputes between neighbours, and allegiances. This was the method used for the first Mau Mau oath. It was a comparatively mild affirmation of the subject's commitment to the organisation's cause.

At first the Mau Mau movement was little heard of, and it probably only worked in the early days, among people who were likely to approve of what was being planned. Obviously it would have been senseless to approach Kikuyu who were working for the Government and ask them to take the Mau Mau oath, for they would have refused and at once reported the movement to the authorities. Since there were a great number of discontented Kikuyu among the squatters on European

Two old men argue a land case in front of tribal officials

farms, the Mau Mau movement, was spread, first of all, in the farming areas. But even among the squatters, there were some who were loyal to the British and who were not willing to take the Mau Mau oath, so it became necessary to do a number of things that were contrary to [Kikuyu] custom if the movement were not to be discovered and stopped in its tracks by the authorities.

It became necessary, in the first place, to force people to take the oath once they had been approached but had shown unwillingness to participate voluntarily [because they would immediately report it to the authorities]. So unless people were coerced into taking this oath, they would be a menace to the movement, whereas if they could be intimidated and forced into taking it, then the movement was safe, because once taken, they would have promised on oath not to reveal the fact.[108]

District Officer Thompson describes the early oathings that took place in Fort Hall, and the areas that stood out against them.

When oathing started in 1951 and 1952 it was chiefly carried out by thugs resident in Nairobi whose homes were actually in Fort Hall Locations. By July 1952 nearly everyone in Locations 4, lower 12 and 13 had been oathed. Most ceremonies took place at the weekend and were organised by Nairobi 'corner boys'. Oathing gradually spread, covering the whole of the lower areas of the District and then moving up through Kandara and Kigumo Divisions.

There were certain islands of resistance to oathing: at Chomo in Location 1 and Ndakaini in Location 16, but the largest island of resistance was that of Senior Chief Njiri at Kinyona in Location 2. These three islands all belonged to the Christian group known as the African Christian Church and Schools, under the direction of Elijah Mbatia. Another prominent area of resistance was at Ichagaki in Location 7; this was a very small one and was centred around the Catholic Mission there.[109]

Some of these first oaths may have been administered by traditional and respected *mwene githathi* who were likely to be in agreement with the initial, relatively mild intentions of the organisation, to get back what were described

---

[108] L.S.B. Leakey *'Mau Mau and the Kikuyu'* Methuen 1952 p. 98
[109] W.H. Thompson *'A History of the Kikuyu Guard'* Ed. David Lovatt Smith p.6

as the 'stolen lands' at Kiambu and Limuru. The later and subsequently more degrading oaths had to be administered by impersonators, as the traditional administrators, having soon realised the true aims of Mau Mau, refused to take part in the horrific acts required by the organisers, and many were murdered for their principles.

The leaders of the Mau Mau movement in the early days found that the oath was such a convenient and easy method of recruiting membership to the organisation, that they intensified their administrations to turn whole communities against the government and more importantly against those Kikuyu that remained stoically faithful to their culture and the government. Those that could not be won over, had to be eliminated. Thus it was that the highly respected Senior Chief Waruhiu, one of the most vehemently opposed to Mau Mau, was the first to go. He was murdered in his car two weeks before the Emergency was declared. The next was Senior Chief Nderi of Nyeri, who, accompanied by two Tribal Policemen, had come across a crowd of several hundred at an oathing ceremony organised by Dedan Kimathi. When he ordered them to disperse, because, by then, oathing had been outlawed by the Government authorities, but also in respect of Kikuyu tradition and culture, they rounded on him and hacked him and his two policemen to death.

The Chiefs and Headmen proved a major headache for the Mau Mau organisers. Having been appointed and salaried by the government they were officially obliged to take the government's side, though secretly, many of them may have harboured leanings towards the stated Mau Mau aims. These leaders exercised enormous influence over the local population, and acted as father-figures to their local communities. The Mau Mau, therefore needed to get them on their side as soon as possible, and to begin with, owing to the dire consequences of refusing to take the oath, most of them succumbed, and took at least the first oath which committed them to follow the aims of Mau Mau and to obey its rules.

> The Headmen in nearly all cases were oathed, because if they failed to do so, they knew they would die. There seemed to be very little hope. Apparently Government was not reacting. No forces were made available. The Chiefs and Headmen were lost. The islands of resistance were small and unarmed and the murders increased daily. Things became really grim in the months of August and September 1952. If an Administrative Officer went on safari, young men would turn their backs on him and spit on the ground.

Ten days before the declaration of the Emergency, I was on safari in Location 3 [Fort Hall] when a Church Elder of the African Inland Mission, who has since been murdered by the Mau Mau, came along to me and said that he could show me a Mau Mau oathing ceremony in session. I had one Tribal Police escort, Mwaura Gakomo who later became a Corporal, and the only weapon we had between us was a walking stick. We sat on the side of a hill and watched about 900 people oathing. There was nothing we could do. The people laughed and spat at us."[110]

It is not easy for Westerners to appreciate the hold oath-taking had on the ordinary Kikuyu man or woman. The effect was very great indeed. It played a significant part in every person's life, and in bygone days was the single most effective instrument for keeping discipline within the tribe. An oath once taken, was completely binding, even if it was forced upon the taker. So it was inevitable that Mau Mau should make as much use of this tool as possible to carry out their evil campaigns, particularly in the early stages. The first oaths were not powerful enough to entice ordinary Kikuyu into committing murders, so the leaders had to intensify the oaths and make them more shocking and therefore more powerful so that those who took them could be thoroughly relied upon to go out and kill 'the enemies of the Kikuyu people'. And the greatest enemies in those early days were the Chiefs and Headmen, particularly the senior chiefs who, while they commanded enormous respect from the people, were accused of being 'government lackeys', and therefore not in favour of the return of 'stolen lands'.

In fact, the Senior Chiefs were wise enough to see exactly what the political hotheads were up to and bravely took it upon themselves as community leaders, to try and prevent the headlong slide out of traditional Kikuyu culture into anarchy.

The oaths grew from small beginnings, but as the pseudo oath-administrators grew in confidence and developed even more heinous acts, they violated more and more of the rules governing traditional oathing until it became something so bestial and horrific that it was contrary to all established law and custom.

The respected leaders of the community, not only those appointed by the government, but also many of the unofficial traditional leaders, while

---

[110] Jock Rutherford *'A History of the Kikuyu Guard'* Ed. David Lovatt Smith p.7

sympathising to some extent with the original aims of Mau Mau, were passionately opposed to the methods they employed. Because they held such influence, they and their families had to be eliminated. A District Officer in Fort Hall illustrates the circumstances in which these murders became commonplace in the months prior to the Emergency:

> Resistance was strengthened by the outcrop of murders that occurred—especially in the northern half of the District—during the months of July and August 1952. I well remember the month of August 1952, in particular August Bank Holiday Sunday and Monday. I was on duty in the Kangema Division and stationed with a batch of Kenya Police recruits on loan for three days; our job was to clean up that area. There was a murder of an old man at Ruathia; he was chopped into two halves because he had given evidence against Mau Mau in the Court at Fort Hall. Further down the road, the whole family of a Chief's retainer had been murdered because the retainer had given evidence at the same Court, and down in the river below Gituge we found the corpse of an African Court Process Server who had likewise been strangled for informing against Mau Mau. That was the pattern and it has largely been forgotten. Certainly during the months of July and August hardly a day went by without the report of a corpse or a missing person, and always they were those who had informed or given evidence against the early Mau Mau oathings.[111]

Chiefs and Headmen, and particularly the Tribal Police force were all targets and many were murdered in the months before the declaration of the Emergency. It is sadly a matter of historical fact that, for at least two years before the Emergency was officially declared, the Mau Mau were tragically highly successful in their relentless slaughter of those that did not toe the line. Later, the Kikuyu Guards, after the formation of that heroic force, bore the main brunt of this fratricide.

The Colonial Government were peculiarly slow at taking these mass oathings seriously, although they were made aware of them. As early as 1947, Senior Chief Njiri Karanja of Fort Hall wrote to the Acting Provincial Commissioner imploring the Government to stop the unlawful meetings. Through his scribe and translator, he wrote:

'I consider it absolutely essential that we should be given powers to

---

[111] Ibid. p.6

prohibit all public meetings except with the permission of the District Commissioners and under conditions imposed by them and that there should be very much more drastic penalties inflicted for disobedience. I am fully aware that it will be difficult to convince the [British] Secretary of State of the desirability of such legislation, when such promises have been given to the right of public assembly and of free speech. But it is not freedom of assembly and freedom of speech that these people [the Mau Mau organisers] want. They want to undermine all the institutions of good government which are largely accepted by the mass of the population and this is part of a definite anti-European movement sponsored by people who have visited other countries and have imbibed their ideas. ...Unless such legislation can be introduced, I foresee the greatest possible danger of all the Administration becoming impotent in this Province with consequent loss of progress that has been made by the mass of the people themselves both in local government and in the preservation of the land.'[112]

Senior Chief Njiri Karanja

He was the most senior leader of the Kikuyu people and was revered by all. He stood out against the Mau Mau because he saw they violated the ancient traditions and teachings of his people. The Union Flag flew defiantly over his homestead at Kinyona, Fort Hall, throughout the Emergency.

One of the failings of British Governments through the ages has been to bide their time; to do nothing; to wait and see what happens. It is an infuriating trait to those whose job it is to report to their senior officials what is happening on the ground in their patch, especially when they can see so clearly what will be the outcome of simply doing nothing. In almost every conflict for the past

---

[112] Frank Corfield *'Historical Survey of Mau Mau'* p.71

four hundred years, Whitehall and Parliament has been slow to the point of negligent in facing up to obvious looming crises. It has been one of the British Government's least admirable features.

True to form, by 1950, the Governor was receiving daily reports from Nairobi of unrest and subversive carryings on. They were being made clearly aware of the implications of the reports they were getting from their senior officials in the field. They were being told that these were primitive people, still mostly uneducated, and when confronted with agitators who had political agendas could easily be persuaded to follow a particular line, especially if that line happened to be about such an emotive issue as stolen lands.

W.H. Thompson was a District Officer in Fort Hall. He knew the area from 1947 and throughout the worst years of the Emergency. In his memoirs, he draws attention to the difficulty of persuading Whitehall of the significance of these oathing ceremonies.

> Though we in the field were beginning to see the devastating effects of these oathing ceremonies, and clearly realised what was at stake, the Government in Nairobi, the Kenya Europeans and the British Government in Whitehall refused, or were at the very least reluctant to believe anything of it.
>
> Looking back in my files, I have found a quotation that sums up the situation in mid 1952: *"Mau Mau terrorism has almost completely shattered the average Kikuyu's spiritual equilibrium to such an unbelievable extent that a new extremism, a new barbarism and a new type of African fanatic is now being created."*[113]

He underlines the refusal of Whitehall to appreciate what was happening in Kenya and the error of which the incumbent Governor was guilty:

> In June 1952 the Governor of Kenya, Sir Phillip Mitchell, of whom we all thought well, relinquished office. In the context of Mau Mau and in hindsight I can see he was too comfortable, too popular with Europeans and, as seen from London, 'a jolly sound, jolly good chap whom we know we can trust'.
>
> As required by Whitehall, the essence of Colonial Government was that it caused no problems, kept quiet and cost as little as possible. In later years [when he was Governor of Monserrat] the Minister of State at the Foreign Office said to me, 'For God's sake, Governor, don't bring

---

[113] W.H. Thompson - *Unpublished personal Memoirs*

your problems here. I can't win elections on overseas matters. The tax on football pools and the price of butter are the vote catchers!'.

Let us hope that now, 400 years almost to the day since King James joined the two countries of Scotland and England together to form the nucleus of Great Britain, this unattractive and exceedingly costly trait has at last been superseded by the actions of the Blair government in March 2003.

In the early stages the big names like Jomo Kenyatta, Bildad Kaggia, Fred Kubai and James Beuttah kept a comparatively low profile in Nairobi as leading members of legitimate organisations such as the Kikuyu Central Association (for which an oath of allegiance had to be taken by all recruited members) and later the Kenya African Union. It was the lower echelons with the power of speech-making who carried out the basic ground-work for those Nairobi leaders, who were occasionally invited onto the platform at local rallies as crowd-drawers. In their rhetoric, Kenyatta's cronies used the common straightforward strategy of 'stolen land' to whip up enthusiasm against the government and against European settlers. Tribal Police, Chiefs and Headmen and those who were anti Mau Mau also attended these meetings, so the speechmakers had to be careful what they said. But clever speechmakers can imply meanings without actually saying the words, and there is no better language than Kikuyu for conveying a message cloaked in ambiguity. These speeches and rallies therefore provided the softening-up process for future oathing and once the first oath was given and received, the die was cast. The first promise of the first oath, was, on pain of death, not to reveal the work of the Mau Mau to anyone.

The introduction to the Mau Mau philosophy was cleverly thought out. The first oath was a mild affair, it simply bound the recipient on pain of death, not to reveal the secrets of the organisation, not to sell any Kikuyu land to foreigners, to carry out the future orders of the Mau Mau leaders and to pay the fees of the organisation. Cleverly, it did not mention the more gory work that was in store for the recipient of this first oath. Subsequent oaths did, and these were the ones that committed them to murderous acts. So the unsuspecting majority of Kikuyu, having taken the first oath, were cunningly ensnared into taking and accepting subsequent oaths.

Those who administered these subsequent oaths were brought onto the scene by Mau Mau organisers to impersonate the traditional administrators who would never dream of taking part in the bestial acts that became necessary to subvert ordinary Kikuyu into murdering their own people—or anyone else for that matter—for political reasons, an act that was completely out of character. So new phoney oath-administrators had to be found to administer these subsequent oaths, the first of which were called *'batuni'* oaths (*'batuni'* is Pidgin English for 'platoon'). It will never be known how many people

Batuni oath-taking - the Aberdare forest 1953
'General' Matenjaguo (left) shows off his unsuspecting victim to the photographer. The woman will be used in the ensuing 'batuni' oath-taking of new recruits that have arrived at the forest hide-out, while the oath administrator, 'Colonel' Gakure Karuri (seated centre) holds his catamite boy who will also be subjected to degrading and abusive sexual obscenities.
(This photograph was taken by the same person as the one on page 129)

actually took the *'batuni'* oaths but certainly from my own experience of interrogations, virtually all those who entered the forest took them, so the figures will be in the thousands. After the platoon oath, the oaths get progressively worse as the ranks rise: 'lieutenant's' oath; 'captain's' oath; 'major's' oath etc., all accompanied by sexual shenanigans with women, animals both live and dead, and finally with catamite boys, who, because of the acts involved, also had to be expendable.

Discovery of the ugly secrets of Mau Mau activity and bringing individuals to book under the law was often difficult and protracted. An interesting example arose during 1953 in the Meru District, north east of Mount Kenya. The interest of the case lies partly in what investigation of the case and the Preliminary Hearing revealed, and partly in the way in which, through the kiMeru-speaking Methodist head of a Teacher Training College, Harry Laughton and the District Agricultural Officer, Victor Burke, a former 8th Army Captain and his local staff broke into the tight *mwiriga* circle which, knowing the event and its implications, reported fully to the two well respected and trusted Europeans.

They discovered the facts and circumstances of the murder by careful and patient interrogation of accomplices in attendance. With police assistance, they put together a formal case warranting the presentation of five accused on a murder charge with seven accomplices at a preliminary hearing prior to a hearing in the Supreme Court.

The accused were five men and seven women whose leader was No. 5 accused, the oath administrator and a novice Methodist pastor M'Imathiu. He had instructed those attending the oathing ceremony to murder the victim because she refused to take the oath. Each person attending was bidden by him to take a part of the body whilst he suffocated the victim. Questioning revealed that the body had been crudely buried in the Location. It was exhumed and examined by the resourceful District Medical Officer, Dr. Geoffrey Bisley. On discovering the victim had been murdered by suffocation and that a palm print fitting that of M'Imathiu was evident in the face and neck, he severed the head, preserving it in the hospital's formaldehyde.

At the eventual preliminary hearing, the doctor, having been asked to make himself available to give evidence, somewhat indecorously and in anticipation of the hearing, had the head delivered by an orderly to the office of the Magistrate (the District Officer), in a hemp sack, for the hearing. The magistrate's introduction to the facts preceded the hearing when the principal exhibit was discovered by him before the hearing as he entered his office, prior to the session. Thrusting his hand into the sack, thinking it might be a delivery of vegetables, he was surprised and 'not amused' when he pulled out of the sack the ungarnished head of the victim by its matted hair.

The report of the preliminary hearing went forward to the

Supreme Court in Nairobi for due process."[114]

The most evil thing about the whole Mau Mau oathing business was that, to the pre-literate Kikuyu mind, the acts that the oaths guaranteed: the murders, the choppings-up, the disembowelling of pregnant women and of live cattle, the killing of children and the slaughtering of ones own family, all these could be justified by those who carried them out, on the grounds that it was not they themselves doing it, it was the oath and the oath administrator; he was the one committing these terrible acts by proxy; the perpetrator was a zombie, a robot, an instrument in the hand of the oath administrator – *or those who empowered the oath administrator.*

Jomo Kenyatta himself confirms the power of the oath in his book 'Facing Mount Kenya'. *Among the Gikuyu there are three important forms of oaths which were so terribly feared, morally and religiously, that no one dared to take them unless he was perfectly sure and beyond any doubt that he was innocent or that his claim was genuine.*[115] He goes into considerable detail and describes the oaths taken for different purposes by the Kikuyu.

The use of the oath by the Mau Mau goes right to the core of the evil of Mau Mau, because the hierarchy *knew* the power of the oath, and knew that those that took it would have no difficulty in performing these terrible acts. This was the all-consuming, manipulative power and evil of Mau Mau.

It must be emphasised, however, that a great many who took the oath did so under duress or in ignorance of what they were doing. They did it, because they were left no option. Some, though, knew exactly what they were doing, and entered into it with eagerness. Many of these were, in those days, known as 'de-tribalised' Africans.

By the 1940s, the Kikuyu Independent School system and some Mission schools were fertile breeding grounds for youngsters who were able and indeed were encouraged, while they were growing up, to opt out of the traditional Kikuyu culture. Some Christian missions were openly vying with each other to get the most number of pupils at their schools in a bid to devalue the opposing doctrine. Such pupils—Jomo Kenyatta himself was one—often bypassed

---

[114] Roy Spendlove - Pers. Comm.
[115] Jomo Kenyatta – *'Facing Mount Kenya'* Martin Secker & Warburg 1938 p. 223

circumcision and warriorhood rituals, aided by their teachers and encouraged by the promise of good 'white collar' jobs if they became a 'Christian' and went through school. They were told that in order to get a good job they would have to abandon their tribal way of life, and emulate the European in dress, speech and manner. It was a disgraceful act by a few of the many Catholic and Protestant Missions and one of their least endearing activities. They refused to see what everyone outside knew: that most of these boys had no intention whatsoever of giving anything more than lip service to Christianity; it was simply a means to an end, so after leaving school, if they could not get into a job immediately, they drifted in somewhat of a vacuum, out on a limb, accepted neither as a Kikuyu nor as a European.

When it became apparent to some, that they were not, after all, going to achieve a 'white collar' job, they were ripe for the plucking by Mau Mau recruiters in Nairobi. Like a drug pusher, the predator went to work on his prey, and it was an easy push-over for him. From the novelty and excitement of the first oath, it was a comparatively easy task for the new tutor to induce his victim to slide all the way down to the lowest depths of depravity. Thus

Dedan Kimathi (left) and his brother Wambararia - Aberdare forest 1953
This photo was left on a forked stick outside a British army (Black Watch) camp in Fort Hall on Christmas Day 1953 with a rude message attached.

some of these, typified by Dedan Kimathi, and 'General' China, became Mau Mau gang leaders, some in the forest and some in Nairobi itself. Later, 'Operation Anvil'[116] cleared them all out of Nairobi and sent them on their way to detention camps, but some, notably Kimathi and Itote ('China') escaped detention and were already actively operating in the forests.

When the oathing ceased to follow Kikuyu tradition and it was seen that the act was being misrepresented for political ends, many of the older generations turned against the Mau Mau. Older men and women could not support an organisation that abused and violated their precious beliefs and traditions. As Leakey points out, an oath, according to sacred Kikuyu law, must *a) be one that should not be entered into lightly; b) should be taken voluntarily and with the approval of the rest of the family; c) had to be administered in public and in front of many witnesses.* Mau Mau oathings were the complete opposite of this. Yes, the older generation would have liked a measure of self-government for the Kikuyu; yes, they would have liked more land and they would have liked the Government to have provided more schools for their children, but not if it meant murdering people, and not if it meant violating and perverting the age-old traditions of the Kikuyu people. It became clear to them that the traditional Kikuyu culture meant nothing to the Mau Mau movement. From this moment on, the movement began to lose the support they had won in the first few months of their existence when their stated aim, to get back the 'stolen lands', attained a fairly general degree of sympathy. But when it became obvious that this was just a cover for something far more sinister, the subjecting of the whole Kikuyu, Embu and Meru ethnic group to the Mau Mau movement with someone like Kimathi, Itote ('China') or another of the other self-styled 'Generals' in the forest, as their leader, they began to lose the active support of all clear thinking and traditional Kikuyu.

It was now becoming clear that the real agenda of Mau Mau was not just the return of stolen lands, it was the complete take-over, not only of the Kikuyu, Embu and Meru group, but of the whole of Kenya itself. In their naïveté, the Mau Mau leaders believed that the other tribes of Kenya making up the majority of indigenous Kenyans, would be won over because the Kikuyu would be seen to be the ones who were victorious in getting rid of the

---

[116] 'Operation Anvil' took place in Nairobi in April 1954. Its purpose was to round up all the 30,000 or so Kikuyu men and women known to be working and living in and around Nairobi, and either repatriate them to their home villages in the Reserves, or if they were known Mau Mau supporters, to send them to Detention Centres (Chap 10).

British Colonial Government and the land-thieving settlers.

The leaders of the movement had assumed that having ousted the Colonials, they would be hailed as heroes and everyone would want them to form the first Independent government. But in this, they could not have been more mistaken, for it was not the case at all. Most other educated Kenyans could see the writing on the wall and therefore did not support the idea of Mau Mau and indeed, many joined the Security Forces and risked their lives in the service of the K.A.R., the Kenya Police and the Kenya Regiment. There had always been feuds between the tribes over tribal boundaries and the stealing of cattle and the abduction of people, so better the Colonial devil they knew, than an untried Kikuyu one to rule over them. Thus, Mau Mau was confined almost exclusively to the Kikuyu ethnic group, that is to say the people of Kiambu, Fort Hall and Nyeri Districts, with a minority of the Embu and Meru people taking a passive role; *little more than 5% of the population of Kenya,* the rest being perfectly happy to provide manpower to fight the insurgents.

Because the Mau Mau leaders realised they were beginning to lose support, they had to coerce people into taking the subsequent oaths. Press gangs would be summoned to go out and bring in as many as possible for oathing and if they refused they would simply be cut down with pangas. Soon there was no escape. Everyone had to take the oaths or be killed. And if it wasn't so serious a travesty and so shocking a spectacle, the whole theatrics would have seemed a complete farce. All tribal decency was outraged and with every oath taken, and some took as many as fifteen, the man or woman was dragged deeper and deeper into the net of filth and degradation. The perverted acts that were indulged are more than is necessary to record here. For those who wish to learn more about the depravity and dehumanisation of it all, there are records in the Kenya National Archives in Nairobi of the kind of things oath-takers were made to do and to suffer. One of the most horrific oaths, that was accompanied by the performance of unspeakable acts, is given at the heading of this chapter.

Some of the most interesting pieces of information that have arrived on my desk since I started on this book are the examples of oaths I have been sent. They are interesting because of the similarity of the oaths from different parts of the Kikuyu, Embu and Meru areas. It is not only the words the oath-takers had to speak that are similar, it is the heinous acts they had to perform while taking the oaths, that are surprisingly alike. I now have records of them from as far afield as Kiambu, Fort Hall, Nyeri and in the settled area of Laikipia.

During my own work in Special Branch, Fort Hall, I had, for the purposes of interrogation, collated a list of acts that were performed at most of the oathing ceremonies in the Fort Hall region. But I had always preferred to believe that the more bestial acts were perhaps embellished over-dramatically during confessions. I had always thought it was difficult to believe they were typical of what was carried out generally throughout Kikuyuland. Now, in my research for this book, I realise I was wrong, as the examples I have received from other areas are virtually identical. One is left, therefore, with the conclusion that there must have been a decree from the highest authority, not only as to the wording of these oaths, but also more importantly, to the vile acts that should accompany them.

A secret document that has come into my hands, now released under the 30 year rule, contains the minutes of a committee set up in 1953 by the Governor, to report on the Sociological Causes of Mau Mau. This committee, which included several leading Kikuyu Elders, found that some of the acts involved in these oaths were beyond reconciliation by any means known to Kikuyu tradition, and that takers of these oaths and performers of these acts could not be returned to their own communities under any circumstances. If they were ever repatriated to their home locations, they would be ostracised by their families for the rest of their lives. This fact has a bearing on the reasons why many of those hardcore detainees who had taken these terrible oaths, could not be repatriated after the end of the Emergency, as recorded here in Chapter 10 on Detention Camps.

I have received nearly 200 letters and communications from all over the world, whilst writing this book, mostly from those who took part in, or lived in the areas affected by the Emergency. Typical of the anecdotes I have received from various sources on the subject of oathing, is the following from Peter Evans who was born and brought up on a coffee farm near Nyeri.

> Many of my young memories go back to the wonderful [Kikuyu] men and women we had working on the farm. We used to have great jokes and talk about all manner of things that young boys ask about. I never once felt threatened or worried by our employees and I was always free to wander far and wide throughout the farm and beyond into the Kikuyu homelands. Then, when the oathings began, it was so sad to see the change come over the men and women. We didn't know immediately what had occurred to make this sudden change, but gradually we learnt that they were being intimidated into becoming members of the Mau Mau movement through the initiation of those

horrific, bestial oathing ceremonies that made them do things against their will in fear of losing their wives and families.

We had a cook named Magura. He was there in my life from the earliest days I can remember. He would not allow us kids to pinch the food from the kitchen and kept us well in order. When we entered his kitchen domain, he was always fair with us and became a good friend.

In 1953, when I was 14, Magura suddenly became very sullen and unhappy. This change occurred after our neighbour's house-servant was murdered by a Mau Mau gang. Magura had been friends with the man and they used to meet up for a chat in the afternoons when their work was finished. A few days later, Magura disappeared and I never saw him again.

I enquired after him many times, as he did not live far away from our farm, over the river. Several years went by until I heard one day that the reason he had left us was that he had been ordered by the local Mau Mau gang to assist them in killing us kids and our Mum, otherwise his family would be murdered. I was told that he stubbornly refused to help them but we could never find out whether or not the Mau Mau carried out their threat against him and his family, though we feared the worst.[117]

The numbers of those who refused to be subjected to these degrading oaths and were cut down for their pains, will never be known. But in Fort Hall alone, there are plenty of records to show that considerable numbers lost their lives in the most horrific manner:

Anyone refusing [to take the oath] was quickly threatened and subjected to savage physical violence. If they refused they were killed in the presence of others attending the ceremony, thereby ensuring that the threats were not seen as empty words. Many very bravely did refuse, but we could never find out, nor will it ever be known how many thousands of 'missing' Kikuyu were executed in this way. The chiefs were for ever reporting the discovery of chopped-up bodies, burnt out huts, missing persons, slaughtered animals and other depravities. I well remember several horrid happenings. On one occasion I was called from my safari tent at dawn and taken to an African Anglican Church where a disembowelled goat was splayed out on the alter cross, and the local lay preacher's decapitated body, was spread out before it. On another

---

[117] Peter Evans. Pers. Comm.

occasion, two young pregnant women of the same family lay disembowelled with their foetuses stuffed into their mouths. Time and time
again we came upon or were taken to see slashed or violated bodies.[118]
The perpetrators of these horrific acts, however, overlooked one important
feature of the culture of oath-taking. They had not foreseen the possibility that
with stronger and even more powerful oath administrators, an oath could also
be undone and the recipient absolved of his or her oath. This was the case,
particularly if the administrator of the absolving oath was known as a
respected *mwene githathi* and the oath was taken in daylight in front of an

A venerated seer with his '*githathi*' stone
*The old man is lifting the Mau Mau oaths from those who wish to confess while
leading tribal officials witness the confessions*

assembly of people. This turned out to be a most handy weapon in the hands of
the Government Administration. The '*thenge*' oath was one of the first to be
used, and was done early in the Emergency by certain witch-doctors in the
presence of Chiefs to pronounce a curse against the Mau Mau. It entailed the
beating to death of at least one goat! Needless to say, the few *mwene githathi*

---

[118] W.H. Thompson. Unpublished memoirs 1978 p.75

who could perform this act were soon eliminated by the Mau Mau.[119]

Another piece of the confessing witch-doctor's equipment was the *'githathi'* stone, which was an object of quite considerable veneration. It was used later in de-oathing confessions, when the confessor was able to be given sufficient protection by the Security Forces. It had been used for generations to exorcise or lift a curse, and was known to have enormous powers. It was a heavy stone, about the size and shape of a bucket. It had seven holes through it, into each hole of which the cursed man would thrust a stick, muttering words the doctor would tell him, liberating the man from his curse or his sins. Traditionally the cursed man would have to pay dearly for this exercise, and would have to part with at least one sheep or goat. But the government paid for the witch-doctor's services for the removal and confessing of oaths.

The District Officer of the Mathira Division in Nyeri in 1952/53 recalls the initiative he was advised to take, to invalidate the oath.

> Another rather later initiative was taken on advice of the *Kikuyu Guards* in our Division. We concluded that we could not expect most people who had been compelled to take a Mau Mau oath to confess that they had done so, for fear of being murdered and of the oath itself. So we decided that everyone should be expected, without *necessarily confessing* anything, to take another oath cleansing them of any Mau Mau oaths they might have taken. We also decided that this cleansing oath should be administered by a prominent witch-doctor from Machakos on the grounds that most Kikuyu believed that the most powerful magic came from Ukambani *[country of the Akamba people]*.
>
> To the best of my recollection, a two shilling charge was levied to pay the witch-doctor (who must have done well out of it, as he cleansed many thousand of Mathira Kikuyu). I suspect that Chiefs and Headmen must have exerted pressure on many of these thousands to come and be cleansed, as nobody was legally obliged to do so. I certainly never authorised any form of compulsion and, with one exception, was never aware of any attempts to do so. The exception was during a particular cleansing ceremony when I found a local Chief looking on while someone who had refused to be 'cleansed', was being thumped by a group of Kikuyu Guard. I immediately stopped it and told the Chief it must never happen again; but I have to admit that I did not *order my Tribal Police to* arrest the culprits and have them charged with assault,

---

[119] Pers. Comm. From John Russell OBE., who served in the Kenya Regiment as a District Officer (Kikuyu Guard) during the Emergency.

which in hindsight I should have done. But the thumping had not resulted in any serious injury and it took place at a time when violence was commonplace throughout Kikuyuland, and everyone's nerves were on edge, so I cannot pretend that I feel much guilt.

Whether in retrospect all this cleansing can be said to have served a useful purpose is a moot point. At the time, I believed it was of value for two reasons. First there was the prospect of persuading some individuals who had been reluctant, or positively unwilling to take the Mau Mau oaths, that they were no longer bound by these. Second, it was evidence which might bring comfort to the *Kikuyu Guard* of further positive action being taken in an attempt to counter the spread of what most of us regarded as an evil movement. [120]

The Kikuyu Guard were at a particularly low ebb at this period. They were being seriously harassed by the Mau Mau and felt that they were not fully supported by the Government who had yet to issue arms to them.

It became common knowledge that nearly every Kikuyu had taken at least one oath, and that most had taken more. The Government therefore set about cancelling out these oaths and releasing the recipient from them. But before this could happen, a full confession had first to be extracted from the taker. The history of this rehabilitation, and the eventual repatriation of detainees is dealt with, at some length in Chapter 10.

[120] Peter Lloyd – pers. comm

CHAPTER EIGHT

THE KIKUYU GUARD

'They have saved their tribe from complete degradation and they have earned a place in Kenya's history'

John Pinney, District Commissioner, Fort Hall

The Kikuyu Guard came into being as a result of a succession of events that led up to the start of Mau Mau activities in the Kikuyu homeland itself, then known as the Kikuyu Reserve[121]. First came the mass rallies in Fort Hall and Nyeri. Then the first mild oathings took place, which the majority of the Chiefs and Headmen probably took. It was not until the more odious oathings began to take place in 1951 that dissention began in the ranks of the more traditional, older Kikuyu. To begin with, in fear of their lives, they held their own counsel, but when the first brutal murders took place of those that would not take part in these subsequent oathings, the Chiefs, Headmen and Tribal Police appealed to the government that they, as Government servants, should at least have weapons to defend themselves against these bands of murderers that were now openly rebelling against the Government and subverting the population.

True to style, the government was slow to appreciate the seriousness of the threat and they refused the requests, saying that it was the Police's job to protect them and the community. The official policy that emanated from Whitehall was not to arm members of a tribe that were reported to be opposing the Government and destabilizing the population. To them it made no sense. How would they be able to tell apart those who were genuinely opposed to the movement, and those who were the prime movers behind it? How would they know that the guns they gave them today would not be turned against them tomorrow? Their District Officers in the field knew the answers to these questions, but it was a long way from the forests of Fort Hall to the corridors of Whitehall where the power rested and where they were not yet convinced.

They did, however, allow Police Posts to be built in the Reserve for the first time, manned by European Officers hastily recruited from the UK under

---

[121] Each tribe had its own demarcated area known as a 'Reserve': a name given to distinguish it from other areas such as Crown lands, forest reserves, national parks or European 'settled areas'.

two-year contracts. This measure helped to give some confidence to the Chiefs and Headmen, but it did not slow down the numbers of murders of those who refused to support the Mau Mau. The Chiefs and Headmen pleaded with the government that they themselves should have some means of actively opposing these criminals who were not simply enemies of the Government but of the Kikuyu people themselves. A District Officer in Fort Hall at the time, later recorded his impressions.

> As this pattern of violence and oathing spread, so did the few who refused the oath grow more terrified, and it became obvious that the Government would have to do something to strengthen them. I myself went on a four-day safari to Location 2 in September [1952] with the object of banding the people together in the hope they would resist oathing. I claim that this was the first attempt to form a Kikuyu Guard, although of course in those days we did not call it by that name. I stayed at Kangari and held three *barazas* [meetings], one at Gituri, another at Gatiaini, and a third at Kinyona. The people there were persuaded to form themselves into three groups to look after their own areas; moreover, on the night of the original *baraza* a road-block was put down by the newly formed guard, which stopped a lorry-load of Nairobi oathers on their way to Kinyona – it is said with the object of murdering Chief Kigo. All three groups were to be commanded by Headman Thigiru, the late and very brave son of Senior Chief Njiri himself. I also promised to try and obtain a rifle for him. The people were very brave and they never let us down.
>
> By this time Kenya African Union meetings had been banned in the Fort Hall District itself, but they continued to be held in towns like Nairobi and Thika and were attended by hundreds, if not thousands of Fort Hall Kikuyu. Kenyatta, Beauttah and Kigondo were usually on the platform. The propaganda followed the set pattern of demanding 'more land, more money, more opportunity and self-determination', but it must be emphasised that they made the mistake of pointing to the Tribal Police who were on duty, controlling the crowds, and saying: 'one day we will get you and teach you a lesson'. The Tribal Police never forgot that.
>
> The Chiefs and Headmen were frightened men. They were very frightened of the forces of Kenyatta and the politicians and without weapons to defend themselves they ceased to have real control – with the exceptions of Senior Chief Njiri and Chief Ignatio who continued to

stand out openly against Mau Mau. [122]

Most Chiefs and Headmen, lowly paid and living in isolated places, unarmed and unsupported by government forces, succumbed to the pressures the Mau Mau put upon them. A visit by a group of thugs at the dead of night, one's wife held, a *panga* (machete) to her throat, who could resist taking the oath? And once taken, knowing it was a binding vow, who could then fail to uphold the promises forcefully extracted?

There was, nevertheless, a significant body of resistance to Mau Mau and all it stood for. The nucleus of the opposition was within the Christian Missions dotted throughout Central Province. Those who had embraced Christianity resisted because they realised there could be no compromise between their faith and the activities of Mau Mau. The resistance was not necessarily out of loyalty to the government, it was because they could not tolerate the degradation and depravity that epitomised the movement. Above all, they did not want to see them as future leaders of the Kikuyu people.

The more perceptive among the population could see that Mau Mau would bring nothing but sorrow and ruin to the tribe. The elders, personified by Senior Chief Njiri, could see clearly that Mau Mau violated all their precious traditions and culture, which he upheld heart and soul. He would have nothing to do with it. In defiance and contempt for the thugs, he flew the Union Flag over his homestead and headquarters, throughout the Emergency. The Mau Mau tried several times to kill the Senior Chief but he always managed to avoid their gangs. They did, however, later manage to butcher his eldest son, Thigiru — a chief in his own right, but not before he had fought many a battle against the Mau Mau.

Supporting these Headmen and Chiefs was a redoubtable force of Tribal Police who only numbered thirty [in Fort Hall] at the beginning of the Emergency. Twenty-eight was the number of fatal casualties they were to suffer in the ensuing months. The Mau Mau made a dead set at them and if they could not get them, they got their wives and families and butchered them for their husband's loyalty. Their worth was soon recognised and the force was expanded to 240 and later to 400. No unit in the entire Security Forces paid better dividends than the Kikuyu Tribal Police.[123]

---

[122] Jock Rutherford '*A History of the Kikuyu Guard*' Ed. David Lovatt Smith p.6
[123] Ibid p.9

The Tribal Police were the natural progression from the traditional 'policemen' of Kikuyu culture. There had always been the *'Njama'*, a local band of warriors who were the local defence force in times of war and at other times kept order at large gatherings, especially at market places. Routledge, visiting Waweru's market at Wambogu in 1902, writes: *'It is a special duty of the Njama or native police to keep order on these occasions...'* So they were not a new innovation, although they now received their pay from the Administration, through taxes paid by the community.

They must have been successful, because the very first thing Kenyatta did when he became Head of State after Independence in 1963 was to get rid of all the Tribal Policemen, every man jack of them. The reward for their loyalty was slim indeed.

The District Officers knew where the resistance lay, they knew who the people were and knew their trustworthiness. They pleaded on their behalf to the government to give them weapons.

The government began to realise they would have to protect these islands of resistance before they too, were overwhelmed by the Mau Mau onslaught. *'The matter was urgent because every night their ranks were further reduced. The Mau Mau were having it all their own way because their activities were still treated as a civil disturbance. Such civil forces that existed in the District had no more than normal peacetime powers. Furthermore, if a well-known Mau Mau thug was captured, no conviction could be obtained, because the Mau Mau oath was an effective silencer and it meant death to witnesses who broke it.*[124].

It is a sad reflection on the British Government that many good, committed and highly principled Kikuyu had to die most horrible deaths, before the government saw that enough was enough, and they responded to the pressures of their officers in the field to allow some of those most at risk to carry weapons.

Fort Hall was perhaps the epicentre of Mau Mau operations from the time when the first mass rallies took place, so it was somewhat natural that it should be one of the first to come up with the idea of a Kikuyu defence force to counteract and frustrate the movement. Senior Chief Njiri was the main power behind the idea in the first place. He knew that there were islands of

[124] Ibid p.9

resistance to the movement, and though he was not a Christian himself, and took little active interest in the missions, he certainly understood that Christian Kikuyu could not support the evils that Mau Mau represented and that they

A meeting of elders called by Senior Chief Njiri *(seated)* attended by District Officer Bob Otter at Kangema, Fort Hall - August 1954
The meeting was to discuss the tactics for defending the population against the Mau Mau insurgents

would want to be able to thwart them wherever they could, and particularly around the mission stations. Njiri knew that the people themselves could not fight the Mau Mau on their own, and that they would need the support and weapons that only the government could make available. So he talked at some length with his District Officers, Tommy Thompson and Tony Soutar and through them to the District Commissioner, Frank Loyd, who presented a case for the recruiting of trustworthy people to the Minister for African Affairs, Edward Windley. With the support of the Governor, they eventually persuaded their masters in Whitehall to allow the arming of small selected bands of known law-abiding citizens. The idea quickly spread to other affected districts in Nyeri and Kiambu, and later, to a lesser extent, to Embu and Meru.

163

Considerable progress was made during the next few weeks. In April 1953 a meeting was held at Nyeri, the Provincial Headquarters, under the chairmanship of General Hinde to decide means of strengthening the build-up. Here it was tentatively agreed to recognise officially the Kikuyu Home Guard and, moreover, that twenty percent of them should be armed with guns. European Officers were to be appointed to lead and build up the movement, and an overall Director was also to be chosen. The security of arms issued was to be carefully monitored. No patrol was to operate with less than two guns and eight spearmen together. All Kikuyu were to be carefully screened before enlistment.

The first allocation of fifty rifles was received in the first week of April 1953. On April 20th, General Hinde formally issued a directive establishing the force as the Kikuyu Guard, and defining its tasks in the fight against Mau Mau as:-

a) *In co-operation with the other forces of law and order, so to deny Mau Mau the Kikuyu Reserves, that they become, in due course, a secure base from which our regular forces can be withdrawn to hunt down Mau Mau in the forests and mountains.*

b) *To provide information of Mau Mau activities and plans.*

The main reason for the success of the Kikuyu Guard was the care with which it was built up. It was never allowed to become simply 'the loyal party'. In fact 'loyal' was the wrong epithet anyway. It was not so much loyalty to the British government that drove people to join the Guard. It was their opposition to the manner in which the self-styled Mau Mau leaders sported themselves, and it was the people's instinctive resistance to the methods they used to gain their ends, and particularly to recruit members to their movement. It was the perversion and manipulation of the sacred oaths that they could not tolerate, and it was the gruesome murders of those who disagreed with them that turned growing numbers against them. These were the prime reasons for joining the Kikuyu Guard. It was not to curry favour with the British, nor was it to show any particular affection for them.

The Guard were to have European officers to instruct them in weapon training, discipline and tactics. This job fell mostly to members of the Kenya

Regiment, some of whom had only just returned from their six months army basic training. The Guards were to live in defensive forts built by the local community, assisted by the Kings African Rifles. Here they would be secure and could hopefully fight off any attacks from Mau Mau gangs. They would also use these forts or Posts as they came to be known, as their base from which to go out and search for the gangs in the Reserves and in the forests that lay above them.

No one could become a member of the Guard unless he could prove he was absolutely reliable. It was the confession system that ensured this was so. Danger lay in expansion that was too fast or too large. It was better to have no Guard at all, than one that could not be trusted and relied upon. After all, it was a fairly risky business to arm Kikuyu people, yet it was one that in the end was fully justified. The confession system was begun in Fort Hall, and was largely devised, established and supervised by a Kikuyu Assistant District Officer, Jerome Kihore, who was later murdered by the Mau Mau just as the tide was on the turn. Few Kikuyu contributed as much as this gallant District Officer did, to the eventual defeat of Mau Mau.

Virtually every adult member of the tribe had taken the first oath and in so doing they swore not to give away any Mau Mau secrets; if they did, they were told they would die, and this, the Kikuyu people being the slaves to bewitchment that they were, the vast majority believed implicitly. One or two, worried by the oath they had taken, went to a Chief or to another officer and confessed what they had done or had been made to do. Jerome Kihore was invited in on these confessions and collated the information that transpired from them. From small beginnings, he and his team laid bare the whole Mau Mau organisation throughout the District. The names of the oath administrators, treasurers, committee members and guards were recorded in a card index system. Every particular of the oaths and the bestial ceremonies accompanying them became known.

The rule was that before any Kikuyu could become a member of the Guard he had to confess fully in this manner and in public, hiding nothing that he knew about the enemy. Only then was he eligible to be taken on probation into the Guard as a junior recruit.

In the course of time, as more and more Kikuyu regurgitated the oaths enforced upon them, a very full picture emerged of the underground organisation. The strength of the card index lay in the recorded inaccuracies as much as in the truths. Time and again, when false confessions had been made and set down, they stood out like the proverbial 'sore thumbs'. Over two and half years, as the de-oathing teams became more and more knowledgeable, and the trickle of confessions became a flood, all became clear. The very first confessions were made in secrecy, but after a while, as confidence in the government grew, and fear lessened, all confessions were made in public.[125]

Gradually the people realised the Government knew a good deal about the oath they had taken and, more importantly, and contrary to what they had been led to believe, they saw that those who had already confessed, had come to no harm. They too, made haste to confess. When they had done so they felt better having got the weight of the filthy oaths off their chests. The Kikuyu call it 'kahungwa muhori' or 'to have the lungs cleansed'. They had also been encouraged to make their own individual stand by giving the names of those members of the Mau Mau secret organisation that they knew.

In Nyeri District, when the idea of the Kikuyu Guard was first mooted, the method of recruiting was left more to the Chiefs and Headmen. Peter Lloyd was the District Officer of Mathira Division at this time.

By late 1952, the known political agitators from Nyeri District who were suspected of conniving with, or more often actively promoting Mau Mau, had all been imprisoned or detained, so I was able to spend more time collecting and collating information about other Mathira Kikuyu living outside the District, mostly in Nairobi, who were allegedly oath administrators or potential terrorists. This information came from several sources: from Chiefs and Headmen, whose reliability I initially doubted; from missionaries, where I found the Catholics more cooperative than the Protestants, and from individuals, mostly committed Christians who, having been compelled to take the oath, secretly reported to their clergy or Chiefs. One or two of these latter, I persuaded to work for me as informers, pretending on the one hand to be actively supporting Mau Mau and on the other, bringing me valuable information on characters resident outside the District whom I could report to the Police for arrest.

The information I collected was unlikely to lead to criminal prosecutions because most potential witnesses were terrified of giving evidence in Court. My purpose instead, was to compile dossiers reliable enough to justify detention orders, so that the offenders could at least be

[125] District Officer Tommy Thompson unpublished memoirs

taken out of harm's way.

Throughout this period (October 1952 to June 1953) Kikuyu Guard units were being formed. Their build-up was gradual but continuous, though there were different schools of thought about the pace at which it should take place. Some more cautious Chiefs felt that all prospective recruits should be thoroughly vetted by those known to be loyal to the Kikuyu Guard, lest units be infiltrated by undesirables. Others believed that those volunteering to join should be made welcome in case they decided to join the other side. I did not interfere with this process as there was no way in which I could reliably have judged whether or not individual cases were wise. Moreover, it was abundantly clear that Chiefs and Headmen's lives were at grave risk if they made mistakes! I simply tried wherever possible to inspire the Kikuyu Guard leaders with confidence, and one way of achieving this was to convince them of the government's determination to defeat Mau Mau. However, the most practical way was to issue them with the means to defend themselves, and this I was able to do once Rifles and shotguns were made available to me for distribution.

Eventually, however, a group of terrorists lead by Waruhiu Itote, the self-styled 'General China', mounted a determined attack on my senior Chief's Guard Post. Mercifully the Chief together with his Police bodyguards managed to escape, but seeing the mutilated corpses of several other individuals I had known, respected and admired, was traumatic. Equally traumatic was the realisation that despite all my endeavours, my Division was evidently to be afflicted by the sort of violence that had been commonplace throughout the District. It was dispiriting to realise that I had found no solution to the problem of containing Mau Mau.[126]

Many District Officers felt much the same. Some had only recently arrived in Kenya from the U.K. and had little time to get to know the people to whom they were expected to show leadership qualities. I myself remember well as a young FIO, having to make decisions of a surprisingly responsible nature over Chiefs and Headmen, about the lives of their own people. Chief Wilson Mirange of Location 14, Fort Hall, was one for whom I had the greatest respect, but one could not help but feel most conscious of the greater age of these older men. They were expected to defer to someone very much younger

---

[126] Peter Lloyd – pers. comm

and it was not always easy to sustain their faith in one, and in times of crisis, their dependence on one. A District Officer had, amongst other things, the power of arrest and detention, albeit for a short period of time, and it was necessary for him to be able to make decisions that were not only just, but in these times of Mau Mau, were life-threatening. It must have been particularly upsetting, never, perhaps, having seen a dead person before, to have seen not only the corpses of people one knew and respected, but also their mutilated bodies, cut to pieces with *pangas* and *simis* (machetes and short swords).

One of the first Kikuyu Guard units to be formed in Fort Hall in 1953   Phil Sykes

With the encouragement and supervision of the local District Officer, a nucleus of trustworthy men who had been through the public confession procedure, banded together under the charge of their Headman or Chief and became the local Kikuyu Guard, when they were officially recognised members of the Security Forces. As such, they were 'marked men' by the Mau Mau, and it became necessary for them to live in a secure compound that they could defend against an attack. At the outset this was usually the headman's homestead around which was a hastily erected barbed-wire fence. This soon proved to be easily penetrated and overrun by the insurgents, and several headmen's lives were lost together with their followers, because of the inadequacy of the defences.

It became clear that better and more easily defended posts were needed, and the 4th (Uganda) Kings African Rifles (KAR) battalion were given the job of constructing old-style forts with stockades and moats filled with '*panjis*' — sharpened bamboo stakes set firmly into the moat which rendered the forts virtually impregnable to the insurgents. The whole of the local population were pressed into service to help construct the forts that began to spring up all over the Reserve. The forts came to be known as Kikuyu Guard Posts.

Tuso Kikuyu Guard Post, Fort Hall
The families of the Guard members lived in the village built close to the Guard post for security

By September 1953, the Guard had been established in Posts and a few had been given weapons with which to defend themselves. They had already suffered four months of attacks by the enemy, and the number of attacks were growing daily. The outlook for the future was enough to depress even the most optimistic of them.

The Mau Mau were now at their most powerful. This was their hey-day. They had a well organised system for the supply of arms, ammunition, equipment and money from Nairobi. Recruits were easy to obtain. The forests of the Aberdares and Mount Kenya were Mau Mau territory in which they could move about freely and live in comparative comfort on the stocks they had built up. They had the backing from most of the Kikuyu population, who, slaves to the oath, did as they were bidden and provided couriers that could travel over the Colony without arousing suspicion. Many villages had their own committee ready to welcome gangs with food, shelter and money. Spies reported the movements of the Security Forces to the gangs. Small wonder, then, that if a Kikuyu Guard, contrary to orders, wandered off by himself to see his family or to look for food, he was seldom see again.

At this period the morale of the Kikuyu Guard was low, and they were uncertain of the future. They could not yet see victory ahead and often wondered where the stand they had made against what they perceived to be 'the enemy', would lead them. The Mau Mau agents were ready with cunning rumours to try and feed the disillusionment many had begun to feel.

The District Officers in the field were quick to sense this feeling of gloom and made it clear to their seniors that the Government would have to take action in order to maintain the trustworthiness and aggressive spirit of the Guard during these difficult months.

The Kikuyu Guard were never paid a salary because it could be seen they were nothing but mercenaries, whereas in fact, they were volunteers engaged in eradicating a disease that had afflicted much of their tribe. The Guard member living in his Post was on full time duty and could not go home unless a strong patrol happened to be going his way. His wife and family could not cultivate their fields because their lives too, were in great danger, so they also had to live in or near the Post. All the usual activities of the district such as trading had come to a standstill because of Mau Mau activities. Most of the shops were empty or shut because there were no vehicles to transport their goods. There was no export of foodstuffs either, for the same reason. Craftsmen no longer plied their trades. Restrictions on movement and the curfew kept everyone near their homes. The Guard member had no income and therefore no means of support, so in order to alleviate some of these hardships the Government made available supplies of food to help them over the hungry periods. The amount of food varied according to the hardship of the locality. Some Posts near the forest had to be fed almost entirely while others in the more peaceful areas were not fed at all.

The Guard were also assisted in a number of other ways. They were let off the Special Tax the tribe had to pay as its contribution to the cost of the Emergency. They were helped with the school fees of their children; they were given free issues of clothes from time to time. Where circumstances allowed any form of trade to be carried on, such as the export of wattle bark or charcoal, they were the first to be given permits. They were told that when conditions improved, they would receive preference in every possible way and be considered before the others, who, by their obedience to the oath, would have to work their passage back to recognition.

The Nyeri District Commissioner knew the debt the Government was accumulating in respect of the Kikuyu Guard. In his handing-over notes to his successor, the outgoing District Commissioner was well aware that the Guard were not fighting on the Government's side because of any affection they may have had for it.

> All trade is now rightly in the hands of the Kikuyu Guard, and there, for some time it will have to stay. The method of exempting Kikuyu Guard members from the Kikuyu Special Tax and of remitting Kikuyu Guard childrens' school fees are well known to you. ...The Kikuyu loyalist has not stayed loyal for love of the 'Raj'. Though he is still deep in the war against Mau Mau, he will expect and indeed demand political recognition sometime in the near future, and this will become apparent through the Kikuyu predilection for politics.[127]

Unfortunately this debt was never repaid as it should have been. In fact, by the time Independence came, only nine years after the Guard was finally disbanded, there was a great deal of animosity still surfacing between those who openly fought on the Colonial Government's side, and the rest who, uncommitted as they probably were during the conflict, after Independence, conveniently made out they had always sided with the Mau Mau. The Guard members have sadly always come in for a hard time and even now, in 2004, those whose fathers and grandfathers fought in the Kikuyu Guard are reluctant to admit the fact, whereas those who took part in many of the Mau Mau atrocities are applauded. I hope this book may help serve to rectify that travesty. (See also appendix 7)

By the end of the year (1953), morale had risen again and the Guard was ready to play its vital role in the big battles that were to come. The year had seen the Kikuyu Guard grow from a few bewildered groups of people, to a large

---

[127] O.E.B. Hughes, District Commissioner, Nyeri. Handing over Notes to his successor Jimmy Butler. December 1954

171

organised force well suited to the task of stamping out the Mau Mau enemy in the Reserves.

The 'enemy' were the Mau Mau gangs that had based themselves in the forest. The leaders of the gangs were those who had earned themselves a criminal record in the back streets of Nairobi. Having managed to evade the arm of the law, they returned to their home village only to find that they were now outcasts or *'mu'undu mu'uru'*. The only future for an outcast was to go to the forest above his home, and there to live as a *'nyakirio na kiano'*, literally 'a blunt arrow' — the name given to someone who is beyond rehabilitation and has to be cast out from society. They always took up residence in an area of forest close to their homestead so that they were within easy reach of it should they need to visit their families for any reason. The forest had forever been home to these 'blunt arrows' and when the first Mau Mau had to hide from the police, they too, went to the forest above their homesteads and were given sanctuary by these pariahs, who naturally became their leaders as they knew how to build shelters and feed themselves from the fruits of the forest. The difference now was that the Mau Mau brought with them weapons stolen from raids on settlers' farms and police stations, so the 'blunt arrows' suddenly became somewhat sharper!

Those who had confessed during their recruitment for the Kikuyu Guard knew all these men because they were local people. So the value of the information they were able to reveal about the gangs and their make-up, was of enormous help to the security forces.

The attacks were not confined simply to settlers on their farms in the White Highlands. The gangs that were formed from local people in the Reserve, usually hid in specially constructed hide-outs in the forest above their own homesteads. Here, it was often too great a distance from settler's farms to organise attacks so they turned their attention closer to home, to those kinfolk who were against the Mau Mau movement. One of the first atrocities that took place within the Fort Hall Reserve was at the tiny village of Ndakaini which stood close to the forest edge near the hide-out of a 'General Mawe', a 'sharpened arrow', who, according to the local Roman Catholic Priest, had, before the Emergency, *'a powerful reputation as a goat thief'*. The District Officer of the area saw the result of the attack the next morning.

'Several days before the attack, this particular village, had chased off a group of Mau Mau who had arrived there to give oaths to the whole village. A week later, the gang came at night and slaughtered some thirty

172

women and children, either hacking them to death or burning them alive in their huts. It was a clear warning to others to cooperate or die. But it had the opposite effect, for those men who escaped with their lives were so angry that they immediately volunteered for the Kikuyu Guard. It became one of my most gallant and stalwart centres of the Guard.

My own headquarters was also attacked by a very large and well-armed gang that had filtered down from the forest along river beds, hiding up by day in swamps and reeds. I was away at the time of the attack which came at about 9 am. We found out later that the main purpose was to capture our local armoury in the village hall. They ransacked and burnt part of the school and two houses together with the tiny three-roomed stone building into which I had only recently moved. But most sadly of all, the six rondavel huts built for the Tribal Police had been the focus of appalling savagery. Three of the wives and four children were slashed to death, the children lay beheaded.'[128]

Mau Mau atrocities against their own people

These two attacks were the work of 'General' Kago[129] and his gang. Kago became the most notorious leader in Fort Hall. He was a charismatic leader but a ruthless killer.

This pattern of attacks was repeated all over Kikuyuland, but as the atrocities grew, so too did the revulsion among many of the Kikuyu themselves. They were torn between fear of the thugs, and disgust at the barbaric behaviour against their own people – often their very own families. A growing improvement in the organisation and recruitment of the Kikuyu Guard meant that the force was steadily being built up to counter these increasingly savage fratricidal attacks.

---

[128] District Officer Tommy Thompson unpublished memoirs
[129] See also Appendix 5

It soon became apparent that the method of building up the Guard round existing islands of resistance was insufficient. Some areas were more affected by Mau Mau than others, and Location 14 in Fort Hall, was one of the worst. In these areas, different recruiting tactics had to be evolved. It is an ironical fact that the conditions then prevailing—almost certain death to any Kikuyu who openly defied the Mau Mau—were instrumental in producing some of the most efficient Guards in the District. The authorities now began to find that those who had taken part in Mau Mau activities and had been persuaded to confess and carry out their public denunciation of the oath, often became the best fighters in the Kikuyu Guard. This extraordinary anomaly came to pervade the entire arena of operations and its rationale and complexity is dealt with in greater depth in the next chapter.

The Mau Mau at this time were concentrating their attention on building up gangs within the forests of the Aberdares and Mount Kenya. Making use of arms stolen in various raids on settler's houses and from the Naivasha Police Station raid, local leaders were recruiting hundreds of repatriates[130] now returning to their home districts from all over Kenya. This stream of people was to provide the forest gangs with a ready source of manpower for the months to come.

In order to combat this build-up of forest gangs, the Security Forces were strengthened by various methods: more Kenya Police personnel recruited from the U.K.; more battalions of British Army, sent out to Kenya from the U.K.; more battalions of Kings African Rifles (KAR) brought in from both Uganda and Tanganyika and by Kenya's own Territorial Defence Force, the Kenya Regiment. Lastly and most importantly, the Kikuyu Guard were now being recruited at the rate of several hundred each month.

Until now, the Kikuyu Guard had been mainly concerned in building up their own strength, the better to defend themselves. The various methods of doing this had now been tested, and once started, the movement grew steadily, despite the many setbacks that were suffered at the hands of the Mau Mau.

At this stage, the British battalions were used purely for tracking down the gangs in the forests of the Aberdares and Mount Kenya. It was the Kikuyu Guard and the Kenya Regiment who were to operate within the Kikuyu

---

[130] 'repatriates' were those Kikuyu who had been working on farms in the European settled area or in domestic service in Nairobi or elsewhere, who had been sent back to their homes as there was no evidence of Mau Mau involvement against them.

Reserve. This was the country in which they excelled. They knew it intimately. They could track the enemy; they could think like the enemy; they could, lightly equipped, move fast by night or by day, even across the grain of the country.

The guiding principle for the future was never to concede a single gain to the Mau Mau. If a Chief or Headman was murdered, another must immediately take his place. Whenever a Kikuyu Guard Post was overrun, and the defenders killed, it was re-built and made operational within a single day. Only in this way could the local population realise the futility of Mau Mau terrorism, and without local support the gangs could not exist.

One of the most effective military units was the Kenya Regiment, made up of young white Kenyans like myself, many of whom were the sons of Settlers. Some of us had been called-up for National Service and had spent six months in Salisbury, Southern Rhodesia, undergoing basic training where our instructors and drill sergeants were from the British Army—mostly from Guards regiments. At the end of our training, we were as fit and efficient as any in the British Army, and had returned to Kenya to take up posts in the various arms of the Security Forces. The Kenya Regiment boys had two great advantages over the British battalions: firstly we could speak Kiswahili, the *lingua franca* of Kenya, so that most, but not all Africans could understand us, and secondly, because many had grown up in the country we understood better the psychology of the African people.

Many of these young men went on secondment as advisers to the newly-formed Kikuyu Guard. They operated under the authority of the permanent District Officers who were responsible for the activities of these young infantrymen who, untutored in the ways of civil affairs had suddenly found themselves thrust into the role of administrators. Their role was to train and discipline the raw recruits, show them how to protect themselves from attack by Mau Mau and lead them in special operations against the Mau Mau gangs in the forest and in the Reserve. In April 1953 the first of these temporary District Officers to be known as District Officers (Kikuyu Guard) or D.Os (K.G.) took up their appointments and were issued with sten guns and Land Rovers. Theirs was an unenviable task. They lived in Posts that were barely armed and liable to attacks by gangs at night. By day, they could expect to be ambushed on any road they travelled. Working in Locations amongst people whose trustworthiness they could, at first, only guess at, they persevered and were soon able to build up a real comradeship with the Guards and fought alongside them in many battles, several losing their lives or suffering severe wounds.

Our role was to train the Guards in weapon handling, defence, guard duties, patrolling, laying ambushes, and raiding local villages that may have been infiltrated or otherwise suspected of harbouring terrorists. We were also involved in night operations, pretending to be Mau Mau demanding food or money. This was to test the local support for the terrorists.

We quickly discovered that most of the Guards were reliable and quite fearless and carried out our orders without question. We had to rely on their local knowledge of the area – where best to lay ambushes and which were the easiest patrol routes – and to consider any suggestion from them which would be better or safer options than our original ideas. Most of them seemed to be tough peasants who just wanted to get on with their lives and could not give a darn for Mau Mau. However, under threat from terrorist recruiters, money collectors and food

The Lari massacre
A Kenya Regiment soldier about to remove the last of the dismembered bodies.

gatherers, the Guard Posts were their only hope of safety. They were unpaid but once a week they got a sack of *'posho'* [maize meal] and once a month a skinny steer from the Administration Department. Some of them had abandoned their *shamba* [gardens or small farms], others had land to cultivate and others had families and plots to maintain. Some had

176

lost relatives to Mau Mau recruiters and were already in the forest gangs, whilst others had had relatives butchered by the Mau Mau.[131]

It is a matter of pride within the Kenya Regiment traditions, now, nearly fifty years on, that without their dedicated instruction and leadership, the success of the Kikuyu Guard would have been severely diminished. Also, and most importantly, with their effective control over the sometimes over-zealous Guards, they were able to ensure the more revengeful among those that had suffered terrible losses to their families at the hands of Mau Mau, did not follow the example of their attackers and vent their anger with unnecessary violence on committed or suspected Mau Mau terrorists. In effect, their leadership and the examples these temporary District Officers set, paid off so well in winning the hearts and minds not only of the Guards themselves, but also of the whole population, that within a matter of months, and sometimes weeks, they were able to leave their Locations, to be posted elsewhere in the certain knowledge that the Headman or Chief left in charge would carry on the work in the same disciplined manner.

The D.Os (K.G) were under the direct control of the District Officer who was a career Administrator in the British Colonial Service. He represented the Crown, the civil authority within his area, and was himself under the District Commissioner who in turn answered to the Provincial Commissioner and thence through the Chief Native Commissioner to the Governor who was chosen by the British Government in Whitehall, London, and appointed by the Queen. So the chain of governmental command was a direct one from the lowliest Headman in his remote village through to Whitehall and the Queen. And that is why, when a Chief or Headman had excelled himself in a particular heroic act or in outstanding work for his people, his achievement was recognised and acknowledged by a decoration received from the Governor who represented the Queen, in a ceremony in Government House, Nairobi.

The following unpublished memoir of a Kenya Regiment soldier seconded as a District Officer (Kikuyu Guard) gives the best description of the work the Kikuyu Guard carried out.

By year's end [1953], paucity of evidence in the forest led us to believe gangs were much reduced in numbers. This was an incorrect assumption

---

[131] Alan Francis - Kenya Regiment District Officer (Kikuyu Guard) Pers. Comm.

because, with great skill, the hard core terrorists had learned to live like wild animals, thereby mostly avoiding Government forces altogether.

This situation required a new tactic to bring pressure to bear on the terrorists. Earlier, despite serious risks, a voluntary Home Guard composed of Kikuyu who were opposed to Mau Mau was initiated by the Administration. Despite the appalling instances of every day murder and violence against those Kikuyu who did not support Mau Mau, a few brave stalwarts clung to their beliefs and traditions in isolated and sometimes ill-prepared defences, in total defiance of the terror sweeping their homeland. Being at first such easy targets, many of them lost their lives. However, with their opposition to Mau Mau proven, slowly but surely the Administration strengthened the movement by encouraging construction of suitable defensive outposts, which in time dominated local areas. By also denying food and other resources reaching the terrorists, the initiative was regarded as successful and by 1954 the programme was being greatly expanded.

In July, my Platoon transferred to South Tetu area of Nyeri District to assist the Administration's Kikuyu Guard programme. In small groups we took up positions in four recently constructed defensive posts in Gikondi above Sagana. The main purpose of our residence within the tribal reserve was to train and strengthen the voluntary Kikuyu Guard movement, which had succeeded elsewhere in denying Mau Mau vital support from the population.

The Administration's District Officer had already informed each group that personnel of Kenya Regiment would be coming to assist them. The Guards were to be armed and trained by us to use durable single barrel [Greener] shotguns, ideal for the defence of the stockades which they had recently built. Once an overall satisfactory level of competence with firearms was achieved, we were to carry out offensive patrols locally. These patrols were intended initially to be more of a flag-showing and confidence-building effort than an actual attempt to engage Mau Mau in force.

With L/Cpl Muirhead and two Privates, each armed with jungle rifles, we moved into the Headman's Post. I carried a Patchett sub-machine gun. As experienced combatants, we made immediate arrangements to assist each other should any of the Guard Posts suffer attack. The first night at our new Post passed in circumstances of mutual distrust and suspicion. On our part, we feared that while we slept these Kikuyu might attack us to obtain our precision weapons, then head for the forest to join their kinsmen. On their part, knowing how difficult it was for anyone to distinguish between loyalist and Mau Mau, they feared that we might set upon and annihilate them at the slightest pretence. Some of these loyalists had never been in close contact with Europeans and probably had instinctive phobias about us. Not all Kikuyu understood Swahili so there were problems just communicating.

At first, Headman Filipo was not much help to me. Unusually tall among his people, he would consider at length any request or suggestion, apparently looking for hidden meaning in everything. We wasted much time while he prevaricated. Although better dressed than his fellow men, by following a custom that was no longer fashionable, he obviously identified himself with an older generation. He must have been born some years before the first Europeans came to Fort Hall. From greatly extended pierced earlobes, copper earrings dangled almost to his shoulders. However, it was this aspect, together with his natural dignity, that made me think I could work with him. Later, I found that once we reached a thorough understanding, he addressed each situation positively.

When we commenced training activity the first morning, we found morale very low and I failed initially to determine the reason. These Kikuyu seemed neither to welcome our presence, nor did they by their actions show us resentment, nor any resistance or disagreement in what we intended doing. Overall, they presented more an appearance of bewilderment rather than a body of men taking arms to defend their customs and beliefs. In hindsight, it was natural that the profound circumstances of the time had led some individuals into confused thinking. They knew well enough that they had embarked on a course that could one day, if it failed, be their undoing. They were a minority standing out against a tide that had apparently swept up the mass of the population to a cause that so far had brought only loss of life to many, misery and intense suffering to everyone. Like any other soldier, I pressed on with the programme that had been outlined for me.

Progress with training at first was slow, but very soon we had in place constant sentry duty and a thorough understanding of drills necessary for defending the stockade in case of attack, day or night. We gave priority to safe handling and use of firearms, knowing well the propensity of this type of shotgun to break its firing pin if the trigger was released without a cartridge in the barrel. We had plenty of cartridges but only one shotgun. With just this one, we trained six Guards. Until more guns came we had to mimic the action of firing in defence, with most Guards making use of a staff or piece of wood .

Later I was attached to a small intelligence unit set up specifically to examine, interpret and act upon all information that could affect the campaign. Every day brought a welter of news and activity. Originally, much of it seemed irrelevant, but from experience we learned never to ignore even the smallest snippets however abstruse. In hindsight, I believe information about Mau Mau was always available to anyone prepared to live closely with Kikuyu People. The Kikuyu Guard programme proved such an opportunity at minimal risk. These people were notoriously reticent. Anyone interested in their welfare had to understand their customs and be extremely patient before anything of value was given.[132]

These Kenyans of European stock who were born and had grown up in Kenya and, perhaps with a local nanny to look after them, could probably speak the Kikuyu language before they could speak English, were of inestimable value when it came to supporting the newly recruited Kikuyu Guard and teaching them the basics of military drill and the use of weapons.

In the areas concerned with the Emergency, it was the career District Officer's job to pull together all the strings of the different arms of the Security Forces within his area, which, besides the Kikuyu Guard, included the Departmental heads of the Army, the Kenya Police and the Tribal Police.

The Kikuyu Guards and Tribal Police were now the main targets of the Mau Mau gangs, particularly the Chiefs and Headmen. They were seen as the major barrier to the successful aims of the Mau Mau and their political masters in Nairobi. The more men and women the Kikuyu Guard recruited the more they frustrated the plans of the politicians. The main objectives of the attacks, therefore, became levelled at the Guards and their Posts, and there were no more intensive battles than in the Fort Hall District. From April 1953, Fort Hall was to become the scene of a bitter and bloody struggle.

At about 9pm on the night of April 28th, Headman William's Post at Ruathia was attacked and overrun by a gang of fifty Mau Mau, armed with at least one automatic. Like many of the first Posts, this one was not tactically sited, but merely consisted of defences thrown up around the Headman's homestead, overlooked by higher ground on the southern side. The gang's objective was to kill Headman William and Sergeant Gadsby of the Kenya Regiment who were stationed there. The

---

[132] Stan Bleazard - Kenya Regiment – unpublished memoirs.

gangsters opened fire from above the Post before rushing the defences; these were so inadequate that they were easily dismantled in several places. This done, the gang swarmed inside, and although the Tribal Police and the Kikuyu Guard fought well, their ammunition was limited and they were soon overcome. The Tribal Policemen were found later. Some had had their hands tied and had then been shot and cut to pieces. Four Kikuyu Guard were also killed. Sergeant Gadsby and Headman William were both lucky enough to escape through the gap by which the gang had entered, and eventually they reached Kanyenyeni Police Station. At least four of the gang were killed, but the defenders lost four rifles and three shotguns to the enemy.[133]

From then on the Mau Mau battles raged throughout Fort Hall and the rest of Kikuyuland to try and defeat the Kikuyu Guard and discourage more recruits from joining their ranks. A District Officer (Kikuyu Guard) explains the daily

View from inside a Kikuyu Guard Post
By mid 1953 the Posts are built with ramparts all round, and outside, a moat into which sharpened bamboo stakes are planted. These two lines of defence make the forts virtually iompregnable

---

[133] Jock Rutherford *'A History of the Kikuyu Guard'* p.15

routine of a Kikuyu Guard Post.

Life in the Posts has become more or less a settled routine. The design of defences is gradually standardised. Wide, deep trenches filled with sharpened bamboo stakes or 'panjis' are dug round the oblong perimeters. Immediately inside rise earthen parapets. At opposite corners, 'blisters' are built out to give a clear view to sentries, and to allow enfilade fire along the line of defences in the event of an attack. Narrow drawbridges span the defences by day and are withdrawn when the gates are closed at dusk. The buildings within are roofed where possible with corrugated iron to prevent fire, while in the centre of each Post looms a tall tower manned by sentries day and night. Each man runs to his stand-to position at the sound of the alarm, and practice of this and other drills is frequent.

First light each morning brings relief to senses strained by the uncertainties of darkness. Only the sentries in the tower and on the gate need remain alert. While the men eat an early meal, the Headman of the Post details the day's duties. Already a small patrol has gone out to make a quick search of the surrounding area for signs of gangster activity during the night. If any are found, the trail must be followed. Later another patrol leaves to go further afield, and the Headman sets out to supervise the works of his labour gangs in the Sub-Location.

During the morning, the women bring supplies of water, fuel and food into the Post, and prepare sufficient for the day's meals. By midday the patrols, if they have found nothing, will be back and will spend the remainder of the day cleaning weapons and talking interminably as only Africans can talk. Although this, their new-found existence is completely foreign to anything they have lived before, the Kikuyu Guard have taken to it readily enough. It is the only reasonable alternative to losing their lives, and is a mixture of soldiers' barrack-lives and active service.

Towards evening, the Locational D.O.(K.G.) arrives, and having inspected their arms and ammunition he hears what has happened since his last visit, and tells them the news of other areas. He instructs the Headman where all his available men are to rendezvous for a dawn sweep next morning, and then drives off to another Post.

A whistle blows and everyone makes for his alarm post. The gate is closed and the bridge withdrawn, while the Headman moves slowly round the defences, naming the sentries for the night's watch.

After a good meal there is only quiet talk to be heard. Between eight and ten o'clock is the time when things happen, and nerves are tightening again. A small group of men by the gate is wondering which

Post has fired a tracer bullet a long way off, when a shot suddenly cracks through the camp. There is a rush to the parapets, but when no other shots are heard it transpires that a shaky sentry has accidentally fired his own rifle and blown a piece out of his arm. Not a word of sympathy is given, during the ensuing chatter. Most move back to their beds; others stay on to peer into the night.

Long before dawn thirty men move quietly out through the gate to join with others as the District Officer has ordered. It is dark, and a wet mist is driving across their way. But to some, this night patrol is better than simply waiting in the Post for something to happen."[134]

Typical of Mau Mau tactics was the ambush laid by 'General' Ihura against two of their most dedicated opponents. It took place at about 9am on 31st August 1953. Assistant District Officer Jerome Kihore who was the architect of the confessional system for the recruitment of the Kikuyu Guard, and Chief James Kiru of Location 14, Fort Hall, were travelling in their Land Rover when they ran into a prepared road block. A tree had been felled across the road at a point where it was impossible to turn round. Before the vehicle had come to a halt, the gang opened fire killing both the D.O. and the Chief. The driver managed to escape and ran to the nearest Police Post, but the gang had already made their escape though not before mutilating the bodies. Chief James was still a young man and had served in the East African Division in Burma during WW2. He was buried at his home within a mile from where the murder took place. The dead chief's father, who had, till then, taken no part in the fight against Mau Mau, was visibly shaken at his son's callous killing. The old man swore vengeance on the killers and all they stood for. He demanded and was given a rifle, and despite his age, was ever since seen to be at the forefront of attacks on Mau Mau, by his local Kikuyu Guard.

Jerome Kihore, was an outstanding example of the finest leaders of Kikuyu Society. A University Graduate from Makerere University in Uganda, he had worked for five years in Fort Hall achieving the appointment of Assistant District Officer. His death was the most telling blow the Mau Mau had yet delivered, for he was the person most concerned in the initial stages of the confession system which had done so much to break the hold of Mau Mau in Fort Hall.

The Mau Mau hoped their tactics would discourage others from joining

---

[134] Jock Rutherford 'A History of the Kikuyu Guard' p.21

the government forces. In fact, they had the opposite effect. Within two months, the numbers of Kikuyu Guard in Fort Hall alone had risen to almost three thousand. Fifty five Posts had been built to house them. The Mau Mau knew that if they were to succeed in their plans they would have to beat the Kikuyu Guard first and it was touch and go as to whether or not they would succeed. The attacks on Kikuyu Guard Posts increased and many were overrun and their occupants killed in the first six months until the forts were built in such a way that they could be more easily defended. Many Guards lost their lives during those first few months and several District Officers and D.Os.(K.G) were ambushed and killed or severely wounded in the most bloody and savage attacks. But with proper training and from the security of purpose built forts the Kikuyu Guard soon began to get the upper hand.

That the gangs in the forest were feeling the extent of the Kikuyu Guard's work is shown in the songs the gangs made up and sang in undertones in their forest hide-outs mostly at night. The following is typical of those songs (within the brackets are explanations of the literal translations):

You Home Guards come to us and tell us your sins

[Kikuyu Guards! Come and confess your sins to us that you may be forgiven]

Remember you Home Guards when you are hunting us you will be in trouble when we come out of the forest.

[Be warned, Kikuyu Guards, when you are hunting us; it will be you who will be the hunted ones when we win this war.]

When you are hunting us, Home Guards, we shall be given our freedom and our lands

[Remember, Kikuyu Guards, when we win this war we shall be free and we shall get back all the lands you stole from us]

Home Guards, you are fools. You were deceived. You gave away our lands because of food.

[Kikuyu Guards, you are fools. You have been deceived by the Colonialists. You have given away our land to the European settlers because you think the Europeans will always look after you (inferring they will not)].

You were deceived by the D.C. into becoming Home Guards. Now you have spoilt your people.

[The District Commissioner tricked you into becoming Kikuyu Guards and by so doing you have brought shame on your tribe.]

184

You should follow that D.C. to Europe and he will give you farms there.

[If you like the District Commissioner so much, you should go with him to Europe and tell him to give you land there.

This song is written by the young men of Kairu in our camp at Nyandarua.

[This song is written by the young men of Kairu, a village in Location 14, who live in our Mau Mau hideout in the Aberdare forest]

We sing in prayer to Ngai to help us beat the Europeans and our enemies.

[We sing and pray to our God Ngai to help us win this war and beat all our enemies (including the Kikuyu Guards)].

We shall be glad when the new day is born and those who are in gaol will be freed and those of us who are in the forest will be able to come out.

[We look forward to the day when those who are detained will be free and those of us who have to live in the forest will be able to come out and live a normal life.][135]

Many songs like these were composed by the more active leaders in the forest in order to keep the men's spirits up and to prevent them surrendering and to make sure there was no sympathy for the Kikuyu Guards.

Slowly but surely the Kikuyu Guards began to win more of the battles that took place around the forts and the ambushes they laid along the tracks that led down from the forest where the gangs were hiding. When the government realised that contrary to their initial expectations, not one of the Guards deserted and joined the Mau Mau and that not one single weapon was lost to the enemy by misconduct, they were issued with weapons more freely and so at last, had the means to defeat the enemy decisively. It is reliably estimated that in the Reserves, the Kikuyu Guard were almost entirely responsible for ridding their homelands of the scourge of Mau Mau. Without them and their informers and the assistance they gained from the population in general, Mau Mau would have continued to grow and persisted for much longer. The gangs would not have had to concentrate their resources in the Reserves and would therefore have been free to go into the settled areas more,

---

[135] Taken from documents captured by the author

with the result that many more lives would have been lost and the struggle more prolonged. The Fort Hall District Commissioner sums up the role the Guard played in his Foreword to '*The History of the Kikuyu Guard*':

> Looking back, it is the headman who has emerged as the key figure. He was the man in daily contact with the enemy; all the others were in his support. It was he, with his small band of fifty men who had to keep the nightly vigil, withstand attacks on his post, and by day go out in the Reserve—where many a peasant was a spy—to chase the boastful enemy. It is to their lasting credit that of the guns issued to the Kikuyu Guard under their command in Fort Hall, not one was lost through treachery or desertion.
>
> Casualty figures can only give a rough indication of the strain suffered. For the period from 21st October 1952 [the day after the Emergency was declared] to 31st December 1954, the Administration lost three District Officers, one Chief, nine Headmen, twenty-eight Tribal Policemen and two hundred and thirty four Kikuyu Guard. The deeds of these men must not be forgotten. They have saved the Kikuyu people from complete degradation and they have earned a place in Kenya's history.[136]

Inevitably there were exceptions to the good behaviour in the vast majority of the Kikuyu Guard. To an unscrupulous Headman, it was a very convenient time to settle old scores and to use his position for personal gain. The fact that some Chiefs and Headmen confiscated property including land, on flimsy excuses associated with membership of the Mau Mau, or of having been present at murders of other Kikuyu, must not be glossed over in a book of this nature. The Guard, though unpaid, were armed by the British Government and supported by them, and such occurrences, however rare they may have been, reflect badly on the Administration. The excuse that in wartime in general and in this conflict in particular, things happen that are beyond the control of the Government as a whole, cannot be side-stepped. Even the legality of the Kikuyu Guard itself must be questioned and answers provided.

These questions were posed by Acting Judge Cram in his summing up of a criminal case he heard at the Supreme Court at Nyeri in 1954. The case concerned six Kikuyu Guards from Ruthagathi Guard Post near Karatina, who

---

were accused of murdering two men they alleged were Mau Mau terrorists. In his seventeen thousand-word summing up, the Judge calls into serious question the legality of the Kikuyu Guard since its inception. He describes it as a spontaneous, unpaid, volunteer movement likened to the Local Defence Volunteers (LDV) that was formed in the U.K. under the threat of invasion from the Nazis in 1940. The LDV and their successors, the Home Guard wore a khaki arm band over their civilian clothes as a piece of uniform to show they were entitled to be treated as prisoners of war if they were ever captured by the Germans. The Kikuyu Guard wore a yellow armband for much the same reason. The British Home Guard were given legal status in 1940. The Judge pointed out that the Kikuyu Guard had no such legal status. He maintained that because there was no legal basis for their existence, this armband did not entitle them to be any different to their civilian neighbours. Specifically, it did not give them automatic permission to be in possession of firearms without a firearms certificate, or to detain any member of the population in any way other than an unofficial member of the population. The Judge held that in the absence of any regulation officially gazetting such a force as approved by law, they were neither military nor police and carry no more legality than a normal civilian. The Acting Judge was therefore implying that the Kikuyu Guard could be held as criminals for carrying firearms, detaining people, causing them bodily harm and killing them. While praising the work of the Kikuyu Guard: '...the debt owed by this Colony and by all races to the Kikuyu Guard is very great and the sacrifices made by many of its members [is] very high', the Judge set forth his interpretation of the illegality of the organisation though he offered no alternative method the Kikuyu people could have used within the law, to defend themselves against the determined attacks they were receiving.

Next, the acting Judge attacks the legality of detaining members of the Kikuyu population for screening or interrogation for indefinite periods of time. He cites the absence of any ordinance up to that date, December 1954, that allowed Headmen or Chiefs to detain anyone for periods longer than 12 hours, and in the case of an Administrative Officer or a Police Inspector to detain anyone longer than 48 hours without the authority of a magistrate, though the Police could detain for up to 14 days so long as the detention was in a prison or a police station. He also cites an Emergency Regulation that allows the detention of persons for up to six months but only into certain specific scheduled places of detention. The Judge implied that these regulations have been consistently flouted by the Kikuyu Guard and that people have been detained *ad infinitum* by Headmen and Chiefs in their Guard Posts and that this practice therefore, is in contravention of International Public Law.

The Judge writes:

> The matter is therefore abundantly clear. The freedoms from arbitrary arrest, arbitrary detentions without trial and arbitrary procedure by Courts, are freedoms which the inhabitants of the United Kingdom have struggled to secure for a period of a thousand years. They are not merely high-sounding words, but laws which protect us in our daily lives, if no longer from arbitrary acts of the Crown, at least from the acts of officials purporting to act with authority. The right to be brought to trial as soon as possible after arrest is a fundamental constitutional right recognised wherever British Administration rules. It is such a common, obvious and well-recognised right that it must be known to all men of any education and it is intuitively recognised even by primitive men.[137]

The Judge made it clear that he was unimpressed by the statement of the District Commissioner in the case before him, that he had made it amply clear to the Chief and Headmen in question that no violence of any sort was to be used in the extraction of confessions. The Judge said that every Kikuyu tribesman knows it is illegal to effect torture for whatever purpose and that it has been the subject of declared policy, not only of Her Majesty's Imperial Government, but also of the Kenya Government.

Acting Judge Cram then goes on to record the statements of various witnesses who stated that they were severely beaten during interrogation in the Kikuyu Guard Post, by, or under the orders of the six accused men, and gives his reasons for believing their statements to be true.

Finally the judge goes into considerable detail upon the matter of the African Appeal Court at Karatina, also in Nyeri District, which was referred to during the course of the trial. The Judge declares, *"On the clear evidence before this Court, it seems long out of time for some action to be taken to halt the career of this Court sitting at Karatina."* He makes no bones about accusing it of *"...judgements to have been obtained by fraud or collusion or to have been incompetently delivered, and indeed a horrid tale both the real and*

---

[137] Acting Judge Cram Summing up - Criminal Case No. 240 of 1954, dated 10th December 1954 p.18

oral evidence discloses. I did not ever contemplate that sitting on this bench in this Colony, I would hear or see such evidence. Were it not vouched for by the Court Officials ...it would be incredible."

The Judge takes the opportunity to lay bare the travesties of injustice that he found in this African Appeal Court run by elders under the supposedly watchful eye of the District Administration:

> There runs through all judicial systems from the most mature to the most immature, one golden thread, and that is a justice seen to be done which does not offend the fairmindedness of mankind. It is this universal sense of justice, equity and fairplay resident in nearly everyone's mind throughout time, that is one of the most hopeful of all signs in humanity.
>
> Now I must solemnly declare that the practices of the African Court at Karatina during the whole of this year are abysmally perverted and run contrary to the most elementary cannons of natural justice. It is a travesty of justice. It is a mockery to mention justice in the same connotation. Indeed it is not justice at all but naked oppression. I do not venture to forecast how long it may be, if ever, before this [Karatina] Court regains its prestige, if it ever had one, of doing justice. But it is long past time the African Courts Officer intervened.
>
> The Elders sitting on the immoral mockeries of justice it would seem, ought never again to be permitted to sit in judgement on their fellow Kikuyu. If I collate the evidence of the records, Registrars, registers and the accused, I find no divergence and almost complete corroboration, and this is how the Court sat and operated and it well knew what it was doing, for it was part of a vast conspiracy to pervert justice to the means and ends of war.[138]

The Judge then proceeds into an extended tirade against the Karatina Court. He describes how the first accused in his Court, the Headmen of the Ruthagathi Kikuyu Guard Post in question, sends out his *'armed bravoes'*, his junior Kikuyu Guards, to sweep 'suspects' into a net. 'Suspects', he defines as anyone who was believed to have had connections with Mau Mau, or anyone of whom the headman was jealous or even anyone whom the Headman disliked. All would be swept into the net and brought before the headman to confess at once from fear, or to sojourn in the unpleasant dens of the

---

[138] Ibid p.18

Ruthagathi Post. Some time later, they would be taken to the Appeal Court at Karatina where the Headman, out of the hearing of the prisoners, informed the Court elders who were to be the judges, the nature of the prisoners' evidence.

The Court then sat and the prisoners were brought in, the innocent with the guilty. At the first pleading, nothing was written down, unless those who saw the uselessness of doing aught else, elected to do so. Then there was a significant pause. The obdurate were given a chance 'to think matters over'. There was ample to influence their minds. Over against them was the Headman with his armed band of bravoes. Against them too was a hostile bench, primed with lies about which the prisoners knew nothing. And behind all was the shadow of the dismal cells at Ruthagathi — the flying whips and threats. Small wonder, therefore, that nearly all the prisoners gave way and pleaded guilty, their pleas recorded with lugubrious solemnity.[139]

Judge Cram explains in detail the records of that Court showing pleas of guilty from *'hundreds and hundreds'* of pleas, and convictions on the same charge throughout the year. *'Day after day, week in week out, month after month, the same charge the same plea and the same conviction'.* Even those that pleaded 'not guilty' were falsely and fraudulently recorded as 'guilty' and were convicted on that plea and fined or imprisoned just the same.

The common fine that was meted out was up to six thousand shillings, an enormous and almost impossible sum for the average Kikuyu to find at that time. This money went straight into the coffers of the South Nyeri District Administration and earmarked for 'African development'. He conjectures that the steep incline upwards of fine money should have attracted attention at District Headquarters; at least the Appeals Courts Officer should have sat sometimes with the Court to see how it operated, but no European ever sat within this Court. *'The innocent with the guilty were snatched from their lawful labours and stigmatised as Mau Mau adherents by these men and by this Court which was no longer a Court of Justice but a mere instrument of economic warfare.'*

The Judge describes the Headman as a man 'full of vanity'; delighted with the interference of the civil liberties of his tribesman and with the torture chambers of Ruthagathi where he extracted his corrupt, forged and tragically misleading 'confessions' and the vast number of convictions to his credit. He

---

[139] Ibid p.19

even accused the Headman's Defence Counsel of preening itself with a certain smugness that even if the Headman was to be found guilty of murder, it could be justified because the murdered person was a Mau Mau sympathiser.

This summing-up by Acting Judge Cram is an important document, because it could be held as a typical example of the deficiencies of the British Administration in 1954 and therefore it should be commented upon in the context of those who may read it 50 years or more after the events took place.

There can be no denial that Judge Cram's demonstration of the illegality of the Kikuyu Guard in 1953 is true, but there must be room for mitigation in the context of the situation that existed at that time. Those Kikuyu who opposed Mau Mau and all it stood for were desperate to counter an organisation whose practices were abhorrent to them, and faced with a worsening situation at the time, the Administration was being pressured to allow them to take up arms against these 'enemies of society'. The Mau Mau were murdering people with impunity, and by so doing had effectively

A Kikuyu Guard meeting to honour five guards for their successful sortie against a Mau Mau gang - Fort Hall 1954

declared war on those that were against them — a war created by the Mau Mau, not by those Kikuyu that were being murdered, nor by the British. The murders of Tribal Policemen and 'uncooperative' Kikuyu being carried out daily in 1953/4 were very real and very extensive. This had to be stopped by whatever means possible. Failure to do so would have been a dereliction of duty by the Government and a much greater crime than to sanction this Kikuyu Guard force, illegal though in strict terms, it may have been. New laws surely only come about because a new situation has developed with which existing laws cannot cope. Here was a situation that had not arisen before but about which something had to be done immediately.

There was no coercion of the Kikuyu to join the defence force. On the contrary, they begged the authorities to allow them to take up arms against an enemy who was murdering their people and stealing their young men and women to go to the forest and thence to Settler's farms to murder the owners and disembowel their cattle. It should be remembered that although they were given free food, the Kikuyu Guard were never paid.

It surely makes sense for the Administration to take what must have been the only course open to them at that time. Cram, again with the best interests of both the Kikuyu and the Administration at heart, wanted, quite rightly, to highlight the illegality of the matter. He did so, and probably as a result, the system was changed forthwith. This is what the Acting Judge was paid to do. But it is unreasonable to show this as a typical example of the shortcomings of the British Administration and use it as a stick to beat the British 50 years later. It is to distort Cram's findings, and put them to a use he did not intend, and condemnation now, does not take into account the absence of options available to the authorities *at the time*. The main thing in 1953/4 was to counter the terrorism by whatever means available, and nice though it would have been to have time to prepare a regulation to make the Guard a legal entity *before* it was formed, in the heat of the battle, so to speak, can those who were responsible for protecting the people, be blamed for allowing an organisation, where later it's legality came to be called into question, which, during its lifetime accounted for 63% of all Mau Mau killed or captured?

The Judge also brought to the attention of the Administration things that were long overdue regarding the Court at Karatina. There is no doubt that what went on was wrong and inexcusable—wrong, that is, in the generally accepted definition of 'Natural Justice' as the Judge makes very clear, and inexcusable, *because they were disobeying orders from their senior officers*. It may be argued justly, that having taken over the responsibility, rightly *or wrongly*, of imposing British 'Natural Justice' on them, the British had a duty to ensure it was carried out properly. Not to have done so in this case, is inexcusable.

The question arises, however, as to whether or not Western Man could have expected his interpretation of 'Natural Justice' to be applied to African peoples even then in 1954. Western culture had one thousand years of judicial evolution behind it. Kenyans, at that time had no more than sixty years of their imposed interpretation of 'Natural Justice'. Before the British arrived in Kenya and started imposing their laws on the Africans, the two cultures interpreted 'Natural Justice' quite differently. Who will be so bold as to say which was correct? 'Correct', that is, in the way that Judge Cram defines it: *'that which serves the people best'.*

In 1888, sixty six years before this case took place, if a Kikuyu man was a persistent stealer of goats, he was not tried before a Court with the niceties of Counsels to speak on his behalf, experts to advise him and a learned Judge who would, we hope, have given an impartial verdict having heard all sides. He was *'burnt alive with grass round his neck, or stabbed with a spear like a sheep.*[140] This was Kikuyu 'Natural Justice'. Something they believed in and had practiced, who knows, for a thousand years previously. (How many times, even within the last 25 years, have I been told by peasant Kikuyu and Masai, 'We do not understand the Western way of dealing with criminals.')

Today, in 2004, mob justice takes place all over sub-Saharan Africa. Not a week goes by that a Nairobi newspaper does not report the stoning of a (suspected?) thief by the crowd. I am quite certain it was the norm, for years after the British began to impose their order, for a suspect goat stealer to suffer mob justice, whether or not he was the real culprit. Everyone knew this, and an innocent man would not necessarily blame the people if he was punished by mistake. *He would look upon it as something between himself and his God, Ngai.* He would accept that Fate or Ngai had decreed that he should be the one to die. Moreover, 'justice', even if it was mob justice, would have been done, and would have been seen to have been done, and the message would still have got through to the guy who did steal the goat, that next time, he might not be so lucky. So therefore the punishment, even though it may have been the wrong person, will have done its job, and at minimum cost to the extremely limited resources available. Life—human as well as animal—was, and still is

---

[140] Routledge *'With a Prehistoric People'* Cass 1968 p.216

not the number one priority in Africa as it is in Western Culture, something Westerners find extremely difficult to come to terms with.

The African Appeal Court about which Cram is so derogatory, is surely a vestige of what was 'Natural Justice' applied up to, and perhaps, well beyond 1888. It is most likely that those who sat on the bench in that Court in 1954 (they were all Kikuyu), were not, *in Kikuyu terms*, considered wicked by the people on whom they sat in judgement. To be able to recognise their wickedness one needs to have a thousand years of judicial evolution and awareness behind one. In the absence of those thousand years, they were accepted by the local community as administering the only kind of justice they knew. If a few innocent people got caught up in the net and had to suffer the same consequences as the guilty, that is the price they were prepared to pay. An illiterate African wrongly accused, does not blame the judge who may have come to the wrong conclusion, he blames the curse that had been put on him by an unknown enemy, or he blames himself for having in some way offended *Ngai* whose punishment this was. Fate or *Ngai*, one and the same thing, he believes, intervened and one cannot control Fate. Western Man, with his thousand years of experience and literacy behind him, knows that Karatina Court was wrong, and the correction of its 'injustice' and the teaching of the manner in which a civilised community works, goes to the very core of the job the British were in Kenya to carry out.

That the elders sitting in judgment in that Court were wrong because they were not obeying orders from their European masters, is an entirely different matter.

In hindsight, where the British may have got it wrong, was to impose their moral codes too quickly or too early. It may have been better to try and change practices which were considered to be wrong, not by imposition or coercion, but by gentle persuasion and sensible arguments.

Maybe there was an error of judgement on the part of the British to impose the British legal requirement for a witness to swear on the bible before giving evidence. Had the traditional oath been allowed to remain as in traditional Kikuyu law, things might have turned out quite differently for Acting Judge Cram. Jomo Kenyatta in his book *'Facing Mount Kenya'* explains very clearly that if the British had carried on with the traditional oathing system in Court cases, instead of the method of swearing on the bible – an oath *'which has no meaning at all to an African, one that has no binding force, moral or religious.'* it would have had a totally different result in court cases. The effect of introducing something as foreign to them as swearing on the bible, *'has meant a fabrication of evidence where bribery and corruption is the order of the day'[141]*.

A good example of where the British did go wrong is given by Juanita Carberry, someone who was born and brought up in Kenya.

> I was very upset at what I saw as the appalling injustice meted out to an African woman in a 'circus' which called itself a British Court of Law. Sixty years later, I am still appalled. The woman had killed her child because it had leprosy. In killing the baby the woman had acted in accordance with the custom of her tribe. It goes against a mother's nature to kill her infant no matter what is wrong with it. Afterwards she was told that under British Law she would have to tell the District Commissioner what she had done, so she walked fifteen miles through the Kikuyu Reserve to Nyeri to do what she believed was the right thing. She had concealed nothing. I asked what would happen to her. 'She'll hang', they told me. So much for British justice.[142]

If the British, and particularly some of the missionaries had been less hasty in condemning practices that had stood the test of time in primitive Africa, we might have been better teachers. Female circumcision is a good example. Set out, perhaps, to change practices, and give good reasons—medical, in the case of circumcision—why it is an unwise practice, but be patient and have good arguments that can easily be understood as to why the British system is better. But be aware it may take many years, if not generations to change traditions peacefully. It took the British over 50 years finally to abolish the slave markets in Zanzibar, and it was done by persuasion rather than imposition.

Even so, when all is said and done, the British were surely better teachers than other Colonial powers — the Belgians in the Congo and the French in Algeria, not to mention the Portuguese and the Spanish!

This in no way excuses the fact that under the British Administration, what went on in that African Appeal Court was wrong. It is to *offer an explanation* for the reason it occurred. It was, surely, no more than a grave aberration or lack of sufficient control by the relevant Officers, and as such, Cram in his position of Supreme Court Judge, rightly brought it to the attention of the Administration (and castigated them soundly in so doing). It should not

---

[141] Jomo Kenyatta – *'Facing Mount Kenya'* – Mercury Books 1961 p.225
[142] Juanita Carberry *'Child of Happy Valley'* Heinemann 1999 p.164

be seen as the norm, indeed, if it was, Cram would not have been so vehement in his lengthy condemnation of it. It should be seen for what it was: vestiges of Kikuyu 'law' being highlighted by a proper authority which was, in fact, changed forthwith. It is wrong, therefore to portray this much publicised case as though it was typical of what went on under the British Administration, and use it as a stick to beat them.

Confirmation that things have now, in 2004, slipped back into the pre-colonial mode, is there for all to see. After Independence, the Kenya Judiciary, at least in the lower Courts, are still following on the lines of that Native Court in 1954. According to the Daily Telegraph on 4th October 2003 the 'Tariff of Corruption' in the Kenya Courts is currently:

To be cleared of murder: 40,000/- to 1m/-
To be cleared of rape or manslaughter: 20,000/- to 500,000/-
To bribe a Judge to deliver a particular verdict: 50,000/- to 1.6m/-
To bribe a magistrate: 4,000/- to 150,000/-
All at the exchange rate of £1 to 132/- (Kenya shillings)

So much for Western 'teaching'.

The murder of the two Kikuyu by the Kikuyu Guard was, of course, illegal, and it is accepted that this was not an isolated case. The reasons were as many, I suspect, as there were murders. In Western terms there is no excuse. Acting Judge Cram found all the six accused guilty, and rightly so on the evidence as given. The only mitigation there can be is that these were Africans, Kikuyu, and this is what happened in Kikuyuland then and still happens even now and even more so. Africa is, after all, Africa, much as some would like to think of it as Europe or America. One only has to listen to Francis Bok[143], from the Sudan, to know that slavery is alive and well all over sub-Saharan Africa. Life is cheap and the taking of it is still not considered the heinous crime that it is in other parts of the world. Acknowledging this and facing up to the realities of it, is to begin to understand Africans and thereby to help them change, and see it our way. The cardinal mistake is to make comparisons. 'Primitive Africa' did not allow the luxury of our high-flown principles of the sanctity of life. The Kikuyu race would not have survived if it had. Up to the time the European

---

[143] Francis Bok *'Escape from Slavery'* St. Martin's Press 2003

powers came on the scene it was a question pure and simple of survival, and sadly, since the European powers left, it has reverted back to what it was before they arrived, though perhaps in not so great an intensity. The wanton murders that occur in and around Nairobi are still terrifying, though today it's mostly about money and wealth as opposed to starvation and survival.

In a letter from Nairobi dated 12th March 2002 from a Kikuyu lady of about 30 years of age, who was commenting on my historical novel '*My Enemy: My Friend*', writes: *...Every time I watch the News here, and as I monitor the political trend and the current situation in Kenya, I cannot help thinking about "my enemy my friend". The same thing is threatening to be repeated in front of our eyes and it is such a pity that the government of the day is allowing it and it's questionable that they do not approve. This I say cos of groupings like "the Mungiki, Kamjesh, Jeshi la .." and others that might have not been made public yet. Last week, "the Mungiki" murdered 20 innocent citizens in one of the estates in Nairobi overnight just like that. So between you and me, you can now see why I relate the current political front with the scenario presented in your book. I am only hoping that the situation will not escalate. Only time will tell....*

So a few of the seeds sowed by the British have germinated.

The Kikuyu Guard was disbanded on 31st December 1954 and a new force of Tribal Police came into being on 1st January 1955. The new force had all the legal backing required, and continued successfully with their aims to rid the whole of Kikuyuland of the Mau Mau terror.

The creation of the new force coincided with a general amnesty not only for those Mau Mau who had carried out murders, so long as they gave themselves up to the authorities by a certain date (January 18th 1955) but also for all outstanding cases against Kikuyu Guards. Leaflets were dropped over the forest and the Reserves explaining exactly what the terms of the amnesty were and what they meant. Very few terrorists took up the offer, but it was a shrewd and convenient method of regaining the faithful Kikuyu's confidence, which had been severely dented by the amount of criminal investigations that had been carried out against them in recent weeks. The C.I.D. arm of the Kenya Police, ever keen to carry out their work efficiently, were investigating instances of 'on the spot' justice being carried out under such excuses as 'attempting escape after capture' or the planting of evidence, often ammunition, on suspects — justice that the Police suspected was either revenge killing or the settling of old scores both of which were against the (British) law. By the end of 1954, so many Kikuyu Guards were either 'under suspicion', or had been formally charged with capital or other crimes that they were becoming disillusioned with the Government who seemed to show their gratitude for the Guards 'loyalty' by charging them with criminal offences. C-in-C General Erskine felt there was so great a danger of them deserting with their weapons to 'the other side', that he declared a general amnesty for both the Kikuyu Guards and the Mau Mau.

Phil Sykes was one of the first intelligence officers sent to Fort Hall at the beginning of the Emergency. He writes:

Mwangi Kimotho was one of the most courageous members of our Kikuyu guard Post at Muriranjas in Fort Hall. This Post was set up by Derek Dansie in 1953 and became his base. I joined him later that year. Mwangi was one of the first Kikuyu Guard to join up.

Derek and I were often called out at short notice to assist some Guard Post under attack from Mau Mau and Mwangi would always be the first to volunteer to go on such sorties. He was the most reliable and efficient member of that team and earned himself high accolades from us and from his fellow Guards.

One day, the C.I.D. came and arrested Mwangi and later charged him with murder. I personally investigated the reason for the charge. I found that on one of the Kikuyu Guard patrols he led, a cache of recently brewed beer was found which the patrol members proceeded to drink, there and then, on the spot! During the drinking orgy that followed, an argument transpired and someone was shot and killed. Although none of the party could remember who fired the shot, Mwangi as leader, was held responsible. If he had been convicted he would have been hanged. That was the law.

Derek and I decided we could not let this happen without a proper defence, so we had a 'whip-round' and managed to get a good lawyer out from Nairobi to defend him. In the end thankfully he was found not guilty.

I only tell you this to show that the C.I.D. were just as likely to take action against the Kikuyu Guard as they were against the Mau Mau or anyone else.[144]

---

[144] Phil Sykes Kenya Regiment and D.O. (K.G.) – Pers comm..

The accusations that the British Administration 'turned a blind eye' to atrocities perpetrated by the Kikuyu Guard are unfounded. Those of us who were in the Security Forces during the Emergency had no illusions about the situation. The C.I.D. were everywhere, and were constantly breathing down our necks. We had it continually drummed into us by our senior officers that the authorities would not hesitate to bring to (British) justice the perpetrators of what in terms of English Law were deemed to be crimes — but what in Kikuyu terms might be considered 'natural justice'.

Routledge, even as early as 1905, sees the efficacy of traditional justice over Western methods. '*The present and avowed object of the East African Judiciary is to suppress native justice altogether as derogatory to the dignity of British Courts. Even allowing for all the imperfections of primitive methods, this shows a point of view at which it is hard to arrive. The effect on the native mind of a culprit, whose guilt is well known, let off because of some technical flaw in the evidence, is disastrous to a degree.*'[145]

---

[145] Routledge '*With a Prehistoric People*' Cass 1968 p.220

CHAPTER NINE

THE PSEUDO GANGS

"You know, Bwana, you will never beat the Mau Mau thinking like a White man. I am an African, a Kikuyu; I know what goes on in their minds. Let me do the thinking for you and together we will bring this war to an end a lot quicker." Mwangi Murabasha to Capt. Ian Feild DCLI

If the Kikuyu Guard were responsible for bearing the brunt of the Mau Mau onslaught in the Reserves, the pseudo gangs finished the job in the forests. The forests of Mount Kenya and the Aberdares at that time covered several hundred square miles. They were thick virgin *podocarp* forests of cedars, olives and podocarpus trees with large areas of bamboo so thick that it was difficult to walk in between the 15 centimetre-thick stems, which reached to heights of 30 metres. In these forests, dangerous wildlife abounded. Herds of elephant and buffalo were common and anyone walking around in the forest had to know how to evade the determined charge of a rhino that came thundering down the path towards you. It was in these forests that the gangs of terrorists lived and hid, and from where they would make sorties down into the Reserves or into the Settled Areas to carry out their murderous attacks.

A clearing in the bamboo forest

Conventional military tactics in those days had few answers to these gangs who had made this dense forest their home and in which they could move about with such comparative ease and with the stealth and silence of a forest duiker. Soldiers on patrol in these forests were weighted down with packs and rifles, ammunition bandoliers and radio transmitters. They moved about on the steep and slippery forest tracks with difficulty and could not help making a considerable noise so that every Mau Mau within half a kilometre could hear them coming and would have plenty of time to move out of their way. Handicapped as they were, the fully equipped British soldier could have little impact on the gangs in the forest other than to destroy their hideouts and keep them moving on.

It was the removal of these gangs from their hiding places in that vast area of forest, and the prevention of their murderous assaults into the Kikuyu homelands and onto the European farms, that spawned the evolution of pseudo gangs. Like the Kikuyu Guard, it was the local people themselves, under the control and leadership of European officers who provided the means for these 'cloak and dagger' operations to work successfully. It was they who carried out the difficult and dangerous task of contacting the real gangs both in the forest and in the Reserves either to eliminate them or to bring them out to safety, and it was they who carried out the 'turning' or conversion of those that had just come out of the forest gangs. And the most extraordinary thing about the whole pseudo gang fraternity was that, apart from the European Officers, its members were exclusively those Kikuyu who had been in the forest—the ex-Mau Mau terrorists themselves. Not only that, but it was usually the *leaders* of those gangs, having been captured and 'turned' by their former colleagues, who became the experts and militant executors of the pseudo gangs and returned to the forest to seek out their erstwhile colleagues, sometimes within a matter of an hour or so from their own capture.

The reasons for this extraordinary conduct are almost beyond Western Man's comprehension. They are buried deep in the psyche of the African Kikuyu people, and may never surface unless or until they are exposed to some traumatic event that involves their survival. *The indigenous cultural modes still permeate the lives of many people who at first sight seem totally detribalised [Westernised]; so that some exposition of this general background is highly necessary for the understanding of Africans today*[146].

Foremost in the Kikuyu subconscious had always been the need for survival. This basic instinct, carried over from previous generations, was paramount. If it were not so, they could not have survived as a people against all the hazards pristine Africa presented for humankind.

---

[146] Dr. J.C. Carothers – *The Psychology of Mau Mau 1954 p.2*

In his fight for survival primitive Kikuyu man saw little fault in taking life—human or other. It was no great sin to chop off an enemy's head, and an enemy could be anyone who threatened his survival, or his family's welfare. Where there was uncertainty about the threat, no benefits of doubt could be given and no chances taken. The name of the game was survival and this meant reducing as much as possible the competition, particularly where food was concerned. Two overriding fears, starvation and bewitchment, lay at the root of most homicide and provided the need to take positive action against a perceived 'enemy'.

For example, the Masai were given to preying on the Kikuyu. They liked their nice plump women and girls but more especially—the Masai staple diet being milk—they liked their strong healthy cows. But at a time when the Masai were severely weakened by disease and famine they came in for much slaughter by the Kikuyu. Francis Hall illustrates this in his letters home from the village of Kikuyu in 1894. Hall had been feeding and protecting several hundred Masai – remnants of the Kaputei section who had been so reduced by famine and internecine wars that they had sought refuge from the Kikuyu with Hall, in Fort Smith, even though it was close to the Kikuyu homeland. The local Kikuyu people, sworn enemies of the Masai, did not like the presence of these Masai within their territory, even though they were unarmed and had no warriors with them.

> The local Kikuyu begged me to send some of the Masai out of the country as there were too many. I had warned the Masai about this, and the following day I started [some of] them off with an escort of 40 of my men. Unbeknown to me, the blackguardly brutes of the Kikuyu followed them at a distance, out of sight, and when they reached the edge of Kikuyu country and my men had returned, they fell on the Masai and carried off as many women and children as they could, killing the men. You may reckon I was a bit mad when I heard of it, and called the Kikuyu Chiefs at once, and after cursing them until language failed me, I ordered them to return all the Masai they had captured, and pay a fine of 100 goats within 3 days, or I would wipe them off the face of the earth."[147]

This illustrates the casual attitude the Kikuyu had towards eliminating those who might constitute a threat to them in the future (and the booty that went

---

[147] Francis Hall – unpublished letters home 5th July 1894

with it); it also demonstrates the kind of punishment they understood and respected. Hall's orders were complied with forthwith.

We have seen in the first chapters of this book that primitive or preliterate Africans, only fifty years before the Emergency, did not have the luxury of such Western characteristics as compassion, forgiveness or tolerance. Pride they had in abundance. Courage was never lacking and respect for age, leadership, seniority or tutorage was an inherent feature, but anyone or anything that was likely to produce rivalry or competition had to be eliminated by whatever means available. These inherited traits can surely not be bred out of a race in a generation or two, so it can be understood that if survival simply meant changing allegiances to one side or another, this was far too trivial a matter to warrant serious consideration.

If, when captured, a Kikuyu was threatened or beaten up, he would be as stubborn as a mule. To an interrogator, he would give away nothing of any value. But when captured and shown respect by his captors, and given arguments he could understand as to why it would be in his own best interests (of survival) to give information, he responded accordingly. When it was pointed out to an intelligent Kikuyu man who had just fallen captive to a pseudo gang team composed of his old friends that it was surely futile to fight with pangas and home-made guns against a sophisticated army who had Land Rovers, radios and Bren guns, and who could call on their air force to drop 500kg bombs on them, he could easily appreciate the argument. If it was then suggested that he could not only save himself and his family but also the lives of others of his clan, simply by changing sides and working for the Government, it was not difficult for him to contemplate such a radical change of loyalties. If, finally, it was suggested to him that a much better way of achieving self rule or independence for Kenyans would be to finish the war in which everyone was suffering, and then to fight with well chosen words in the corridors of power in Nairobi and London, the job was done and he would come to the fold like a lamb. Faced with sensible arguments, presented, not by Europeans, but by his own peers, the intelligent Kikuyu were bold enough to admit their mistakes, confess, and join the stronger side. The oath certainly held many back from 'turning', but we found that a combination of intelligent argument, respect for the person, and the imposition of strong leadership on them were more likely than anything else to overcome the powers of the oath.

Violence never entered into the conversion of a captured man. Once a man was captured or had surrendered, there was simply no need to inflict pain to get information from him. Any information of value could only be obtained if it was given voluntarily.

It is impossible to understand the actions of Mau Mau, the 'atrocities' that followed and these apparently anomalous changes of loyalties, in isolation of the Kikuyu's traditional tribal culture, their psyche and their inherent beliefs.

As a young man I was seconded from the Kenya Regiment to Special Branch Fort Hall and took a part in this work in 1954/55. I still retain a copy of all the seventy or so hand-written interrogation reports that I carried out which was part of our work under the District Military Intelligence Officer (DMIO) Capt. Ian Feild M.C. I also have copies of documents that were taken from forest hideouts or from captured, surrendered or dead Mau Mau personnel. Added to this, I have the entire collection of letters home that I wrote during that time, which my parents so carefully and so wisely kept, and these act as a kind of diary of events. More importantly, I have received invaluable assistance from many of those who were involved in the same work, who are also keen to see that a true history not only of the methods we used but also of the extraordinarily heroic deeds so many of our Kikuyu friends carried out during that time, are recorded for posterity.

Our main job was the gathering of intelligence, and our Commander in Chief, General Sir George Erskine, writing the Foreword to a book by a neighbouring DMIO, Capt. (later General Sir) Frank Kitson, sets out the reasons why our work was so important in this particular conflict.

> The need to develop a first class intelligence system is obvious. In these internal security situations you must develop your intelligence service to meet your needs and you must not be content with a general picture and trends. You must know your enemy's mind, his organisation and every detail you can possibly find out about him. Only when you know this will it be possible to deal with the root of the trouble and the leaders. Even when you have the information, it is often difficult to make use of it quickly enough through the orthodox security forces. The secret of success of the Special Forces [in Kenya] as developed by Frank Kitson, was that they put themselves in a position to follow up their information

instantaneously and do something about it.[148]

The first idea of pseudo gang operations against the Mau Mau came quite early on in the Emergency in Fort Hall. John Dykes, a Sergeant in the Kenya Regiment and one of the few Europeans who could speak fluent Kikuyu, was seconded to Special Branch in Fort Hall as a Field Intelligence Officer (FIO). His job was to interrogate terrorists who were captured or who had surrendered. Soon after he began his work, he realised there was a potential for gathering information by pretending to be a real Mau Mau gang visiting a hut at the dead of night – something the real gangs did regularly.

Having discussed the possibilities at some length with my Special Branch Constable and my Tribal Policeman, Mwangi, together with the headman of my local Kikuyu Guard Post, we decided to try it out one night on a hut close to the main road where I could park the Land Rover without raising any suspicions. It was in August 1953 when the real gangs were top dogs in the Reserve and roamed almost at will. I decided not to tell my boss what I was planning, as I wanted to satisfy myself as to whether it was a real possibility. During my interrogations I had established roughly how the gangs operated in the Reserve, and what their tactics were for gathering food and recruits from the local population.

The first time I went out, I took six Kikuyu Guards, as well as Mwangi, and the Police Constable both dressed in their civilian clothes. We went to the first hut we came across which was quite close to a main road. We had decided that I would stay outside with the Police Constable and three Kikuyu Guards, while Mwangi and the other three guards would try to gain entry to the hut. By chance, the hut was only occupied by a woman, and Mwangi, who was armed with rifle, was immediately accepted as a genuine Mau Mau together with the other three. He told the woman that he was a leader from Nairobi and was looking for recruits to join his gang. The woman immediately accepted them and prepared tea for them. She proceeded to tell them all she knew about the local Mau Mau set up; who was responsible for gathering food for the local gangs, and who they should contact for recruits. All their questions were readily answered, and within half an hour, Mwangi had more information about the local set-up than I could have expected from a week's formal interrogation of the woman.

---

[148] Frank Kitson *'Gangs and Counter Gangs'* Barrie & Rockliff 1960. Foreword by Gen. Sir George Erskine

This one operation proved beyond doubt that not only were the Mau Mau in total command of the locality, but also that this type of operation was going to bring us much more information than simply interrogating prisoners. I did another trial run and this time was nearly caught by the local police who happened to be on patrol in the same area. This made me realise I was going to have to tell my boss what I was doing so that he could get the area cleared of all other operations for that night.

My immediate boss was Capt. Ian Feild who was the DMIO, who reported to the head of Special Branch. Ian was very interested in my ideas and said he would bring up my request for operating clearance at the next District Military Operations meeting.

Unfortunately the District Commissioner immediately vetoed the idea of carrying out these kind of pseudo gang operations saying that it was unjust and an unacceptable method of warfare. His actual words were, 'it is not cricket, my man.' So I was not officially allowed to do it, but nevertheless I did carry out a few more operations, though I found we had to be more careful of our own forces than of the Mau Mau. Soon others were doing it openly in other areas, and eventually our DC relented and from then on we began to get information pouring in.[149]

I was posted to the same area of Fort Hall some months after John had carried out these first trial runs, and by the time I arrived the methods he and others had initiated were well-practised. Our work was fascinating and exciting, but what made it even more interesting was the fact that we were now allowed to follow-up the information we gained from our own interrogations. Once we gained the confidence of the person we were interrogating, if he or she had something of operational value to give us we were allowed to follow it up, and if possible to act on it. Later on, much of the initial interrogation work was done, not by us Europeans, but by members of our team, who were, without exception, all ex-Mau Mau activists themselves.

As FIOs, besides our interrogation work we formed a network of informers in our allotted areas of the Reserve. These informers, who were given numbers rather than names, provided us with the information about the gangs in the forest and their supporters in the Reserve. The informers were usually ordinary members of society who had a particular grudge against the

Mau Mau for some reason. There were a few people who had managed to slip through the net and had not taken the oath, so were not bound by it. Such people were more likely to become willing informers. Some were even double agents, giving information to both sides – a very hazardous occupation. They were paid according to the value of the information they fed us, and were usually worked or 'operated' not by us Europeans as it was too dangerous for them to be seen talking to a member of the Security Forces, but by members of our team who dressed in ordinary civilian clothes and were *in cognito*.

Like all informers, they lived a perilous existence, and sadly many, living in such a close community, were compromised and had to pay with their lives. So it meant that contacting them had to be done with the utmost care. Certainly, at the beginning of the pseudo-gang operations, it was the informers who provided us with a picture of the past, present and future activities of the gangs. Later on it was the gangs themselves that provided us with all the information we needed.

While the operational members of our teams, except for ourselves, were exclusively ex-Mau Mau terrorists, members of the support team were mostly

Part of our pseudo gang team - Nyakianga, Fort Hall, March 1955
All are ex-terrorists except the Tribal Policeman in uniform

ordinary civilians. But all were Kikuyu, and all were totally trustworthy.

If an informer had information for us, he would leave a note in a 'Dead Letter box' (DLB) often with just his number written on it. This would be sufficient for his 'operator', one of our team, to know he had something to tell us. The operator would meet the man casually in the road, so as to raise no suspicion, and the information would be passed quickly. If it was too dangerous to meet in daylight, the operator might have to visit the informer's hut at night, and this would involve a more serious operation involving us and the team, as there was a dusk to dawn curfew in operation throughout the Reserve, and anyone found breaking the curfew would be in danger of being shot without question.

It was often the informer's information that someone was coming down from the forest on a certain night to collect food from a relative. The FIO might then decide to try and capture the food gatherer by means of a 'reception party'. This would entail a team of five or six led by the FIO, setting off at dead of night in a Land Rover to a place some distance from the target hut. The team would be dressed as a bona fide Mau Mau gang. The FIO would blacken his face and wear a black wig and the team would wear clothes that had either been captured from other terrorists or that they themselves had worn in the forest.[150]

Pseudo gangsters - Nyakianga 1955

Two of our ex-terrorist pseudo gangsters in full dress. They are armed with home-made guns, a simi, knives and a whistle. By 1955 the clothes of the terrorists in the forest are wearing thin and are much more ragged than when they first went to the forest in 1953, so the pseudo teams have to copy them.

Once the team had arrived in the area, the vehicle would be hidden away from the road (so that any other Security Force's vehicle passing and seeing an empty Land Rover on the side of the road, did not stop to investigate). The team would move off, led by the informer's operator who would know the

---

[150] Details of pseudo gang work and other operations are given in the author's historical novel *'My Enemy: My Friend'* ISBN 095447130X

precise location of the target hut. From now on, the team would behave exactly as a Mau Mau gang, acting as if they were walking through the Reserve at night. The leader of the 'gang', the FIO, would be at the back of the group, which was normal procedure, so that in the unlikely event that the 'gang' met up with a real gang en route, it would be easy to pass themselves off as bona fide Mau Mau. The FIO, even though he was heavily disguised, could easily be recognised as a European at close quarters, so he had to remain at the back and out of sight as much as possible.

When the target hut was reached, a previously arranged plan would be put into operation. It would be likely that only two of the team would try to gain entry to the hut, while the others remained outside. The FIO would be one of those who remained in the background while the pseudo work was going on.

The object of the operation would be to capture the food gatherer and there would be many ways of doing this without raising suspicions too early in the proceedings. This would require the utmost caution and split second decisions by the two 'pseudos' in the hut. Posing as part of a bona fide gang like this could only be possible if those who were carrying out the task had been Mau Mau themselves. Any Kikuyu who had not spent time in a gang and who had not lived in the forest, would immediately arouse suspicion. Apart from his knowledge of the forest hideouts, the clothes he would be wearing and his lack of strong bodily odour would immediately give him away.

The two pseudos in the hut would probably try and trick the food gatherer to come outside for a moment on the pretext, for example, of handing him some ammunition, and once outside and out of earshot he would be pounced on, and a hand slapped over his mouth. His hands would be tied together and he would be rushed back to the the Land Rover, bundled in and taken back to the team's headquarters.

Having got him safely back to the team's base, one or two members of the team would immediately go to work on the new recruit to try and 'turn' him. This would be done as soon as possible after his capture while he was still in a state of shock having realised he had been caught by a government patrol posing as a bona fide gang. Most Mau Mau would be terrified of falling into government hands, having been told by their leaders they would be tortured and die a horrible death, an idea impressed upon them in order to discourage any thoughts of surrendering. When they realised they were in government hands, but being interrogated by friendly Kikuyu, who might well have been in the same gang as they were only a short time ago, they were so amazed that they usually 'talked' well for the first few hours. It was not advisable to leave them to rest and sleep before the initial interrogation took place. Once they felt rested and secure, with a good meal in their bellies they would be more inclined to think up devious ways of telling lies. One had to strike while the iron was red hot and that would be within an hour or so of capture. The FIO might sit in on this 'turning' session if he spoke Kikuyu, as it had to be done in their native tongue, but the main conversion would be carried out by those who knew the right questions to ask, and the right arguments to put to them.

The main object of this initial conversation, would be to get the man to tell where their hideout was and who was in it; what weapons they had and how they deployed their sentries. Clearly, the best person to carry out this task would be someone who had been in the same gang from which the person had just come. The man being questioned would be amazed to see his old colleague was still alive and working for the government, and the interrogator would know exactly what was going through his mind having been in the same position himself, perhaps only days before. He would therefore be able to ask the most appropriate questions and know whether or not he was receiving the correct answers. Naturally it did not always work like clockwork, but once the FIO had set up the facility and had one or two ex-terrorists in his team to help him with the questioning, the conversions came more quickly and more easily, and the information collected was of a much higher standard.

Once the captured man had started giving answers that were known to be true, the next stage would be to get him to agree to take the team back into the forest to the hide-out from which he had so recently come. This was the tricky part, because once the man realised he was not going to die, and once he saw how his friends were living in comparative luxury at the expense of the government, he was not so keen to go back to the forest with all the dangers and privations that involved. However, if he began to object, it was threatened that if he did not take the team back to his old hide-out, he would be handed over to the Criminal Investigation Department of the Police (CID), and would be charged with consorting with an illegal organisation and land up in a detention camp. Whereas if he agreed to take the team back into the forest, and they were successful at getting out at least some of the gang, he might be accepted into the team and share the luxuries of life that he saw around him. Given these alternatives, very few elected not to lead the team back into forest.

Once agreement had been reached, and there was no going back on his story, the man would be given a good meal and allowed to rest. The team would then prepare itself to carry out a sortie into the forest that same evening. It had to be arranged quickly, because the captured food gatherer would be expected to arrive back in the hide-out with his load of food, within 24 hours, and this was an important factor in the ensuing operation.

Firstly and most importantly, clearance had to be obtained from the military for the operation to take place in that sector of the forest. The team could not afford to run into a patrol of the Security Forces that were carrying out their own operations in the same area. The FIO would approach his DMIO for this clearance, which would be obtained through the highest military authority in Nairobi. Sometimes it was impossible to give such clearance and the operation had to be called off. Losses by 'friendly fire' could not be risked in this type of special operation.

If the operation was sanctioned by Nairobi and the decision had been made to go ahead, the team would be dropped off by vehicle at the forest edge, with a rendezvous for collection later. They would move off through the forest, now shrouded in darkness, and once again, act as a normal Mau Mau gang. From this time forward, the FIO would leave it to the food gatherer and his operator to lead the 'gang' through the forest towards the hide-out which may entail a walk of several hours along elephant tracks with all the hazards of meeting herds of buffalo and other dangerous wildlife. Not until the team got close to the hide-out would they halt. When they were within earshot of the hideout and could see the glow of the camp fire and perhaps glimpse the thatched bamboo huts, they would know for certain the hideout was occupied. The FIO would then discuss with the other members of the team a strategy to enter the hide-out. The two main objects of the attack would be firstly to capture as many weapons as possible and secondly to capture the leaders of the gang. It was therefore of the utmost importance to have a clear picture as to where the main weapons were kept and where the leaders might be found. This information would be obtained from the food-gatherer guide. The team had the advantage of complete surprise and they had to be able to use this in the most economical way and to the best advantage possible. It would be unlikely that the inmates would have time to gather their weapons and use them, therefore it was unlikely that they would stand and fight. They would simply dash away from the hide-out as soon as they realised the 'enemy' was in their midst.

In an ideal situation, some members of the team would go to the leader's hut first and try to capture him before he could arouse the rest of his gang. At

KENYA, THE KIKUYU AND MAU MAU

the same time, other members of the team would go to the huts were they had been told the weapons were kept. By this time the rest of the gang would probably have realised what was happening and would be fleeing from the hideout in all directions. Only if any had managed to secure their weapons and began firing at the team, would the team use their weapons in self-defence, though they would try to capture as many of the gang as possible. It was well known that when a hide-out was discovered, and the inmates scattered, many of those that fled would give themselves up at a later date, having been able to slip the lead from their masters. So it was unnecessary for the team to go into the hideout with all guns blazing unless they fell into an ambush situation. The main object was to capture people, not to shoot them.

The leaders and anyone else captured would then be hand-cuffed and brought down through the forest to the rendezvous and interrogated, when the whole cycle of events might well start up again. Sometimes the teams would stay in the forest for several days and try to visit other hideouts, the locations of which might be remembered by recently recruited members of the team. To remain for several days in the forest acting as a *bona fide* Mau Mau gang was pretty uncomfortable, particularly for the FIOs, as tents could not be used and cooking had to be carried out Mau Mau style in case any real gangs happened to come into the temporary 'hide-out', though if this did happen it would be a real bonus as the chances of capturing the gang were greatly increased.

One of the most successful FIOs in Fort Hall was Ian Pritchard with whom I worked for several months until I left to return to my civilian work in Kenya's national parks in May 1955. The following is an extract from a letter I received from Ian soon after I left. It gives a good example of a typical forest operation.

I've had tremendous luck with forest c & d ['cloak and dagger'] work recently. On one job we took 6 chaps and 16 rounds of ammo. One of them was 'Gandezia' the 'Doctor' and 2 i/c to 'General' Thiga. My chaps interviewed him and next evening he led us to 'Major' Long's hide-out on the Tuso [river] as per your list. Dave Arrowsmith and I walked into the hide-out followed by my team. As I walked up to the gate of the hideout I saw them all sitting around the fires just as it was getting dark. They took no notice of us, thinking we were coming for a meeting. Unfortunately at the critical moment, somebody came through the gate and asked me who I was. I simply said "Mbuthia", but he was so close, he saw I was a European and went "oooooeeee". The inmates immediately took up their weapons and began firing at us. We had to lob

212

grenades into the melèe and unfortunately killed three and wounded others that thankfully turned up later having given themselves up.[151]

Ian Pritchard and his team - Nyakianga March 1955
Mwangi Murabasha is second from the left

Mwangi Murabasha who made the remark that heads this chapter was known to have been a particularly active member of a notorious Mau Mau gang. He played a leading part in a really nasty ambush and murder of a European D.O.(KG) and had personally killed several Kikuyu Guards. He was captured by the Kikuyu Guards and given to Capt. Feild, our DMIO, to 'dispose of'. The Kikuyu Guard had stripped the man of all but his underpants and he had suffered considerably at their hands. He was wet and shivering both from fear and from cold. His hands were tied tightly with string behind his back. The string was tied so tightly that it was eating badly into his now very swollen hands.

Ian Feild had only recently arrived from the UK and was shocked at the

---

[151] Ian Pritchard GM. Letter to author dated 9th May 1955

state of this man, and the inferred 'disposal' the Kikuyu Guard made to him about the man who was clearly expecting to be taken out and shot. Instead, the DMIO took him to Ian Pritchard's camp at Nyakianga where Ian had only

Kimani Kirugo and Mwangi Murabasha, Nyakianga, Fort Hall - March 1955
Our two ex-terrorist pseudo gang leaders. Kimani was a 'Captain' in 'General' Ihura's forest gang and is in the photograph on page 129, second from left.

recently started his work as an FIO and was feeling his way by setting up a network of informers. Mwangi was interrogated by Ian who immediately realised the man was no ordinary Mau Mau, but a highly intelligent, if ruthless combatant. To begin with Mwangi remained sullenly silent, but Ian went on talking about the conflict in which they were both engaged, saying how stupid it was that good Kikuyu land was lying idle, producing no food while people went hungry; where brothers were killing brothers and sons fighting fathers, which made no sense. Still Mwangi said nothing and Ian went on talking gently almost to himself. Gradually Mwangi began to join in. When this happened, Ian sent for mugs of hot sweet tea for them both. When Mwangi began to answer a few questions, Ian sent for clothes for the man, and within two hours, Mwangi, who by now was sure he was not going to be taken out

214

and shot, was given a decent meal and allowed to sleep, but in a secure cell. Mwangi was intelligent enough to understand and believe what Ian was telling him, and the next day agreed to work for him. Within a week, Ian had given the man a Sten (sub-machine) gun. He became the first member of the 'Muranga Kundi' that went on to achieve so much in the Kangema Division of Fort Hall.

Much of what Ian learnt about the Kikuyu and the Mau Mau, came from Mwangi, who remained with Ian throughout the two years he was working in pseudo gangs. The successes were as good as any within the area of operations and Ian admitted to me, before his untimely death from a water skiing accident some years later, that Mwangi was the inspiration and brains that accounted more than anything else to the success of the pseudo gang operations in Fort Hall. Mwangi epitomises the young Kikuyu man caught with 2,000 years of evolution crammed into 25 years of his young life.

Sometimes it was possible to carry out the interrogation and conversion there and then, on the spot where they were captured. Another Fort Hall FIO recounts such an encounter.

'Captain' Njatha was one of 'General' Kago's officers during the heyday of the gang that terrorised the Fort Hall Reserve during the early years of the Mau Mau campaign. He had taken part in wholesale murders of many Kikuyu in the western area of the Reserve including the Ndakaini massacre, when that village refused to supply food and recruits to the gang. He had also taken part in the murders of at least two District Officers, Jimmy Candler and Richard Wood-White. When Kago was killed by the Kikuyu Guard in March 1954, Njatha took over the remnants of his gang. Hunted down and harassed by the security forces, they had remained in the forest above their home area of Location 9, and had continued terrorising villages near the forest. Several times we thought we had him in our grasp and had sent pseudos out to try and locate him, but he always managed to slip through our fingers. Eventually Njatha's following dwindled to himself and just three others.

One day I was walking through the forest with four of my team on a different pseudo operation when we came across a man on his own. We were in our pseudo outfits so the others were able to stop and talk to the man, while I kept a low profile at the back. My chaps discovered the man was part of Njatha's gang, so they told him that by chance, they also happened to be looking for Njatha as they had important information to give him. I kept my face well hidden all the time and the man was totally unaware of us acting as pseudos. My chaps played their part very well. The man led us straight to the hide-out where there were three others, one of whom was Njatha. He immediately became suspicious of us and we had to make a grab for him. He fought like mad, but we managed to pin him to the ground before he could use his pistol, which we snatched from him, while we put the handcuffs on. The other three managed to escape.

We decided to try and 'turn' Njatha there and then as we wanted to catch the other three who had escaped. So we tied him in a sitting position to a tree and began talking to him. He knew one of my team who had been in his gang several weeks before, and was surprised to see him alive and the rest of us dressed as a Mau Mau gang. Njatha was no fool, but to begin with he was extremely rude and insulting and would undoubtedly have chopped us up, given the chance.

We talked with him for over an hour explaining what we were doing and how we operated and why we wanted this war to end so that people could get back to a proper life. At the end of an hour or so, he was beginning to show interest, so I told the rest of the team to leave me alone with him so that I could talk to the man on my own.

I told Njatha that he was now faced with only two alternatives. He could either come back with us to Fort Hall in handcuffs and we would hand him over to the

Europeans preparing for a pseudo gang operation in the Aberdare Forest

CID who would bring a case against him for the criminal activities he had committed, including the Ndakaini massacre, or he could come with us now, and perhaps become one of our team. I told him I was the boss and if he showed us where the other three of his gang would be hiding

216

(they always had a rendezvous, the location of which everyone knew so that they could meet up after getting separated), I would promise to give him back his pistol to show good faith and might even give him the opportunity of working in our team.

From that moment on, he changed completely. After my assurance he would not be killed if he complied, he agreed to show us the rendezvous and we all went off, with him still in handcuffs. When he got close to the rendezvous, he made the bird-call showing the others he was in the vicinity, and with him in front we just walked in to where they were sitting, in a forest clearing, and collected the other three without even a fight.

Having secured the others, I immediately took the handcuffs off Njatha and handed him his pistol with 6 rounds in it. It was a risky thing to do, I know, but by then I had been in this work for over a year, and knew pretty well, the reaction to showing trust and respect for a man like this. We allowed him to talk to his colleagues for a few minutes and were not surprised to find that he and the other three were following us back all the way to our rendezvous with the Land Rover. After several more hours of discussion, and with the permission of my DMIO, Njatha joined our team and within two weeks was created Sergeant-Major by common assent of the team. He became one of the keenest and most loyal members of my team. But I had to watch him like a hawk to see there was no bullying of the junior members. Together with the team, he was subsequently responsible for getting many terrorists out of the forest and was given a pardon at the general amnesty by the Governor, in January 1955.

I lost contact with him after the Emergency, until one day he turned up at my house in Nairobi and asked if he could work for me. I gave him a job as a gardener and he became one of the few Kikuyu in whom I had complete trust to guard my family whenever I was away on safari. As far as I know he is retired and living on his family farm at Fort Hall to this day." [152]

This conduct is almost impossible for those in the Western world to believe. It is certainly difficult to understand. But in our work with pseudo gangs, the 'turning' of these hardcore Mau Mau was a daily occurrence. The initial work on the 'turning' was done by one or two members of the team themselves,

---

[152] Anonymous FIO Fort Hall - pers. comm..

preferably by someone who had been in the same gang as the man. It was not done by the FIO. Having set the thing up, the FIO would leave it to his team, as to which member or members were the right ones to carry out this initial and very delicate task. But the FIO would always keep an eye on what was going on and made it his business to be kept informed as to progress. It would be he who would give the final decision as to whether or not the person should become part of the team.

The 'turning' had to be done as soon as possible after capture and always by ex-Mau Mau. They had the advantage of knowing what was going through

A pseudo gang team after a successful encounter in the Aberdare Forest
April 1955
The man sitting in the foreground has been accidentally shot in the foot. He now has to walk several miles to the forest edge before he can be transferred to hospital by Land Rover .

218

the man's mind at the time. They would remember only too well, what they themselves had been going through at that same traumatic time, perhaps only weeks or even days before. They would know the astonishment that would greet the man at the time when he first realised someone from his own gang was now working for the security forces, and they would know the relief in the man's mind, at realising he was not going to be tortured and die a horrible death as he had been led to believe by his gang leader — that he was, after all, going to survive.

There were failures, of course, as not every person captured was prepared to turn in this way, but the successes far outweighed the failures, and this is due entirely to the Kikuyu mentality, both of the 'turner' and the 'turned'.

The pseudo gang teams became so adept at turning people that had just come out of the forest or had been captured, that it became a comparatively simple matter to hand a captured man over to the team and let them deal with him. Within a day and sometimes within a matter of an hour or so, he would be 'turned' and would often be willing to lead the team back into the forest to his erstwhile colleagues. The turning could only be done by sensible argument and persuasion. Once there was any form of coercion, the man clamped up. Any form of torture or beatings up was utterly useless and counter productive. Respect for the person was the key to unlocking his acquiescence.

Occasionally combatants came out of the forest and were prepared to lead us back in, for other, quite exceptional reasons.

On 8th November 1954 a man was brought in to me for interrogation. His name was Njeroge Muchoki. Both his arms were broken and he was, naturally, in considerable pain. His story was that he had been with a gang above Location 9 in Fort Hall and had been sent down to the Reserve at night by his leader, 'Major' Gathigira, to fetch food from his family. When he arrived at the family homestead he found no one at home. The huts were empty, the animals gone and the food stores empty. As he dared not go to another homestead for fear of being captured by them and turned over to the Kikuyu Guard, he returned to the hideout empty handed. His leader was so incensed to see he had returned without any food, that to punish him, he took up a piece of bamboo and while two other men held his arms outstretched, slammed the bamboo down on his arms which smashed them both.

Later that night, in great pain, he managed to evade the sentries and slipped away from the hideout. He gave himself up to the Kenya Police at

Tuso Police station, close to the forest edge early the following morning. The Police sent him on to me for interrogation.

I asked Njeroge if he would be able to lead me back to the hideout and he said in effect that it would be a pleasure! I already knew from previous interrogations that this particular leader had carried out many acts of violence against members of his gang and had been responsible for the murder of several Kikuyu Guards and their families.

As it was a large gang, my DMIO said it would be too dangerous to attempt a pseudo gang operation on it, and it was decided Njeroge should go with me to the hideout and that we should be accompanied by a section of the British Army Black Watch Regiment who were stationed on the Kinangop, the other side of the Aberdare mountains. Arrangements were hastily made, while Njeroge's arms were set in plaster by a doctor in the Fort Hall hospital. That afternoon I drove Njeroge the hundred or so miles around the mountain to the camp of the 1st Battalion, the Black Watch at South Kinangop. Major Tony Lithgow the Officer Commanding, decided he would like to join the patrol that was already kitted up and ready to move off. By the time we reached the forest edge, it was dark and the whole sortie was carried out with Njeroge attached to a piece of string leading me through the forest with the rest of the patrol of eight fully armed British servicemen following behind. Although I had some idea of the location of the hideout, it would have been totally impossible for me to find it. The whole success of the operation rested entirely on Njeroge and his guidance to the hideout. We walked throughout the night, mostly on game paths, up to the moorlands of the Aberdare range at over 10,000ft (3,000m) and down the other side.

At 4.15 am, after only a couple of breaks for tea, we halted and Njeroge told me we were now close to the hideout. Major Lithgow asked me to go ahead with Njeroge to recce the hideout and try to discover the layout so that we could plan the action. Njeroge crept on a few yards with me beside him, hanging on tightly to the string. Then he stopped. He whispered in my ear that we had now arrived at the hideout. It was pitch dark and virtually impossible to see even a few feet ahead. The snores of the inmates confirmed that we were indeed in the middle of the hideout. I was about to turn round and head back to report to Major Lithgow, when a shot suddenly rang out from the direction where I had just left them. (It later transpired that a food party from the gang was by chance, following up the same route as us, and while the others were sitting waiting for my return, this food party had literally stumbled into the last man of our party who, in consternation and fright, had fired at the intruder.) In the split second that followed the gunfire, the hideout simply erupted with bodies fleeing in every direction. It was a second or two before I came to my senses and opened up with my Patchett sub-machine gun indiscriminately in the direction of the fleeing bodies, which I could hear but could not see. At the same time, I found myself shouting at the fleeing people. I was unaware of what I was saying as it was a spontaneous reaction and probably made no sense at all.

After all the commotion had died down and the crashing of bodies through the forest had ceased, Major Lithgow came up with the rest of the patrol and with torches we set out to see what damage, if any, had been done. Njeroge, by this time, was dancing with delight. All the tension of the past eight hours suddenly released, he was the hero of the moment and everyone was praising his guidance through the forest most of which was done in total darkness. With our torches, we searched the huts and Njeroge, who, by this time had slipped his string 'lead', went straight to the hut where the leader Gathigira slept. He gave a great shout of joy as he shone his torch on the body of his tormentor who lay there with a bullet through his head. It turned out that he was, in fact, the only casualty. This was justice indeed. We found several precision weapons in the camp, together with home-made guns, pangas and cooking pots. Several of the inmates gave themselves up during the following days. Njeroge, who was a driver before he joined the Mau Mau, made a complete recovery and became our team's official Land Rover driver.

Several years later, in 1960, I had been posted to Mountains National Park as acting warden while the Warden, Billy Woodley, was on overseas leave. Woodley also carried out pseudo gang operations during the Emergency, and after the conflict was over, he employed several of his old pseudo gang members as Rangers in his Park. One day when I was on a five-day patrol with a group of rangers in the Mount Kenya National Park, we had arrived at Klarvill's Hut, on the upper slopes of the mountain. After our evening meal, we were sitting round the fire chatting when the talk turned to the Mau Mau Emergency.

Now Sergeant Kamau, who was in charge of the group of Rangers, had not been particularly friendly towards me during the few days since I had taken over from Warden Woodley. He was Woodley's man and had, I later found out, been one of the leading members of Woodley's pseudo gang team. He was a proud man and I was an intruder, and therefore demanded little respect. It was the same on this patrol. Kamau had led his Rangers at full speed up the mountain hoping that I would soon tire and show my weakness. (He was, I believe, disappointed.)

Not all the Rangers were Kikuyu, and those from other tribes, began to wander off to their sleeping bags when the talk turned to the Emergency. Sergeant Kamau had been listening with some disdain to what was being said. So far he had not thought fit to join in the conversation. At length, someone asked me if I had had any exciting moments to relate during the conflict and I told the story of Njeroge and the Black Watch. When I got to the bit about shouting at the fleeing gang, Sergeant Kamau suddenly got up from where he was sitting and came round to where I was standing leaning up against the hut. I could just see his face in the light of the camp fire. He was a big burly man, much taller than I, and for a moment I thought he was going to attack me. Instead, without saying anything, he took my hand in both of his, and shook it vigorously. I was nonplussed. He then addressed the gathering, still holding my hand, and said that what I had been relating was perfectly true. He could vouch for it as he had been one of those in the hideout that night. He said he had always wanted to meet the *Mzungu* [European] who had dared to walk up through the forest at dead of night and attack the gang and then, when they were fleeing the camp, had shouted to them to come and fight instead of running away!

I lost no time in telling him and the gathering that the real hero of the night was the man Njeroge Muchoki who, with two broken arms in plaster, had led us through the forest, over the moorlands and found his way in the blackest of nights, directly to the hideout. A truly amazing feat. At least I had the satisfaction of knowing at last, the words I had shouted at the fleeing terrorists that night!

The complete absence of any bitterness towards me was so typical of the Kikuyu. The man Kamau was genuinely pleased and excited to meet me and from then on, during the remaining months I had at the Mountain Parks headquarters, continued to show me the greatest respect. I still have a photo of Mount Kenya with his greetings and signature on the back, presented to me by him and the other rangers as a memento when I left the Park on Woodley's return some months later.

The downside to pseudo work in the forest was that within a comparatively short space of time, those who managed to slip away without being caught, would warn other gangs who would be more sceptical of a strange 'gang' appearing, and later, at the height of the pseudo gang operations, some hardcore gangs would stand and fight, and these had to be eliminated instead of being captured. But even so, the knowledge that pseudo gangs were operating in the forest, limited the movements of the real gangs so much, that in the end, they were unable to move about freely in the forest and into the Reserve to obtain food, for fear of meeting a pseudo gang, and eventually they had to give themselves up or starve to death.

Towards the end, when they did come out for food, they got a bad reception from the population, mostly from the women in the Reserve. After three years of killings and little opportunity of growing sufficient food in the

Women take part in a public ceremony agreeing not to send any more food to their menfolk in the forest

The women wisely understood that if their husbands and brothers remained in the forest gangs, they would sooner or later be killed by the Security Forces. So in a public display of solidarity they ceremonially dumped their food carrying baskets (kiondos) on the ground to demostrate their opposition to the men remaining in the forest, in the hopes that this would persuade them to come out and give themselves up to the authorities.

gardens, the women grew tired of the war and losing their menfolk either to the Mau Mau or to the Security Forces. They became thoroughly disenchanted with Mau Mau and all it stood for. They just wanted to get back to normal living again. They began to join in with ferreting out the few remaining gangs in or on the edge of the forest where they were hunting for food. If a gang or if individual terrorists searching for food, happened to be spotted by the Kikuyu Guard or even by women, word would get around quickly that there were some Mau Mau in a certain area and the local women would gather together and in a surprisingly short time, would throw a large cordon round the unfortunate gangsters to corner them, and by sheer weight of numbers would simply hack them to death. Frank Kitson writes of an occasion where he witnessed this somewhat gory scene. He was on his way in a Land Rover to oversee an operation in the Kiambu District, near the forest.

> For the first half of the journey, the Reserve was much as usual, but as I got nearer my destination the tracks and paths became congested with people, mostly women, moving in the same direction as myself. There were hundreds and hundreds of them, all carrying their pangas [machetes]. Dressed as they were in their gaily coloured frocks, the scene was reminiscent of a major sporting function in England, such as a football match or the Derby. Our Land Rover nosed its way through the crowd and we eventually reached the forest edge, where I was told there were thought to be two gangsters hiding in the bracken.
>
> As I drove round the cordon the women had now formed, I saw the line of cutters start to move slowly forward. It was a wonderful sight to see the way they all hacked their way through the undergrowth leaving a swathe of cleared ground behind them as they went. Naturally they only cleared the undergrowth: they did not try cutting down the big trees. Suddenly I saw one of the Kikuyu Guards who was interspersed with the cutters raise his rifle and swing it round in front of himself. For a moment I thought he had seen the gangsters, but there was no bang. Instead about thirty women dived on the spot indicated. There was a mass of seething and struggling bodies. I caught a glimpse of a small furry body and two tiny horns. The women had thought it was a Mau Mau but it turned out to be a little buck. There was a moment of turmoil and then the scrum broke up. The lucky ones each came away with a bit of the animal.

Kitson goes on to explain that later that day, the same women were rewarded with two terrorists. The first one had already been shot by the Kikuyu Guard and Kitson wanted to search the body for documents, before the crowd set upon it.

> We just managed to get to the body in time and I hurled myself on it to get the papers from his pockets while Eric [Holyoak] held the crowd at bay. By now their blood was up and they were determined to have their sport. I think I should have been carved up as well had it not been for the fact that another terrorist was seen at that moment and all eyes turned in that direction.[153]

In his book *'Mau Mau Detainee'* Josiah Mwangi Kariuki writes that while he was detained in Manyani Detention Camp in 1955, he met a 'pseudo-gangster' from Location 12 in Fort Hall. It is difficult to understand how a member of a pseudo-gang had been sent into detention. Someone who had genuinely taken part in pseudo-gang work, by so doing, would have committed himself to work against the Mau Mau, so unless he was one of the volunteers, sent to help in the rehabilitation process, it is impossible that he would have been in detention himself. He would certainly not have been allowed, for security reasons, to mix with other detainees in July 1955 when the pseudo-gang operations were at their height. Kariuki gives his own thoughts as to why men joined the pseudo-gangs, but from the reasons he gives, it is unlikely that he ever spoke to a genuine member of a pseudo-gang.[154]

In the same way, a book was written purporting to be a record of Dedan Kimathi's writings. It is entitled *'Kimathi's Letters'* and is edited by Maina wa Kinyatti. In case this book is ever taken to be a true record of Kimathi's writings, there is ample evidence that anything that was written down by Kimathi, did not survive the Emergency. The editor in his Preface tells that four sackfulls of Kimathi's papers were captured in 1955 and these are retained in the Public Records Office in London and in the Kenya National Archives in Nairobi, and cannot be made public until the year 2013. I have to disappoint Mr. Kinyatti. According to the Kenya National Archives, they hold no such documents, neither does the Public Records Office at Kew, in London. Furthermore, Kimathi himself, though partly educated, wrote very little. His scribe, Gathura Muita did all his writing. Gathura survived the Emergency and became a personal friend of mine later. He was our very efficient clerk at the

---

[153] Frank Kitson *'Gangs and Counter Gangs'* Barrie & Rockliff 1960 p.204
[154] Josiah Mwangi Kariuki *'Mau Mau Detainee'* Oxford University Press 1963 p.95

Mountains National Parks Headquarters in Nyeri. One day in 1960, he took me to the hideout on the moorlands under the very tall *ericaceae* or 'Giant Heather'*(Blaeria filago)* forests which abound on the moorlands.

The hideout, which was known as '*30 X 30 Nyandarua*' was, in fact, within the Aberdares National Park, but it was never found by the Security Forces because it was so well hidden. I was the first European ever to see it. It was an ideal place for a hideout as the bushes grow up to five metres high and provide complete cover both from air attack and from the ground. Here Gathura spent many months with his master, and travelled with him to other gangs throughout the Aberdares. He spoke freely about his work, and told me that Kimathi spent hours dictating poems and songs to him, which he kept in a Kenya Police Muster Roll book, taken, he understood, from the Kenya Police station at Naivasha during the raid by the Mau Mau in 1953. Gathura told me that when Kimathi was being hunted by the Police and the Kikuyu Guard who eventually captured him, they became separated, and Gathura gave himself up to the Police in Nyeri sometime later. The Muster Roll, a book of some 250 pages, was burnt on the orders of Kimathi, at the hideout before they left together. Gathura himself burnt the book together with other papers and letters. He was certain that none of Kimathi's writings ever survived. Gathura still lives at Njabini on the Kinagop, on a plot given to him after Independence by Jomo Kenyatta. (See also Appendices 2 and 8 for bona fide Kimathi letters)

It is a pity, in fact, that apart from some of Karama Njama's book '*Mau Mau from Within*', no authentic records were written by those Mau Mau who took an active part in the fighting. Even in Njama's book, he fantasises on many issues, typical of which is 'General' Kago's demise, which is a complete fabrication, as the records written at the time confirm.[155] (See also Appendix 5 'The rise and Fall of 'General Kago')

Several books written by those purporting to have served in the forest, such as '*We fought for Freedom*', by Gucu Gikoyo, '*Freedom Fighter*' by J Wamweya, '*War in the Forest*' by Kiboi Muriithi and Peter Ndoria all published by the East African Publishing House, were simply figments of the authors' vivid imaginations and unfortunately bear little relation to the facts, consequently it is difficult to believe that any of the authors actually took part in the conflict at all. The only authentic writings of those that took part are

---

[155] Donald L. Barnett & Karari Njama '*Mau Mau from Within*' Modern Reader Paperbacks 1966 p.355 (See also appendix 5 The Rise and Fall of Kago)

those that were captured during the Emergency and were subsequently translated and typed out and issued to those of us who could make use of them in our interrogations.

After the Emergency, and when Kenya finally became independent of the British in December 1963, those Kikuyu who 'turned' to work with the security forces were dubbed traitors and were given a hard time by the population. This was a travesty of justice and was brought about purely by ignorance of the pseudo gang operations and what the teams had achieved in terms of saving lives. The ignorance came about because the type of person who took part in pseudo gang work was not the sort that shouts his own praises from the rooftops. He is a withdrawn character, given to actions rather than words and on returning to his family tends to keep his head down, and his secrets to himself. He is a hard man on the outside but usually has a pretty soft centre. He is not well-suited to civilian life and unfortunately often turns to a life of crime. So his exploits remain untold unless some literate friend or colleague recalls his deeds and commits them to paper and to history, something I have yet to find. Such men as these, though few in number, were responsible for saving many lives, particularly those of the more uncommitted and lukewarm fighters who were too scared to give themselves up, and would therefore have remained in the forest to die of starvation or be killed by other arms of the security forces if they had not been sought out and captured by the pseudo gangs. Without the pseudo gangs the conflict would have dragged on into a war of attrition where conventional warfare would have taken months if not years to rid the forest of the remnants of the gangs.

If it had not been for the Kikuyu Guard, the Tribal Police and the pseudo gangs, the Government forces would have had an impossible task to hunt out these terrorists in the forest and in the Reserve. Guerrilla warfare tactics would have lasted for several more years and this would have seriously affected the date of the Lancaster House Conference and would have undoubtedly put back the date for Independence. The inescapable fact is that, in the end, and for the most part, it was the Kikuyu themselves that brought an end to the fighting. They saw the folly of trying to win a measure of self determination through Mau Mau. They realised that that road would clearly lead to greater disasters. Instead, the vast majority of Kikuyu decided to follow the road that led to peaceful and controlled' transition to self determination and were prepared to fight for their beliefs, if necessary against their own people, in the same way that the reformers fought with Francis Hall at the start of the British influence fifty years before, against those of their own people who shunned progress and continued in the old ways, and for much the same reason: that they had the foresight to see that they could make a better life for themselves by siding with the British who offered the means to achieve that end.

Many courageous deeds were carried out by Kikuyu fighting to rid their homeland of Mau Mau, not because they were 'loyal' to the British, but because in the end, they realised Mau Mau was an evil organisation led by murderers and outlaws who were terrorising the countryside for their own ends and their own glorification. The majority of Kikuyu may have agreed with the Mau Mau objectives at the beginning, but in the end, they realised the leaders were simply a bunch of thugs out for what they could get, and wanted to see an end to them and their prostitution of the Kikuyu culture. That they succeeded so admirably in their task has never been properly recognised in post-Independent Kenya, especially in Kikuyuland.

CHAPTER TEN

DETENTION CAMPS

The system of British rule in Kenya and of its Protectorates or Dependencies throughout the world in 1950, was ultimately answerable through Parliament and Whitehall to a British electorate. It relied on a delegated local Government for the exercise of its power.

The decision to resort to force, to quell an uprising in a Colony or Protectorate such as the area in which the Kikuyu people lived, was dependant on many complex issues, not the least of which was the degree and nature of the force applied and the legal basis of that force coupled with the dangers involved in the failure to act. Apart from the very real threat of violence, Mau Mau was perceived by Whitehall not only to be a cancerous growth that had to be lanced before it infected the whole body of the country, but also a serious barrier to the overall economic growth, leading to planned constitutional change, i.e. to internal self-government and eventually to total independence from Great Britain. These reasons then, together with the growing unease among the field officers reporting from the Kikuyu homelands, were the trigger for Whitehall to act.

The legal basis of operations against the Mau Mau insurgents was the obligation the British Government, and therefore the British people, had under international law, to protect the inhabitants of its Dependency against a felony, using the minimum force necessary. The manifestation of this obligation was the British Parliament's Colonial Laws Validity Act, 1865, which was the legal basis and, before the existence of the United Nations, the internationally recognised authorisation, not only for the British presence in Kenya but also for the use of force in order to protect the people of the Dependency.

When the Emergency regulations came into force, anybody within certain specified areas could be stopped and searched. In practice, most operations took the form of 'pursuit to capture'. Buildings and huts could be searched and anyone suspected of having taken a Mau Mau oath or known to have associations with Mau Mau could be detained. Those detained or captured had to be passed to the Police, who, for a conviction, then had to show that the person had broken the law. This was often very difficult if not impossible to prove. Witnesses or informants were reluctant to give evidence, or were impossible to trace, or it was simply not possible to get them to Court because of the distances involved.

Under Emergency Powers, the Government could issue Detention Orders that were the legal basis for the arrest and internment of those who were suspected of Mau Mau involvement, but against whom no case could easily be brought, or no conviction envisaged through lack of witnesses. Thus, within a short period of time, thousands of Kikuyu were brought in to District Headquarters throughout Nairobi and Central Province by the Police and other Security Forces, for Detention orders to be signed. At first the orders had to be signed by the Governor himself, but later, because of the numbers involved, they could be signed by Provincial and eventually District Commissioners. In the end more than 80,000 men were detained, together with a handful of women. Detention Centres or Camps sprang up in remote areas of Kenya holding up to several thousand inmates each. The Kenya Prisons Service were responsible for running the Detention Camps and because of the sudden influx, prison warders had to be hastily recruited and trained.

The detainees were not convicted criminals; they were held under a particular set of Emergency regulations that provided for certain specific measures. A detainee was entitled to a certain standard of food, housing, and medical facilities; if medically fit, he was obliged to work for certain hours during the week for which he would receive remuneration.

Whatever the rights and wrongs of detention, at the time there was no alternative. In 2004, everyone is familiar with the implications of terrorism and the arguments used to justify detention without trial. But in 1952, Kenya criminal law was based on English Common Law expressed in a criminal code set out in a Criminal Offences Ordinance passed by the Governor in Council. It was, however, not within the Governor's powers to change or suspend this Ordinance. As in England, once laws had been passed as an Act of Parliament, they could not be changed until a new Act was passed.. The situation in 1952, therefore, presented the Governor with the necessity to seek Whitehall's reluctant approval for the introduction of Emergency Regulations that enabled the Executive, amongst many other things, to undertake a process of detention without trial for those Kikuyu who were suspected of having affiliations with the now proscribed KAU and the Mau Mau organisation itself.

Detention was first and foremost a method of holding in a secure system those who were committed to take part in criminal activities through an obligation to oaths they had taken, but against whom it was difficult, if not impossible to produce evidence. Secondly it was a detoxification clinic for those on their way back from the effects of the oath – back to the society they left the moment they took (or were forced to take) the oaths. The intention of the Mau Mau hierarchy was that the oaths must be so shocking that once taken, they would never be broken. In this, the hierarchy were completely successful. As intended, the taker, particularly of the second and subsequent oaths, became slaves to their imposed obligations. Such was the gravity the Kikuyu man or woman attached to the taking of an oath and such was the enormity and trauma involved in the physical act of taking these degrading subsequent oaths, that only a rehabilitation centre with specialist treatment could purge their effects. Even to a hardened Kikuyu, brought up in the harsh realities of life in that primitive society, even he or she could not but be affected by the depravity and bestiality of the acts without some deep-rooted and lasting damage to his or her mental state. These people had to be taken out of society until they could be cleansed through voluntary confessions. The real 'peddlers' of these acts, those who came to be known as 'Z' category detainees, the ones who invented and carried out the terrible oathings, were not so easy to detoxify. Fortunately they were in the minority, though they caused a great deal of trouble before they were eventually able to be released. Some, in fact never recovered and went to their graves with the dark shadow of the oaths still dominant in their pathetic lives.

Above all, detainees were not political prisoners. Mau Mau was not a political organisation in the sense that it pursued nationalism through peaceful means. It aimed firstly, at domination of the Kikuyu ethnic group through intimidation and the annihilation of any opposition that got in its way. Secondly, it aimed at the removal and repatriation of all immigrants including Europeans and Asians, and thirdly it required the removal of the lawful Government by whatever means necessary, followed by the take-over of that Government. Fortunately for Kenya it got hung up on the first aim, which precluded the achievement of the other two.

So it was recognised that detainees were not prisoners and that they might have committed no crime other than passive affiliations with Mau Mau, a proscribed organisation. Some, though, had been in the forest, captured by the security forces and released from prosecution by the general amnesty of 1st January 1955. They may have taken part in terrorist raids on their own people in the Reserve or in the settled areas. Others had been implicated in actively helping the Mau Mau organisation, either by supplying food or arms and ammunition. Most had taken at least one oath and many had taken several. All had one thing in common: there was insufficient evidence to prosecute them but sufficient evidence to connect them with the illegal Mau Mau organisation. Many had been forced to take the oath against their will, but having taken it, were obliged to carry out its demands. They had to be taken out of society until cleansed and freed from the oaths' obligations. Not to have detained them in a secure unit would have been an act of gross dereliction of the Government's duty.

One of the first camps to be set up soon after the declaration of the Emergency was at Marigat, 80 miles north of Nakuru, close to Lake Baringo where the Njemps[156] people reside. It was typical of the twenty or so camps that came to be built specifically to house the detainees. It was at the beginning

Detainees arriving at a detention camp

of the Emergency when detainees were starting to arrive in their hundreds. Within a few days there were some 2,000 detainees in the camp, looked after by 50 warders. The 'A' frame huts were made of corrugated aluminium: ten detainees to a hut and four warders to a similar size and type of hut. The same

---

[156] The Njemps are an offshoot of the Masai people.

design was subsequently copied for virtually all the camps throughout the country. It was here, at Marigat, that James Breckenridge was sent to start a rehabilitation scheme in conjunction with the Prisons Service officers who ran the camp. The idea was to be able to get the inmates to confess their associations with Mau Mau, so that they could be cleansed of the oath, screened to make sure they would not re-offend and then to be repatriated to their home locations as soon as possible. It was the intention of Government to get them out of the camps quickly, but not before they had certain assurances they would not go back and join a local Mau Mau cell.

The detainees were expected to work while they were in detention and were remunerated at the rate of eighty cents per day, which was the normal wage for a farm worker at that time. The project on which the Marigat detainees worked was an irrigation scheme for the local Njemps tribesmen. 3,000 acres of flat semi-desert land was developed for a variety of crops such as rice, maize and sorghum, fed by channels dug from the Marigat river. Vegetables and tomatoes were also grown and a tomato-canning factory was subsequently built there. Work started at 6am and finished at 3pm when the detainees returned to camp to a meal cooked by the residents of each hut.

James Breckenridge, who knew something of the Kikuyu language, came to know many of those in the Marigat camp. He realised that there was little for the men to do after their main meal of the day, and knowing how 'the devil finds work for idle hands and minds'—the particular 'work' in this case being clandestine oathing—he proposed to start voluntary evening classes.

We broadcast a message over the public address system saying that we were intending to start evening classes, and if any teachers were interested, we would like to talk to them. I wanted them to learn simple economics, the three R's and particularly the essential facts about the civil administration (the average African had no idea why he paid taxes, except that he thought the District Commissioner needed a new car!).

As they were suspicious of our intentions, there was little response for several days. Then four men came all together. We had a lengthy talk about the project. We told them that we, the authorities, would provide as much guidance as possible, and keep some control — we knew that it would provide an opportunity for Mau Mau propaganda to be introduced which had to be avoided at all costs. My four volunteers said they would give it a try. The following evening, after their meal, we were astonished to find four groups of twenty men sitting down near the perimeter of the barbed wire fence, writing on their bare knees with a thin stick. (The African's skin leaves a white mark when scratched and they lick their hands to rub out mistakes and write again.)[157]

It is known that a considerable amount of Mau Mau propaganda work went on in these detention camps. Mau Mau committees were formed by the hardcore adherents amongst them, and these secret committees worked overtime to try and prevent people attending evening classes or any kind of rehabilitation. Josiah Mwangi Kariuki, a political Mau Mau adherent, though not an active fighter, was one of those detained. In his book '*Mau Mau Detainee*', Kariuki gives an interesting insight into what usually happened in these camps.

In Lodwar [Detention Camp] we created the best [Mau Mau] organisation among the detainees of any camp I was in. Robinson Mwangi was elected camp leader while Joseph Kirira became chairman of the camp committee.

Each room chose its own leader who was then responsible to the camp leader for the carrying out of executive decisions. The camp committee consisted of one member elected from every room, making twenty-two in all plus the camp leader, his assistant and myself as educational member and political adviser. This committee met once a week, but special urgent meetings could be called at any time by the chairman or the secretary in consultation with the camp leader.[158]

All the inmates knew of these committees, and knew there were those ready to report them the moment they were suspected of colluding with the authorities. The committees were never slow to convict a suspect at a 'kangaroo court', and it was all too easy for the convicted person to suffer an 'accidental fall', perpetrated by the 'executioner', when out working while the warder in charge was looking the other way. So anyone who wanted to approach Breckenridge in the first few months of the rehabilitation process, was risking his life in no uncertain way.

Two Kikuyu Community Development assistants, Benjamin and Kariuki were sent to assist Breckenridge in his work. They took over the day-to-day supervision of the teachers and the supply of slates to the pupils, when paper was in short supply. They also supervised the workshops where men who had been craftsmen were encouraged to practice their trade and teach

---

[157] Breckenridge '*Forty Years in Kenya*' Published privately p.186
[158] Josiah Mwangi Kariuki '*Mau Mau Detaianee*' Oxford University Press 1963 p.109

others. One day, one of the detainees approached Benjamin and asked him if he could discuss something that was troubling him. It soon turned out that he wanted to confess his associations with Mau Mau. Benjamin took him straight to Breckenridge.

> The detainee was very nervous, for if word got back to the compound, he would have been killed. He was very hesitant at first but soon gained confidence, and said that he wanted to get rid of this awful burden. We let him talk, and he admitted that he was a member of the [Mau Mau] society — a confession that in itself, broke the oath. He was reluctant to say what the ten oaths he had taken consisted of or tell us what part he played in the organisation. Having promised that we would not divulge his visit, we suggested he should return to the compound, work for a day or two then come and see us again if he still felt like it. There was no point in pushing him at this early stage and we did not want to frighten him in any way.
>
> He returned three days later and said he wanted to make a full confession. This was a real break through. He started slowly but once he got going, he couldn't stop and told us everything that he knew about Mau Mau. Within a day or two his whole facial expression had changed from a harassed, strained and dried-up looking skin and a permanent frown, to a natural, shiny, oily complexion with a smile. It was very interesting for us subsequently, to observe this changed expression and complexion, whenever a man confessed.[159]

This man, the first of Breckenridge's successes, was taken out of the compound and put in a room of his own, safely away from the rest of the detainees. Subsequently, he agreed to make a tape recording of his confession, with the idea that it should be broadcast over the public address system of the camp. This he did, and at the end of his piece, Breckenridge came on and explained that this man was known to all the inmates and that he had made the confession voluntarily, and that he was prepared to talk to anyone who doubted the truth of what they had just heard.

The result, though not immediate, was positive. One or two men came to see him, including those sent by the committees to try and find out the name of the man who had made this confession, so that action could be taken against him or his family. Only one visitor at a time was allowed, in case someone

---

[159] Breckenridge *'Forty Years in Kenya'* p.187

tried to do the man harm. But among them were a few who were genuinely interested and told of many more who would like to confess but who were terrified of the intimidation by the strong-arm men of the committees. In view of this, a new compound was built for those who, it was hoped, would confess. Soon they had taken several confessions, and it was not long before the trickle became a flood. Naturally it was not possible for those who confessed to mix with the others, either for meals or in work parties, so provision had to be made for them, and soon they were able to be repatriated to their families in the Reserve.

Before long, James Breckenridge's wife Caroline, who had been the camp's secretary, joined him in the work of rehabilitation. She had kept a card index on all the inmates and through this had begun to follow each detainee's progress closely. She describes what happened in the hundreds of cases of confession she herself witnessed.

The man first puts his name down on a list to visit the confession team. He has already listened to the tape recording of others who have confessed, but who have been removed from the compound for their own safety. The confession team is made up of five Kikuyu. Most are older men and not to be trifled with. The leading member is usually a tribal Court Elder who has experience of Court work. One of the team is a scribe who takes down the important passages of the coming confession. The man is invited to sit down on a chair opposite the team, in somewhat similar fashion to that of a formal interview. He gives his name and other particulars, all of which are written down. He is then asked what he wants to say to the team. He starts slowly and hesitatingly, but as he gains confidence, his words flow more easily. The team help to smooth the way for him by asking the odd question, which he enthusiastically answers, and the team then know that the man is in earnest.

Gradually, the man begins to show signs of relief. He starts to smile and is clearly happier in himself. Sometimes he runs away with himself, and the scribe cannot keep up with him. Some get so carried away that they talk all day, and do not allow the team to take a break. Hurry is useless, and the team know they will have to hear the man out and maybe carry on the next day. And when the next day arrives, the man is a changed being. He is smarter, happier, and his skin has taken on a shine that all healthy Africans have. It is as though a great burden has been lifted from him, and he can walk tall again and be himself. The final act was to stand on a chair and speak his confession out loud to all those within the compound who had already confessed. This done, there was no going back.

Some of the things many wanted to confess were the finer points of what they were made to do at the oathing ceremonies, and awful though they were, the team knew that allowing them to go through the details of that traumatic experience, exorcised, to some extent, the effects. They called it 'vomiting the oath'[160].

The effect of these oaths on the psyche of the person was terrible to perceive. The acts which they were made to perform in order to make the promises indelible, were bound to have a deep-seated effect on the mental state of the taker. But the change after detoxification was even more remarkable. Caroline Breckenridge, writes: '... *the difference in the physical appearance of those under the power of the oath: the slit eyes, and almost wild animal-like appearance that I have seen hundreds of times, was pitiful to witness. But directly a man or a woman voluntarily confesses and throws off the oaths, the change is almost tangible. The gloss returns to the African skin; the man regains his dignity and is happy once again. The woman particularly becomes a real woman again. Her clothes take on a neatness quite absent before.*[161]

Other camps were following the same routine and other rehabilitators were finding the same situations in their camps and dealing with them in a similar way. The Breckenridges were not the only ones who were engaged in this delicate and often distressing work of rehabilitation, but as a successful husband and wife team they were moved to different Camps in order to teach the same system there. In one of the camps they were sent to at Athi River near Nairobi, the Moral Re-Armament (MRA) people were invited to try and rehabilitate the inmates. They had to admit that they were completely out of their depth with these people, and were obliged to give up and return to the UK. The Breckenridges found that the principles which had worked so well in Marigat bore much the same result in the other camps. The same straightforward open treatment gave the same encouraging results. Caroline Breckenridge records one success at Athi River that typifies what happened.

We met one man at Athi River whose name was Kimani. He was a B.A. from Fort Hare University in South Africa, and had proved quite impossible for the MRA people to handle. Without waiting for a

---

[160] Breckenridge *'Forty Years in Kenya' p.188*
[161] Ibid. p.216

confession from him, James, who had realised the man's potential, told him that he wanted him to help me plan an educational system in the camp as none existed there. Kimani was surprised at being singled out to do this work. When we began, I found that he knew much more about it than I did, so I let him carry on. I was really only interested in seeing what he made of the job. To begin with his attitude was reserved and only just civil enough to be acceptable. However, I ignored this and after a week, he suddenly announced 'you really do want me to do this work, don't you?' When I replied that of course I did and I considered it such important work, he told me in that case, he wanted some days off 'to do some hard thinking'.

Two days later Kimani got to his feet before the whole camp, holding a photograph in his hand. The photo was of himself in cap and gown. 'You see this photo? It is of a man with a Bachelor of Arts degree. Now you may think it is the most marvellous thing for an African to hold a B.A. degree and that I deserve respect. Well, look at me, and see where it has got me. I am a detainee, degraded and penniless, with an oath on my mind and turmoil in my heart. So my degree did not teach me much. But here I have learnt something worthwhile. I know which direction I am going. From here I am going straight to the confession team and confess all that I know about Mau Mau. When I come out from that room, then you can respect me.'

Though we do not usually divulge what was said in the confession, he has given us permission to record one part of it. When he returned from South Africa in 1950 with his degree, Jomo Kenyatta personally met him at the airport and congratulated him. He took him straight to the offices of the KAU and had him oathed within an hour of him landing.[162]

It is difficult therefore to reconcile Josiah Mwangi Kariuki's statement in his book *'Mau Mau Detainee'*, that very few detainees were persuaded to confess and were rehabilitated, and that those who did confess, did so only because they were either hungry or were 'persuaded' to by fair means or foul.

Soon the 'bogey' of 'confessions' appeared. The officials in charge there [Athi River Detention Camp] did not beat people [into making confessions] but they used many other means, some more subtle than others. Rations were reduced and this forced the weakest to surrender.

---

[162] Ibid. p.231

Joseph [Karira] told me that prostitutes were brought into the camp to speak words of love and to dangle their legs before the detainees to remind them of some of the things they were missing. They were not allowed to taste these joys, merely to recall them, before the ladies were taken out. Some three or four people were rehabilitated in this way, but such devices could never move a true nationalist. We say that the love of a woman cannot be compared with the love of one's country: they are as different as earth and heaven.[163]

Josiah Mwangi Kariuki, however, would have us believe that Breckenridge was a bully and a sadist. In his chapter on rehabilitation, he describes a beating-up by the Camp Commandant and Breckenridge, whom he calls 'Rochester' in which they beat him to within an inch of his life.

One day they called me and told me they now wished me to confess. As usual I refused and I also told them clearly that they could only rehabilitate someone when he decided to be rehabilitated, and that any confessions extracted under force were not binding. At this point I was given a strong blow by Rochester.

Slowly I rose to me feet and I was then taken to another open place near the ration stores where three other men were called to come and help screen me. They were Jonah and Elijah, both from Nyeri, and a clerk from Kiambu. Four Europeans were also present, Rochester, Buxton and two prison Officers. They said that this was my last chance to confess. I gave the same reply as before. Slowly and significantly they started on me. Europeans only; the African screeners took no part in what happened: people said that the Europeans thought they could do it without going too far and that they were frightened the Africans would deliver a fatal blow. Many of the detainees working nearby could see what was happening and after what seemed a long while, just before I mercifully fell unconscious I saw Kiragu Wamugure, a great friend from Lodwar, standing among a group with tears streaming down their cheeks at my extreme suffering. My face was puffed up and split open, my right knee was fractured just below the kneecap by a club, and my chest was pierced by a strange instrument like a black truncheon with nails in it. I failed to die, but the scars on my knees and chest will always be with me and I still suffer from severe attacks of pain in my abdomen and thorax. I was shaved completely, the blood flowing from that operation too. The

[163] Josiah Mwangi Kariuki 'Mau Mau Detainee' Oxford University Press 1963 p.109

screeners eventually carted me away, my clothes splotched red with blood, and paraded me in triumph past the barbed wire compounds, telling my friends to come and see what their leader looked like now. I was thrown into a cell and for two days no food was brought near me; even if it had been, I should not have been able to open my mouth to put it in. The evening of my beating up, a detainee hanged himself in Compound 4. His sleeping companion, Jimmy from Embu, told me that he had seen my treatment and had said that he could not stand living in this hell any longer. He had used the rope which was issued by the Government to tie up our shorts.[164]

It is notable that Kariuki's 'beating up' was apparently done in full view of *'many detainees working nearby'*. Would those who were beating someone *'to within an inch of his life'* really want the performance to be witnessed by so many people? In a personal communication to me, James Breckenridge assured me that Kariuki's remarks were quite ridiculous and totally untrue. James added *"Kariuki eventually joined us at Karaba in the Mwea where, together with most of the others, he made a full confession of all the oaths he had taken and subsequently helped in the successful screening of other hardcore detainees"*.

———————————

John Dykes, a Kenya Regiment interrogator and one of the few Europeans who spoke fluent Kikuyu, was working at Mackinnon Road Detention Camp in June 1954. No 1 Compound housed the 'core of the hardcore' and Dykes was working through each one to see whether or not they were as bad as they had been made out. He was having little success in getting any of the men to talk, until a man was brought to him whom he recognised. It was someone he had saved from the hands of the police during an operation in Nairobi some months previously. The man, Manlik Wachira, had been responsible for executing several Kikuyu men and women in Nairobi who refused to take the oath. For some reason—perhaps because he had had a disagreement with those who had ordered the executions, or perhaps because Dykes spoke Kikuyu—he had given the names of several of the ringleaders to Dykes, and because of this, Dykes managed to have the charges brought against him reduced.

Dykes records his second meeting with this man.

———————————

[164] Josiah Mwangi Kariuki *'Mau Mau Detainee'* Oxford University Press 1963 p.129

I then went to the [Mackinnon Road] camp and saw the officer in charge of Compound No. 1, containing the people regarded as the most senior and hardcore Mau Mau whom I was to interrogate. He warned me that the compound was dangerous and that a few days before an inmate had been killed as the result of an altercation in the cook-house. The interrogations took place in a small room with just the two of us in the room.

Manlik was of course surprised to see me and even more surprised that I recognized him. After the usual warm greetings of old friends, I began to ask him about the inmates of Compound 1, and what was going on there. Unlike all the others I interviewed that morning, Manlik, on the promise that I would not divulge him as the source of my information, told me everything that I suspected had been going on. I learnt the whole story of what was happening in the camp. He told me that silence from the inmates was assured by continual re-oathing and that the Mau Mau had complete control of the camp. The penalty for either refusing to take the oath or divulging any information about Mau Mau, was death. He asked if I knew about the death of the man in the cook-house and went on to say that in fact this person had been murdered because he would not retake the oath. I knew that he himself would be killed immediately the inmates suspected that he had given me this information, so I had to make sure that no one would know from whom the information came, when I passed it on to the authorities. Manlik had complete faith in me not to divulge his name.

I continued to interview the rest of the compound of fifty of so people, and when finished, I reported to the commandant what I had found out, without divulging the source of my information. The men whose names I gave as the ring leaders were immediately taken out and sent to a camp on an island on Lake Victoria, thus breaking up the controlling committee, and sending the culprits out of harm's way.[165]

In this way, all the really bad hats from all the camps were collected together in one or two special camps, while the rest were prepared for rehabilitation.

One of the young men who was detained in the same Mackinnon Road camp was Francis Njuguna. He was a Kenyan athlete whose main discipline was the 440 yards. He had taken part in the Madagascar Indian Ocean Games in 1952 having qualified at the 1951 and 1952 Kenya Athletic Championships. In 1954, when he was 22 years old, he was detained during Operation 'Anvil'

---

[165] John Dykes – Pers. Comm

in Nairobi, in April of that year.

On Saturday 8th April I was heading home to Kabete to see my parents. I had to pass through Nairobi from Makongeni Railway Estate where I had been staying with my brother. While walking along Bohra Road, I was detained by British Soldiers accompanied by Kenya Policemen. They asked me for my I.D. card which I gave to them together with other documents including letters from the Chief and Priest. They were all in the same folder. The British soldier took them from me and threw them into a dustbin. I dare not protest as I feared I might be shot. We were being thrown around and hit. They were beating people and assaulting them. I remember being hit with the butts of guns and with batons. I was led away to a lorry with other Kikuyu, Embu and Meru people. We were taken to Langata Barracks where I stayed for about two weeks. We were then transported to Mackinnon Road Detention Camp. I stayed there for about one and a half years. Conditions at Mackinnon Road were terrible. We were not allowed to wear any clothes. We were housed in large cages of 250 people some of whom were old enough to be our grandfathers. It was all very humiliating being naked all the time except for a blanket we were given. When people died of typhoid, there was always a rush to volunteer to bury them as it was something to get us out of the compound as they had to be buried outside the camp. People were dying in that camp of typhoid. Many, many died. What annoyed me most was that I had not even taken the Mau Mau oath. The interrogators always told me I was a Mau Mau treasurer, but I always told them I had never taken the oath.

There were bad people in the Mau Mau, but there were also bad people in the Security Forces. That is what war always brings. We look upon those Mau Mau as freedom fighters. They brought us Independence. If it had not been for them we would still be under the British rule.[166]

John Dykes was in Mackinnon Road Detention Camp at the same time as Francis Njuguna, carrying out his interrogation work. When I asked him about Francis Njuguna's allegations he replied:

It is an unfortunate fact of present day life that there are still some people who want to rewrite Kenya's history for personal gain or personal prejudice. They refer to the Mau Mau terrorists as 'freedom fighters

---

[166] Transcription of an interview of Francis Njuguna by Cheryl Bentsen 1992 Contributed by Peter Lloyd

against a tyrannical colonial power'. Whereas it was an armed insurrection by terrorists against the inhabitants of their own country that had a fully constitutional Government with legal status recognised throughout the world.

At the age of twenty two, it would have been virtually impossible for Francis Njuguna, living as he did in Nairobi, to have escaped taking the oath. By the time of 'Operation Anvil' in 1954, every Kikuyu male over 18 years of age living, working, or even at school in Nairobi, had, by then taken the oath willingly or been forced to take it. Otherwise he would have been one of the hundreds murdered for refusing to take it. If by some extraordinary means, for example through an extended stay in hospital, he had escaped taking it, he certainly would have had to take it in Mackinnon Road Detention Camp. It was impossible to avoid taking it there, or at any other Detention camp or centre that I ever visited. Every Camp had its Mau Mau committee and anyone refusing to take one or more oaths would have met with some kind of 'accident'.

The claim that inmates were kept naked in Mackinnon Road is pure fantasy. On my visit, I went into the compounds and everyone was wearing normal clothes. Can you imagine the screams of horror from left wing M.Ps who came from London to visit all these Detention Camps with monotonous regularity, if they found any of the camps run contrary to the Kenya Prison's Ordinance and international standards. There would have been an almighty outcry. Njuguna's 'innocence' from having carried out any Mau Mau work prior to his arrest and detention, is impossible to believe. Every detainee had to have a Detention Order signed by a magistrate, or the District Commissioner and he would not sign it unless sufficient evidence had been produced from Special Branch, the Criminal Investigation Department (CID) or another policing authority to justify the order. Yes, the compounds contained up to 250 people and yes, they slept in hangar-type buildings, but the compounds were adequate otherwise there would have been eruptions from the Red Cross and other organisations that had free entry to all the camps. There may have been outbreaks of typhoid fever, but if there were, they would have been dealt with quickly, and it is possible there was the odd death, but anyone who knows about typhoid knows that unless it is dealt with quickly and properly, it spreads like wildfire, and there is no history of this happening at Mackinnon Road or any other detention camp.

Mackinnon Road may not have been the best administered detention centre, but it still had to meet standards that were acceptable to the Kenya Government and our British overlords, the general public and the world at large. Finally, while I cannot claim to be an authority on Mackinnon Road, Manyani or Wamumu Detention Centres, I do know that as a chief interrogator, I had to report to General Headquarters in Nairobi that it was pointless keeping an intelligence team at any of them in order to find out what was happening in the camps, as the 'honour of silence' insisted on by the Mau Mau committees was absolute and complete, and no amount of intelligence gathering was going to break the silence until the committees themselves were broken up through the removal of certain individuals, and the rehabilitation teams started their work[167].

Later, Njuguna goes on: *"At the Mission school I was in, we were all brainwashed with Christianity. There was a lot of brainwashing through Christianity in Africa....We were made to feel that they [the mission school teachers] were doing us a favour by taking us in their schools and giving us European teachers to teach us. It was as though it was a favour to us, so this is a kind of brainwashing."*

After the Emergency Francis Njuguna distinguished himself as secretary to the Kenya Olympic Committee and was also a member of the Kenya Films Censorship Board.

By 1957, 60,000 of the 80,000 detainees had been released and sent back to their families, but there remained some fifteen to twenty thousand committed adherents who were proving a much more difficult task. These had been kept in Manyani Camp and at distant places such as Mageta and Seiyusi Islands on Lake Victoria, but were now being moved to the Mwea and to Hola.

Terence Gavaghan, an Administrator with an impeccable record of service in Kenya was given the job of releasing these recalcitrants by rehabilitation. Gavaghan wrote of his experiences during this time and the result is a unique history of how he learnt to cope with these people and how, in the end, it was possible to bring most of them to a state where their families would accept them back into the fold. The book is entitled *'Corridors of Wire'*, and though written as a novel with the characters having fictional names, it is, nevertheless, a factual history of how these remaining detainees were

---

[167] John Dykes – pers. comm..

eventually constrained and brought to bay. In the 'Historical Note' that introduces the book, he gives an overall view of what lay ahead.

In successive sweeps of city and countryside, some eighty thousand suspected activists and adherents were arrested and detained: nearly one in three of adult male Kikuyu.

...As the tide [of the campaign] turned in favour of the Government, it was deemed safe and politically necessary to screen and release some three quarters of those detained. Many had been held for up to four years. The generally severe but peaceable process of filtering them through a series of camps, and interviews became known as 'rehabilitation', and the channel to release was called 'the pipeline'. The controlled outward flow was mainly achieved by religious and community development workers through thousands of personal and group encounters. Inevitably it slowed as the more stubborn adherents were reached and the pipeline finally dried.[168]

Medicine men at a cleansing ceremony

Interestingly, the ones that had committed terrible crimes under the influence of the oaths, did not usually find it difficult to confess their crimes voluntarily and come out of their oath-induced malevolence once the right key had been

---

[168] Terence Gavaghan *'Corridors of Wire'* 1994 Published privately. P.ii

found to unlock the store that housed all the malice. District Officer Henry Wright's cook was a self-confessed Mau Mau executioner who admitted in his final confession to 35 different 'executions' of 'traitors'. Wright described him as *'a grand chap who goes out of his way to please me with his cooking!'*

It was the oath administrators themselves, the ones who thought up the vile acts; they were the difficult ones to rehabilitate, and some of them remained irreconcilable until well after Independence and could not return to their homes as their families would have nothing to do with them. They lived out their lives as outcasts, never to be expunged of their hideous inventions.

The handling and treatment of these recalcitrant detainees by the authorities, has, over the decades, been the subject of considerable attention by writers and journalists. Allegations not only against those who were directly responsible for the welfare and treatment of camp inmates, but also against the British Government who sanctioned that treatment, have been made by some American academics, who, with the documented history of their own forebears' treatment of North American Indians, should be the least qualified to make these outrageous accusations on the treatment of indigenes. It has been declared that conditions in some of the Kenya detention camps were worse than those of the notorious Japanese prisoner of war camps in World War II and even to Auschwitz. These are such scurrilous accusations that it is necessary to address the subject in some detail to refute them, and put the facts as they occurred in their correct context.

With the benefit of first hand information from officers who were there at the time and who were responsible for what took place but who have not spoken up before, together with very detailed research into the Public Records Office at Kew, London, I have been able to piece together and record exactly what took place in the detention camps and why extremely harsh treatment was occasionally necessary. Some of the most important files in the National Archives were, under the 30-year rule, not available until 1987 and beyond, and therefore I have had the benefit of seeing these official documents to which authors of earlier works may not have had access.

To some extent, a casual observer could be forgiven for not believing the facts that emerged from these detention camps. It is, by no means easy to understand the degree of force necessary to control these fanatical men. The most irreconcilable of them were not normal Kikuyu people, though they were not insane. They had become obsessed by the bestiality of oath-taking and by so doing, had become sub-human – a description not lightly used but one approved by those who had to deal with them daily. Coupled with this, as Carothers points out in his study of the Mau Mau psychology, there were probably genuine mentally disturbed cases that helped to swell the numbers of these extremists. *'There are in all societies, African, European and others, always a number of unstable, emotional aggressive people who are a constant menace to society. In Europe, they spend much of their lives in institutions (mental hospitals, prisons etc.). It is safe to assume that in a land like Kenya, where such institutions are a relatively recent innovation and as yet of limited accommodation, far more of these people live at large than is the case in more developed countries.'*[169]

Manyani Detention Centre

A visitor to the camps who had no experience of these people might be shocked at the treatment he saw being meted out. But it should not be forgotten that this was still an age where, in some schools in England, boys were being beaten on their bare buttocks by the senior boys for certain transgressions, with the direct approval and regulation of the school authorities, a matter of which I had some personal experience!

---

[169] Dr. J.C. Carothers – *The Psychology iof Mau Mau* 1954 p.4

One District Officer who was posted to the Mwea to take part in the rehabilitation of 'Z' category detainees, on arrival there, saw the methods that were employed to control these people, and refused to work there. Without listening to those who had to deal with them, and without waiting to see or hear why such treatment was necessary, he got back into his vehicle and reported to his seniors in Nairobi the same day. He expected to be expelled from the Service for his refusal to carry out his duties, but the Commissioner responsible for his posting, realised his temperament was quite unsuited to cope with the measures that were needed, and instead posted him to an area of Kenya where his subjects were more agreeable. It is unfortunate however, that he did not stay at the camp a little longer to find out the reason why such treatment was the only way to restore the most affected internees, instead of taking every opportunity in the world's media since then, of castigating those who had the extremely responsible, difficult and unpleasant task of dealing with them.

It would be a mockery to refer to these people as political prisoners. They were unstable, emotionally disturbed and extremely violent men. It has been well documented that Jomo Kenyatta himself, when he came out of detention completely disowned them. They were an embarrassment to him. His son Peter Mwegai, from his first Kikuyu wife, worked with Breckenridge in Karaba camp on the Mwea in the rehabilitation process of these people and no doubt reported on them to his father. Breckenridge recalls that Peter did an excellent job. In every case I have come across in the research for this book, I have found none of those who actually witnessed these people and their behaviour while in detention, describe them as normal human beings able to make reasoned decisions or judgments. Even the Attorney General of Kenya visiting the Mwea Camps that were holding the very worst of the recalcitrants, having witnessed at first hand the treatment of new intakes, even he described them as unable to respond to 'the orthodox methods of non-violent persuasion'. Professor Junod of the International Red Cross, an expert on African prisoners, who was invited to visit the camps at Mwea to advise on the treatment and reconciliation of these hardcore detainees advised that '*if a short, sharp, physical shock when they first arrived at the Mwea was the price to be paid for their early release and repatriation, then it would be a price worth paying*'. As the Colonial Secretary Alan Lennox-Boyd said in the House of Commons at the time of the Hola incident, ' *Men with extreme mental reversions, demand extreme measures*'. It is not necessary, therefore, to try and hide or play down the harsh measures that had to be taken in order to deal with these humans on the edge of society. They had to be controlled so that they could be eased out of their oath-imposed stupor, ready to start back on the road to sociability and re-absorption into their communities. But it does no justice to those who were able finally to divest themselves of the horror, nor to those in charge of them, to describe their treatment without being thoroughly aware of their mental state at the time.[170] Sadly, some were so badly affected that they were beyond reconciliation and their own people shunned them. They had to end their days as *mu'undu mu'uru* – outcasts, never to return to their own communities.

Most of the men who arrived at the Mwea from Manyani, Mackinnon Road and other detention centres, had been refusing to work in their previous camps. Some of them even refused to 'slop out' or clean away their own garbage, or to change their clothes or to have their hair cut. The only variation to their existence had been to keep re-oathing each other with different novelties thrown in, or tattooing each other with acacia thorns into which they would drip juice squeezed from tomato leaves. The group was often led by a crazed fanatic with long dreadlock hair who purported to be sent from some obscure god to instruct them. He would see 'omens' in a fish rising from the surface of Lake Victoria or in the flight or call of certain birds.

By 1957, after the fighting war was over, there still remained a number of these hardcore Mau Mau that had been sent back and forth through the pipeline and filtered through the various camps until they arrived at the Mwea, in Embu District, and Hola, near Garissa, to be rehabilitated and hopefully repatriated to their homelands. There were several camps at the Mwea each having various grades of hardcore detainees. Rehabilitation and repatriation went on at these camps, though the throughput slowed as the more extreme members were left behind. These proved more and more intractable as the manic effect of the oaths plagued and twisted their minds. They had been sent to the Mwea because they had refused to carry out the most basic hygiene and daily routines such as the removal of their toilet buckets, the cutting of their hair and even the changing of their clothes. These 'Z' categories – 'the core of the hardcore' were so degraded that even their families who were allowed access to them, wanted nothing to do with them until they returned to some form of decency. The feeling was often mutual, and some detainees, if they

---

[170] See appendix 3 for letters written by ex-detainees after they had returned to their families.

were not restrained in time, would throw the contents of their slop bucket over their unfortunate visitors.

These people were not 'political prisoners' as some have made them out to be. They were not *'True African Nationalists fighting for the freedom denied to them by the British'* as Josiah Mwangi Kariuki, assisted by John Nottingham in their book *'Mau Mau Detainee'* has made them out to be. Far from it. At the outset they were committed to violent revolution as they had shown in their murderous forays against their own communities in the Reserves who refused to join their cult, and against other lawful settlers on Kenya land, with which the vast majority of Kenyans were in agreement. When they were thoroughly shunned by their own people, a few of them who were unable to accept they had been wrong, turned to more and more bestial shenanigans with each other. If these people had not been detained and had been allowed to roam the streets, there would have been another 'Rwanda' or a 'Congo', a 'Sierra Leone' or a 'Uganda' with one tribe or ethnic group attempting to annihilate another.

The difficulty, as Terence Gavaghan explains, was that these hardcore members like all the rest before them, also had to be released as soon as possible.

> By 1957 there remained over fifteen thousand men (and some women) behind the wire, mostly classified as 'hardcore', or 'irreconcilable'. They were not amenable to any form of external discipline or inducement to abandon the violent code of Mau Mau. Their personal identities were lost or denied within often impenetrable compounds. They declared themselves to be 'the people of the wire'.
>
> A new and concerted effort was mounted by the Governor, in consultation with the [British] Secretary of State under a special Government Minister charged to reduce this solid mass to less than six thousand within two years, a total judged to be the worst that could be tolerated during the political changes leading up to independence (then only six years ahead).[171]

This formidable task was delegated to Terence Gavaghan himself, under the title of 'Administrative Officer-in-Charge of Rehabilitation. He was to work closely with senior officers of the regular Prisons Service and the Ministry of Community Development, but he was to report directly to the Minister for

---

[171] Terence Gavaghan *'Corridors of Wire'* 1994 Published privately. P.iii

African Affairs. No oral or written instructions or guidance were given to Gavaghan, and although the broad purpose and its political significance was made plain, the methods to achieve it were left unspecified and had to be worked out by Gavaghan who had no precedent from which to work.

He set about his task with typical enthusiasm and dynamism. At the head of a combined team he evolved a new approach based upon clearly defined imperatives: *to re-establish control and order in the camps; to eliminate any sources of fear from any quarter; to find and follow some common objectives with those of the detainees; to set and achieve targets of self-renewal through work and individual expression, and progressively to offer a return home without shame*[172].

The policy was that an all out effort should be made to release these last detainees, as soon as they were fit to go home. The reason for this was that although the fighting war was at an end, the Emergency Regulations could not be relaxed until all the detainees had been repatriated to their home locations. This ending of the Emergency powers was frustrated by the most hardcore of all detainees themselves, because they did not want to be repatriated; they resisted it as hard as they could, as they knew only too well that if they were taken back to their home locations they would not be welcomed by their families and would, in fact, be ostracised because of the enormity of the acts of oathing to which they had succumbed.

Gavaghan soon found that work was the secret to begin the task of rehabilitation. He had found that once they had begun to work, by force if necessary, the detainee's rehabilitation became easier, both for them and for those trying to carry out the rehabilitation. Somehow, the positive action of picking up a shovel and digging an irrigation trench that allowed water to flow down through it to a rice paddy, gave them an incentive. This proved the trigger that began a cycle of actions that restored some purpose and meaning in their lives.

But the Mau Mau had a most sinister and primeval method of frustrating the order to work, or even to move from one large compound to another smaller one or from one camp to another. The action to which they resorted, grew to be a dreaded event in the camps housing the 'Z' category detainees. It

---

[172] Ibid p.iii.

became known as the 'Mau Mau pyramid'. It started with one or two of those whom the warders were trying to force compliance with their orders. They would start a gruesome moaning sound and others would take up the chorus, the moan rising in crescendo to a howl. This was done by 'ululating', something Kikuyu women did when they were being beaten by their husbands, or when they wanted to attract the attention of others some distance away, perhaps across a valley. They also did it at large gatherings, when praising a national leader. It is done by rapid movements of the tongue up and down while issuing a loud yell. It is very piercing and extremely intimidating. It was unusual for men to carry out this extraordinary behaviour which sounded more like a chorus of howling wolves. Once a few started the howl, like neighbourhood dogs, others would pick it up and soon the whole camp would be howling. At the same time, those who were the initial perpetrators would lie on the ground while others lay on top of them with more and more clambering on top until a kind of heap or pyramid was formed, which, if there were enough of them in the compound, soon became a seething mass of thrashing arms and legs. It was a terrible scene to behold and with the whole camp in uproar, extremely intimidating. There was little the warders could do either to prevent it happening, or to stop it once it had started. The only thing was to leave the compound and let the thing burn itself out.

Senior Superintendent Cowan describes an incident where this happened.
There were some eighty detainees in Thiba Camp [in the Mwea] who had refused to participate in any rehabilitation activities, and we decided to compel them to do so. Fifty warders with shields and batons were detailed for the purpose, reinforced with one hundred recruits in training at Karaba.

The detainees were ordered by Terence [Gavaghan] to proceed outside the camp to the playing field. This they refused to do, whereupon they were warned that force would be used if they persisted in their refusal. They were given five minutes to make up their minds. They still refused. The warders, equipped with shields and batons, were then ordered to surround the detainees, which took place without incident; but when a small party of warders were detailed to remove ten detainees one by one, general uproar ensued. The situation became difficult to control, which led to a number of detainees being hurt, four requiring hospital treatment. It was on this occasion that I witnessed what has been described as the pyramid effect and the Mau Mau howl, which I personally found to be a profoundly distressing spectacle. When the detainees scattered, chased by warders with batons, they appeared instinctively to form themselves into a violently vibrating almost symmetrical heap, writhing and howling in anguished submission. Those on the outside kept burrowing in until only their feet and part of their legs were visible – truly a horrific and primordial sight. Never again at the Mwea were disciplinary measures attempted with detainees en masse.[173]

This behaviour may well have had its origin in a relic from former times, as a method of intimidating attackers during battles, when surrounded by overwhelming odds there was no means of escape – not unlike the formation of the famous British Army 'Square' in the nineteenth century. It was frightening to experience for the first time and officers and warders were indeed intimidated by the chilling sounds and the formation of the 'Mau Mau pyramid'.

In order to get them to work, Gavaghan devised a scheme that came to be called 'The Dilution Technique'. The idea was that the most recalcitrant among the new intakes should be separated into single individuals, the moment they arrived at the Mwea camps. Each one was then put into a compound with ten 'co-operators'. 'Co-operators' were men who were already on the road to recovery and who had accepted the discipline of the camps and were waiting to be repatriated to their homeland. They had realised the futility of carrying on their protests and had submitted to the process of rehabilitation. They had not necessarily confessed in the way that the more tolerant ones had done with the Breckenridges, but they were on the road back to normality. The co-operators were happy to go to work on their new intake, and no one could do the job of turning them round better. Much the same routine as we carried out in our pseudo gang work.

Superintendent John Cowan describes how this worked at Thiba Camp in the Mwea;

One hundred and sixty ['Z' category] detainees arrived by train every Thursday. They were divided into two batches of eighty, for admission to two of the four camps. On approaching the camp, the detainees were split into four parties of twenty and held some half a mile away. Half the existing camp population—several hundred detainees—were waiting for them in a tight semi-circle outside, a short distance from the perimeter.

[173] John Cowan MBE, Unpublished memoirs.

The party of twenty were drawn up in one line in front of the semi-circle, for a short talk by the senior rehabilitation officer, after which several particularly well known detainees from the semi-circle would get up, one after the other, and relate their Mau Mau oaths and activities. When the detainees had spoken in this way, both newcomers and the existing population, would be formed up and march back to camp singing, usually a song with words like *'Mau Mau amekimbia'* 'Mau Mau has run away', to be confronted by the remaining inmates within the perimeter. Both halves would be formed into a tight semi-circle, and detainees who had not previously spoken would address the newcomers.

When it was perceived that this procedure had served its purpose, five newcomers were separated and taken to a compound where they were shaved, searched and re-clothed in new clean uniforms. They were given a further talk by the senior rehabilitation officer, who emphasised the standards of order, discipline and obedience required together with the punishment for non-compliance. They then joined in normal camp activities and were subjected to detailed screening at which the vast majority confessed their Mau Mau oaths, most, on the day of their arrival.[174]

Over periods of several hours of conversation, I have had the privilege of discussing the subject with Terence Gavaghan as well as reading his factual novel *'Corridors of Wire'*. The experience has been most revealing. He told me there were some of the very worst of these 'Zs', that even the co-operators could not budge. These few had to undergo what can only be described as 'shock treatment', a procedure that Gavaghan calls 'Splitting The Rock'. I learnt that you had to treat them much as you would a favourite horse that had spent some years away from his own stable in the hands of a sloppy stable-lad who had allowed the horse to deteriorate into bad habits. When returned to its original stable, the horse had to be punished for its bad habits, but it had to be rewarded when it was doing something right. Referring to the analogy, Gavaghan was emphatic that, "Above all you had to love the buggers", and he went on, "You could never allow yourself or those under you to overstep the mark. If I ever saw the slightest indication that any of my staff actually enjoyed using what inevitably became 'necessary physical force', they would be gone within the hour — African or European". He instanced a Junior

---

[174] John Cowan MBE, Unpublished memoirs.

Officer, only recently posted to the Mwea camps, whom he found wearing kid gloves when dealing with mob control. This man was immediately removed.

So a form of discipline had to be devised that allowed prison staff to use the kind of force necessary to make these degraded sub-humans work and to keep even basic human cleanliness going, but to keep within the law in so doing.

The Kenya Minister for Legal Affairs, Attorney General Griffith-Jones, set out the parameters in a new draft regulation within which prison staff could operate to keep order within the camps and to keep basic cleanliness going, for medical reasons in particular. The memorandum setting out the problem and a new regulation for dealing with it, was written after a visit by the Minister to the Mwea Detention Camps, and following detailed discussions with the Officer-in-Charge of Rehabilitation, Terence Gavaghan, and the Prison Officer-in-Charge, Senior Superintendent John Cowan. The memorandum was sent to the Governor for his approval.

For the sake of clarity, I include the complete memorandum here.

"DILUTION" DETENTION CAMPS.[175]

USE OF FORCE IN ENFORCING DISCIPLINE.

1. INTRODUCTION.

In the application of the "dilution" technique of rehabilitation of the more intractable detainees there are two main objectives: firstly the conversion of the bad detainees, and secondly, but no less important, the maintenance of progress in rehabilitation of the co-operative detainees. The maintenance of strict discipline is a prerequisite to the attainment of these twin objectives. Success depends on the overwhelming predomin-ance of the reformative influences on the bad detainees over their disruptive influence on the co-operative detainees.

Psychology and symbolism play a decisive part in the process, and at no stage more vitally than at the very beginning, i.e. on the arrival at the "dilution" camp of a new intake of 'Z' detainees. Experience has shown that, on a new intake, two essentials must be substantially achieved if any appreciable prospects of success are to be preserved:

---

[175] Public Records Office, Kew, CO822/1251

255

firstly, discipline and authority over the new arrivals must be immediately established, and secondly, all physical symbols and souvenirs of their Mau Mau past, and of the camp from which they have come, must be removed from them. Thus, in the latter regard, their hair and beards (if any) are shaved off with clippers; this also facilitates their ready identification. In the important days immediately following arrival and "dilution", they are made to take off their own clothes and put on camp clothing, and any souvenirs (e.g. metal bracelets, made by themselves, which are a feature of Manyani) are taken off them; the purpose is to condition them psychologically to shed the past and look to the future, with its prospects of potential release. The establishment of discipline and authority over the new arrivals necessitates the use of force on any who defy authority and resist the impact of discipline. This use of force, and the responsible concern of the officers engaged therein regarding their own position in relation thereto, have been the subject of anxious consideration by the Government and prompted a recent visit to Kandongu Camp in the Mwea by the Ministers for Legal Affairs, African Affairs and Community Development, accompanied by the Acting Secretary for Defence and the Commissioner of Prisons. The purpose of the visit was to witness a new intake of Z detainees from Manyani and to observe the procedure and technique of reception. A description follows. Mr. T.J.F. Gavaghan, the District Officer i/c Rehabilitation, Mwea Camps, conducted the visiting party and explained the operation as it proceeded, and also himself participated in the proceedings and maintained in conjunction with the senior prison officers, direct personal control over the proceedings.

2. DESCRIPTION OF RECEPTION OF NEW INTAKE.

The intake consisted of 80 Z detainees from Manyani. They arrived by train at Sagana, in a third-class coach attached to a goods train. The disembarkation area was cordoned off by a Police G.S.U. armed with rifles and automatic weapons. Disembarkation took place at a siding, by which four lorries were drawn up, each with a "guard" of 10 warders (unarmed save with truncheons in their belts, and barefooted) under a warder N. C. O. On each lorry were two detainees of the last intake.

Disembarkation proceeded smoothly and without incident, under the direction of European Prison officers.

The detainees, each with his basket or bundle of possessions, were mustered, squatting in rows. A roll was called, each man answering his name and joining a party totalling 20 detainees, which was then allotted to a lorry. Each party mounted its lorry; the detainees were ordered to sit on the floor of the lorry, the two "Co-operator" detainees from the last intake started chatting to them at once, and the 10 warder-guards also mounted the truck and stood in it among the detainees.

The lorries moved off at 15-minute intervals (in order to stagger their arrival at the Camp). The journey to the Camp was about 7 to 8 miles and occupied, say, 20 to 25 minutes. The visiting party moved off ahead of the first truck in order to observe the truck's arrival at the Camp.

On arrival at the Camp, the detainees were hustled off the truck and into a cul-de-sac catwalk dividing two barbed-wire compounds. Here they were met by some 40 detainees of the last intake, with hair-clippers and clean camp clothing (a pair of shorts and a loose "sailor's blouse" for each new arrival.) Also in the catwalk were European prison and rehabilitation staff (including Gavaghan, Cowan (Prison Officer in overall charge of the Mwea Camps), McInnes, (Cowan's Community Development opposite number). Woods (Officer-in-Charge, Kandongu Camp), the Kandongu Camp Rehabilitation Officer, and one or two lesser European prison officers on the camp staff); the African warder guards from the truck accompanied the detainees to the catwalk and remained there during the proceedings but were mainly occupied in searching the detainees possessions.

The detainees were ordered to squat in two rows, one at each side of the catwalk. The "receptionists" from the last intake then handed out the camp clothing to each man and set about shaving their heads with the hair-clippers, talking to the new arrivals as they did so. The detainees were ordered to change into the camp clothes. Any who showed any reluctance or hesitation to do so were hit with fists and/or slapped with the open hand. This was usually enough to dispel any disposition to disobey the order to change. In some cases, however, defiance was more obstinate, and on the first indication of such obstinacy three or four of the European officers immediately converged on the man and "rough-housed" him, stripping his clothes off him, hitting him, on occasion kicking him, and, if necessary, putting him on the ground. Blows struck were solid, hard ones, mostly with closed fists and about the head, stomach, sides and back. There was no attempt to strike at testicles or any other manifestations of sadistic brutality; the performance was a deliberate, calculated and robust assault, accompanied by constant and imperative demands that the man should do as he was told and change his clothes.

In each of these cases, which the visiting party witnessed on this occasion (and it watched the reception of all four parties of 20), the man eventually gave in and put on the camp clothes. Gavaghan explained, however, that there had, in past intakes, been more persistent resistors, who had had to be forcibly changed into the camp clothing; that some of them had started the "Mau Mau moan", a familiar cry which was promptly taken up by the rest of the camp, representing a concerted and symbolic defiance of the camp authorities; that in such cases it was essential to prevent the infection of this "moan" spreading through the camp, and that accordingly a resistor who started it was promptly put on the ground, a foot placed on his throat and mud stuffed in his mouth; and that a man whose resistance could not be broken down was in the last resort knocked unconscious.

When changed and shorn, the men were made to squat in similar rows, facing the exit from the catwalk. They were then given a "pep-talk" by an African Rehabilitation Assistant in the vernacular. The gist was that they were on the way to release if they confessed and obeyed all orders, that instructions given in the Camp were orders to be obeyed immediately, that they would now be given an order to proceed to the adjoining compound and subsequently to attend a rehabilitation class, and that they would obey. The order was then given. Each man was asked in turn if he intended to obey. If he said "Yes", he moved on immediately; if he said "No" or did not answer, he was immediately struck and, if necessary, compelled to submit by the use of force in the manner described above.

The above process was conducted at speed and with urgently and constantly applied momentum. One party had just about been dealt with and moved into its compound by the time the next party arrived from the railway station, the interval between arrivals being that between departures from the railway station, i.e. 15 minutes.

Of the total intake of 80, about a dozen needed minor "persuasion" and 4 or 5 pretty rough treatment. One man had to be manhandled to his compound, but was subdued by the time he got there.

The European officers themselves carried out the violence necessary, the senior ones leading and directing. The African staff took little or no part, except that the man who was manhandled to his compound was so manhandled by four African warders on Gavaghan's direct instructions and the force which they applied, while not gentle, was primarily motive.

The use of force ceased as soon as a man gave any sign of

complying, or readiness to comply, with the orders given. The whole process, however, was one of rush, hustle and prompt and, if necessary, enforced discipline. The purpose is to compel immediate submission to discipline and compliance with orders, and to do so by a psychological shock treatment, which throws off balance and overcomes any disposition towards defiance or resistance.

The detainees comprising these Z intakes are particularly ugly customers and there is no doubt whatsoever that the use of methods of non-violent persuasion and normal camp punishments for disobedience would be, and indeed have proved to be quite useless and ineffective in their case. With possibly a few exceptions they are of the type which understands and reacts to violence and offers no appreciable prospect of responding to gentler treatment.

It will be observed that two types of force are involved that required to overpower and manhandle, and that entailing the striking of blows. The legal implications of these two types of force are discussed later in this paper.

3. PRACTICAL CONSIDERATIONS AND SAFEGUARDS.
The following practical points arise from an examination of the procedure described above: -

(a) the use of force could only be justified and permitted for the purpose of enforcing discipline and compelling compliance with authoritative orders; its purpose could not and must not be punitive or to injure; the pain caused is an inevitable consequence of the use of the force but must not be the primary intention or design underlying its use;

(b) serious injury must be avoided; kicking with boots or shoes should not be permitted; vulnerable parts of the body should not be struck, particularly the spleen, liver or kidneys; accordingly any blows should be confined to the upper part of the body and should avoid any area below the line of the chest, front or back

(c) the psychological effects on those who administer violence are potentially dangerous; it is essential that they should remain collected, balanced and dispassionate, and should consciously and resolutely resist the natural upsurge of temper and hot blood;

(d) equally important as self-control, is the close and deliberate control of participating subordinates by the officers in charge of the operation;

(e) the force should be carried out, where necessary, by senior and responsible European officers, assisted by dependable subordinate

European officers under immediate and effective direction and control; the use of African staff for this purpose should be avoided save where absolutely necessary in a sudden crisis;

(f) officers engaged in these unpleasant duties must be selectively chosen for their qualities of character, and any officer who shows the slightest sign of a lack of the necessary objectivity and self-restraint must be promptly relieved;

(g) every detainee included in a "dilution" intake should be medically examined before leaving his previous camp and any to whom force is applied should be medically examined again immediately after completion of the intake;

(h) by these and any other means it must be ensured that any force used is necessary, reasonable and in no way excessive, and that no serious injury is caused.

Consideration has also to be given to the need to impose discipline on the recalcitrant at other times than on the arrival of a new intake. The most obdurate and persistent resistors could gravely undermine the discipline of the Camp if their defiance and refusal to obey orders were not promptly and effectively visited with compulsion. To charge and punish them for a "prison" offence, achieves little or nothing, for they take a perverted pride in their incorrigibility and derive satisfaction and encouragement from the distinction which in their eyes, ordinary punishments afford them. The difficulties of maintaining discipline in a camp of marginal detainees in the face of determined defiance by a number of obdurate resistors are manifest, and undoubtedly the task of the officers responsible for discipline in these camps and for converting the obdurate detainees would be simplified if they were authorised to apply force of the beating type (as well as the overpowering type) on persistently refractory detainees at any time. Nevertheless, the risks entailed in any such general authority are considered to be too great to be undertaken; the dangers of excesses, the impracticability of constant and personal control and restraint by responsible officers in all parts of the camp at all times, and the insidious infection of violence, combined to eliminate any certainty of assurance against abuse. The problem of "dilution failures", however, is a difficult one. If sent back up the pipeline, e.g. to Manyani, their influence is most harmful, particularly on future "dilution" intakes, and there are already indications that this influence might eventually reach such aggregate proportions as to wreck the "dilution" scheme; already, comparatively few rejects have had a most deleterious effect on the 3,000 to 4,000 detainees at Manyani awaiting "dilution" – and this despite segregation. It is, therefore, hoped that arrangements now under examination to move such failures to a holding camp or camps, with a view to re-injecting them into the "dilution" process after a time, and in the meantime to prevent their contaminating pending intakes, will prove satisfactory.

In any consideration of the use of force on the lines described above, two considerations are of primary consideration:–

(i) the lack of any practicable alternative method of dealing with the worst types of detainees, with whom we must now deal if we are not to resign ourselves to holding them in detention for the rest of their lives;

(ii) the necessity to maintain discipline in the dilution camps and to support and protect the officers charged with this most difficult, dangerous and unenviable task.

4. THE LAW RELATING TO THE USE OF FORCE ON PRISONERS.

The only reference in the Prisons Ordinance and Rules to the use of force on prisoners is contained in section 18 of the Ordinance, which provides for the use of weapons against the escapes or attempts at escapes, combined outbreaks or attempts to force outside doors, gates or the enclosure wall of the prison, or the use of violence by the prisoner. Under section 19 of the Ordinance, prison officers have the powers, protections and privileges of police officers in arresting escapers and for the purpose of conveying prisoners to and from a prison (power to use necessary force in making arrests is contained in Section 20 of the Criminal Procedure Code).

The authority under section 18 to use weapons must necessarily imply an authority to use lesser forms of force, if adequate, for the like purposes. Accordingly, it may be taken that the use of force on prisoners, and on detainees (the relevant provisions for the Prison Ordinance and Rules being applied to detention camps and detainees by reference — Regulation 18 – 20 of the Emergency [Detained persons] Regulations, 1954) is contemplated and authorised by law, to such extent as is necessary, for the following purposes:-

(a) to prevent escapes or attempts thereat;

(b) to prevent combined outbreaks, attempts to force outer doors, gates or enclosure walls;

(c) to counter violence used by prisoners;

(d) to arrest escapers or to keep prisoners or detainees in custody while in transit.

It will be observed that there is no express mention in the law of the use of force for the maintenance and enforcement of prison discipline. Section 52 of the Ordinance, however, provides that all prisoners (and, by reference, detainees) are subject to prison discipline, and Rule 20 (24) of the Prisons Rules, 1949, requires prison officers to maintain proper discipline among the prisoners. Section 84 sets our "prison offences", i.e. offences by prisoners against prison discipline, and succeeding sections deal with trial and punishment thereof.

There must, therefore, it is considered, be implicit in the disciplinary provisions of the Ordinance and Rules an additional authority to use force, to the minimum degree reasonably necessary, for the following purposes:–

(a) to arrest offenders against prison discipline (section 18 does not extend to this) for the purpose of their trial and punishment for prison offences;

(b) physically to prevent offences against prison discipline; and

(c) to enforce physical compliance with orders, e.g. to move prisoners, or prevent prisoners from moving, in accordance with lawful orders disobeyed, and to e.g., wash a prisoner forcibly if he refuses to wash himself when ordered to do so.

It seems, therefore, that it would be legally justifiable to strip a prisoner of his clothes and forcibly introduce him into other garments if he refused to perform these acts for himself when ordered to do so; to manhandle him from A to B if he refused, when ordered, to move himself; and to shave his head and search his person if he refused, when ordered, to submit thereto. Such action would be without prejudice to the prisoner also being tried and punished for prison offences committed by disobeying orders, and any violent resistance by the prisoner, or attack on prison officers, in the process of compulsion could legitimately be met by such counterforce as might be necessary to overpower him.

There still remains, however, the force used in the Mwea Camps to compel new intakes to submit to discipline, i.e. the blows struck in order to make a man do for himself what he is ordered to do, as distinct from the force used to overpower him and do forcibly for him what he is ordered to do and refuses to do for himself. This form of force is not "necessary" in the orthodox sense, and is therefore probably not included in the express or implied authority mentioned above, being an authority imported by reference to the treatment of convicts in prisons. Nevertheless, it is the crux of the whole psychological problem of disciplining the more thug-like 'Zs' on dilution. It has been found to be the most successful means of receiving these thugs into the dilution camps without undermining the system of discipline in those camps. Not only do 75% of those who have to be beaten on arrival subsequently turn and volunteer to confess, but the shock treatment on arrival sufficiently subdues the new intake collectively to allow the balance of discipline to be held over the rest of the camp notwithstanding the disruptive influence of the new arrivals.

If we accept the necessity to enforce discipline on the defiant 'Zs' on intake into dilution camps, not only by force to overpower and manhandle but also, if necessary, by force, i.e. beatings, to compel submission to discipline the authority to use force should, it is considered, be provided expressly and in the direct context of the treatment and disciplining of detainees in detention camps. The authority would then be construable in relation to the particular and exceptional circumstances of detention, its underlying purpose of rehabilitation and its special requirements of discipline. The importation of authority to use force on detainees merely by reference to and analogy with the treatment of convicts in prison would, it is thought, leave the officers concerned in the use of force by beating, open to prosecution for, in effect, carrying out accepted executive policy; their only protection would be the Attorney-General's discretion not to prosecute, and it would be neither constitutionally correct nor politically advisable that the discretion of a quasi-judicial authority, independent of the Executive, should be relied on as the means to implement executive policy with respect to a practice of questionable legality.

The Prison Rules, 1949, of England (1949 No. 1073) contain, *inter alia*, the following provisions under the heading "DISCIPLINE AND CONTROL" –

Rule 29 (i) "Discipline and order shall be maintained with firmness, but with no more restriction than is required for safe custody and well ordered community life;"

Rule 34 (i) "No officer in dealing with prisoners shall use force unnecessarily and, when the application of force to a prisoner is necessary, no more force than is necessary shall be used."

The Prison (Scotland) Rules, 1952 (1952 No. 565 [S.18]) contain in rule 179 the following provisions –

(1) No officer in dealing with prisoners shall use force unless its

use is unavoidable, and no more force than is necessary shall be used.

(2) An officer shall not strike a prisoner unless compelled to do so in self-defence."

Both the English and Scottish Rules go on to provide, in relation to the use of force, that: "No officer shall deliberately act in a manner calculated to provoke a prisoner."

(It is perhaps interesting to note that the UK Rules are framed in limitative terms; they limit an assumed or implied power to use force rather than confer an express power to use force. This reinforces the view that there is an implied power to use force, where necessary, beyond the strict confines of section 18 and 19 of our Ordinance).

With the UK Rules as a partial terminological guide, the following draft regulation has been devised, which, supported by precise administrative instruction limiting the use of beating to the time of reception of new intakes and importing the necessary safeguards, is considered to be adequate to provide sufficient legal cover without being too ostentatious and politically provocative.

"Discipline and order shall be maintained with firmness. Force shall not be used in dealing with detained persons save when necessary to enforce discipline and preserve good order, and no more force than is necessary shall be used. Moreover, save by or under the personal direction of the officer-in-charge or, in the case of his absence or incapacity, the senior prison officer present in the camp, force shall not be used under this regulation except when immediately necessary to restrain or overpower a refractory detained person, or to compel compliance with a lawful order or to prevent disorder".

The above draft is designed for incorporation in the Emergency (Detained Persons) Regulations, 1954, immediately before Regulations 16 and 17, which deal with punishment for minor and major offences against camp discipline.

5. CONCLUSIONS

It cannot be over-emphasised that the use of force on persons in custody is ordinarily abhorrent and illegal, and, even within the strictly limited confines discussed above, potentially dangerous. Its only justification is the necessary enforcement of discipline; it must never be used punitively (save by way of corporal punishment awarded formally and by due process for a proved offence) and, needless to say, it must never be used to extort confessions. When necessarily applied, it must be applied responsibly, deliberately and dispassionately, with adequate safeguards against causing serious injury, under the immediate control of a senior

European officer, and in no greater degree and for no longer than its purpose necessitates.

The subject is fraught with difficulties, dangers and pitfalls, and, if the solution is unorthodox, the reason is that it is designed to meet an unorthodox problem and to afford some prospect, which would otherwise be lacking, of reforming and releasing the worst type of detainee, whom experience has proved to be irredeemable by gentler methods.

7. SUMMARY OF ACTION PROPOSED.

(i) The present shock treatment for new intakes at dilution camps, involving the use of force as described, should continue.

(ii) The Emergency (Detained Persons) Regulations, 1954, should be amended by the insertion of a new regulation in the terms of the draft set out above.

(iii) Administrative instructions should be issued by the Commissioner of Prisons restricting the use of force by beating to the reception of new intakes and recording the safeguards mentioned above against causing serious injury (which have already been introduced in practice).

(iv) Arrangements are being examined and will in due course be made, to remove "dilution failures" to a holding camp, with a view to giving them a subsequent chance of passing through the dilution process, and in the meantime to avoiding their contaminating pending intakes at Manyani.

Signed: Griffith-Jones, Minister for Legal Affairs.

———————

This memorandum, together with its new draft regulation, was laid before the Governor, but before he could sanction its use, the Governor felt he must send it to Whitehall for the approval of the Colonial Secretary, the Rt. Hon. Alan Lennox Boyd. In his covering letter to the Secretary of State, dated June 25th 1957, having spoken at some length to Gavaghan, the Governor, Sir Evelyn Baring, wrote:

In this covering letter to the enclosed papers [the memorandum], I wish to put before you two ideas. The first is that the so-called 'Dilution Technique' in camps for detainees is giving very hopeful results indeed and is in fact the only way of dealing with the more 'dyed-in-the-wool'

Mau Mau men who will be our problem in the future. The second is that its successful implementation depends on our ability to deal with a small number of very difficult men; and if we are to do this successfully, risks are unavoidable.

An administrative officer named Gavaghan, who has taken charge of all the Mwea camps, has introduced a number of changes and the result with the Manyani 'Zs' who go there, has been good. He staggers the arrival of the detainees, bringing them from the [railway] station in batches of twenty with intervals between each batch, and he has introduced a modified dilution technique mixing one new arrival with ten co-operators.[176] He insists that any step taken to deal with refractory detainees must be by the [European] staff and not by the co-operating detainees. He has introduced more Kikuyu warders and over half the warder staff on the Mwea are now Kikuyu. He has generally improved co-operation and organisation all round. As a result, the Mwea is now again taking Manyani detainees and dealing with them successfully.

The Governor goes on to explain to the Secretary of State that although the rate of intake from Manyani into the Mwea is still somewhat low, it should be possible to increase it soon.

We find that with the type of men from Manyani with whom we are now dealing, there are a certain number who arrive determined to resist and to cause others to resist [the 'Z' cases]. We also find that the resistance of these men breaks down quickly in the great majority of cases under a form of psychological shock. It was for this reason that the Ministers mentioned in Mr. Griffith Jones' memorandum, visited the Mwea and saw the treatment of the new intake.

Gavaghan has been perfectly open with us. He has said he can stop the secret beatings [by prison staff] such as that which occurred in the case of Jasiel Njau[177]. He has said he can cope with a regular flow of Manyani 'Zs' and turn them out later to the district camps.[178] But he can only do it if the hard cases are dealt with on their first arrival in a rough way. We have instituted careful safeguards: a medical examination before

---

[176] A 'co-operator' is someone who has confessed and has been rehabilitated but not yet repatriated.

[177] Jasiel Njau was beaten to death by a warder who was subsequently tried and found guilty of murder.

[178] District Camps are those camps in the Kikuyu homeland that began the repatriation system near the home location

and after the arrival of the intake; the presence of the officer in charge all the time and the force used being by European staff only.

We have felt that either we must forbid Gavaghan and his staff to proceed in this way, in which case the dilution technique will be ineffective and we will find that we cannot deal with many of the worst detainees, or, alternatively, we must give him and his staff cover provided they do as they say they are doing. That is the reason why the Attorney General has prepared a new draft regulation and that is the reason why, unless you disagree, I will accept the proposals and sign the new regulation in the first week of July.

Put another way the problem is this. We can probably go further with the more fanatical Mau Mau in the way of release than we had ever hoped eighteen months ago. But to do so there must with some, be a phase of violent shock. I privately discussed this question with Dr. Junod of the International Red Cross, who I knew well in South Africa and who has spent his whole life working with Africans and most of it with African prisoners. He has no doubt in his own mind that if the violent shock was the price to be paid for pushing detainees out to the detention camps near their district, away from the big camps, and then onwards to release, we should pay it. I agree that if we get into trouble [we] would be quite prepared to ask Dr. Junod, at the invitation of the Kenya Government, to visit us again and examine the methods used.

…We cannot leave the position at the Mwea as it is, for any length and so I shall be very grateful indeed if you could reply by telegram so that I can sign the new regulation. We must either do this or greatly slow down the flow and thereby undoubtedly increase the number of persons who prove irreconcilable over a long period of years. As the International Red Cross visitors remarked, the greater the number of detainees brought into comparatively small camps near their homes, the smaller will the number of those so near being irreconcilable that they have to go to Hola, prove to be.

Signed E. Baring[179]

The new regulation was not approved by the Colonial Secretary immediately. He insisted that before he could give the (British) Government's approval he would have to have a full discussion with the Governor about his 'doubts and hesitations' of so punitive a regulation. The Governor flew to the UK on 13th

[179] Letter addressed to the Secretary of State for the Colonies. Dated June 25th 1957 (PRO No.CO 822/1251)

July to meet with the Secretary of State. After their discussions the draft regulation was amended before it was approved, and while the initial 'shock' treatment was modified, it remained essentially the same:

"Those who refuse to obey a lawful order such as moving from one compound to another or changing their clothing, should be compelled to do so by means of 'overpowering force'. And those who commit a major offence by disobedience of a lawful order 'in such a manner as to show a wilful defiance of authority', should be summarily tried under Regulation 17(a) of the Detained Persons Regulation and the penalty of corporal punishment not exceeding twelve strokes inflicted on the spot".[180]

The Governor Sir Evelyn Baring leaves Nairobi for London by air

While this provision was made available to officers, the records show that it was seldom necessary to carry it out. It was, however, necessary to 'overpower' the occasional man with whom it was impossible to reason. These were men were so crazed and psychologically affected by persistently taking oaths, that they were, for all practical purposes, out of their minds. It should be remembered that in 1957 there was no moderate method of immobilising a

---

[180] Corporal punishment had been used as a means of punishment in Kenya prisons for several decades. It could only be used under the strictest limiting provisions and was used mainly for cases of rape, personal injury or repeated failure to carry out an order. Up to 25 strokes could be inflicted but the usual number was 12. One of the main provisions was that it could only be administered in the presence of a European Prison Officer.

person, such as has been perfected by civil authorities all over the world, with, for example, the use of C.S. gas that is now (2004) in common practice.

It has been necessary to go into detail to show why such punitive measures were needed to control these irreconcilable men. It is of the greatest importance for any student of Kenya's colonial history to understand the type of individual these 'Z' Category men were, and the effect that continual oath-taking had on them. They had entered the realms of insanity and were constantly in a trance-like state. It is equally important to appreciate the lengths the authorities went to, to ensure that any 'overpowering force' was carried out within the law, and that there was no conceivable alternative. The new regulations ensured that such force was carried out within specific parameters. The force was not haphazard or slapdash, with warders and officers meting out their own form of 'justice' as the mood took them. If the law was broken, as it was with the case of Jasiel Njau, the only detainee to die as a result of beating at any of the Mwea camps, the perpetrator was brought to justice immediately. That the International Red Cross was also given access to the detention camps where 'Z' detainees were housed, and that they were consulted at some length is evidence that everything possible was done to avoid the use of force, but where it proved impossible to persuade these intransigents to carry out orders without the use of force, everything was done to minimise actually bodily harm to the men. Nothing was hidden from the world's press, the British Government or from the International Red Cross[181].

Sadly there was an exception to the strict order, in another camp, not under the control of Gavaghan or Cowan. This happened at Hola Detention Camp, on 3rd March 1959 when eleven inmates died as a result of being beaten by the warders. Much has been made of this tragedy over the decades by those who would exploit this failure in the administration of the camp and it was, without

---

[181] Amongst those who visited the Mwea camps and were given unrestricted access to them were:
Phillipe Junod International Human Rights Investigator, who, on a visit to the Mwea Detention centres, remarked to the Commandant, *'Compared with Algeria you are angels of mercy'*.
Dame Margery Perham Oxford Historian; humanitarian.
Barbara Castle MP Labour Cabinet Minister.

doubt, a blot on the otherwise relatively unblemished record of the Detention Camps. It was also inexcusable. But like so many unnecessary tragedies, it was the culmination of several errors, omissions and sloppy management that brought about the tragedy. However, those who would censure the British over it, should, perhaps, dig a little more deeply into the archives to learn the true nature and facts of what actually happened, before they point the finger of blame too wildly and too accusingly.

It has not been easy to get to the bottom of exactly what happened on that day, but from the Public Records Office at Kew and extracts from Hansard, together with the assistance of some of those who were there at the time, I have been able to piece together as near true a picture as is possible, now that many of those who witnessed the incident are no longer with us.

Hola was a prison camp in the Coast Province of Kenya, which had been expanded to take detainees during the Emergency. Extra hutted compounds had been built that housed some two thousand of the original fifteen to twenty thousand Mau Mau adherents that Gavaghan had been under orders to reduce through rehabilitation and repatriation to their homelands. By March 1959, the numbers of detainees at Hola had been significantly reduced, and only a few of the most intractable members remained. Eighty five of the most intransigent of these resided in one compound. They had refused to be subjected to camp discipline and had also refused to work. Up to that time, it had not been deemed necessary to force detainees at Hola to work – work that involved digging channels for the nearby Tana River irrigation scheme for the local Pokomo population, and something they desperately needed, to grow better crops.

These eighty five people were the last remaining 'Z' detainees and it was necessary to repatriate them as soon as possible, so that the Emergency powers under which they were being held, could be lifted, and the Government could turn their attention to granting Internal Self-government leading to Independence for Kenya. It was not possible simply to send them back to their homes, as their communities would not accept them in the state they were in, and it would be irresponsible to allow them freedom to roam the countryside in their state of mental instability. Yet, because there was insufficient evidence to try them in a Court of Law, it was only under the Emergency powers that they could legally be detained, and without those Emergency powers there would be nowhere for them to go. The government was therefore in somewhat of a cleft stick over them, and it had to do something quickly to rehabilitate them.

It had already been established that the secret of their restoration lay in getting them to work. This had been found to be the trigger to rehabilitation over and over again. Thousands of ex-detainees were admitting openly that either their confession in the early days, or, for the more committed ones, their manual work later, was the one thing that brought them out of the awful web of Mau Mau filth, and gave them something positive to occupy their bodies and their minds.

The Commissioner of Prisons sent Senior Superintendent John Cowan, to Hola, to report on the best method of persuading these eighty five intractable men to go to work like the rest of those in Hola. Cowan, was the Prisons Officer-in-Charge of the Mwea camps, where he had been co-operating with Gavaghan to rehabilitate and repatriate successfully, thousands of detainees. Unlike the Mwea, 'the Dilution Technique' had not been used at Hola to pacify and subdue the new 'Z' category arrivals.

Cowan spent two days at Hola with the Officer-in-Charge of the camp, Superintendent Sullivan. He discussed with Sullivan, in some detail, how best to get these eighty five out to work in order to speed up their restoration. Sullivan had not worked at the Mwea, so did not have the benefit of seeing the best way to handle these intractables, something of which Cowan had, by now, had considerable experience.

After his visit to Hola on 7th and 8th February 1959, Cowan's report to his Commissioner, entitled *'Discipline – Hola Camp',* dated 11th February, was based on his experience at the Mwea, where small numbers of the intractables, around twenty at a time, were removed from their compound and made to work. This had proved highly successful and many 'Z' detainees had begun to work and had started on their way back to recovery and normality in this way. There had been a few cases where 'necessary force' had to be used in order to get them to work, but this had involved nothing more than several warders surrounding the man and physically giving him no alternative but to work, this procedure being carried out under the supervision of a European officer. Never had it been necessary to beat or kick a detainee unless he had continued to show open defiance against a lawful order. Batons, which some warders carried, could only be drawn and used in self-defence.

Exactly the same procedure was proposed by Cowan for Hola. On the specified day, twenty detainees at a time would be removed from the compound, while the rest of the convicts and detainees would remain in camp so as to allow as many warders and European officers as possible to be

271

available. The first twenty or so intractables would be taken down under close guard, supervised by as many European Officers as possible, to the work site, but they were not to be given tools or implements until later. Only one small group of twenty should be taken at a time, leaving other groups for later, when all was seen to be working well with the first twenty. All members of the staff would have been briefed with precise instructions as to how the operation would be conducted, and the appropriate action to be taken in events that might transpire during the operation, including manhandling any who might refuse to work.

Cowan's report concludes:

> Although discipline in a camp is intangible and cannot be measured by facts and figures, a brief visit to Hola leaves one in no doubt that the discipline amongst the detainees has been allowed to deteriorate. It is a problem that can best be solved by firmness and by intelligent co-operation between the authorities concerned. I believe the present prison Officer-in-Charge [Sullivan] is fully aware of the delicacy of his predicament and he has already done much for Hola by his enthusiasm and his infectious good humour. Wisely, I think, he has postponed a definite trial of strength until he was sure of his ground, but he appears able and willing now to put it to the test, as indeed he must, with his present staff. This does not imply a brutal and harsh regime but a high standard of personal example and insistence always on immediate obedience. The alternative 'peace at any price' can only lead to danger and disorder.[182]

This report, that came to be known as 'The Cowan Plan', was copied to the Attorney General for his approval. The Attorney General sanctioned the Plan under the existing regulations that allowed 'necessary force' to be applied where a lawful order was given, in this case to move to the place of work, and carry out the order to work. To order the detainees to work in in this way did not require new legislation. It had been done successfully many times before at the Mwea under the legislation of 1957.

Cowan also proposed that he himself should go to Hola to supervise the operation, or, if not him, that two of his experienced Superintendents from the Mwea should be provided. But the Commissioner of Prisons considered these

---

[182] Senior Superintendent Cowan – Report to Commissioner of Prisons dated 11th February 1959 Command Publication No. 816 *'Further Documents relating to the deaths of 11 Mau Mau detainees at Hola Camp in Kenya'* July 1959

precautions were unnecessary. A request by Sullivan for a Senior Superintendent 'with appropriate powers of summary punishment', was also turned down by the Commissioner. Cowan assumed that in any event, a copy of his report would be sent to Sullivan as a matter of course, to leave him in no doubt as to the measures and safeguards to be taken. Cowan himself was due overseas leave at this time, and although he offered to postpone it in order to supervise the operation, his offer was not accepted, nor was another experienced officer from the Mwea sent in his place. Furthermore, Cowan's report was never sent to Sullivan. Sullivan himself, in a Situation Report to the Commissioner dated 13th February, two weeks before the incident occurred, raised questions of the Commissioner appropos of the impending operation, but these were never answered. The reason for these serious omissions has never been explained, but they were clearly errors that originated in the office of the Commissioner himself. The Disciplinary Commission of Enquiry chaired by the then Solicitor General which took place several weeks after the incident, concluded that '*these omissions constituted the main causes of the tragedy that followed*'.

On 20th February Sullivan received an order from the Commissioner to carry out the operation as soon as was feasible. Sullivan replied that it would

Compounds at Hola Detention Centre

273

be carried out on Monday 2nd March, but because of illness among the warders, he decided to carry out the operation on Tuesday 3rd March 1959.

The work the 'Z' Categories were to carry out was some distance from the camp and entailed a walk of approximately half a kilometre down a main road outside the camp. However, instead of splitting the compound of eighty five men into batches of twenty and taking each batch out separately – a crucial part of the Cowan Plan, Sullivan, for some reason that has never been explained, decided to take all eighty five out together.

The detainees were closely guarded by some one hundred and fifty warders while Sullivan himself followed behind in his Land Rover. As they arrived at the work site, Sullivan left them in the hands of a senior (African) warder and returned to the camp on some other business. At the camp gate he met Officer Coutts, his European second in command, and instructed him to go to the work site to assist in the operation.

When Sullivan returned to the site, some twenty minutes later he found the place in complete chaos with six dead detainees and some twenty five to thirty others injured, some severely. A bowser of water stood close by.

It has never been possible to establish exactly what happened to precipitate this tragedy, and those officers, warders and detainees that gave evidence at the subsequent Coroner's Court did not even agree amongst themselves. However, one person who gave independent evidence to the Court, was Anthony Peters, the Officer in charge of the Hola Irrigation scheme, employed by the Ministry of Works. He was in his Land Rover going to the same place of work as the party of detainees. As he came up behind the party, he saw that a fracas was taking place between the detainees and the guards who were using their batons. He saw at least two bodies lying on the side of the road. As he had no authority to give assistance, and did not want to become involved, he turned his car round and went back to the camp. He did not see Superintendent Sullivan nor any other European at the site where the fracas was taking place.

Taking the Peters evidence and sifting through the rest of the evidence, it is possible to piece together the most likely account of what actually happened.

Superintendent Sullivan having returned to the camp, the eighty five detainees were left in the hands of a senior African warder who had at least 150 other Africans warders to assist him. When they arrived at, or were close to the site of their work, some of the detainees were issued with shovels and told to start digging. They protested and refused. The warders then proceeded to manhandle them to work, even though there was no European Officer present. Immediately some of the detainees started to howl and form a 'Mau Mau pyramid'. Others, who did not want to form the pyramid, tried to walk or run away and were thought to be trying to escape and were caught or restrained by the warders. Other warders trying to prevent the 'pyramid' and stop the howling, became involved in a fight and a warder was attacked with a shovel and provoked into drawing his baton to defend himself, whereupon other detainees went to their comrade's assistance. Batons were only allowed to be drawn in self-defence, but clearly other warders now saw their colleague being attacked and felt it was correct to draw batons. Within a matter of seconds, a fight broke out that soon deteriorated into a battle. The unarmed and outnumbered detainees were, no doubt, spoiling for a fight with their warders between whom there was known to be no love lost, and with no European officer present to see what was happening, the warders were also able to vent their feelings with impunity. At this point, Coutts arrived, but too late to effect any control whatsoever in the hopeless situation, though the battle probably subsided from that moment.

After some semblance of order had been restored, the bowser of water that happened to be close-by was used by the warders in their panic to try and bring round those detainees that had collapsed from the baton injuries. It may even have been that some detainees were actually asphyxiated or drowned by having too much water thrown over them while they lay unconscious or semi-conscious on the ground. By the time Sullivan returned in his Land Rover, six detainees lay dead and another five died subsequently of their injuries. Twenty two were taken to hospital in lorries and detained there with injuries ranging from severe bruising to broken limbs.

That, however, was not the end of the story. A radio message was sent by an operator in the camp before it was known exactly how the deaths had occurred, and before Sullivan had been able to inform the radio operator accordingly. The garbled story that emerged was that a number of detainees had died either of poisoning by drinking from a contaminated water bowser, or possibly by over-drinking the cold water in the extreme heat of the day. This message somehow reached the press in Nairobi and was sent to London and came out the following day in the media, as the cause of death.

The next day, the Commissioner of Prisons, Mr. J.H.'Taxi' Lewis, instead of going to the scene himself, sent his deputy, Campbell, to Hola to find out exactly what had happened. Campbell was accompanied by two senior government officials. A meeting took place at the camp with the three government officials on one side and on the other side Sullivan, with his four European prison officers, the District Commissioner, Mr. W.H. Thompson who chaired the meeting, and District Officer Marsden. No record of that meeting has ever come to light, but whatever transpired, Deputy Commissioner Campbell himself, together with the other two decided to keep to the story of poisoning, although they must have had grave suspicions as to how the deaths had been caused. Whether the party had to leave in a hurry because of deteriorating weather conditions (they flew to Hola from Nairobi in a light aircraft) or for some other reason, Campbell and his party left apparently without visiting the scene of the incident and without talking to Peters or to any other independent witnesses. More astonishing still, was the fact that they did not even go to the hospital. If they had done that, and it was only a matter of a short distance away from where they were holding the meeting, they would have seen twenty two detainees with severe bruising and limbs in plaster and could not possibly, thereafter, have failed to realise the truth. Questions were undoubtedly asked at the meeting about the use of force to get the detainees to work, because Campbell would have been privy to the Cowan Plan, but according to Campbell's subsequent report, the meeting concluded that although there were 'a few minor scuffles during the walk to the workplace', the deaths had been caused by detainees drinking too much contaminated water.

The three officials spent less than four hours at the camp. On their return to Nairobi the same afternoon, they reported to a meeting of Ministers at Government House. The Government Press Officer also attended this meeting, at which the story of poisoning was given as the official reason for the deaths.

At the subsequent Disciplinary Commission of Enquiry, the Government Press Officer, Robert Lindsay stated:

> There was no information open to us at the [Government House] meeting other than what was contained in Campbell's report. There was a good deal of discussion as to whether violence was the cause of the deaths of these men, and in answer to questions, the three officials that had just returned from Hola, gave it as their opinion that the deaths had not been caused by violence. The impression given was that there had been 'scuffles' but that they had not seemed serious. ...We were left with the emphatic impression that the most likely cause of death was the drinking of large quantities of water in the extreme heat, some of which was possibly contaminated.

It was then decided that I should draft a Press announcement. I did so and the draft was agreed by all those present including the three officials who had visited Hola.[183]

Thus it was that the garbled version of the incident was broadcast to the world and made official. When it came to be known subsequently, that the detainees had, in actual fact, been beaten to death, the authorities were quite understandably, accused of creating a cover-up.

Cowan's report to the Commissioner of Prisons was closely referred to by W.H. Goudie, a Senior Resident Magistrate who carried out the subsequent inquest at Mombasa, some two weeks after the incident. Cowan, who had returned from the UK especially to give evidence at the inquest, was shocked to hear his report picked on by the Magistrate who found that: *"the expression 'they should be manhandled to the site of work and made to carry out the task' would be construed by any reasonable person as carte blanche to use whatever force might be necessary, including the use of batons'"*.

Cowan strongly denies the implication that it was his report that led to the deaths. He points out that the use of batons was never mentioned in his report, nor was their use contemplated by him. *"Sullivan and the Commissioner knew what I meant; they knew the prison jargon and were conversant with the difference between 'compelling force' and 'overwhelming force'. Had I envisaged a wider audience [for the report] I would have been more explicit. As it was, the press and the media seized with relish on the magistrate's words, and totally misconstrued them. The damage was done."* In his memoirs, Cowan concludes: *'The situation at Hola offered no greater risk than many I encountered in the Mwea [camps] but it needed experienced staff and specific precautions. It got neither'.[184]*

The Magistrate's report at the inquest concludes:

...I find the evidence as a whole to be so conflicting and unreliable as to make it impossible to be certain as to the exact nature of everything that happened on this morning, when things must have been, for a considerable part of the time, quite out of the control of one man. The reason for this uncertainty is to be found partly in the contradictions and covering up generally of prisons staff, but in my opinion, mostly to the blatant lies of all the detainees themselves, whose sole concern seemed

---

[183] Disciplinary Commission of Enquiry into the Hola Disaster 29th June 1959
[184] Senior Superintendant Cowan – unpublished memoirs

to be to paint the blackest possible picture against the entire prisons staff irrespective of how patently impossible, even ridiculous their evidence sounded. I have had the misfortune in this inquiry, not to be able to feel that a single witness of the Hola Prison staff, warders, or the detainees, were making any real attempt to tell me the plain unvarnished truth.

...I find that the medical causes of death in the case of each of the eleven deceased was in accordance with Dr. Rogoff's finding in each case. These findings are shown in detail on the Post Mortem Report Forms... but for the purpose of further pursuance of this Inquiry it may be said broadly but without undue regard for scientific accuracy, that in each case death was found to have been caused by shock and haemorrhage due to multiple bruising caused by violence and contributory factors in such shock or haemorrhage.[185]

The magistrate then assigns the cause of death to each deceased as: fractured

District Commissioner Thompson (*back to camera*) with Prisons Officer Superintendent Turner (*facing*) briefing the press at Hola after the incident

jaw; fractured skull; fractured knee-cap; laceration of mid-brain etc.

He concludes: *I find the evidence is conclusive that the violence inflicted*

---

[185] W.H. Goudie, Coroner's Report

on all the deceased was inflicted in the course of a major operation... to compel detainees who had refused to work on any work not directly connected with their own well-being... to do manual work on the ALDEV Tana River Irrigation Scheme.

The Observer newspaper saw the camp in a slightly different light, in a report on Sunday May 31ˢᵗ 1959. Their reporter, George Clay, having visited the Hola camp the day before, writes:

> There were surprises all round when three months and many miles of red tape later, the Kenya Government allowed a press party to visit Hola. The group of officials who came to meet us at the airstrip...were more than eager to show off the remarkable experiment in rehabilitation which is being conducted at Hola. Though the pride and enthusiasm with which they demonstrated the good that has been done, could not altogether wipe out the memory of the bad, it did help to put the incident in much better perspective than that evoked by the Kenya Government's evasions and secretiveness.
>
> One major fact that the visit helped to bring home is that Hola is not just another barbed wire concentration camp crowded with rebellious prisoners. For 590 men, many of whom fought for years in the forest with Mau Mau, it is a prison without bars. And there is nothing to prevent 133 who are confined within the barbed wire of the 70 yard square 'closed camp', from attaining the same measure of freedom overnight.
>
> District Commissioner Thompson, senior administrative officer for the Hola area, says, in fact, that the metamorphosis could be effected in five minutes. "All a man has to do, to get out of the 'closed camp' is to ask," he told the visiting Press group.[186]

The subsequent Disciplinary Commission of Inquiry held on 26ᵗʰ June 1959, chaired by the then Attorney General found:

> If a copy of Cowan's report of 11ᵗʰ February had been sent to Sullivan, it is scarcely credible that Sullivan would have carried out the operation in the manner in which he did carry it out. Sullivan executed an entirely different plan to that proposed by Cowan and he abandoned those measures of safety and control, upon which Cowan insisted and which formed the basis of Cowan's thinking. ... Unfortunately the issue of an

---

[186] The Observer, Sunday 31ˢᵗ October 1959 *'Surprises All Round at Hola'*

279

interim Press Release pending verification of the facts was not thought necessary, and thus it was that the cover up story, seized upon with such spiteful relish by unscrupulous politicians, gained credence. [187]

In the end, Sullivan was charged with gross dereliction of duty. With certain mitigating circumstances taken into account he was required to retire from the Prison's Service without loss of gratuity.

The last word should go to the Colonial Secretary himself in his speech to the House of Commons in reply to the motion of censure, following the Hola disaster.

Mau Mau is a conspiracy based on the total perversion of the human spirit by means of the power of the oath, by witchcraft and by intimidation, all of which combine to place its followers mentally almost in another world, in which the pursuit of their twisted aims was the only important thing. To achieve this end, extensive organisations were set up of a type I think hitherto unknown. Every location in Nairobi, for instance, along the Mau Mau seedbed had its Mau Mau committee and its 'court', which dealt with the vilest forms of murder and of torture. Armed gangsters, the counterpart to the forest terrorists, were the instruments of what passed as Mau Mau justice, and so well did they do their work that the African population of all tribes was reduced to abject terror. There has been horrifying evidence of the workings of the Mau Mau court and the bodies of men and women killed by terrorists could be found practically every day. Evidence to convict their murderers, some of whom were known to the police, was unobtainable.

In the early days of the Emergency, courageous Africans came forward to give evidence against Mau Mau in open court. Many of them were murdered as a result. Often witnesses giving evidence when a trial was adjourned could not be found the following morning. Their bodies would be discovered months later in improvised graves or floating in the rivers. We do not know the extent of these murders but when the turn of the tide of Kikuyu opinion came, many hundreds of bodies were dug up, the vast majority being Kikuyu who had tried to do their duty as good citizens.

I do not think I need dwell on the bestiality of Mau Mau. Everyone knows, or should know, of the Lari massacre and everyone is acquainted

---

[187] Disciplinary Commission of Inquiry in to the Hola disaster dated 29th June 1959 Command Pub. No. 816 of July 1959

with the horrible ritual of the graduated oathing ceremonies and activities. Originally, the oaths differed little from the normal Kikuyu oath used in tribal ceremonies, but as the terrorists grew more brutalised, their moral degradation was reflected in the characteristics of the Mau Mau oath.

This developed sexual and sadistic aberrations, which, in the higher forms of the oath, included murder and cannibalism. All this ritual played its part in building up the Mau Mau mind, and the activities to which they were driving themselves tied them more and more to it.

All this came very much to light in the Report of the Parliamentary Delegation to Kenya in July 1954. …The report dealt particularly with the demoralising effect of these frightful oaths and it recommended that an inquiry into the psychology of Mau Mau should be undertaken. As a result, the Carothers' inquiry took place.

What is clear from both these reports is that the taking of the oaths had such a tremendous effect on the Kikuyu mind as to turn quite intelligent Africans into entirely different human beings, into sub-human creatures without hope and with death as their only deliverance.[188]

---

[188] Hansard 1959 Vol 607. Col 310

CHAPTER ELEVEN

LOCALISATION

'There will never be another Empire where people from the colonial power handed over in so brief a period, the machinery of government to those whom they governed.'
Eric Burr

'The desire to do the best for one's charges was, almost without exception, the driving force behind the colonial servant and we all knew that by so doing, we were working ourselves out of a job.
J.A. Golding *'Colonialism – The Golden Years'* Birlings - 1987

Although the British Government might be blamed for leaving the country to its own devices too quickly, the local administration cannot be shown to have been slow to hand over leading positions in the Civil Service to local Africans. It's just that they were not given the inducement, the money or the time to do the job properly.

In 1956 Winston Churchill wrote:

There has been no lack of critics, at home and abroad, to belittle Britain's colonial achievements and to impugn her motives. But the record confounds them. Look where you will, you will find that the British have ended wars, put a stop to savage customs, opened churches, schools and hospitals, built railways, roads and harbours, and developed the natural resources of the countries so as to mitigate the almost universal, desperate poverty. They have given freely in money and materials and in the services of a devoted band of Civil Servants; yet no tax is imposed upon any of the colonial peoples that is not spent by their own governments on projects for their own good.

It had always been the British Government's objective to hand over the government of Kenya to local people, black, white and brown. It was the timing of the hand-over that they never made clear, any more than they did the make-up of that government, and what the percentages of each race would be.

In hindsight, the ideal would have been to have made a proclamation in the 1930s that self-government would take place by a certain year following a period of constitutional development with a programme of education running parallel with it, so that as and when local candidates were considered ready to take over, expatriates would no longer need to be recruited – rather on the same lines as their mandate in Hong Kong. There is no doubt Kenya would have benefited enormously from such a declaration when stirrings about land issues first surfaced. But it was not done, and by the end of the decade, World War II made such a task impossible.

When Prime Minister Macmillan started forcing the pace of political change in Africa from 1957 onwards, the urgency to grant self-government and Independence that followed, had to be accompanied by an inordinate rush to localise the civil service, and Kenya, along with most other African states, has been suffering from the severely truncated period of localised civil service education ever since. Had expatriate officers been allowed to stay on for another decade, hand in hand with an accelerated programme of education and training for the civil service, they would have been independent of local pressures and a bastion against corruption. As Okelo-Odongo, Assistant Treasury Minister in the newly formed Independent Government pointed out in an opposition debate in the Kenya Parliament in 1964, *'In the Civil Service nothing is needed more than courage and integrity, and certainly the British Colonial Service had that!'*

Perhaps the most difficult thing a young African finds when he is put into a position of authority and responsibility is to discipline his subordinates. He is loath to report any wrongdoing in the workplace and will always try to avoid discharging a person for a misdemeanour or for underperforming. It is a trait little understood by Westerners. To a Western employer, to fire a man for incompetence is something that is taken for granted and comes naturally to him. Not so in Africa. Endearing feature though it may appear to be, as it implies, incorrectly in my opinion, a kind of misplaced compassion for one's fellow-men, it is a great disadvantage when it comes to managing a company or a country.

An explanation for this characteristic maybe that, apart from those few whose leadership was inherited such as the Masai *laibon*, the moment manhood began at circumcision, one lived as part of a small, tight community of one's peers. It had never been part of tribal custom to order or discipline one's peers – not, that is, unless or until they reached a venerated age when they would automatically assume authority over their families. This part of their culture is particularly applicable in the case of the Kikuyu where before the appointment of Chiefs and Headmen by the British, there was no tribal hierarchy and all administration was done on a family basis.

The necessity to be able to hire and fire people was something that I personally found had to be drummed into those Africans who had gained positions of responsibility, over and over again. The overwhelming reluctance throughout the African workforce, to remove those who were unfit for their job, has had serious repercussions in these first decades of Kenya's independence. It is something that, given more time, would surely have been focused upon by the outgoing colonial administration.

In 1946, the British Government published a White Paper (official policy) on 'Localisation' a word meaning the replacement of the expatriate workforce by local people. The Paper speaks of expatriates *supplementing locally recruited staff*. It goes on to state that *'if the progressive advancement along the road to self-government within the framework of the British Commonwealth of Nations is to be a reality, the public services must be adapted to local conditions and must, to the greatest extent, be staffed by local people. It is already a fully accepted principle that there should be no barrier to the appointment of a colonial candidate or a locally recruited public servant to any post which he is qualified to fill.'* One of the points the White Paper emphasised was that *'the structure of the service must permit the putting of the right man or woman in the right place, irrespective of race or colour, and with equality of treatment and opportunity, on the basis of efficiency and merit.'*[189]

Unfortunately the Mau Mau uprising six years later, got in the way of all this. The British Government had to put a massive amount of resources into quelling the insurgency and by the time it ended seven years later, the impetus for an extended period of self-government leading to Independence had been lost. It is surely reasonable to conjecture that if the Government had, in the 1930s, instigated a programme which would lead to self–government in, say, thirty years time, with full Independence to follow later, Mau Mau might never have taken place, though given the characters involved, it remains a somewhat dubious possibility.

That the British were serious in their intentions of handing over the country to internal self-government (ISG), is quite clear. In 1954, the Lidbury Commission Report on the civil services in the east African territories, which

---

[189] *'Organisation of the Colonial Service'*, Colonial No. 197 (HMSO 1946)

the British Government accepted in full, laid down certain principles regarding the question of localisation.

It may be taken for granted that it is the ultimate objectives of the east African governments, as they move towards self-government, to staff their public services as far as possible from their own resources. It is a settled aim of policy in East Africa that there shall be equality of opportunity for every indigenous community in the public service.

So far as the public service is multi-racial, each race [African, Asian and European] must make its full contribution. The essential principle is that there shall be no barrier in any part of the service which is in fact (even though not in name) one of race. Grading by race rather than responsibility must disappear. Selection for appointment shall be based on qualifications, experience and character.

Any temptation to lower standards in the service must be firmly rejected. The men must come up to the standards not the standards down to the men.[190]

However, Terence Gavaghan, appointed Senior Assistant Secretary in Charge of Localisation and Training in Kenya wrote of the 'philosophy of localisation', shedding light on certain attitudes that shaped the apparent lack of policy.

The doctrine of trusteeship, the fashionable device of administrative scaffolding, the hangover from the exclusive traditions of the old Indian Civil Service, the still pervasive sense and fact of social inequality between the races, the uneven growth of education, the demands and influence of the Settler community, the lack of political guidance and time-scale from the Colonial Office, all these contributed to a degree of inertia which was often concealed behind the incessant demand for 'the maintenance of standards'.

In other words, the sacrosanct tenet of maintaining standards in those early days, served to preclude virtually all Africans to responsible posts in the civil service because of their lower academic qualifications and their inexperience of taking authority and responsibility, while, at the same time disregarding their superior inherent qualifications of language and local conditions. But how could an African achieve better academic qualifications? Dixon, a lecturer in the Uganda Institute of Public Administration, writes that '*the*

---

[190] The Lidbury Commission – Report on the Civil Services in East Africa 1953-54

greatest obstacle to localisation was the absence in virtually every colony of a sufficient pool of local candidates educated to a standard which would befit them to carry on the administration of their country, and an inadequate flow of secondary school leavers to University to maintain the needed output.' Even by 1961 less than 700 Kenyan children were achieving first or second grade Cambridge School Certificates annually, a number which was thought to be painfully low.

Not until 1960, less than three years before Independence, were strides made in the education process of Kenyans. The Royal Technical College had been opened in Nairobi in 1956, and by 1960 some 339 students were working for technical and professional qualifications.

The most positive action in Kenya was left until after the Lancaster House Conference in 1960. This was to establish the Kenya Institute of Administration with funds from Britain and the United States. This college at Jeannes School just outside Nairobi, was opened in July 1961 with the following objective. *'The core purpose of non-professional administrative training is to secure a cadre of Africans well able to carry on the process of government under whatever political form. This will be done as rapidly as is consistent with the maintenance of such standards as will ensure that the efficiency of administration does not sink to a level which will endanger the prosperity and progress of the nation'.*

Once the College was built, training hastily began in Accounts, Personnel and Office Management, with latterly, five departments in all: Public Administration, Executive Training, Local Government, Community Development Training and Cooperative Training. The students were mainly from the pool of African clerical officers. But gradually training was extended to administrative officers themselves, such as District Officers.

In 1960, Terence Gavaghan, as Under Secretary i/c Localisation and Training, and fully in charge of the whole programme of Localistaion, saw his job thus:

> The inescapable conclusion is that Localisation must have as its definite aim, the introduction of a minimum proportion of Africans at all levels in which they are not at present, adequately represented. The two most important motives are
>
> 1) to enable the territory as rapidly as possible to have a civil service drawn almost entirely from the people of the country, enjoying terms of service with the capacity of the local economy.

2) to ensure by the date of transfer of power, that the composition of the local civil service so increasingly reflects the social and political pattern of the country as to be generally acceptable and to make it a contented, effective instrument of orderly transition and future stability and progress.[191]

In another report Gavaghan discusses Whitehall's dragging of feet over the issue.

As to the hypothetical question of whether localisation [Africanisation] and training should or could have been done differently, I find it hard to make an honest answer that does not also reflect regrets about my own personal attitudes and deficiencies. I do, however, regret that we were not more open-minded and conscious of our own short historical and cultural perspective in comparison with, say 2,000 years of Chinese experience of bureaucracy from which Britain had so much to learn. But [as colonial officers] we were only able to perform within the values and attitudes of our Whitehall masters and we were fallible people feeling our way in a new situation for which we had not been trained. The programme of African training could, of course , have been done better and should have been based upon an earlier and longer run-up, more studies, more resources and a wider range of advice. Africanisation was not merely a process or technique of establishment management, it was, or should have been the instrumental manifestation of a profound philosophical, moral and political conviction that colonialism, necessary though it was in the first instance, must eventually give way to independent choices in which our role would be to make available to our companions and successors, as broad and effective a selection of possible actions as we could offer, or indeed comprehend. [192]

A.R. Thomas, who served in the Colonial Office from 1952 to 1973 in a reply to a question posed to him in 1983 as to how far there was an official policy of 'localisation' within the British Government, wrote,

On the grounds of cost alone, there was always a bias on the part of the Colonial Office towards employing local officers in preference to expatriates, subject to the extent that it could be done without an unacceptable sacrifice of standards or prejudice to the British

[191] Gavaghan *Localisation and Training of the Kenya Civil Service – interim report 1960*
[192] Gavaghan, Terence J.F., Oxford Development Records Project, 1985, Rhodes House Library p.146

Government's ultimate control. There was some recognition in the early days that localisation had merit for its own sake in associating local people with their own affairs and as a long term basis for equipping territories for self-government. It is nevertheless arguable with the advantage of hindsight that a certain complacency and lack of imagination was shown by the British colonial authorities between the wars, and particularly immediately following the second World War, in not foreseeing the pace of political advance and in not pursuing more active and positive programmes of localisation at an earlier stage. When special localisation schemes came to be adopted later, there was ...a shortage of experienced officers in senior grades from whom candidates for the higher posts could be chosen without doing damage to the traditional criteria for promotion. This need not have been the case had it been possible by adopting a more positive policy at an earlier stage to appoint more officers locally into the basic grades of the Senior Service. The countries of Africa were, by Western standards, primitive when we took them over and it is not surprising that the efforts of colonial governments in the earlier years should have been concentrated on the basic tasks of administration, law and order, communications, and public health, rather than directed to raising educational standards at a level at which recruitment to the senior grades of the Service could acceptably take place. [193]

In a study by Eric Burr on Localisation in Britain's African Colonies and Dependencies, writer after writer tells of 'a galloping crash programme on the eve of Independence'

Given the circumstances that the colonial government of Uganda had to cope with, the shortage of funds for capital works and the fact that we had such short notice of impending independence, I cannot see that many mistakes were made. In the early days of Independence the new Ministers and such civil servants as there were, gave the British personnel who had agreed to stay on, every cooperation. It took some three of four years for them to understand the meaning of power and how it could be used to further their own aims, and when this stage was reached they wanted the Britisher out of the way as soon as possible

I suppose some of the blame must be put on the British administrators, but considerable pressure was put onto them [by

---

[193] Localisation and Public Service training - Eric Burr, Rhodes House Library p.4

Whitehall] in the early sixties to get the countries ready for Independence.

Another contributor to the study, my brother-in-law John Wild who served in Uganda from 1938 to 1960 and who chaired Uganda's Constitutional Conference in 1960 states:

It seems to me there was little more we could have done in the very short time that we were allowed by outside influences [i.e. Whitehall]. The disasters that have befallen Uganda in the last decade or so, have not, I am sure, been due to any shortcomings in our Africanisation policy and practice. We just needed more time.[194]

In perhaps the foremost work on Localisation, edited by Eric Burr and published by the Rhodes House Library in 1985, many of the contributors write of the considerable pressures that were put upon them to 'get the countries ready for Independence as quickly as possible', and that 'there was simply not the time to do it'.

Creating the vacancies for qualified Africans posed a dilemma between the desire and pressures for localisation on the one hand and the need on the other to retain an experienced civil service. There was a need to avoid an administrative breakdown though many expatriates were likely to want to leave as self-government progressed to independence.

Branch of Civil Service	Total	Europeans	Asians	Africans
Central Government	89	82		7
Provincial Administration	364	290		74
Executive class	1,636	781	709	146
Clerical class	4,446	483	1,512	2,451
Secretarial class	373	327		46
Lower grades	52,375	4,087	2,090	46,198

But by 1961, only two years before independence the balance was still loaded

---

[194] Wild J.V. , Oxford Development Records Project, 1985, Rhodes House Lib. p.143

very much in favour of the Europeans[195] (See table above)

In the end, it could not be seen as a success. J.A. Golding writing in the 1980's after he had retired from a distinguished service in the African colonies and Protectorates wrote:

> Between 1967 and 1980 I made regular visits to most of the newly independent states in Africa, and with one or two notable exceptions I found there had been a steady deterioration in economic and political stability, and in law and order. Countries that had been self-supporting and often with a healthy export market now had to rely on regular aid in cash or kind, and shortages of food and other necessities were commonplace; and the lot of the ordinary man was not a happy one.
>
> I trust that this is only a transitory phase, but fear with the ever-increasing birth-rate and decreasing productivity, the time will come when the period of colonial rule will be acknowledged as having been a golden age of justice, peace and plenty.[196]

Roper echoes the sentiment:

> That something has gone wrong with Localisation in Africa is apparent. Uganda, Tanzania, Lesotho, Zimbabwe, Ghana – I cannot speak for other countries – can hardly be called success stories. Agricultural chaos; industrial collapse; economic disaster; coup after coup; tribal wars; corruption; famines; military rule; breakdown in security, etc. Are we really to blame? In the days of Amin's rule in Uganda, a Permanent Secretary from Uganda at the East African Staff College asked the Minister giving the opening address whether there was not some way in which the former colonial power could take over the country again and let the people enjoy freedom again. In later discussions [at the same meeting] the British came in for some adverse comments because they failed to go back to Uganda and take it over again.[197]

I myself witnessed the same sentiment in 1977 when I returned after fifteen years to meet some of my old Masai friends at Amboseli who had recently been evicted from part of their land to make way for the National Park. Lengu ole Mbaa, the elder with whom I worked within the National Reserve could

---

[195] Source: Rhodes House Library – Gavaghan – Localisation and training of the Kenya Civil Service Nov. 10th 1960 Annex III pp.1-2
[196] J.A. Golding – 'Colonialism – the Golden Years' Birlings 1987 Introduction
[197] R.F. Roper, Oxford Development Records Project, 1985, Rhodes House Library p.141

not understand why the British handed over so quickly, something that was working well. "Why," he asked me, "Why did you (the British) have to go away and leave us? We were all getting along well. We had our differences, but we always discussed them through and came to an agreeable solution. After you deserted us, the Government just came in and stole our most important dry-weather grazing areas for a national park, and told us to get out. They made promises to us that they never kept, and now our cattle are suffering. Why did you go? Were you frightened of the Kikuyu who are now our masters? Did the Mau Mau win the war?"

The result of this dispute was that in revenge, the Masai, who owned the land up to the time the Amboseli National Park was gazetted, but did not kill its wildlife, decided to make sure the important wildlife in the National Park were not going to be around for tourists to see. Rhinos were once, one of the most numerous animals on the plains of Amboseli. Although it had been a wildlife preserve for more than a hundred years, once the landowners were told to get out, every single rhino of the hundreds there had been on the plains, were killed together with all the lions. Since then there have been no rhinos at Amboseli, though thankfully a few lions have recently returned.

There can surely be no doubt that many of the ills Kenya now suffers from, can be traced back to the handing over of the country to an administration that was simply ill-prepared and under-qualified for the job. If the firm hand of the British had been maintained from the top down, during, and immediately after the granting of self-government, the chances of seeing the country through to an efficient state with a minimum of corruption would have been much greater. As it was, the corrupting influence of minor officials at the bottom of the ladder, and some also at the top, who should have been summarily removed, were allowed to stay at their posts, and infected their workmates so that the disease crept through the ranks to pervade the whole system until it became impossible for any official to keep his job unless he joined the band-wagon. It has been impossible to find a cure for the malady and this state of affairs is still retarding progress, and denying Kenya its rightful place as the leader of the whole of eastern Africa.

EPILOGUE

"Self-government is better than good government."

Kwame Nkrumah

If Mau Mau was the reason for Britain's indecent haste to rid herself of the financial burden and irritation of Kenya, then those Kikuyu who sowed the wind in 1952 are still, in 2004, reaping the whirlwind of their misguided act. If, on the other hand, the Mau Mau Emergency was just a drop in the ocean of the British Government's overall course of action, then the speed with which she handed over government to one that was ill-prepared and demonstrably under-qualified was at best flawed, at worst profoundly irresponsible.

Those Kikuyu who have been led to believe that Mau Mau was a 'war of independence', waged to free their people from the oppression of colonialism, when they take a closer look at the evidence, will find a very different 'can of worms'.

Instead of being able to build on the progress made towards Internal Self Government (ISG) up to 1952, the Mau Mau intervention was, without any qualification, an entirely destructive interlude. It was seven years of wasted time and opportunities. It necessitated financial and human resources to be diverted into the complex and profoundly unsettling activities I have described in earlier chapters. It was a wasteful, cruel and entirely unproductive episode at a stage of Kenya's development which undermined the prospects for the successful transition to independent statehood. The momentum towards ISG that was gained up to 1952 was lost, and sadly was never regained.

Although the Mau Mau Emergency cost some £55m, over half of which came directly from the British taxpayer, money was not the reason why the British Government decided to leave Kenya so suddenly, any more than it was the possibility that remaining there until the job was finished, might involve the lives of more of its soldiers and airmen and indeed of its civilian countrymen.

Another agenda was permeating through the corridors of Westminster at that time – an agenda that had more extensive and far reaching effects on the people of Britain. The repercussions of this new agenda would affect not only Kenya but the whole Empire.

Clyde Sanger, in his biography of Malcolm Macdonald, the last Governor of Kenya, records that up to the late 1950s, the timetable for Kenya's independence was to be around 1975, fifteen to twenty years ahead. However, by 1960, Prime Minister Macmillan's mind was not focused on Kenya, nor on any other part of the Empire – not in a positive sense, anyway. It was towards Europe. Europe and the Common Market was the subject that was occupying the minds of Her Majesty's Ministers towards the end of the '50s, particularly those of Chief Whip Ted (later Sir Edward) Heath and the Prime Minister, both of whom believed it was now time for the sun to be setting on the British Empire in order for it to begin rising on the British presence in Europe.

In 1959, towards the end of Baring's term as Governor, the first repercussions of this somewhat sudden, and in hindsight, disasterous change of priorities, began to manifest themselves in Kenya. The Minister of Defence and his senior staff arrived in Nairobi with the sole purpose of impressing on the Governor that it was no longer possible to maintain the British Government's commitment in Kenya. They were the heralds that brought the edict from Whitehall that Kenya (and most other African colonies) must gain its independence within the incredibly short period of the next four years. This was a bolt from the blue that had been unthinkable to most of the Colony's administrators, and certainly quite preposterous and extremely worrying for the settlers.

(During their visit to Kenya, the Minister of Defence, Duncan Sandys, and Marshall of the Royal Air Force Sir William Dickson, together with their retinue, descended on me at Amboseli where I was warden and therefore responsible for their lodging, welfare and entertainment. They were taking a brief break from their meetings in Nairobi. It was a private visit to give the party a rest and an opportunity to see one of the best wildlife areas Kenya had to offer at that time. I had had very little warning of their arrival by air, as they had come straight from a meeting at Government House and were somewhat irritable on arrival at the airstrip, still in their pin-stripe suits. I am happy to say that 24 hours later, when they left in their two Vickers Valetta aircraft, the largest ever to land on the grass airstrip, they had seen and photographed the 'big five': lion, leopard, rhino, buffalo and elephant, and they were considerably happier and in a much better state of mind to carry on their deliberations with the Governor. I received most appreciative letters from them later, letters that sing the praises of Amboseli and the magnificent wildlife spectacle it provided in those days. It was during this time that I heard about the programme that had been laid before the Governor and was about to be made public. In common with most Kenyan Europeans, I was dumbfounded. Four brief years seemed ludicrous in the extreme, and a dangerously short length of time to hand over a country to an administration that would, by any standard, be under-qualified and ill-prepared.)

It was not that there were no good African men and true, to take up positions in a new Government. Every Colony or Dependency in Africa had its budding statesmen who had been educated and groomed under British tutelage: reliable leaders of good calibre and strong character, who were being prepared and mobilized to set the country on the right lines during an extended period of self-government prior to total independence. The trouble was, there were not enough of them. It needed a few more years to train up more and to sort out the wheat from the chaff. As one observer has commented:

> The fundamental weakness of ISG was not the fact of its introduction, it was the short length of time that it was programmed to run. There was a need for not less than ten to fifteen full cycles of political and institutional life, i.e. budget years, to give the newly emerging institutions under localisation plans, to become embedded in the habits and minds and disciplines of localised officers, both at the centre of government and at the periphery. Such a period of benign tutelage might well have contributed to a less painful and crippling infancy for the new state. But the impatient preoccupations of Whitehall pre-empted the scope for this and Kenya was dragged along in the slip-stream of other people's expediencies. [198]

The governance of a country like Kenya with its extensive tribal and ethnic differences was complex and sophisticated. It had been continuously evolving over the previous seventy years and this evolution needed to reach a conclusion. Structures of government, both local and national, required careful management by well-educated, well-qualified and experienced senior staff, with large numbers of competent and reliable middle ranking staff. Despite changes that had led to the induction of substantial numbers of such staff since 1945, they inevitably remained a scarce commodity supplied by a slow, if steady production line. Those who understood the structures and had so assiduously nurtured Kenya's institutions while laying the foundations for ISG, knew that so short a timetable as four years would have catastrophic effects, perhaps for generations to come. But they were powerless to do anything about it.

Senior Kikuyu leaders have recently complained to me that the British

---

[198] Roy Spendlove *Pers. Comm.*

were too dilatory in educating the Black communities and in training up administrators, and therefore too slow in giving independence. This is a wholly unfair and contemptible criticism. It was way beyond the capability of any European power from 1939 up to and beyond 1950, to instigate new schools and colleges and the facilities required to produce qualified teachers and administrators in their Dependencies. Britain had to use all her resources for fighting and then recovering from a war to prevent the whole world sliding into the abyss of an oppression that would, if it had been allowed to succeed, have meant regression not for one particular race but for all mankind. And if the Jews and Gypsies of Europe could suffer the fate they did in the 1930s and 40s at the hand of the Nazis, what, one might ask, was in store for Africans?

Nevertheless, it is a sad reflection that once Macmillan had proclaimed his intention to the world through his 'Wind of Change' speech, and its meaning had been digested by all those eager, clamouring politicos emerging in ever increasing numbers throughout the Empire, there could be no turning back – just a relentless cry of *Uhuru!* Freedom! Independence now!

Following Kenyatta's dramatic release from detention in 1960 and two constitutional conferences in London, a general election took place and on 1st June 1963 Kenyatta became Prime Minister. ISG then ran for just six months before independence was finally won on 12th December that same year. A severely truncated period, therefore, of six months of ISG had to suffice. This meant that instead of being appointed to the leading positions by the British, to ensure they would be well-established by the time ISG came along, any budding statesmen had to take their chances along with the pretentious and unqualified self-styled politicians when the clamour was for 'democracy' (Africa style) and 'elections' (Africa style). Those who landed the plum jobs were the ones who could shout the loudest at the election rallies and could make the wildest of promises to the masses. They were not the moderate, restrained, maturing statesmen. Western-style elections (Africa style) did not favour those who were sober-minded, who could see what the future held and were honest and candid enough to tell their audiences; they, and any who were hostile towards corruption, were soon eliminated, and power was grabbed by those whose height of ambition was a white Mercedes, a white mansion and a white woman.

Thus the country was handed over to a government, most of the members of which were inexperienced, untried and were certainly unworthy of the title of statesmen. A Western style democratic election process was installed that was totally unsuited to the voters of a country that had only comparatively recently been introduced to the system that had taken nearly a thousand years to evolve in Europe.

Corruption and nepotism soon cast their ugly shadows over the entire system, and ever since have been the progenitor of retrogression, and show yet no signs of diminishing. And as the West should continue, quite rightly, to refuse to indulge in no more than a token trade with countries that are dominated by corrupt officials, the regression will persist.

Had Kenya remained peaceful from 1945 onwards, and continued towards the stated aim of ISG, this would have been achieved in due course, and by the mid 1950s, Kenya would have been a thriving economic state.

In 1950, a strong association of young Kenyans was formed. Known as the 'Young Kenya Association', it was composed of all races and it was way ahead of its time. One of the far-sighted prime movers behind this was Francis Erskine, a second generation white Kenyan whose father Derek, took Kenyatta's children under his wing, when Kenyatta was jailed at the beginning of the Emergency. Who knows what this association may have achieved if its life had not been cut short by the Mau Mau.

> In 1950, we set up the 'Young Kenya Association' to help guide our fellow Kenyans towards independence from Whitehall. Dr. Michael Wood and his wife Susan were committee members along with some responsible African and Asian men and women who were anxious to see their country achieve self-government as soon as possible. We were in touch with the Colonial Office, Whitehall, who were as keen as we were to relieve themselves of the burden of Kenya. The 'Wind of Change' was already beginning to blow and by early 1951 we were told that we might expect to get Internal Self-Government by 1954. Alas all our hopes were dashed when an extremist terrorist organisation called Mau Mau raised its ugly head. Its basic aim was to kill enough whites to scare them all out of the country and grab Kenya for the Kikuyu. So the result was that the poor old Brits got lumbered with Kenya for another 9 years at great expense to the British taxpayer. So these so-called 'Freedom Fighters' actually *delayed* our movement to self-government which was given in such haste that most of the wrong people got the important jobs in the civil service[199].

To conjecture further, if the Mau Mau conflict had never taken place, the

---

[199] Francis Erskine Pers. Comm.

appointments of suitably educated and qualified Africans to the more responsible posts in local and national government under the watchful tutelage of British expatriates would have accelerated. Speeding up the throughput of qualified administrators would have meant that both middle ranking and senior posts within the Administration would gradually have been filled by local people. The economy of the country would have grown with the help and expertise of White as well as of Black farmers, and the tourist industry would have developed along with the increase in global travel. All this would have led to a smooth transition to ISG perhaps by as early as the mid-1950s. The transition would have been supervised by the British with appointments to senior posts in government carefully monitored to make sure they were filled by trustworthy, responsible and properly qualified people without the interference and burden of corruption and nepotism. When Independence finally came, the Localisation programme would have run its course and the consequent independent government, both local and national, would certainly have been more qualified and unquestionably less corrupt. Jomo Kenyatta may well have been the person best qualified to head that government, but he would, by then, have been fully groomed, tutored and equipped to take over and run the country responsibly. More importantly, he would have had ministers who had also been groomed for their work, whom he could rely on to take over where the British had left off. *For it was every British Administrator's aim to hand over the country as a going concern.*

Those of us who worked in the Colonies and spent the major part of our lives there, all have one thing in common. We wanted the best for those Kenyans we left behind. Now, in 2004, when we return, we find a population returning to something like it was in the 1880s. The goal of 'life, liberty and the pursuit of happiness' that we wanted so much for the inhabitants, has been lost; fear has again crept back into their lives—fear of poverty, because there are not enough jobs to go round; fear of famine because the traditional wasteful methods of farming are still pursued and have not been overtaken by technologically efficient methods to keep pace with the population explosion; fear of disease because medical institutions are often staffed by those who have won their positions through corruption and not through expertise, and in urban areas where policing is virtually non-existent, fear for one's life through attack by murderous thieves, because life is once more a question of the survival of the fittest.

Post colonial Africa leaves little room for doubt that the Great Scuttle of the late '50s and early '60s was, in developmental and human terms an unqualified failure. To those who know Africa, the reasons for this are plain and simple. Decisions were made in the cosy atmosphere of the panelled offices of the Colonial Office in Whitehall, by people insulated from a clear understanding of 'Africa' and all that that term implies; they were made in the absence of a full appreciation of the far reaching impacts they would have on the future of the peoples in those far distant lands. Impatience for change at any cost is, even now, one of British politicians' more objectionable and arrogant conceits. In Kenya's transition from Colony to sovereign state the disasters of Darfur and Rwanda, of Ethiopia and Angola, of Uganda and Biafra as well as the unfolding collapse of balanced governance in Zimbabwe have, thankfully, so far been averted. But in 2004 the Kenya government cannot afford to be complacent in its search for a way out of the domestic and human crisis into which its economy and peoples continually drift. They must be ever mindful of the fateful dangers of inter-ethnic and inter-tribal confict that has ravaged the greatest part of the continent since the European powers pulled out and left them to their own devices. In 1952 Kenya had unbounded commitment for all its peoples; even in 1959 the signs still showed promise. But at the precise moment when help was most needed, the 'Drill Sergeant' turned 'Midwife' suddenly left the patient's bedside and the child entered the world already scarred and with severe complications from which even now, forty years on, it is still suffering.

The tragic reality of Kenya's haste into independence is that the first forty years of 'standing on its own feet' have been spent in squandering its precious economic resources such as its forests and wildlife and dissipating the institutional foundations such as the judiciary, so carefully and honourably laid by dedicated professionals whose affection for and service to Kenya's peoples is now little more than a wistful memory. Africa's poverty, we are told, can be met by greater aid from the 'rich' countries of the world. Such delusions may serve the short term ambitions of finite politicians on both sides of such deals, but the challenges of modern Africa will not be met by naïve grand standing.

How then may they be met?

The modern reality of all states in Africa south of the Sahara, whether or not historically colonial, is that population growth has not been matched by sound and enduring structures and methods of resource management backed by the rule of law.

Could it be that Kenya with a new, more liberated and enlightened President, could lead post-colonial Africa into a modernised prejudice-free attitude where substantial, but not exclusive expatriate expertise would execute a controlling influence over its finances, its civil service and its government departments? Could it be that an offer of substantially increased aid from the 'rich' could, with the total complicity of the Kenya Government (thereby circumventing the dubious efficacy of United Nations involvement) be tied to conditions that give control to experts, *both local and expatriate, according to their qualifications.* Such a scheme would require an invitation from the Kenya Government to be based on a clear contractual arrangement by an executive agency set up especially for this work and initiated by and working on behalf of a body such as an 'Alliance of Democracies'[200] or the G7 countries, with subventions from them. The British with their unique experience of Africa should take a leading role in such an agency, which would determine and effect the contract with the Kenya Government and have bi-laterally agreed legal powers to employ and dismiss experts both local and expatriate on behalf of each department concerned, and would have total control over the country's finances. Perhaps such a far-sighted and liberated male President has yet to be born... but a woman?

All sub-Saharan African states, no matter how poor they appear to be at present, have the ability to be self-supporting without the necessity for aid. All have enormous potential not only as a net provider for themselves but also as a contributor to the world's economy. It is surely time this potential was realised. It is surely time corruption and nepotism which every Kenyan recognises as the greatest barrier to progress is finally buried. It is surely time those states stopped wasting their resources, and blaming the climate for their self-induced poverty; stopped begging a living from the rest of the world and blaming donor countries when they think they are not getting enough. It is time they set aside their pride for a while and admitted that if they want to achieve Western living standards they must first accept Western principles of probity and community conduct strictly backed by the rule of law. They must accept that they need advice and restraint in such basics as resource

---

[200] 'An alliance of countries where democracy is so rooted that reversion to autocratic rule is unthinkable'. An idea proposed by Ivo Daalder and James Lindsay in the Financial Times magazine of 6.11.04

management and financial integrity. Above all, it is time the rest of the world stopped pouring its cash into the pockets of a few billionaire African autocratic dictators and their cronies, under the guise of aid.

It is also time the West stopped kidding itself that the way to 'help' the poorer nations is to increase aid money with few, if any, strings attached. For there will always be the Idi Amins, the Saddams and the Mugabes, waiting in the wings. And like all megalomaniacs, their progression from initial genocidal tendencies, will be to dominate their neighbours and then their neighbour's neighbours and the West will, yet again, find itself having to send its sons and daughters to sort out the problems, to feed the starving, to stop the genocide, to free the oppressed, and to depose the perpetrators through battles that will take yet more innocent lives. Left to their own devices, African states will continue to throw up these dictators with monotonous regularity as they have in the past. Throwing money at them under the guise of aid, did not prevent their rise to power in the past, nor will it in the foreseeable future. On the contrary, it will simply serve to keep them in power.

Undemocratic one-party systems favour the rise to power of the criminally paranormal. Post-colonial Africa is littered with examples too numerous to mention. The difference now is that the weapons so easily available to them are far more sophisticated and dangerous. Better by far we learn from lessons from our colonialist past, from administrators like Sir John Kirk and Francis Hall, firstly to try to persuade with sensible argument, and if that fails, to coerce with threats and finally to take decisive action before the suicide bombers act; before the anthrax spores are spread and before the 800-seat jumbos are hijacked, while we *can* still persuade, while we *have* the ability to peacefully coerce a little and while there is still an opportunity to effect the kind of control we know is the right way to proceed to a future where the whole world, regardless of colour or religious orientation, can enjoy the goals of life, liberty and the pursuit of happiness.

The last word must surely go to Alan Liddle who was a comparatively young District Officer in Kenya at the time leading up to Independence. This entry in his journal harks back to the last paragraph of my Preface on page 13. It sums up the reason why the British were in Kenya and the reason why those of us who spent the greatest part of our lives in the service of that country, are proud of the work we did and the legacies we left behind.

In March and April 1960, *barazas* [meetings] were held in every location in Kitui district explaining what the approach of *Uhuru* would mean. I was on safari for a number of days running eight *barazas* in my division, while the DC, and other DOs did the same in the three other divisions. Senior Chief Kasina at Migwani made plain his views, and probably those of most of the older generation of Akamba, at the end of my *baraza* at Migwani as he delivered a wringing endorsement of Britain's sixty odd years of running Kenya. Several younger men had put points to me after I had spoken, fair enough points in their way, but considered impertinent by Kasina. Finally he lost his patience and leapt up beside me, and, in his curiously high pitched voice, said: 'Do you know what *Uhuru* is? I'll tell you what *Uhuru* is. When I was young there were those of the Akamba who still remembered Arab slave raiders. The British came and stopped that. I remember as a boy the Masai raiding our land to try to take our cattle. Then the British came and stopped the tribes fighting each other. The Kikuyu, Embu, and Meru combined and caused the barbarous Mau Mau rebellion. The British stopped that. The British brought us education, showed us how to improve the use of our land, brought us water supplies, and much else. What did we do for the British? We gave them askaris for the KAR and the Kenya Police. We fought for them as our friends in their wars. We can be proud of that. Today we have peace and improving conditions. Do you see that? (pointing at the Union Jack flying above his office). That is *Uhuru*.' The young smirked, the old looked embarrassed, Kasina looked defiant. I could have hugged the old boy, but it would probably have been against Queen's Regulations![201]

---

[201] Alan Liddle – *Colony to Nation* p.163

Appendix 1

This is part of one of the many letters I received from White Kenyans who grew up on farms adjoining the Kikuyu Reserve. It illustrates the close ties, affection and respect the two races had for each other. The writer, Andrew Barnett's boyhood friends were Kikuyu from the neighbouring areas and he spoke Kikuyu before he spoke English.

The Kikuyu man who looked after our garden had been in the K.A.R. during WW2. He was at the defeat of the Italians at Addis Ababa and witnessed the reinstatement of Haile Selassie. He taught me the K.A.R's favourite marching song *'Funga Safari'* and I used to follow him around the garden pretending to march and singing the song. When we came to the end of the song, Gichohi would come to attention and pretend to salute an imaginary officer with his right hand, his left hand pretending to hold his army .303 rifle. Sometimes he would get me and my sister together with Wahome, the cook's son, and Maina, our *ayah's* son, and issue us with wooden planks as rifles and march us up and down and make us 'present arms'. Worst of all was 'inspection'. "Corporal Maina", he would shout. "Stand to attention, you bloody *shenzi! Viatu yako ni mbaya sana. Hakuna polishi!" [Your shoes are filthy. You have not polished them]"* "But I have no shoes Bwana Gichohi." "Shut up you bloody fool. Listen to me. I am your sergeant and if I tell you to polish your shoes you bloody well find some shoes and polish them!"

Gichohi's claim to fame for us children was that he could go into a trance and speak as an authority on any subject. We would sit in a circle and he would place the palms of his hands over his eyes and drone out some mumbo-jumbo that we would not understand. After about 5 minutes he would drop his hands and slowly stand up in a trance. Where his eyes should have been, there would be red skin – probably the inverted skin from his upper eyelids. It was a horrible sight but we kids were fascinated. He would dance around chanting complete rubbish. All very harmless stuff but highly entertaining for us kids.

I once fell out badly with Gichohi. He reported me to my mother for swearing in Kikuyu at some staff who didn't do what I wanted them to do. I tried to tell my mother that a Kikuyu boy had told me these words and I didn't know what they meant. But she wasn't to be taken in. She told Kiritu our cook to catch me and give my backside a good tanning with a large wooden kitchen spoon. This Kiritu did, out at the back of the kitchen in front of all the staff. It was a real humiliation for me, but a very good lesson.

Kiritu was also a good friend of mine. He used to tell me all sorts of Kikuyu legends. One story he told me that sticks in my mind was why some people are black, and others white.

He said that all people were black to start with, and then a great lake appeared in the north and all those close to it rushed to wash themselves in it and became white. By the time those who lived in Africa got to the lake, most of the water had gone, and they were only able to wash the palms of their hands and the soles of their feet.

African and European tastes are completely different. I could never get my mother to accept this. One rainy day when the women came out of the tea to the weighing station not far from the kitchen, [*the Barnetts lived on a tea estate*] my mother took pity on them and decided to give them all a cup of tea before their trek back to their homesteads. It was early afternoon and the house servants were off (they had a break between lunch and 4.30 pm when tea was served). My mother brewed a large kettle of tea and handed it round to the dozen or so women sheltering from the rain. What my mother did not understand was that all Africans like their tea stewed in a pot with the milk and sugar all together.

I happened to pass by while the women were drinking their tea, and heard screams of laughter. My mother, not understanding Kikuyu, did not realise that the women were all saying *'Ni doori'* 'It's piss!' The women were too polite to say anything to my mother, and I hadn't the heart to tell her either!

304

Appendix 2

THE KIMATHI LETTERS

contributed by Laurie Slade

In 1954, my father, Humphrey Slade (HS), received two letters purporting to come from Dedan Kimathi.

In the family, we never thought they were written by DK, but we assumed they were written on his behalf. DK was known to be foremost among the forest commanders of Mau Mau, and his reputation was such that we did not think anyone would dare to take his name in vain.

The envelope of one letter – it is not clear which – survives. It bears a Nyeri postmark, and is addressed to: Mr. H. Slade, P O Naivasha.

At the time, HS owned a farm of approximately 500 acres in North Kinangop, on the lower slopes of Mount Kipipiri close to the Aberdares. In 1952, he became a member of the Kenya Legislative Council, elected on an exclusively European franchise. He represented the Aberdare Constituency, a massive area, embracing the districts of North Kinangop, South Kinangop, Naivasha, Gilgil, Ol Kalou and Thomson's Falls (now Nyahururu).

HS's political views in the early 50's were complex. On the one hand, he had been elected on a manifesto advocating self-government for Kenya, a common electoral roll for all races, and the development of a society without a 'colour bar'. On the other hand, he was also advocating the continued dominance of British 'standards and ideals', and the maintenance of a 'culture bar', with other races only allowed to participate in public life if and when they were capable of matching up[202].

HS modified his more hardline views radically in later years. He committed himself wholeheartedly to the principle of majority rule in Kenya, once the Lancaster House Conference of 1960 had set the timetable for progress to independence. He urged the rest of the European community to do likewise maintaining that though the burden of political leadership was shifting, there was still scope for all races to contribute to the development of the new nation. He never wavered in that belief[203]. In the early 50's, however, he was uncompromising. The Mau Mau movement, in particular, he regarded as a rebellion. He criticised Government initiatives to provide amnesties for forest fighters, rather than put them on trial. He also encouraged resistance to

---

[202] *An Address to Voters in the Aberdare Constituency from Humphrey Slade, a Candidate for Election to Legislative Council* – May 1952 (Papers of Humphrey Slade in Rhodes House Library, Oxford)

[203] See for example – Address to E.A European Pioneers Society, 26.9.1962, responding to the toast *Our Country* (Papers of Humphrey Slade in Rhodes House Library, Oxford)

Mau Mau among Kikuyus in his constituency, helping organise a group for this purpose known as *Njamba Cia Kumurika*, or *Torchbearers*[204].

So it is not clear what Dedan Kimathi (DK) felt HS had to offer, in terms of any agenda DK was wanting to pursue.

An earlier letter was received by HS, also purporting to come from DK. Like the subsequent letters, this first letter invited HS to meet with DK. HS later told me that he took the first letter to the Police, and offered to set up the meeting DK requested, so as to enable the Police to capture DK. In effect, he was offering himself as bait for a trap. His offer was not accepted by the Police, but they kept the letter. When the second and third letters arrived, HS did not mention them to the authorities. He never attempted to reply to any of the letters.

The last time he and I looked at the letters was shortly before his death in 1983. He believed the letters were historic, but did not know what to do with them. After he had read once more DK's complaints about the injustices of the situation, HS commented: 'What he was asking for doesn't seem so unreasonable now.'

In 2000, the letters were donated to Rhodes House Library, Oxford, along with other papers left by HS.

Laurie Slade
London
21 August 2004

Author's Note

I have no doubt these letters are genuine and that they originated from Kimathi. The reason I am so certain is that the person who wrote them, Kimathi's scribe, was employed in the Mountains National Park after the Emergency where I came to know him well. His name was Gathura Muita[205]. *Before the Emergency Gathura was a schoolmaster in Tetu, Kimathi's home Location. When Kimathi went to the forest in October 1952 after the brutal murder of Chief Nderi, he asked Gathura to accompany him as his scribe. Gathura, who spoke excellent English, spent the next two and a half years in the forest with Kimathi working as his scribe and his confidante. In 1955, Gathura, now completely disillusioned with Kimathi and life in the forest,*

---

[204] *Humphrey Slade – Random Notes and memories* (undated) by Wilfrid Hopcraft; Address by Rev John G Gatu, Memorial Service for Humphrey Slade – 19.8.1983 (both from Papers of Humphrey Slade in Rhodes House Library, Oxford).
[205] The person in the photo on page 93.

surrendered to the Security Forces and later joined a pseudo gang team led by Bill Woodley.

After the Emergency, Bill was appointed senior Warden of the Mountains National Park which included the highlands of both the Aberdares and Mount Kenya[206]. One of the first people he employed was Gathura as his clerk.

When Bill went on six months leave in 1960, I stood in for him. During this time, I came to know Gathura well and we talked a lot about his time in the forest with Kimathi. He told me that although Kimathi knew a little English, he could not write it. In fact, Gathura wrote everything for him – English, Kikuyu and Swahili. We had long discussions about his life in the forest – how Kimathi saw himself as the future leader of the Kikuyu people and how gradually he became more and more obsessed with the delusion of his own importance and power. Gathura was reluctant to talk about the murderous deeds carried out at the hand of Kimathi, but occasionally he would let slip something that would convey the hideous things that went on in Kimathi's hideouts. One day he took me to Kimathi's derelict hideout on the moorlands of the Aberdares amongst the giant heather, and it clearly brought back some appalling memories for him.

When Bill Woodley returned to take up his post and I left for another assignment, the senior staff of the Park kindly gave me a leaving present of a large framed photo of Mount Kenya by Arthur Firmin. I still have the photo and cherish it greatly. On the back of the frame, the staff wrote messages of goodwill to me. One of those who wrote was Gathura Muita[207]. A 36-word facsimile of his handwriting, therefore, remains with me and though I am no handwriting expert, it is quite clearly the same handwriting as both these Kimathi letters. I have no doubt, therefore, that they are perfectly genuine, and both are written by the same person but dictated by Kimathi. They would have been dictated in Kikuyu and translated into English by Gathura.

I have asked two colleagues who had experience of Kimathi during the Emergency to comment on these letters and they both believe that during 'General' China's interrogation by Special Branch, he agreed to write a letter to Kimathi asking him to join cease fire talks. This was done in order to lead Kimathi into a trap where he would be taken prisoner while attending the meeting, but the plan was probably vetoed by the Administration once they got

---

[206] The two parks have now been split and his son, 'Bongo' Woodley is currently Warden of the Mount Kenya National Park
[207] Another was Sergeant Kamau (see page 221)

wind of it, as being unacceptably dishonest. As the first letter shows, Kimathi would dearly have liked to take part in the negotiations as it would have given him considerable prestige and would have done him no harm for his bid to lead the Kikuyu people. So his anger at being snubbed by Government and excluded from the talks, in the second letter, was entirely predictable.

DLS
August 2004

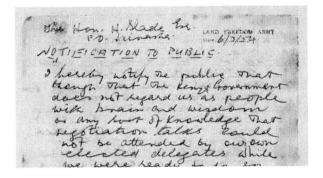

One of Kimathi's original letters written by Gathura

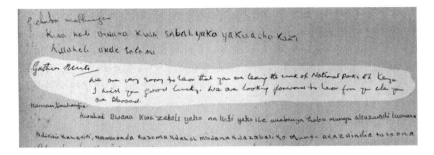

Gathura's message to me on the back of the photo of Mt.Kenya

Original wording   *Interpretation*

G & M Defence Council
Land Freedom Army
Date 10/3/54

H. Slade Esq.
P.O. Naivasha

LET US MEET AND
NEGOTIATE PEACE

Dear Sir,
On 28th April[208] 1954 I received a
long letter from General China who
is now under Government arrest and
who has been charged as a terrorist.
He stated that he did write to the
Government and asked for cease fire
talks to which two officers one
being sent by the Governor Sir
Baring and the other by Gen.
Erskine C in C. East Africa. He
talked the matter over by these two
delegates as to how we both should
end the war. He was asked several
questions some of which he said he
had to write to me and ask me with
my council to discuss out and stress
our views.

My cabinet met on 1/3/54 and I
replied direct and accordingly and
agreed to send 4 delegates as regards
to my proposal of Aug. 1953 when I
wrote to the Governor, President.

I am sure now that this is not an
Emergency but a rebellion of which
we must care for both people and

LET US MEET AND
NEGOTIATE PEACE

Dear Sir
*On 28th February 1954 I received a
long letter from general China who
is now under Government arrest and
who has been charged as a terrorist.
In the letter, he said that he wrote to
the Government asking for cease
fire talks. He spoke with two
officers, one from the Governor Sir
Evelyn Baring, and one from
General Erskine, C in C East Africa.
He discussed with these officers how
it would be possible to end the war.
Some of the questions he was asked,
he said he could not answer until he
had written to me so that I could
discuss them with my council and
give my answers.*

*My cabinet met on 1/3/54 and we
decided to send 4 delegates to a
meeting with the Government where
we could discuss my proposals set
out in my letter of August 1953 to
the Governor.*

*This is good news and I now believe
that this is no longer an Emergency
but simply a Rebellion[209] which we
must make sure does not harm the
people and the wealth of*

---

[208] This must be February, not April

[209] He probably means something more akin
to disobedience or disorder

Original wording

wealth also for the country as well as whole heartedly. Difficulties have aroused on either sides and over everybody and as well as over everything a life. Plans have ever now and then been made which none of which is ever successful.

To achieve a level best let us not plan the weapons but the cure on human hearts for this disease is now so serious throughout the country and will shortly affect seriously our neighbouring territories however so hard we prevent.

Here I am going to stress some few points which undoubtedly will make us to realise our sincerity and sympathy.

1. Let us know who we are and where we are, where we came from and where we are going to.
2. If an old machine is out of order we must buy a new one without delay
3. We are not fighting for an everlasting enmity but are creating a true brotherhood between white and black.
4. What you teach the child is what he/she will aim at all he/her life.
5. Let us not hate what we really love.

Interpretation

the country. The difficulties that have arisen on both sides have affected everybody and the life of the country generally. Ideas for waging this war or for ending it have, so far, been unsuccessful.

Let us stop planning even worse weapons and ideas for killing, and instead think how we can cure the disease which is affecting the whole country so seriously and may even start affecting our neighbours however hard we might try to prevent it.

I shall now put a few points for discussion which will show our sincerity for the task ahead.
1. *We must first make clear our identity, our authority and our present position. Then we must declare what our objectives are from these discussions.*
2. *The analogy is that the present system is not working so we must find a new one without delay.*
3. *On our side, we are not fighting because we hate the Europeans. We only want to create understanding and an alliance between Whites and Blacks.*
4. *The analogy is that good teaching (by the European) lasts a lifetime.*
5. *The analogy is that we do not hate what we have been taught (by the Europeans)*

Original wording

6. Let us dismiss all sincerityless leaders who have led us astray and reform our own new system to govern and to rule.

7. War is just a nice worldly game but not so often at games those which break off sincerity.

8. I ask the Kenya Government to cancel the £500 price offered for my head and to arrange for a cease fire talks to which I shall gladly attend with my other three delegates whenever I shall be called up.

9. If no troops surrounding Reserves there would be no war. Those Home Guards are ours. We love them heartedly and we shall not attack them whenever troops and Polices are cleared up.

10. I have offered to become a bridge that will join your Home Guards and my Mau Mau into one love and true brotherhood without further blood spilt.

11. Remember you call us Mau Mau while I call you Gicakuri and Kamatimu but once we get these nick names cleared off so the butter will become better

12. British Government is our true teacher who will never forget. She brought light and she reared us up. The only trouble with British Government is she beats us hardly and chase us from our homes to bushes. British Government taught how to write but as well as to fight.

Interpretation

6. *We must get rid of all those leaders that are not up to the job of leadership and start a new system of government*

7. *War is one way of settling disputes, but it always brings the worst out of people*

8. *The Kenya Government should rescind the £500 price on my head and should arrange for talks on a cease fire which I shall gladly attend with three other delegates. I shall be ready whenever I am called*

9. *If the Security Forces leave the Kikuyu Reserve, we shall not continue the fight. The Home Guards are our friends and our brothers. If the Security Forces leave the Reserves we shall not attack the Home Guards even though they were fighting for you.*

10. *I offer to become a bridge between your Home Guards and my Mau Mau that will bring them together once again without further blood spilt.*

11. *Although you call us Mau Mau and we call you Gicakuri (lit.' 'those who stir up trouble') and Kamatimu, (lit. those who carry spears', i.e. the aggressors) it is bad to use these derogatory names, and we shall do away with them and this will sweeten our relationship.*

12. *We shall never forget the British Government who was our true teacher. She brought us*

Original wording

Interpretation

13. I am sure the peace we are seeking is just around the table while we are biting teeth and lips with weapons looking for a season blindly.

14. To any wise Briton I prophecy that within the twentieth century British Empire reign will have to be melted away if care is not to be taken for British sovereign is let out with children of a beast while the sovereign should be laid to children of man, and for only that, the world say that the British teach love whilst besides they have a great tunk of enmity on fire.

I myself did serve Europeans but I have never served an imprisonment or ever have I been arrested in my life except in 1952 when I passed a night arrested by Chief Muhoya at Ihururu and was released without any charge. This is in August 1952 when he had caught me as a Mau Mau after he received of my bad fame from Laikipia. Commander M. Baldock of Ol Kalou lived with me at Ol Kalou. He loved me and my work was ever satisfactory.

enlightenment but now she beats us and chases us from our homes to our hideouts in the forest. The British taught us how to write but they also brought conflict between us.

13. *I believe we can achieve peace if we sit round the table and stop killing each other blindly.*

14. *I prophecy to any wise Briton that by the end of the twentieth century, the British Empire will have ceased to exist, unless they stop being so aggressive. The British are known in the world for their good works but if they are not careful they will only be known for their aggression towards less fortunate people.*

I worked for Europeans and I have never done bad things or been in prison except when I was arrested by Chief Muhoya at Ihururu and was released without charge in August 1952 when he was told of my involvement with Mau Mau by someone from Laikipia who reported me to him. I worked for Commander M. Baldock of Ol Kalou. We liked each other and he always praised my work.

Original wording	Interpretation
15. In conclusion I should want you to know that no one wants to stay in bushes if Reserves are peaceful. But, Mr. Slade, How can the rate come out of the pit while the cat watches to catch it? My desire also was to stay in Reserves but death penalty was imposed on me for which I ran away.	15. In conclusion I want you to know that none of us want to stay in the forest. But we have to stay here if we continue to be hunted down in the Reserves. How can a rat leave its hole when the cat is waiting to catch it when it comes out? I wanted to stay peacefully in the Reserve in my home, but when the death penalty was imposed on me I had to hide away.
16. My dear British Empire, why you being so strong and powerful loosing your arrows with a mongoose while a lion looks to jump upon your shoulders.	16. My dear British Empire (Government) why do you pay so much attention to a little mongoose when a lion is about to attack you?
I send you with my writings to your elected members and the Government officials. Let you all let us meet and negotiate peace if necessary or let me know the Government proposals. I am only the worst Field Marshall Sir Dedan Kimathi who now turns to being the best Field Marshall D. Kimathi K.C.G.E. God bless your all F.M. Sir D. Kimathi	I am sending this to you as the leader of the elected members but I am also sending it to the Deputy Governor. Let us meet and try to negotiate peace or else let me know your suggestions for an alternative. I may have been your worst enemy, but now I am trying to be your best friend Sir Dedan Kimathi, Field Marshall D Kimathi K.C.G.E. God bless you all F.M. Sir D. Kimathi

Kimathi received no reply to this letter and so, angry at not being invited, and no doubt in a fit of pique he wrote the following letter to Humphrey Slade.

Original wording

Interpretation

Land Freedom Army
P.O. Naivasha
Date 6/3/54[210]

The Hon. H. Slade Esq.

PUBLIC NOTICE

<u>*NOTIFICATION TO PUBLIC*</u>

I hereby notify the public that
though the Kenya Government does
not regard us as people with brain
and wisdom or any sort of
knowledge that negotiation talks
could not be attended by our own
elected delegates while we were
ready to do so and as now the Kenya
Government has nominated its own
delegates to attend the negotiation
talks, I on behalf of all my followers
and the Defence Council and as
President of the Council and The
Knight Commander of the African
Empire and the Supreme
Commander-in-Chief of the Country
of Kenya notify that the terms
proceeding and the discussions will
not be considered and are in all the
circumstances extremely rejected as
this encourage a further progress of
rebellion.

The Government should consider of
either to continue with fighting or to
co-operate with our own elected
delegates.

Marshall D. Kimathi

*I hereby notify the public that
because the Kenya Government does
not regard us as people with brain
and wisdom or any sort of
knowledge, our elected delegates
were not invited to attend the
negotiation talks although we were
ready to do so. Now, the Kenya
Government has nominated its own
delegates (General China?) to
attend the negotiation talks.*

*On behalf of all my followers and
the Defence Council, I, as President
of the Council and Knight
Commander of the African Empire
and Supreme Commander-in-Chief
of the country of Kenya, notify the
public that the discussions that took
place preceding the terms of these
negotiations are completely rejected
as we believe they will only
encourage a prolonging of the (Mau
Mau) rebellion*

*The Government should consider
carefully their options. They should
either continue with the fighting or
cooperate with us and our own
elected delegates.*

---

[210] This should be 6/4/54 as this letter was
written after the previous one and has the
correct date at the end of the letter

314

By F. Marshal D. Kimathi, K.C.A.E.
& Supreme C in C of the Country of Kenya
and the Land Freedom Armies
Nyandarua
6/4/54

Copy to the
Acting Governor,
P.O. Secretariat,
Nairobi

Dedan Kimathi was hunted down by Superintendent Ian Henderson[211] with the Kikuyu Guard and the Kenya Police. He was shot and wounded and captured.

He was later tried and found guilty of the murder of Chief Nderi and several others and hanged.

----

[211] Ian Henderson with Philip Goodhart *'The Hunt for Kimathi'* Hamish Hamilton 1958

Appendix 3

These are two letters sent to District Commissioner Thompson who was in charge of the rehabilitation of hardcore detainees at Hola Detention camp. They were sent to him by ex detainees after their rehabilitation and release back into their home community. The letters speak for themselves.

Kiambu
23ʳᵈ October 1959

Dear Mr. Thompson,
Please treat this letter as personal.
What shall I say that will in the smallest degree express my sincere appreciation for all the troubles you took and the wonderful effort you showed towards my release.
My delight is due to the fact that it was this untiring effort plus your cleverness in handling the affair that I now find myself free. Every hour of the day I certainly feel deeply indebted for the battle you fought so relentlessly towards my eventual release. I fully realise how difficult and hard it was to tackle this problem with the authority and this alone leads me to believe that this battle would never have been won so easily without the courage and devotion you had. I therefore wish to acknowledge your great kindness, effort and energy such a wonderful achievement involved. To Nyambura my girl friend, my release has been nothing but a blessing from heaven, and I assure you that of all the people that share my happiness for my release, Nyambura tops them all. Believe me, not a single hour of the day passes while we are together without discussing you. You may be amazed to hear that to you we always feel that we have a great friend.
We are wedding on December 12ᵗʰ and now that all the arrangements are through, we are therefore both looking forward with great eagerness to seeing you here during this great and memorable occasion in our life. To Nyambura and myself, let me assure you that your presence shall be regarded not only as a blessing, but also as a pride, honour and good omen. We shall never be more honoured I assure you. We are sending you a joint wedding card in the immediate future in the hope that your response will be affirmative.
One other point before I close is that as you well know I have been in Detention Camps for seven years and I know enough what sort of life this is. Before I left Hola, I remember I pledged before you that I resumed my normal life, I shall maintain my behaviour and see that I am not going to implicate myself with the public activities. This pledge believe me I have always observed and it would be very foolish and unrealistic and would rather call it

madness to try to astray myself by implicating myself in this type of dirty activity. This would be a self betrayal even before the ink that revoked my detention order got dry.

Anyone who may attempt to convince you that I am engaging myself in the country's wrong affairs is lying you. I shall never forget the little sermon you so generously gave me while in your office. This sermon has always been in my memory and let me assure you this minute that I shall never, repeat NEVER let your golden words down. Should I forget the bitterness of seven years then I should be considered something more than a lunatic. I hope you always take me to my word. May I hope that when you come up you shall spare me some minutes of discussion.

Please convey my best wishes to the Commandant, Mr. Paul Mungai.
Yours sincerely,
Fred M. Koinange

---

11 Kerugoya
2ⁿᵈ January 1960
Dear Sir,
I should have written this letter soon after my arrival but I thought to delay for sometime in order to have something to tell you about the condition of this new world for me. But before I come to that I have to mention my indebtedness to your prolonged endeavour to expel me from the Detention Camp. Although it was a part of your duty to prepare for the release restrictees in Hola, I feel that you took special interest in my case. It is because of that reason that I must have special gratitude to you.

It is not an exaggeration to say that during my stay I learnt that you had changed you heart before you advised us to change ours soon after your taking over the charge of restrictees at Hola. Has every European and African followed your example of changing the heart practically instead of theoretically much of the existing racial controversy in Kenya would have been avoided. I wish and hope that the remaining restrictees will enjoy your stay at Hola and they will at last enjoy your success in Hola with restrictees.

Our journey from Hola was quite good and enjoyable. The convoy leader, Mr. Kimani, treated us courteously throughout the way to Embu and he safely handed us over to the D.C. Embu.

When I reached home I met all members of my family who became extremely happy to see me with them once again after seven years. Everybody in the country is busy in the shamba and the season looks favourable. I fitted myself in the community here both socially and in the business. I should mention that many people here are economically awfully bad. They cannot manage their living, but that is because the chances of going out for employment are limited. I am not sure of my economical position too, but with God's help things will shape favourably.

I wish you happy New Year and hope that you will try to fit yourself into the changing conditions of our new Kenya where we all expect to remain good citizens.

Please convey my best wishes to your staff who have worked with you in the struggle of our Release.

I beg to remain,
Yours sincerely,
Romano Njamumo Gikunju

Appendix 4

I received this letter from an ex-colonial administrative officer just prior to the publication of this book. It is an important addition as it typifies the kind of work carried out by a District Officer, and later a District Commissioner, before, during and after the Mau Mau Emergency.

20 Sept. 2004.

Dear David Lovatt Smith,

I do apologise for the delay in responding to your letter of 30th July, and for the copy of your 'History of the Kikuyu Guard'. I do not remember ever seeing the original, and I am delighted that something was, and is being, done to acknowledge the role of the Kikuyu Guard.

I took over Kangema Division, after Jimmy Candler was killed. I have not looked out my diaries, so I will detail very roughly from memory some of my experiences before, during and after Mau-Mau.

Arriving in Kiambu as a Cadet in 1951 where Noel Kennaway was District Commissioner, when Terry Gavaghan and Oliver Knowles were the other District Officers. It soon became very apparent there was a simmering resentment by some Kikuyu, particularly within the many ex-servicemen, caused by unemployment and the wealth of European coffee farmers when Kikuyu were not allowed to grow coffee. This resentment was giving rise to rebellious talk which in turn was being fanned by the political leaders, notably Jomo Kenyatta and the others to be detained later in Turkhana and Marsabit on the declaration of Emergency. There was talk of secret oathing ceremonies. I had had some slight intelligence experience gained during my previous service in the Royal Navy based in Singapore at the end of W.W.II, and for a short while in the Foreign Office, before transferring to the Colonial Service. Together with a Special Branch Kenya Policeman, having obtained information, we actually walked in on an oathing ceremony in the District. We could not bring any charges as there was no evidence of any criminal activity, but our reports were forwarded to the Police and to my superior officers, but there was little support, however, to these and other warnings from other Districts.

Later, in 1952, following a massacre of 92 out of a clan of 93 Gabbra on the shores of Lake Turkhana, I was despatched to Marsabit, where 'Windy' Wild (ex Group Captain S.A. Airforce) was sole District Commissioner of a

District the size of Wales. During the next 12 months, I spent most of my time on safari, initially placating the Gabbra who wanted us to supply arms for a good retaliatory raid. During the year, the Emergency was declared and we had twelve second-ranking political detainees who were sent to live in comparatively loose detention in a camp near the District Commissioner's Boma *[Headquarters]* on Marsabit mountain. Among the twelve was Richard Achieng Onyieko.

In the Spring of 1953, I was then moved to Fort Hall (Muranga),where Frank Loyd was D.C., and took over from Ginty Tannahill as D.O.I. Tony Soutar was D.O.2. Jimmy Candler was D.O.Kangema, Donald Clay D.O. Kigumo, and Tommy Thompson D.O. Kandara.

The Northern half of Muranga was, and is, the heartland of the Kikuyu tribe. It is there that Kenyatta wrote "Facing Mount Kenya". It was the area where most of the bloodiest fighting took place. Initially the resistance to the Mau Mau was lead by a few courageous Chiefs such as Senior Chief Njiri, who denounced Mau Mau oaths as contrary to Kikuyu custom and by strong leaders of Christians such as Ignatius Morae, in Location 10. The Catholic Consolata Missionaries were particularly strong in their condemnation of the evil of Mau Mau, and these small church elders provided some of the earliest to stand against the whole concept of Mau-Mau. Initially, Chiefs and Headmen had to be protected, and the only security force available was the small contingent of Tribal Police allocated to the District. These men were armed with old S.M.L.E. rifles and given 2 rounds apiece. The Chiefs and Headmen's homesteads, were traditionally surrounded by cut thorn bushes to keep the sheep and goats protected at night, and this thorn fencing would be strengthened with a few strands of barbed wire.

The danger of this situation was that having so few Tribal Police, these Chiefs and Headmen became soft targets for armed Mau-Mau, and several of their homesteads were overrun, with serious loss of life and loss of the few rifles we had. The Chiefs and Headmen had their own personal retainers and they suggested that some of their loyal adherents should be armed, so as to support the few Tribal Police who were so vulnerable. This was rejected at first by the authorities in Nairobi, but after persistence it was agreed they should have shotguns issued, initially on the basis of 2 guns per Chief or Headman. These men were then called Home Guards, forerunners of the Kikuyu Guards. Tony Soutar, who had joined the Colonial Service from the Army, took over the responsibility for initial arming, discipline and general training in methods of defence and attack. He issued these Guards with distinctive arm-bands so that everyone was in no doubt who they were and what their job was.

I cannot commend the Tribal Police highly enough. I feel very strongly that many of them should have been awarded medals and compensation paid to the relatives of those that were killed by the Mau Mau. I suggest that even now, it is still not too late to do something for them.

As the conflict developed, and following General Erskine's appreciation of the position, it was decided to build up the body of these Kikuyu Guards. Officers, mostly from the Kenya Regiment, were recruited and General Hinde was appointed to oversee this build-up and eventually he was successful in obtaining arms and equipment for them in quantity. Initially we had four District Ofiicers (Kikuyu Guard) posted to the District, one per Division: Keith Foot, I think, to Kandara, MikeToomey to Kangema, Paul Berry to Kigumo and Derek Dansie to me at Kiharu. They were shortly followed by four more, Dick Wood-White [*later ambushed and killed by Mau Mau*] coming to me, so that we had one each for two Locations, two per Division, and eight for the District.

When a Chief's or Headmen's headquarters (soon to be called Kikuyu Guard Posts) were ransacked and destroyed by a Mau Mau gang, the re-building of that Post had to be completed in one day, otherwise the Mau-Mau would attack again and easily over-run a partially built Post. This operation required all the occupants of the Headman's area to participate. Early in the morning young men and women would leave to cut poles from wattle trees which were common in the area – planted to curb erosion and provide a cash crop from the bark for tanning; women with children and old men would then cut lengths as required, some to build walls and roofs and some for sharpened spikes. As the younger men and women arrived with poles, work started to cut a square moat. The earth was then watered and stamped until malleable, and a stout wall to act as a rampart could be built inside the moat. A central tower was then erected, roofed with corrugated iron sheets, or flattened tin from old kerosene cans. At first floor level, a bullet-proof walling or rampart was required, giving the defenders a good field of fire with adequate protection. All had to be ready before dusk, and the local people then realised that their safety was at stake, so they brought their sheep and goats, and personal possessions into the fort, abandoning their mud and wattle huts. This was the beginning of villageisation, which gave the people the protection they needed from the forest gangs. The fighting in Kangema was pretty non-stop in June, July and August 1953. We also developed the tactic of strengthening the Posts with extra Tribal Policemen and a group of us would then leave ostentatiously, but return after dark and wait for the Mau-Mau to attack, so that they were caught by fire from the defenders in front and from us behind them to their consternation.

Jerome Kihori, one of the two very first Africans to be made District Officers *[later ambushed and killed by the Mau Mau]* became a good personal friend of mine. He refused to take enough care of ·himself, he travelled everywhere by Land Rover and although well-armed himself, and always with four armed guards, he knew he was a marked man, but still carried on bravely. He took to himself a roving duty, going wherever there was fighting or need of extra force, but operating particularly in Kangema and Kiharu Divisions. He was one of the bravest men I've ever known.

I remember an interesting fight with a large Mau Mau gang on October 4th 1953. We had some150 Kikuyu Guard, a platoon of 4 K.A.R. and some 50 Kenya Police, but we were still out-numbered and possibly out-gunned, too. Idi Amin was the 4th K.A.R. Sergeant Major and, when his platoon came under fire and was taking cover, bravely stood up and charged down the slope shouting: "Hapana fikiri! Fanya charge tu!" *[Don't worry, just charge them]* which dreadful Swahili was understood by his men and officers. Many Kikuyu Guard were wounded, but we ended with few serious casualties. A K.A.R. officer was shot and his orderly severely wounded. I was myself hit a glancing blow by a bullet on the waist-band.

Dick Wood-White, one of my D.O's (K.G.), was killed within a few days of returning from a very brief spell of leave to get married. We were all very depressed at his funeral so soon after Jimmy Candler's and Jerome Kihori's, but in fact the end of the real fighting was approaching, as the Mau Mau gangs were on the run and the Kikuyu Guard were gaining progressively more confidence. The Mau-Mau were, however, still getting recruits from Nairobi and the Rift Valley farms, but they were less hard-core than the early gangsters, and quite readily accepted de-oathing and release from detention when captured. Employment of these men became a problem for the Administration.

The Army still considered the forest to be a 'no-go' area. At Easter 1954, we organised a party to test the jungle; I made up a party comprising Jock Rutherford, Derek Dansie, Phil Sykes and about 20 experienced Tribal Police and Kikuyu Guards, and we went into the forest above Location 10, and carried on up, discovering the remains of a burnt-out R.A.F. Blenheim bomber that had crashed (the Mau-Mau had claimed they shot it down of course), and we camped on the moorland after climbing to the top of "the Elephant",– one of the peaks of the Aberdares. This had an excellent effect on the morale of the Guard.

A point worth noting was that in the early days of 1954, it became part of the policy of the Administration in Fort Hall to recognise that if an area was quiet, with no Mau-Mau attacks, then that was an area colluding with the gangs. It became axiomatic that a Headman or two would have to be replaced, the area should be "swept" by a large patrol (the Army was always keen on that exercise), and villageisation implemented rapidly. Old rondavels would be cleared and then burnt, generally providing a fire-cracker display as rounds of ammunition and guns hidden in the thatch roofing exploded. Location 14 remained to the end perhaps the most solidly pro Mau-Mau of all, and it was here, near where Jimmy Candler and Jerome Kihori had both been killed in ambushes, that one of the earliest villages was burnt down, to be re-settled in a clean and orderly manner at a later stage.

I would like to mention also the work of Tony Soutar throughout a long two years in the District, in which, with his Army experience, he was to provide enormous back-up to the divisional District Officers, Tribal Police and Kikuyu Guards, and all their officers. When Jimmy Candler was killed and I was posted to take over his Division, Tony immediately customised my Land-Rover with a home-made barrage of Verey lights, to be used to frighten off cattle on the roadways, which was a common device used by the Mau-Mau to make it easier for them to ambush vehicles. These Verey lights were not capable of giving mortal wounds; they bounced off the cattle and stampeded them excellently.

After the Emergency in 1959 when I was District Commissioner Taita – the only District in Kenya that was not 100% for either KANU or KADU *[political parties]* – Jomo Kenyatta came to address a large *baraza* (political meeting) accompanied by a contingent of recently released ex-detainees. Kenyatta, who I found had great personal charisma, was by then, obviously going to be President of a newly independent Kenya within a few years, so we laid on a full 'Guard of Honour' for him and his retinue. The local Taita were noted for their musical prowess and there was also a strong Christian ethic. Large numbers of children turned out in their best clothes and sang songs of welcome and a hymn or two. This upset some of Kenyatta's retinue of minor politicos who started to murmur that they should be singing 'Songs of Freedom'. Jomo ignored them and asked one group to repeat their song. Few of the non-locals would have understood what it was but Kenyatta knew that it was, in fact, the 23rd Psalm. When it had finished he turned to me resplendent in my white shorts and shirt for once, and introduced his personal secretary and aide, Richard Achieng Onyieko who I had recognised from our first meeting at Marsabit. Onyieko did not recognise me, but I reminded him of our last meeting at Marsabit when the detainees lorry in which he was travelling from the day's work was stuck in the mud and we had to get all the passengers out to push it. Jomo roared with laughter at Onyieko's obvious discomfiture.

I hope these few reminiscences will help your readers to visualise some of the work we, in the Administration, had to carry out.

Yours sincerely,

Bob Otter.

Appendix 5

THE RISE AND FALL OF 'GENERAL' KAGO

Little is known about Kago Mboko's early life before his name first surfaces as a 'Sergeant' in 'General' Matenjagwo's Location 12 gang in June 1953. There is, however, reference to him in Joram Wamweya's book 'Freedom Fighter'[212] where Wamweya describes his own escape from Manyani Detention Camp with Kago. Unfortunately he gives the date of their escape as 4th July 1954 a year after Kago is first mentioned in official interrogation reports[213] and 3 months after his death. However, as Wamweya's book was written some seventeen years after the events took place, one assumes that the year given is incorrect.

'General' Matenjagwo, 'Brigadier' Gakure Karuri and 'Sergeant' (later 'General') Kago - Aberdare forest June 1953

If Kago was detained in Manyani, it was quite in character that he would try to escape as his exploits in the forest later, proved him to be a man of action and a leader *par excellence*. My interrogations of members of his gang show that when he arrived in the forest in April or May 1953, he gathered together the largest gang ever recorded in Mau Mau annals. At one stage he led some five hundred men (some reports give greater numbers) and

[212] J. Wamweya – *'Freedom Fighter'*, E.A. Publishing House, 1971 p.85
[213] D. Lovatt Smith unpublished Interrogation Report No. 59 *et al* February 1955

was responsible for much of the mayhem in Fort Hall during the latter half of 1953 and the first three months of 1954.

On his arrival in the forest above Fort Hall, he joined a gang led by 'General' Matenjagwo and quickly rose through the ranks to become a 'Sergeant'. His exploits are described in somewhat glowing terms in a book by Gucu G. Gikoyo who claims to have been in the same gang.

> At this point [in the meeting], General Matenjagwo asked Kago to stand up and told us to look at him. He was a tall man of dark complexion[214]. I was later to know him for a brave man, well versed in the strategies of war, who dearly loved his men and never fought lying down.
>
> 'The man you all see is a very brave man whom you should respect and obey whenever it is your privilege to serve under him. No war can be fought without able commanders.'
>
> Having said this, the General turned to Sergeant Kago and asked him to address the gathering.
>
> 'I, Kago,' said the Sergeant, 'am here with you because this is my country and I would like to impress on you that this is going to be a very tough war. To fight it successfully, one must fight in anger. Should any one of you ever see five, ten or even twenty of your colleagues fall, do not exclaim 'Oh!' in distress. Should you do so, you will get scared and will scare others. Instead of exclaiming in fear, you should always feel angry at the death of your colleagues. With anger will come courage and positive action that will encourage others. Show the others that death is nothing, for a war where there is no killing and getting killed is no war at all.
>
> 'The British', he continued, 'are sending their sons here to fight us and deprive us of our birthright, not because they think they are just but because they know that loot is always sweeter than their own goods. You should be ready to thwart the expectation of their greed and to ensure a future for our children.'[215]

There is no doubt that Kago was the prime mover in some of the worst massacres of Kikuyu Guard in Fort Hall during that time. He led the gang that

---

[214] Kago was actually quite short as the photo shows.

[215] Gucu G. Gikoyo – *We Fought For Freedom'* E.A. Publishing House 1979 p.68

attacked Ndakaini village killing all but two of the 35 men, women and
children inhabitants when they refused to take the oath. His gang also attacked
Kandara Divisional Headquarters[216] in September 1953, leaving a trail of
destruction behind him. Several African and European District Officers were
murdered by him or his lackeys, including Jerome Kihore, Jimmy Candler, Ian
Patterson and Richard Wood-White as well as Headman Thigiru, son of Senior
Chief Njiri.

Richard Wood-White's murder is described by Gucu G. Gikoyo one of
those presumably on the attack.

> The general [Kago] decided on the spot that a hundred of us
> should go out and waylay any government vehicle on the roads and
> destroy it. The group under Captain Kihara took positions on the
> southern side of the Mathioya River, while we, under Muomboko, stayed
> on the northern bank. As we lay waiting, the District Officer came in a
> Land Rover from our side of the road. We attacked the Land Rover.
> When the District Officer's bodyguards saw how tough things were
> bound to get, they took to flight leaving their master behind. We got
> hold of the thug who had insulted our people and hacked him to pieces
> before setting his Land Rover on fire. We removed three sub-machine
> gun magazines fully loaded from his jacket pocket before we finished
> him off.[217]

Whether or not Kago himself was involved in this murder we shall never
know, but it was typical of the callous but organised way he carried out his
attacks.

A personal experience of one of Kago's typical exploits is told by a
policeman who was living on a coffee farm near Thika.

> In February 1954, I was Chief Inspector in charge of Thika CID. Three
> other European policemen from Thika were staying with me in a
> manager's house on a coffee estate not far from our police station.
>
> I was in bed asleep one night when I was awakened by an unusual
> noise outside. As I groped my way back to consciousness I realised to
> my considerable alarm that the noise was obviously a large Mau Mau
> gang passing through the coffee plantation just a few yards from the

[216] W.H. Thompson, District Officer, Kandara Division, unpublished memoirs.
[217] Gucu G. Gikoyo – 'We Fought For Freedom', E.A. Publishing House 1979 p.132

house. I was quite certain my last moments had come and with them, those of my colleagues as well. The gang must surely know there were Kenya Policemen in the house, and were now coming to get us. By the sounds they were making, it was clear there were hordes of them. They were blowing bugles and whistles and were shouting and joking and laughing without any attempt to conceal their presence. They were clearly in high spirits singing bawdy songs about the uselessness of the KAR. They continued to pass by for some minutes and every moment I was expecting the rather flimsy wooden back door of the house to come crashing in, or to hear the breaking of glass as they entered through the French windows.

But to my surprise and not a little relief, they kept on going and eventually the cacophony died down into the distance and I went back to my bed still clutching my trusty Patchett sub-machine gun, but slept no more that night. The next morning at the Police Station I was told that a large gang had passed through the area heading towards Fort Hall. It later transpired from intelligence that it was indeed Kago's gang and that they had been to Thika to pick up recruits and were heading back for their forest hideout above Fort Hall in high spirits.

Obviously their intelligence, however, was somewhat lacking, for what a coup it would have been to have got four White policemen in one simple operation![218]

A 4,600-word journal[219] written by one Njuguna Gakuru who went to the forest with Kago in April 1953 recounts accurately the operations carried out by his gang from the time they entered the forest until Kago's death on 30th March 1954. The diarist was killed on the same day and this journal was taken from his body. Beside Kago, several leaders are mentioned including that of 'Captain' Njatha Kagiri[220].

One interesting passage describes the attack on Ndakaini village and the burning of an aeroplane belonging to a settler.

---

[218] Roger Dracup – Pers. Comm.
[219] A copy of this diary is in my possession
[220] See page Chapter 9, p.215

While at Makiama [hideout] they planned of attacking Ndakaini. They therefore left on 16.6.53 to Ndakaini led by Captain Njatha Kagiri and General Kago.

People for burning houses and attaching [collecting] cows and goats were led by Captain Kariuki Nduati....The shops and the camp [Kikuyu Guard Post] were attacked by Kago and Njatha Kagiri. They fought from 8 o'clock at night until morning of 17.6.53. Their drivers took two lorries and packed them with their capture [booty]. Women and girls also helped to carry the goods. They returned triumphantly being cheered by women all the way. When they arrived they prayed that those things might be blessed for the welfare of the Kikuyu Govt.... They then proceeded to Kinangop so that they could go and eat the Kibata spuds [potatoes]. Afterwards they were greatly irritated by the tracer [Tripacer] aeroplane which hindered them from lighting a fire. They then sent forth a scout ...together with 14 others including Muiruri Muhuha. Those people were instructed to go and burn the aeroplane. Before they left their camp they were blessed by Kihongo s/o King'ara. When they arrived where the aeroplane was, Muiruri Muhuha knew the positions of the sentries of the Security Forces. He was the first to open fire, and all the sentries and Europeans fled. They [the Mau Mau] all entered the [sentry's] tents, and others went to the aeroplane and took all the things that were there, as much as they could carry. This was on 27.7.53. They then returned to their hiding place having burnt the aeroplane. They were cheered of such a daring act after their return.[221]

It is particularly noticeable that in the whole journal, there is no mention whatsoever of politics or Kenyatta. Nor is there any reference to the reason they were fighting.

All those I interrogated who had been in Kago's gang spoke well of his leadership qualities, and there is no doubt that he had a certain charisma, flavoured with a pathological love of homicide.

The harsh regime of the forest gangs is brought to light by a story I received from a KAR Company Commander.

---

[221] This was the burning of the Tripacer aircraft belonging to Mr. Nimmo on his North Kinangop farm, a well documented attack.

I was commanding a Company of 4 KAR in one of the so-called 'Forts' on top of the Aberdares [Fort Jericho] in November 1953, when a boy of about 15 was sent up to my camp by the Kenya Police.

The boy had been Kago's batman in the forest, up to a few days before. The boy told me that his mother whom he had not seen for several months had given information to the Police about the Mau Mau. Apparently it was not information that concerned Kago or his gang, but nevertheless it was important information.

Kago had come to hear about this and in reprisal, had sentenced the boy to death. The boy heard about this from a friend who had overheard the conversation between Kago and the gang leader, a man called 'General' Matenjagwo, and wisely decided to escape before the sentence was carried out. He escaped before they could catch him and walked in to a Kenya Regiment camp on the Kinangop. On interrogation the story came out and when it transpired that he knew where the gang's hideout was and was willing to lead a party there, I was immediately contacted by radio as the hideout happened to be in my area of operations.

When he arrived, the boy told me that Kago's hideout was only about two hour's walk from my camp. So I set off immediately with two platoons led by myself and the boy.

After only about 45 minutes, we came to a place where the game track we had been following, divided. I decided to take the left fork, against the advice of the boy. After less than 5 minutes, we overlooked an enormous valley with a stream at the bottom. Following along the same track, we were suddenly confronted by a burst of fire followed by yelling and shouting at us. We had been trying to avoid an ambush situation but had walked right into it. The boy who was by my side at the time, was killed instantly and I suffered a slight wound in the leg.

When my chaps had regained their composure, they chased after the gang who were still shouting and firing at us. We joined battle with them and gradually they dispersed and melted away into the forest. The boy was our only casualty apart from my slight wound. We later found we had killed three members of the gang. One of them we were later told was the famous 'General' Matenjagwo.

I could never bring myself to decide whether the boy was going to lead us down the wrong path in order that we should not find the hideout and thus save his erstwhile companions, or whether he was trying to save us from the ambush he knew would happen if we took the one we did, the left-hand path where he knew there would be a sentry.[222]

On the death of Matenjagwo, Kago styled himself 'General' and took over the leadership of the gang. The Government had put a price on his head of £500, the only other with such a high value being Dedan Kimathi himself, which gives an idea of the importance the authorities attached to his elimination. His demise is often made into that of a hero with fantasised episodes, and although it was during a long drawn out battle between his gang and the security forces, his personal end was quick and ignominious. John Blower of 'Blowforce' who had been hunting Kago unsuccessfully for some weeks recounts the operation leading to his demise after one of his attacks on his favourite target: Kikuyu Guard Posts, this time at Kiriaini in Location 2, Fort Hall.

Unfortunately there had only been ten Kikuyu Guards in the Post at the time, and although they put up a brave fight until their ammunition ran out, they were soon overrun and butchered to a man.

It had been an easy victory for Kago, who would doubtless be encouraged thereby to make further attacks against similar targets. But fortunately retribution was at hand.

On the evening of 30th March 1954, the local FIO, George Hales', in a daring encounter with one of Kago's men reported that a meeting was planned that night between Kago, Ihura and other local gang leaders, followed the next day by a raid on Kangara village to obtain blankets and other supplies[223]. On their way back to the forest, they would make a night attack on Kinyona Kikuyu Guard Post with the intention of killing Senior Chief Njiri. Such advance notice of his plans obviously offered a splendid opportunity to trap Kago, and it fell to Donald Clay, the Kandara District Officer, together with his police

---

[222] Pers. Comm. from Capt. R.G. Winstanley K.A.R.
[223] In a personal letter to me in 2003, George Hales told me that his informer was actually in the hut where Kago and his bodyguards were eating. *'I was waiting for him outside the hut but I did not stay long enough to inquire what the meeting was about as I had a very close call to prevent myself being identified. My informer advised "immediate retreat"!*

counterpart, Jeff Hedger-Wallace, to concoct an effective counter plan, which they proceeded to do with commendable speed and efficiency.

Tracker dogs were brought up overnight and we were warned to stand-by for an early start. A spotter plane was to be sent from Nyeri, and army, police and Kikuyu Guards were instructed to take up positions along the forest edge to block the terrorists expected line of retreat.

Having received instructions by radio, Colin O'Driscoll and I with all our men and weapons, crammed into the Land Rover and truck, and left Kinyona at about 3 am. The tracker dogs team failed to pick up the scent from where they were told the meeting was to be held, because unbeknown to anyone, the location of the meeting was changed by the leaders at the last minute. It seemed that our quarry must have given us the slip once again. Disappointed, we were beginning to think of breakfast when we received a radio message instructing us to proceed at once to a certain point where tracks of a large gang had just been found crossing a ridge-top road nearby.

The tracks were indeed very clear and we set off at once in pursuit. We had not gone far when we came across the body of an elderly Kikuyu man lying in a pool of blood. He had only recently been killed, his back horribly slashed while he was still alive, and then his throat cut from ear to ear. It was a typical Kago-type murder like so many I had seen before, providing us with yet more incentive, if we needed it, to catch up with the gang.

It was, however, a long chase. We had set off in pursuit about 10 am, and they must have had at least an hour's start on us. We kept going along the swampy valley bottom, through wattle plantations and across scrub-covered hillsides without any sign of our quarry apart from their tracks. The spotter aircraft had been over several times ranging across the country ahead of us, eventually dropping a couple of orange smoke markers, indicating, at last, the position of the gang, while a fusillade of shots directed at the plane, forced it to climb swiftly out of their range.

Hurrying on, we soon had some of the gang in view and opened up with our two inch mortar in their direction. Soon we were exchanging rifle fire with them as they headed up a ridge separating us from the next valley. The chase continued into the afternoon with a succession of minor skirmishes in the course of which we inflicted some casualties on the gang. So far we had remained free of casualties ourselves, but lying

332

beside the path, I found the body of Ian Patterson, a D.O. (K.G.) whom I knew, with a bullet through the heart. He had been with a group of Kikuyu Guards pursuing the gang from a different part of the ridge and must have been hit by a rear-guard ambush.

It was only just before dark, when contact with the terrorists had finally been lost, that I heard Kago himself had been killed during one of the running battles in the afternoon. He had been wounded and had been found in quite thick bush by one of our Kikuyu Guard men. Kago had put up his hands and shouted to the Kikuyu Guard "Don't shoot, I am General Kago", whereupon the Guard who had greater reason than most to hate the man because of what had been done to his family by the man, raised his rifle without a word and shot him dead. The distinctive black and white colobus monkey skin hat for which he was well-known, was found lying nearby.[224]

The story is then taken up by Ian Feild, District Military Intelligence Officer, Fort Hall who was asked to verify that the body was indeed that of the famous 'General'.

The news of Kago's death was instantly broadcast around Fort Hall, but as he was such a key figure, we had to be absolutely certain the body really was that of Kago. The job of proving this to be true was given to me. I drove off early the next morning to collect the body and took it to his home village. There, his relatives inspected the body as though it was a prize sheep. One looked at his feet, others at his teeth and more at his hands. They admitted they had not seen him for some years, but eventually announced with some pride, that it was indeed Kago Mboko.

Their deductions were not all that convincing, so to make absolutely certain I took the body, still in the back of my Land Rover, all the way to Nairobi, to CID headquarters where they kept records of all detainee's fingerprints. Having taken his fingerprints as he lay in the vehicle and compared them with their records, they pronounced him No. D169005 Kago Mboko, escapee from Manyani Detention Centre on 28/29th April 1953.

---

[224] John Blower – unpublished personal memoirs

I took the body back to Fort Hall where John Pinney, the District Commissioner, gave orders that it should be cremated in the grounds of the District Headquarters there and then.[225] .

Kago's funeral pyre

Following the death of Kago and the positive identification of his body, the District Commissioner John Pinney gave orders that it should be burnt forthwith

Kago was undisputedly the most prominent and ruthless Mau Mau terrorist leader of all. He and his hordes had been responsible for more deaths of Kikuyu Guards, European and African Administrators, Kenya Regiment members, missionaries and ordinary Kikuyu people who were either relatives of Kikuyu Guards or those who simply refused to toe the line, than any other leader. If Kimathi was the 'Hitler' of Mau Mau, Kago was undoubtedly the 'Himmler'. To those of us who knew most of the terrorists in the Aberdares, and the feats they achieved, it is a travesty that an insignificant little road in Nairobi is named after such a universally renowned leader of men, when one of the main thoroughfares bears Kimathi's name, a man who never led a single attack during the whole of his Mau Mau career.

From the moment of Kago's death in March 1954, resistance to the Mau Mau by the Kikuyu populace in Fort Hall began to harden and the tide against the insurgents generally throughout Kikuyuland began to turn.

---

[225] Ian Feild – pers. comm.

Appendix 6

A DISTRICT OFFICER'S WIFE'S MEMORIES OF LIFE IN MAU MAU COUNTRY

Jimmy Butler, to whom I was married in India in 1942, served in the Indian Police from 1939 until Partition in 1946. He joined the Kenya Administration in 1949 and we went to live in Kenya with our family.

Jimmy was a District Officer in the Samburu areas to begin with and in 1953 we were sent to Nyeri, the centre of operations against the Mau Mau insurgents. In 1954 Jimmy took over as District Commissioner, Nyeri, from Ossie Hughes. We were allotted a small bungalow on the outskirts of Nyeri beside a deep ravine. At the time, I had two small children and was 8 months pregnant with my third.

As my husband was away on safari for much of the time we were allotted

Nyeri District Headquarters staff - 1954
District Commissioner Jimmy Butler seated centre

an armed guard who slept in the house with a blanket over his head and our cat on his stomach. I was also given a shotgun. One night I was woken by my little dog who slept in the same room when my husband was away. I looked out of the window and saw men with pangas moving around in the garden bushes nearby. I fired my shotgun in the direction of the bushes and bruised my shoulder badly. There was a shout from the bushes. I woke up the guard who was too frightened to go and check in the garden.

I took a couple of aspirins to calm myself and lay down on the bed with my loaded gun beside me. I did not want the baby to come too soon. There was no more trouble that night. In the morning we found traces of blood in the bushes.

On the day I went into labour, there was a battle going on in the forest close to the small hospital where I was to be delivered of my baby. The doctor was too busy with the wounded to pay much attention to me. The wards were full of groaning bodies with the occasional dead bodies covered in blankets, in the corridors. I was put into a small room and my baby son arrived safely after three hours. My husband eventually turned up, his clothes covered in blood from carrying the wounded to hospital.

My elder four year old son attended a nursery school in Nyeri, until the European woman who was running it was murdered by a Mau Mau gang.

One evening I watched a Kikuyu Guard patrol corner a Mau Mau in the garden. There was so much firing and shouting going on that I had to put the gramophone on so that the children could not hear the noise. My non-Kikuyu servants cowered in the kitchen, but my loyal Kikuyu ayah [*nanny*] Rebecca stayed with me and the children in the sitting room. One morning, Rebecca told me that my Mkamba servant Nzioka and his Kikuyu wife Wanjiru had disappeared, leaving their baby in their hut. Nzioka's body was found with his throat cut in the servant's latrine. Wanjiru had been abducted, and we later heard she had been sent to the forest by her abductors as a 'comfort girl'. The baby was taken by it's mother's family. My only other non-Kikuyu servant, as a result of this, asked to be relieved of his work and went back home. I was, however, able to employ two Kikuyu servants in their place. They were both Christians and had suffered terribly at the hands of Mau Mau.

There was a young White nurse who used to drive around the villages in a Red Cross van, treating the sick families. She came to me one day and told me that she had received threats from the Mau Mau who told her she must give up her work otherwise she would be killed. This particular day she had been asked to treat one of the Chief's children and she wanted to go to him. As I had a Land Rover with a driver and a guard, she asked me if we could go together.

We went to the old man's house and my friend treated the child after which the Chief's wife brought us tea while we all chatted together. It was happy occasion.

Soon afterwards she was travelling in her van with the Red Cross emblems painted on it, when she was ambushed on the road and killed very unpleasantly indeed. On the same day, the Chief had a visit from a Mau Mau gang who chopped off both his hands. It was all shocking news for me. However, when my husband went to Government House some weeks later to be invested with the M.B.E., he was surprised to see the old Chief there at the same ceremony collecting his own M.B.E. from the Governor Sir Evelyn Baring. The old Chief was in great spirits and as defiant as ever.

After my new baby had been weaned, I worked in the District Headquarters typing reports and generally helping where I could. I also helped with the women's clubs in Nyeri township and nearby villages. The clubs were known as 'Maendeleo ya Wanawake' *[lit. advancement of women']*. It was mainly teaching sewing, cooking and childcare. I was provided with a Land Rover and driver and two armed guards. The idea was to try and get the women to resist helping the Mau Mau, some of whom were supplying food and ammunition to their men folk in the forest. Young girls were selling themselves to British troops at three bullets a time.

One day I arrived at a village to find the women sitting round the walls of a new hut that was in the process of being built, but as yet had no roof. There was a tense atmosphere when I arrived and I asked them what was the matter. 'Memsahib', they replied, 'they have taken our men and our young girls to the forest. This war is bad for everyone and we want it to end. Please tell your husband to try and end the war quickly.' The Headman's wife told me that the Mau Mau gang were still nearby and that I should be very careful as they would kill me. She said that the women would protect me as they knew I had small children. We all had tea together in that desolate place and I tried to lift their spirits and told them that the Government was doing everything possible to end the war. My two guards looked very nervous and stank to high heaven like men do when they are frightened. I was very afraid of being ambushed on my way back and the road was a quagmire because of the rains. At one stage I had to get out and help push the vehicle getting covered in mud in the process. It was dark when I eventually arrived back home, and my husband reminded me that we had to go to a reception at the Outspan hotel. Luckily trusty old Rebecca had bathed the children and put them to bed and so after a quick bath we arrived at the Outspan where a rather tetchy Barbara Castle *[Labour member of Parliament and Cabinet Minister]* who was touring the areas affected by Mau Mau, was somewhat annoyed at being kept waiting by the District Commissioner and his wife.

Pam Gwyer (Butler), 1ˢᵗ May 2004[226]

---

[226] Pam Gwyer – Pers. Comm.

Appendix 7

The following report was written by Hugh Walker, a District Officer who was responsible for some of the most politically active areas of Kikuyuland. The report was written in reply to a request from his senior Administrator for his measured views on the conflict between those Kikuyu who had collaborated with the Government – the 'loyalists'– and those who had either been fighting for the Mau Mau or who had agreed with their aims – the 'other' Kikuyu. The report was written in January 1961, after the end of the Emergency but before Kenyatta had been released from detention.

After talking with many loyalists it would appear that in most ways the rift is as wide as ever. This is due to several factors:

1. The poor timing of the Lancaster House Conference and the declaration of the end of the Emergency, which had to be made for political reasons before the Conference began, resulted in the widespread belief that Independence was imminent and had been won by Mau Mau.

2. The inescapable fact that many criminal acts were perpetrated by loyalists in the name of Government during the height of the Emergency, as well as the opportunities taken of settling old personal scores all of which necessitated an Amnesty, and that many obtained privileged positions and land by association with Government.

3. The mass release of those detained early on in the Emergency who never experienced the miseries it brought in the Reserves and who only saw the benefits on their return that had been made possible by closer administration and the vast sums of money expended in the fight against Mau Mau. These they almost justifiably claim only came about as a result of their activities. They are still as revolutionary-minded as ever — many never

having confessed (taking the oath) and believe that only extremism can rectify such problems as landlessness and unemployment and reverse the privileged position of the loyalist and landed.

4. The growth of KANU *[Kenya African National Union – political party]* with the appointment of such ex-detainees, terrorists and ardent Mau Mau supporters as its Office-bearers and their infiltration even into local government.

5. The inhibition of loyalists from joining KANU, even as an investment, despite their association with a government which is progressively divesting its powers—apparently in favour of the extremist element—because they see the confidence of the "other" Kikuyu increasing daily, and who will soon be in a position to treat the loyalists as they have always threatened. They thus cling to Government as the protector of minorities!

6. The continued detention of Jomo Kenyatta used as a platform by all political parties and the conviction that he will eventually be released, leaves the loyalists no alternative but to remain silent or agree with the majority that he should be freed. The few notable exceptions amongst loyalist leaders themselves differ, either from a sense of conviction or reality (i.e. the Muhoyas and Makimeis as opposed to the Wanyutu Wawerus and David Waruhius) and indicate a split viewpoint that makes the "others" believe that all are really against his release in their heart of hearts and that the day of reckoning will come when he is released.

7. If the loyalists are examined it will be seen that over 50% were those with land or property as they had more to lose than the majority of Mau Mau active wing who were recruited in large numbers from dissident landless. Conversely, the other half contained landless who hoped to obtain land, property or money by helping Government. It has been said that the emergence of the "haves and have-nots" will tend to obscure the differences between loyalists and Mau Mau as many Mau Mau also have land. However, many of those loyalists who assisted Government acquired (more) land or property—often illegally—through their position of strength, and therefore many ex-terrorists and detainees who had their land confiscated or taken by others on

'Land Consolidation' feel even more strongly against them than in 1952.

8. Of the Kikuyu tribe, the percentage of loyalists has been estimated at 5% at the start of the Emergency and 10% thereafter. Even doubled, are they a leaven which will count after Responsible Government [Self-Government] has been attained?

What is the present position? Loyalists will not drink with ex-*(sic)* Mau Mau for fear of provoking old animosities; Gichuru exhorts all to forget who was responsible for their detention and in the same breath not to drink with them! The women are told to ullulate for Kenyatta so that God in heaven can hear (are they not the guardians of all the old atavistic customs of the past?); youth wings of young thugs, KANU askaris and ex-detainees "old boys" associations and others released who will not speak or report; Christian girls and married women being circumcised; intimidation and fear returning as fast as they came in 1951/2; songs exalting all to submit to detention, imprisonment, exiled to islands etc.; deifying Kenyatta in the quest for land being taught to tiny children. Are all these not pointers to the continuance of division amongst the Kikuyu?

9. There seem no reasons why it should not continue. Through external pressures Kenya's Independence is only a matter of time. There is no need for oaths or violence at present. As the Europeans appear prepared to concede Uhuru soon, the only quarrel is with those who continue to delay it. The extremist elements of Mau Mau are well infiltrated into KANU and now local government. Will the obedience to law, accepted temporarily as a means to an end, be enforceable by the leaders with such office-bearers and supporters upon whom they now depend for their political existence? The loyalists firmly believe that when in power the present political leaders will come out in their true colours and fulfil their secret promises of future extremism made to keep their present supporters docile.

10. To the Mau Mau the loyalists were traitors to their own people for, but for them, Uhuru would have been attained long ago. Maybe the Mau Mau did not realise what they were up against, but to them their 'failure' in 1953/4 was due only to a small

percentage of their own people betraying them, and it was these same people they now publicly castigate as responsible for the continued detention of Kenyatta and thus the delay of Uhuru.

11. Again, out of the Emergency, the Kikuyu have benefited far beyond other tribes! Closer administration has brought Land Consolidation, hospitals and health centres, schools, youth clubs and nursery schools etc. even Administration Offices and Police Stations and, above all, money circulating in the Province as never before through cash crops and an increase in trade. There appears no side on which prosperity has not come out of evil. Who is responsible? The Mau Mau claim the credit as, but for their struggle—despite its cost—none of this would have happened. However crooked thinking this may be, it is indisputable that Central Province is now the kingpin of Kenya and that on the Kikuyu the future of Kenya largely depends.

12. These unpalatable observations may be condemned as nonsense but the 'others' are the majority even if they include unthinking old men and women who believe all they are told. A generation or more is needed for people to recover from a Civil War. Time is not on our side and about the only remedy is political compromise. This, again, cannot be successful without stable conditions of law and order. To the Mau Mau the division in the tribe was caused by a minority of loyalists, and Government, as their backers, should encourage them to join actively in politics with Independence as the goal. Only if the loyalists are prepared to join a political party and criticised from within as members instead of doing so from outside, forlornly sitting on the government fence, would there be a possibility of a rapprochement on a political basis. After all, the common aim even of loyalists and unaffected tribes is also Independence.

13. At present, the divisions within KANU itself do not augur well for Kikuyu unity and the loyalists, not being members of any party, are an added reason for disunity. Children are openly calling after all ex-Home Guards and serving loyalists 'andu a KA(N)DU'. They are the mouthpieces of their parents echoing what they hear without fear of reprisal, and a true indication of the general feelings of the 'others'. This vilification of the

opposition party acronym (KADU) *[Kenya African Democratic Union political party]* into the Kikuyu word 'kandu' meaning food, is not only a by-product of our encouragement of multi-political parties, but also an indication of future relations between such parties – particularly towards the loyalists [who are] mentally expelled from the tribe for blowing neither hot nor cold.

14. The conditions in which the breach between the loyalists and the Mau Mau may heal depend initially on two factors: the settlement of the Kenyatta issue as soon as possible and the will and ability of Government to maintain law and order whatever the result of his release (or continued detention) may be. Without positive indications of the intention on the part of Government—particularly after the election—every means from passive resistance to positive rebellion will be used to attain Independence now rather than by planned stages. It may well be, however, that the loyalists will go the way of all minority groups unless they can come to terms with the majority – and who are better qualified to do so than the Kikuyu themselves? It is, however, up to Government actively to encourage and assist them to do so whilst ensuring stable conditions now and until Independence, and, as far as is humanely possible, that the future government will be a responsible one, for in the continued division of the Kikuyu lie the seeds of another Congo.

Hugh Walker,
District Officer Limuru.
30th January 1961

Appendix 8

Franz Hvass farmed on the Kinangop close to the Aberdare forest. He was in the Kenya Police Reserve and was very active in hunting the forest gangs on the Rift Valley side of the Aberdare mountains. The forest gangs came to know him and wrote letters to him which they left on a forked stick close to his farm. The threatening nature of these letters failed to intimidate Franz Hvass, who came to Kenya from his native Denmark. Franz's son, John, with whom I worked in pseudo gangs, provided me with copies of these letters that were written in broken English. The first letter was intended primarily for the Governor:

From H.W. Kahinga. - Governor and Prime Minister of Kenya,
To: E.Baring - Ex. Governor of Kenya

Original wording

A notice is hereby given to all Europeans who are fighting people of Kenya that you have been cursed by the Mighty God that you have to be fought by 51 Tribes of the wild wide in this year without, an doubt because you have disturbed his people of this country where he owned this land you to them. N.B. You had better to take care and clean in your body and mind that you are like Goriat who was very storng because he weighed 1680 lbs. and his helmet weighed 150 lbs. and we all Kenya people are David who killed that giant with a small tiny thing. Everybody knows that you have killed many people in this country without any reason why, except robbing their lands and wealthy which their God giveth them and blesses it for them. Its better you increase your weapons because they are not enough for the 40th. And Mau Mau war at all, because they directed by their God at all times, whenever they go in this country. My people of Kenya are very eager to visit Rift Valley for whether it is fitile or not because they wish to cultivatetheir land in this-year whatever circumstances or case may be. N.B. There is no any British Empire and there will be no any British Empire in Kenya any- longer except I myself, but if you want to remain here in Kenya, you better be as traders and stay in Towns but not to be as settlers looking how their lands alike any more. That means that we only want to leave those stranger or foreigners who are going with trades, (Tradesman). As from today, it is better to pack out your luggages and rags. Only 60 lbs. per person but no more than, because I drem last night that you are leaving here without a notice given to you because you have no mercy to other tribes. All the matter is settled frankly without any amicably ways by the mighty God. N.B. You be prepared at all times because my soldiers are on the way there coming to consume you, now they are fresh eaters. You have the great danger of life because cattles are becoming short. Please do not ask about that fellow who passes there because he is one of my soldiers, who is collecting tins and cattles for making tined food from your meat and beef. The European meat is very good and fat because you consumed our lands and you sucked our blood. We want to refund our land and blood that you sucked. Waiting to see your reply soon telling me on which day you are leaving here.

Bye bye ex.Governor of Kenya
Very thin but wiser than you, H.W.Kahinga
Governor and Prime Minister 2/7/53

Interpretation

Notice is hereby given to all Europeans who are fighting the people of Kenya that you have been cursed by Almighty God because you have upset all 51 tribes of Kenya by taking their land. You had better make sure your body and mind is clean and prepare for your end.

Goliath was also a strong man. He weighed 1,680 lbs, and even his helmet was 150 lbs. But like David, the people of Kenya will kill their Goliath easily.

Everybody knows that you have killed many people in this country with the excuse that you want to rob them of the land which God gave them so that you can become wealthy. You had better get more weapons because however many you have they will not be enough to beat the Mau Mau who are always directed by God wherever they go.

The people of Kenya are eager to go and look at their land in the Rift Valley so that they can cultivate it this year even if it is not fertile enough. You can be sure they will do this whatever the circumstances.

The British Empire is coming to an end, and Kenya is no longer part of the British Empire. You can stay in Kenya but only as shop-keepers in towns. You may not be settlers in the country any longer. If foreigners want to come, they can stay only as traders. So as from today, you had better pack your bags, but you may take only 60lbs [approx. 25 kilos] with you. I had a dream last night that you were told to leave Kenya without any notice because you have no mercy on us or on other tribes. This decree is now settled without friendship but by the word of Almighty God.

You had better prepare yourselves to leave at any time because my soldiers are coming to 'eat' you. They are now flesh eaters. So you are in great danger because we have little meat left and my soldiers are hungry.

If you see someone passing on your farm, do not worry. He will be one of my soldiers collecting your old tins for us to make tinned food from your flesh. TheEuropean flesh is very good and fat because you consumed our land and you sucked our blood. We now want to restore that balance.

I await your reply telling me which day you are leaving.

Good bye ex-Governor of Kenya, E. Baring

[signed] *Very thin, but wiser than you, H.W. Kahinga, Governor and Prime Minister* [dated] *2/7/53*

The following letter was written by a gang leader who was close to Dedan Kimathi. He had been told by Kimathi to go to the Rift Valley side of the Aberdares and put an end to Hvass' and his operations in the forest. This letter was to warn Hvass that he was coming to kill him.

Original wording

A Notice is hereby given to all your Tribes and Familes that, as from today up to date that I am coming on that direction of Rift Valley because I have removed from my old camp Kariaini by name where I was residing for six months and kill 20 Europeans Soligers and thirty one African Solidgers and also I killed 16 Home guards and I caught 47 Home guards as prisoners of war because now they art fighting against you. So I am quite sure that my soldiers will do better there for killing and consuming Europeans because they are CANUOS that IS, MAN EATERS.

I hope to stay here at about one or two months and finish all of you. Now, we are not joking because the time is over. Hoping to arrive there on next Sunday what-so-ever. You must be prepared for waiting me on the said day. I am on my way coming there. Kariatni is near Uthaya Division, if you wish to come and see me before leaving here, it is better to follow – on the T. Falls Road through to Nyeri and when reaching Nyeri to follow Uthaya Road where there is 16 miles and then to push on up to the line of the Aberdares Ranges where it is 8 miles away. My convoy have got enough weapons which I took from Naivasha Prison where I reached on the month of March in this year. This matter is concerning Dr.Leaky who is directing all forests of Kenya - because I am wanting to dig my lands which are on Rift Valley sides very soon.

The following are my Generals and Captains *[a list of names follows]*…and also my doctor is ready to do, postmotom to all Eurpeans who will be killed. His name is Mwangi s/o WaMbugu. Uthaya Division. He is specialists for his work as a doctor. Hoping to see you on Sunday

[signed] Kibira Gatu. Uthaya. 29.7.53.

Interpretation

Notice is hereby given to all people[living on the Kinangop] that as from today I am coming in the direction of the Rift Valley [i.e. the Kinangop], because I have left my old hideout at Kariaini where I was residing for six months having killed 20 European soldiers and 31 African soldiers. I also killed 16 Home Guards, and I captured another 47 Home Guards who are my prisoners of war and who are now fighting against you. I am sure my soldiers will do well against you now because they are now cannibals or 'man-eaters'. I hope to stay here about one or two months by which time we will have finished all of you. We are not joking. Your time is over. I hope to arrive there by next Sunday without fail. So prepare yourselves to wait for me. I am on my way.

Kariaini is in Othaya Division and you can come and see me if you wish. Follow the Thompson's Falls road through Nyeri and take the Othaya road for 16 miles up to the edge of the Aberdare forest. We are 8 miles into the forest.

My troops have got plenty of weapons which they took from Naivasha Police Station in March this year.

Tell Dr. Leakey who is in charge of the forests [incorrect] *that I am going to dig my shambas on the Rift Valley [side of the Aberdares] very soon. I hope to arrive there by next Sunday without fail. So prepare yourselves to wait for me. I am on my way.*

The Following are my Generals and Captains: [There then follows a long list of names.] *My doctor is Mwangi son of WaMbugu he is a very good doctor and will perform postmortems on all Europeans who will be killed.*
Hoping to see you on Sunday
[signed] *Kibira Gatu, Othaya, 29.7.53*

Finally, Dedan Kimathi himself wrote a letter to Franz Hvass. It is a rambling, almost incoherent letter, written in English by Kimathi himself. The original was given to the C I D, but Hvass copied the letter beforehand. The letter was written early in 1954.

Original Wording

Land Freedom Army

Within the remaining 46 years the reign of British Empire will have to be melted out for the reason that the British Sovereign is laid upon the children of the beasts more than being laid upon the children of men. Britons teach love whilst besides they have a chunk of hatred on fire. Many present laws of Kenya make us laugh more than fear and obedience. Kenya needs justice with less law. Boms etc, are cheered by us as a pleasant sounding tune at a dance. Does it mean that none of you agrees with each other, or does it mean that all British subjects have been fooled by God as well as stated in the Bible?   The Government ask us to offer freely and to surrender, but how can a rat come out of a pit whilst the cat watches to catch it? Let us not do childish nuisance if so.

The 3rd world war I am sure is about to break out, How shall we defend? All the world big nations watch Britishers loosing their sincerity to may be laughed at last. Mr.Michael Blundell is an antrax to both cow and calf. Your white gentlemen fighting every colony they govern, so they against mine are so fools and always do like little children I am sure they are here to earn money but not to do their duty. Weapons are waisted for nothing here by roaming and gosping, Lacs and bombers are just as hawks or eagles after a dead best which they never get. Let God kill me if bombers have killed twenty of my troops. Only 4 in April 1953 in Fort Hall District and one in Nyeri in Nov.1953 but no more. Only bamboos and other trees you fight against awakening the wild beasts from their resting places.

[Rubber stamp) Marchal D.Kimathi

Interpretation

[Heading] *Land Freedom Army*

The 46 remaining years of the British Empire will have to be forfeited because the Queen is more interested in wild animals than in people. The British teach love between men, but actually they have much hatred as well.

Many of the laws of Kenya make us laugh. We cannot respect them nor be obedient to them. Kenya needs justice with less of the British kind of laws.

The bombs you drop make a pleasant sound like drums.

Do all British subjects agree with the Government when they ask us to surrender? Or are they just being fooled by God? How can a rat come out of its hole while the cat is waiting to catch it? Let us not be so childish.

As the British are so stupid, how will they defend us when the 3rd world war breaks out? The other nations of the world are laughing at the British when they see them losing their good sense.

Mr. Michael Blundell is like anthrax in cattle.

You white people are fools to fight against my soldiers. I think you are here only to earn money from Kenya, not to teach us and rule us properly. Your weapons are wasted on us. You never find usbecause you talk too much in the forest. Your bombers are just like hawks or eagles that are impotent. I will be damned if your bombers have killed even twenty of my troops. They killed only 4 in Fort Hall District in April 1953 and one in Nyeri in November 1953. No more. All the bombs do is to kill some bamboos and disturb the animals from their resting places.

[signed] *Marshal D. Kimathi [Rubber stamp] 'Marshall D. Kimathi_*

In his memoirs[227] Franz Hvass includes copies of documents taken from captured terrorists. The following is an excerpt from one of these documents. It is a diary written in English in a small notebook marked "Platoon Company of Kimathi". *It needs no interpretation.*

The big chief Mwenja works for Mr. Oberholzer. I live with him here with Bwana Kiburu, no teath infront. I came from the forest one day with my best friend Mburu. It was a Monday. We came from the forest at 8 p.m. along with Kanuthia. We left because we were chased away by Police. Kamau went in front ready for anything, he had a bow, which he was able to kill anything. When we arrived at Lereko, Kamau told a Ndito *[young woman]* who was carrying a toto *[child]* called Waweru to throw him away as he was hindering our progress, and he wanted to talk to her. She agreed to throw the toto away. Kamau told the Ndito now she belongs to them and they will look after her every day. No one must touch her she is ours. Kamau told us don't be afraid God is bigger than the European. The Police are not as big as a mountain so they can't see us on the other side.

---

[227] In his unpublished memoirs held for safe-keeping by his son John, Franz Hvass, who was Danish by birth, wrote at length about his experiences and encounters with the Mau Mau.

1873   *Sultan Barghash of Zanzibar ratifies the 1845 treaty with the British by closing all the slave markets and prohibiting the export of slaves from his dominions.*

1885   *The Berlin Conference divides up eastern Africa into European spheres of influence.*

1887   *First recorded contact with the Kikuyu by the Count Teleki and Ludwig von Höhnel expedition.*

1888   *The Imperial British East Africa Company (IBEAC) is founded and British administration of the country under its influence is started.*

1895   *Her Majesty's Government proclaims the British East Africa Protectorate, taking over from the IBEAC and leasing a ten-mile coastal strip from the Sultan of Zanzibar.*

1896   *The first four British settlers arrive at Fort Smith.*

1901   *The Uganda Railway begun in 1896 from Mombasa reaches Lake Victoria Nyanza*

1902   *The Uganda Protectorate which had extended to Naivasha is transferred to the British East Africa Protectorate*

1907   *Legislative Council formed in the new centre of Nairobi*

1920   *The British East Africa Protectorate becomes Kenya Colony and the Zanzibar Protectorate*

1952   *Mau Mau Emergency is declared and arrests are made of Jomo Kenyatta and other suspected leaders*

1960   *Official end of the Emergency is declared and Jomo Kenyatta is freed from detention*

1963   *Internal self-government declared on 1st June with Jomo Kenyatta as Prime Minister and full independence from the British given on 12th December*

Bibliography

BARNETT, Donald L. and NJAMA, Karari (1966) *Mau Mau From Within* Modern
 Reader Paperbacks, New York

BENENSON, Peter (1959) *Gangrene* Calderbooks, London

BEWES, Canon T.F.C. (1953) *Kikuyu Conflict* The Highway Press, London

BOK, Francis (2003) *Escape from Slavery* St. Martin's Press, London

BRADLEY-MARTIN, Esmond (1978) *Zanzibar – Tradition and Revolution* Hamish
 Hamilton, London

BRECKENRIDGE, James and Caroline *40 Years in Kenya* Published Privately

BURR, Eric (1985) *Localisation and Public Service Training* Oxford Development
 Records Project, Rhodes House Library, Oxford

CAMPBELL, Guy (1986) *The Charging Buffalo* Leo Cooper in association with
 Secker & Warburg, London

CARBERRY, Juanita (1999) *Child of Happy Valley* Heinemann, London

CAROTHERS, Dr.J.C., (1954) *The Psychology of Mau Mau* Report to Kenya
 Government

CARTER, Judge Morris (1934) *The Kenya Land Commission* H.M.S.O.

CORFIELD, F.D. (1960) *The Origins and Growth of Mau Mau* Sessional Paper No. 5
 1959/60 Colony and Protectorate of Kenya, Nairobi

COUPLAND, R. (1939) *The Exploitation of East Africa 1856 – 1890* Faber & Faber,
 London

FARSON, Negley (1949) *Last Chance in Africa* Victor Gollancz, London

FOX, James (1982) *White Mischief* Jonathan Cape, London

FRANKLIN, Derek (1996) *A Pied Cloak* Janus, London

GAVAGHAN, Terence (1994) *Corridors of Wire* Published privately

GIKOYO, Gucu G. (1979) *We Fought for Freedom* East African Publishing House,
 Nairobi

GOLDING, J.A. (1987) *Colonialsim – The Golden Years* Birlings, London

HARDY, Ronald (1965) *The Iron Snake* Collins, London

HENDERSON, Ian with GOODHART, Philip (1958) *The Hunt for Kimathi* Hamish
 Hamilton

HEWITT, Peter (1999) *Kenya Cowboy* Avon Books, London

HOLLIS, A.C. (1905) *The Masai* The Clarendon Press, Oxford

HOLMAN, Dennis (1964) *Bwana Drum* W.H. Allen, London

HUNTER, J.A. and MANNIX, Dan (1954) *African Bush Adventures* Hamish Hamilton, London

HUXLEY, Elspeth (1935) *White Man's Country.* Chatto & Windus, London.

INGHAM, Kenneth (1962) *A History of East Africa* Longmans, London

JOHNSON, Sir John (2002) *Colony to Nation* The Erskine Press, Norfolk

KAGGIA, Bildad (1975) *Roots of Freedom 1921-1963* East African Publishing House

KARIUKI, Josiah Mwangi (1963) *Mau Mau Detainee* O.U.P., Nairobi

KENYATTA, Jomo (1938) *Facing Mt. Kenya* Martin Secker & Warburg, U.S.

KINYATTI Maina wa (1986) *Kimathi's Letters* Heinemann, Nairobi

KITSON, Frank (1960) *Gangs and Counter Gangs* Barrie and Rockliffe, London

LAMB, David (1983) *The Africans* Random House Inc., New York

LEAKEY, Dr. L.S.B. (i)   (1936) *Kenya* Methuen & Co, London

   (ii)   (1952) *Mau Mau and the Kikuyu* Methuen & Co., London

   (iii)   (1954) *Defeating Mau Mau* Methuen & Co., London

   (iv)   (1977) *The Southern Kikuyu before 1903* Academic Press, London

LONSDALE, John - Various papers incl.:

   (i)   (1990) Journal of African History *Mau Maus of the Mind*

   (ii)   (1995) *The Prayers of Waiyaki*

   (iii) (2002) *Jomo Kenyatta, God and the Modern World* James Currey, Oxford

   (iv)   (2002) *Authority, Gender and Violence*

   (v)   (2002) *Kikuyu Historiography – Old and New*

LOVATT SMITH, David (2003) *My Enemy: My Friend* – Mawenzi Books

MAITLAND, Alexander (1971) *Speke and the Discovery of the Source of the Nile* Constable

MAJDALANY, Fred (1962) *State of Emergency* Longmans, London

MEINERTZHAGEN, Richard (1957) *Kenya Diary* Eland Books, London

MILLER, Charles (1972) *The Lunatic Express* Futura Publications Ltd., London

MOORHEAD, Alan (1960) *The White Nile* Hamish Hamilton, London

MOXON, Robert M. (1986) *East Africa – An Introductory History* East African Educational Publishers, Nairobi

MURIITHI J. Kiboi and NDORIA, Peter N. (1971) *War in the Forest* East African Publishing House, Nairobi

ROUTLEDGE, W. Scoresby and ROUTLEDGE, Katherine (1968) *With a Prehistoric People* Frank Cass

RUTHERFORD, Jock, Ed. and published by David Lovatt Smith (2003) *A History of the Kikuyu Guard*

SORRENSON (1967) *Land Reform in the Kikuyu Country* O.U.P.

SPEKE, John Hanning (1862) *What led to the Discovery of the Source of the Nile* Blackwood, London

STONEHAM, C.T. (1955) *Out of Barbarism* Museum Press, London

SWANN, A.J. (1910) *Fighting the Slave hunters of Central Africa* Seeley & Co, London

THOMSON, Joseph (1885) *Through Masailand* Sampson Low, London

WAMWEYA, Joram (1971) *Freedom Fighter* East African Publishing House, Nairobi

WILLS, Colin (1953) *Who Killed Kenya?* Dennis Dobson, London

WILKINSON, J. (1954) *The Mau Mau Movement: Some General and Medical Aspects* East African Medical Journal

Also the National Archives, The Public Records Office, Kew, London. *Various papers and articles.*

Index